Two Centuries of
Parasitic Economics

Two Centuries of Parasitic Economics

The Struggle for Economic and
Political Democracy on the Eve of the
Financial Collapse of the West

BASIL AL-NAKEEB

ISBN-13: 9781523827954

ISBN-10: 1523827955

Library of Congress Control Number: 2016901840
CreateSpace Independent Publishing Platform
North Charleston, South Carolina

1. Banking 2. Investment 3. Jesus Christ 4. Political Science 5. Taxation I. Title

Acknowledgments

I am grateful to Roderick Grosvenor, my school principal, for letting me attend economics classes as a listener at an early age.

I am also indebted to the late Nobel Laureate and father of econometrics, Professor Laurence Kline, for inviting me to attend the University of Pennsylvania's Wharton School as a visiting scholar, and to Vahan Zanoyan, then managing director of Wharton Econometric Forecasting Associates. Furthermore, I am obliged to Professor Fakhri Shehab, the former chief economic adviser to the Emir of Kuwait and senior research fellow at St Anthony's College, Oxford, for his incisive economic views and invaluable discussions over the years.

To Dr. Abid Al-Aziz Al-Wettary, former deputy director of the Organization of Arab Petroleum Exporting Countries (OAPEC), I would like to extend my gratitude for inviting me to publish my first article in the OAPEC Journal.

I'm thankful to Professor Imad Moosa, professor of finance, RMIT, Melbourne, Australia, for his excellent technical contributions and opinions when we worked together and subsequently. I appreciate Dr. Usama AlJamali's penetrating economic interpretations, Dr. Hamid Majid's priceless comments, and Hamad Al Benali's excellent input.

My thanks to Dr. Pam for her extensive comments on the manuscript and general encouragement, to Ayden Majid for her comments and encouragement, and to Jacqueline Ramey, Aileen Cho, Nanette Day, and Linda

Kleinschmidt for their tireless editing. I am delighted by and appreciative of William's line editing and most valuable comments.

I'm indebted to my wife, Iman, for her encouragement, to my daughter, Sema, for her invaluable corrections, and to my son, Talib, for his understanding and patience.

And most of all, I'm indebted to my parents, who made sacrifices for my education and helped me in innumerable other ways. To all of you, I offer my enduring gratitude.

B. S. T. Al-Nakeeb

Author Note: Readers' comments are most appreciated. Besides submitting your comments in the comments space where the book is sold, you can also forward them to **parasitic.economics@gmail.com**. In the latter case, please provide your full name and title to possibly have your full comment or part of it published in the first pages or on the back cover of future updates of the book, unless you request not to publish it. I will also try to answer questions on the subject matter. Thank you.

About the Author

B asil Al-Nakeeb (b. 1949) is an independent scholar. He has helped establish four investment banks and a consumer credit company. His professional career, spanning four decades and three continents, has mostly focused on stocks. His last stock recommendation sent the stock limit up four days in a row. He extended Leontief's input-output matrix (for which Professor W. Leontief received the Nobel Prize a year earlier) to optimize national investment plans. He guided his research team to decompose the secret currency basket of the Kuwaiti Dinar, earning huge interest spreads. He has written articles and given talks on economics and finance. He holds an MSc. in Financial Economics (from the University College of North Wales) and is a Chartered Financial Analyst (CFA). Al-Nakeeb lives in Dubai with his wife and son.

Contents

Detailed Contents

One

*Knowledge will forever govern ignorance; and a
people who mean to be their own governors must arm
themselves with the power which knowledge gives.*[1]

JAMES MADISON

The lyrics of the song "Ain't We Got Fun?" describe the anxious, hard
times of 1921 in a fatalistic tone, yet with an alarming resonance today.[2]
The old familiar problems are back, like the poor getting poorer and the
rich richer. Decades ago, celebrated economics professor Joseph Schumpeter
observed, "More and more, the world seems about to sink in chaos, anar-
chy, or even a new barbarism," but he might as well have been speaking of
today.[3] Imperceptibly, the wheel of time has spun a full circle. After decades
of decent living, mainstream neoclassical economists are guiding the West
(Western democracies) to the poverty of the 1920s.

Crises are not accidents. The public is unsure whether economic disasters are repeating like *Groundhog Day* because economics has lost its relevance or because the high priests of economics have lost theirs.[4] Too many
economic pundits cannot let go of what someone once taught in the 19th

1

century. However, what is at stake is more profound than economics per se. As someone once observed, big powers collapse from within, while small nations collapse from outside forces. This is especially true in an age where the big powers have nuclear weapons. Two intricately intertwined common denominators of disintegration from within are moral and economic decline. In a democratic setting, the interpretation of moral decline must include democratic decline, as public choices in the absence of a healthy democracy do not represent the interests of the majority.

Several intellectual heavyweights have doubted the correctness of the West's present economic path. Niall Ferguson (b. 1964), a renowned Harvard University history professor, in his thought-provoking book *The Great Degeneration,* asks, "What exactly has gone amiss in the Western world in our time?"

Another scholar, Eamonn Fingleton (b. 1948), published an insightful article in 2010 in the American Conservative warning that the financial health of the United States has been deteriorating since the 1970s. He cites similarities to the more gradual decay of the Ottoman Empire in its final phase: free trade, heavy expenditure on wars funded by a burdensome foreign debt, and extensive foreign direct investments. The Ottomans reached the zenith of their power in the second half of the 16th century and remained resilient for another two and a half centuries, until 1854. Then the decline began with trade deficits and the accumulation of foreign debt. Fingleton notes that it took the United States a tenth of that time to fade from its peak economic power to dependence on foreign debt, prompting him to warn that the United States is at risk of financial implosion. He also sees confirmation of decline in the disappearance of US industries and the ballooning of trade deficits.

Fingleton's warnings are certainly persuasive, with one proviso. The comprehensive Ottoman defeat during World War I diminished the possibility of repairing that economy; the United States, on the other hand, still has a sufficient, if shrinking, margin for changing direction. Nevertheless, the Ottoman economic decline is symptomatic of the decline of great powers.

The lessons of history are valuable, but the most instructive are those from the recent past. The speed of collapse is accelerating. In the 1960s, the crumbling *economics of imperialism* led to the fastest mass-collapse of empires in history: the relinquishment of the British, French, Belgian, Dutch, Portuguese and Spanish empires.[5] Faster still was the more recent disintegration of a great power, the Soviet Union, when its economy imploded. Hence, whether at the center, right, or left of the political spectrum, macroeconomic efficiency ought to become a prime concern for everyone. Another lesson from those cataclysms is that a moral revival is a prerequisite for political and economic revival, which together represent the West's only line of defense against certain decline.

Complacent economists respond defensively that the United States still has a dominant economic position. In that, they confuse elevation with direction. What matters most is tomorrow. Someone descending from the peak of Mount Everest would have to persist for a long time before crossing paths with anyone traveling in the opposite direction—America and China did pass each other, heading in opposite directions, in 2014.[6]

The stack of bad policies, rooted in moral decline, which the United States has endured during the past three and a half decades, are testimony to American economic resilience. Across the North Atlantic, a parallel moral decline has nurtured similarly flawed economic policies that have victimized Western Europe, requiring comparable solutions.[7] Economic healing calls for identifying the causes of unrestrained indebtedness, industrial migration, economic-cycle amplification, chronically high unemployment, spreading poverty, and anemic growth; these and a host of other problems have constrained Western economies to operating well below their production-possibility frontiers.[8] Improving long-term macroeconomic performance will require strategic economic measures. The familiar fiscal and monetary policies are incapable of curing this malaise; the most they can provide is temporary relief from symptoms that in time will reappear. The flawed macroeconomic system needs new foundations. It will also require an unbending political will to pass the much-needed reforms, despite the anticipated opposition of special interests. Moreover, without the public's participation, public interest will not take precedence over private interests.

In Search of Reliable Signposts

In these troubled and confusing times, where can the public turn for dependable economic information and guidance?

Transitions are blurred processes without distinct beginnings and ends, but 1978 might have been the last year before the onset of the age of corruption.[9] The decline that followed has been steady and pervasive. For example, US economic statistics reflected economic conditions fairly before the massaging of the data began in the 1980s. Politicians found it easier to "lower" unemployment and inflation rates by changing their statistical definitions instead of the reality on the ground. Statistics was made an early victim to cover up the incompetence of the new economics. Such are the characteristics of the new age: things appear better than they feel, the ends justify the means, and *parasitic capitalism* no longer embarrasses its preachers and practitioners.

Should investors trust the credit ratings?

The moral decline that inspired "creative" statistics has proliferated; credit agencies have lost all restraint in their ratings, generously awarding "Triple A" to debts that default long before their maturity.

Can shareholders trust corporate accounts?

Accounting firms too have not been immune from the general decline in ethics; they have misled shareholders and would-be investors by overstating corporate profits and have sometimes issued confident reports about companies on the verge of bankruptcy.

Do the media deliver reliable economic information?

To distract attention from the errors plaguing Western economic policies, media coverage of the 2008 meltdown trumpeted a tale of global economic crisis, even though most countries outside the West only experienced a mild slowdown in their growth. China's diminished growth rate was still the envy of the world. Most economies in Asia, Latin America, and Africa, and in North, Central, and Eastern Europe, continued to grow. The growth rate of the BRICS countries, at 4 percent, was six times faster than that of the G-7, at only 0.7 percent. Now, in early 2016, Cyprus, Greece, Italy, Portugal, and Spain are still in the grip of depression, while Great Britain,

France, and Ireland go through double- and triple-dip recessions.[10] The disintegration of the euro is looming. The survival of the European Union is uncertain. The West is experiencing calamities, but the media consistently water down the muddle.[11]

Could the big commercial and investment banks have provided quality advice?

It must have been tempting to listen to them. Having comprehensive economic and investment research provided by the input of the highest paid and distinguished investment managers, economists, and analysts with qualifications from the West's most prestigious universities, the big banks did not seem to lack first-rate advice. Yet, the 2008 crisis revealed a pitiful reality: those big institutions were clueless and only colossal government bailouts kept them from sinking. If the insights of those "top-notch" experts could not save their employers from de facto bankruptcies, should anyone risk listening to them?

Did the Federal Reserve (Fed) offer the public a reliable assessment of the state of the US economy in 2008?[12]

Despite evidence to the contrary, the Fed avoided reporting disagreeable facts and maintained an optimistic outlook for as long as possible. At first, it denied there was a recession. Later, it admitted a mild one and then a regular one. Only when its shareholders, the big banks, were on the verge of bankruptcy and it needed to mobilize an enormous package to rescue them did the Fed scream disaster. The recession deepened further until it became the *Great Recession*. Had it been the 1930s, without Keynesian economics and with a much smaller government, the Great Recession would have been another Great Depression. If the Fed's economic radar, employing a thousand-odd economists, cannot detect the worst economic calamity since the Great Depression, then what can it detect?

Did the government's neoclassical economic advisors provide reliable guidance?

The 2008 crisis exposed the wide gap between reality and the perceptions of those economists. First, they arrogantly assured the public that their theory predicts that a recession is impossible because the deregulations they have instilled have made markets efficient, with near-instantaneous adjustments. The deepening crisis baffled them. Their elegant and costly mathematical economic models proved useless because their underlying theory was not valid, although they don't admit it. Their *sophisticated economics* reeks of intellectual snobbery, contrived complexity, commonsense deficiency, and lack of utility. Their occupations provided them with comfortable livings, at a prohibitive cost to the world. Moreover, since most of the government economic experts previously worked for the banks, most notably Goldman Sachs, their expert opinions are hardly more enlightened than the disastrous advice given to the banks.

To whom could the public have turned for reliable economic advice?

A rare breed of competent economists was in fact offering excellent advice, but regrettably, the public could scarcely hear their warnings above the din of the media-picked "experts." Dirk Bezemer cited twelve economists who predicted the crisis.[13] Of these, seven were from the US: Dean Baker, Michael Hudson, Eric Janszen, Kurt Richebächer, Nouriel Roubini, Peter Schiff, and Robert Shiller. The other five were Wynne Godley and Fred Harrison from the United Kingdom (UK), Jakob Brøchner Madsen and Jens Kjaer Sørensen from Denmark, and Steve Keen from Australia. I think of them as the Magnificent Dozen.

For my part, I was not engaged in making public forecasts and made no explicit forecast of an impending crisis, but perhaps an implicit one. In July 2008, I liquidated my entire stock portfolio and went off on holiday to beautiful Cape Town, South Africa; I realized my largest cumulative profit ever. I must admit, however, I did not suspect that the economy was in such bad shape.

Macroeconomics in Crisis

Politics aided by neoclassical economics have reversed the brief benevolence and prosperity that followed World War II. Mahatma Gandhi, with his undoubted moral authority, once declared, "Poverty is the worst form of violence." Does this imply that the mainstream economists who formulate the policies that are impoverishing hundreds of millions are committing crimes against humanity? Would they ever cease and desist of their own accord?

Macroeconomics has lost its creativity and utility. Aside from the Keynesian stir during the 1930s, the macroeconomic pot has been intellectually stagnant, despite feverish activity. Consider how much technology has advanced since the Great Depression. We now have air-conditioning, cars with automatic transmissions and tons of gadgets, giant aircrafts are flying millions of passengers daily, space exploration, computers, mobile phones, the Internet, and big-screen TVs. Yet, illustrious universities, Nobel Prize committees, and the media hail minor tweaks to 19th century economics as great accomplishments, making the delivery of real value-added macroeconomics that much trickier. A knowledge revolution has swept the world, while mainstream neoclassical macroeconomists have clung to theories from two centuries ago. Is it any wonder the West is in perpetual difficulty? As will become clear in due course, the same forces that have thwarted the development of macroeconomics have also frustrated the development of political science and public finance, fields that are vital for the development of a compelling macroeconomic theory and effective policies.

Adam Smith used the term *political economy* when referring to economics. It is a good description. An appreciation of the realpolitik is essential for understanding why macroeconomic theories sway like reeds in the political winds. Unlike microeconomics, macroeconomics is very political. Doubtless, Marxist economics supports the proletariat, while Keynesian economics upholds the middle and working classes, and neoclassical macroeconomics backs the ultra-rich plutocracy.[14] With the demise of Marxism and the undercutting of Keynesianism, neoclassical macroeconomics has had the field to itself for decades without an effective challenge from a theory that champions the interest of the majority. Unfortunately, macroeconomics now serves a microscopic minority.

Economic propagandists have bent reality to convince voters that giving the ultra-rich a larger slice of the national economic pie is in everybody's interest. Universities indoctrinate freshmen students that rationality is driving macroeconomics, whereas political agendas have tainted macroeconomic textbooks, journals, and theory, rendering them unreliable, and unscientific. Identifying where economic science ends and dogma begins is a challenge of the first order. Sadly, intellectual curiosity and scientific objectivity have sustained too few macroeconomists.

Another grim problem facing macroeconomics is an unwarranted mathematical complexity that ignores Leonardo da Vinci's wise advice: Simplicity is the ultimate sophistication.[15] Complexity has been the fashion for some time; its practitioners are typically the first to get lost in the intricate math they weave, arriving at wrong conclusions and misguided policy recommendations. They fail to observe two universal tests for any fruitful endeavor: relevance and common sense. As John Maynard Keynes observed, "good, or even competent, economists are the rarest of birds." The economic muddle in the West today is testimony to the accuracy of his assessment. The risk to the majority of people and the economy is the dearth of good economists not mathematicians.

Thus, mainstream neoclassical macroeconomists used complex methods to conclude that the deregulation has rendered markets so efficient that fiscal intervention has become unnecessary to counter recessions. During the late 1990s, the chief economist at the World Bank, Joseph Stiglitz, observed that this misconception at the US Treasury and the International Monetary Fund (IMF) made the East Asia crisis worse, yet they were still clinging to it by the time the Great Recession hit.[16]

Voltaire's notion that "common sense is not so common" is especially pertinent to neoclassical macroeconomics.[17] By contrast, Viscount Takahashi revolutionized macroeconomics, instinctively and profoundly, without fancy math.[18] The math best follows from a distance to add finer touches and rigor to an economic concept once common sense, rationality, qualitative analysis, and observation have established its validity. Mathematical economics is not a substitute for these essential tools. The careless application of mathematical economics has produced misconceptions that have become accepted truths, leaving young economists the unenviable but critical task of cleansing economics of many misguided hypotheses.

There are plenty of examples of economists' abuse of mathematics. For instance, it is the basis of securities markets efficiency theories, which supported deregulation and less supervision of securities markets, resulting in financial fiascoes like Enron, Bernie Madoff, and the sub-prime crisis, and the future crises emanating from the unregulated derivatives market. The truly sharp investors never trusted those fairytales; their outstanding investment performance is testimony that markets are not so efficient.[19]

Macroeconomics also suffers from chronic problems of habitual vagueness and hedged bets. These practices have blocked accessibility of the subject for no justifiable reason, preventing the public from participating in informed debates. The public needs to understand the *real* economic issues that are affecting the lives of hundreds of millions.

Yet, the most solemn problem facing macroeconomic theory is its blatant disregard of morality, rendering economic policy without a compass pointing to the true economic priorities.

The Economic Efficiency of Morality

Contrary to popular economic dogma, depriving macroeconomics of morality renders it irrational and as inadequate as medicine without chemistry. In the chapters to follow, *the unified theory of macroeconomic failure* will show that morality is a most critical, yet widely neglected, economic variable.[20] It may come as a cultural shock to many economists that economic efficiency and economic morality go hand in hand and that morally deficient economic policies are, necessarily, economically deficient too. Moreover, the reverse is equally true: inefficient economic policies are necessarily immoral. Hence, morality is a quick and sure test of macroeconomic efficiency. This stance is not driven by moralism but by uncompromising economic logic; those in doubt need to ponder this matter deeply.

For now, let us illustrate how the lack of a moral compass renders economic policies terribly misguided, inefficient, and unintelligent. Following the Great Recession, a morally correct economic policy would have expedited a faster and more cost effective economic recovery instead of an anemic one. Morality and public interest required bailing out the delinquent mortgage borrowers instead of the banks, hitting multiple birds with one stone:

1. Offering government funding to delinquent mortgages at near-zero interest (as offered to the banks) would have made most delinquent mortgages instantly affordable and sustainable, benefiting millions of homeowners.

2. The easy credit terms would also have had the important benefit of stabilizing house prices, the first step toward a recovery in housing construction and employment, benefiting millions of workers and the economy.

3. The resultant higher rates of employment would have increased federal tax receipts and saved the Treasury billions in unemployment and social security outlays, thereby recovering the cost of the mortgage support, in part or in full.

4. The proceeds from low-cost government funding to homeowners would have repaid the banks' nonperforming home mortgages, clearing their balance sheets of those dubious debts and stabilizing their situation.

5. Banks that remained in difficulty despite repaying their doubtful home mortgages were necessarily engaged in large, misplaced, speculative bets, well beyond their capacity for sustaining the resultant losses. Those banks should have folded, as they did in Iceland.

6. The foregoing tack would have had the additional benefit of not clogging the courts with a foreclosure tsunami.

7. Those still unable to sustain servicing their mortgages, due to job losses or otherwise, would have been able to sell their properties at attractive prices, given the subsidized mortgages attached.

8. At some point in the future, once those mortgages are sufficiently paid down and the economy is in full recovery, commercial mortgages could then progressively replace government funding for those who could afford it.

9. This morally correct economic policy, by achieving a broad-based recovery instead of restricting economic support to the sickly banks, would have saved trillions of dollars in subsequent aid to those banks in the form of multiple quantitative easing. It would have also preempted the $16 trillion in secret funds, which the Fed provided to international banks and corporations and which the Government Accountability Office (GAO) discovered by sheer chance, following the first full audit of the Fed ever.[21]

The preceding example illustrates that economic morality and efficiency are inseparable, two sides of the same coin. Instead, Western governments' immoral economic policies saved zombie banks with taxpayers' money only to have those same banks foreclose on home-owning taxpayers, leaving them without shelter in the freezing cold and Western economies lingering in a twilight zone between feeble recovery and recession. Treating bank shareholders as first-class citizens and mortgage borrowers as second-class subjects is acceptable under financial feudalism but not in functioning democracies. Immoral economic policies, besides their economic irrationality and inefficiency, are a violation of democracy itself, because millions have been suffering unnecessarily for a few to benefit immensely. In other words, moral economic policies are not just economically more efficient, but also consistent with democratic principles.

The economic irrationality of immoral policies hardly stopped there. Where is the economic rationality in the US federal government lending $700 billion to the big banks at very low interest rates by borrowing from their subsidiary, the Federal Reserve, at a much higher interest rate?[22] For its part, the Fed went on to magnify this economic absurdity many times over, under the label "quantitative easing," by offering its parent banks trillions of dollars more at cheaper rates than it charges the Treasury and, ultimately, the voting taxpayers.

The prominent neoclassical economists did not object to the immoral, inefficient and irrational economic policies cited above; they either did not grasp the flaws of those policies or they found them acceptable.

Iceland's handling of its debt problem is a valuable demonstration of the duality of economic morality and efficiency. The enormity of the Icelandic banking debt, at 11 times Iceland's gross domestic product (GDP), made the moral economic choice easier because the immoral alternative was economically catastrophic. By putting its people ahead of the banks' lenders and shareholders, Iceland, relative to its size, quickly recovered from the most devastating financial quandary in history.[23]

Iceland's moral solution was also the most cost-effective. Instead of squandering public resources on supporting irresponsible banks, it let them go under. It could hardly afford to let politicking by the failed banks stop the intrinsically capitalist process of creative destruction, which wiped out their equities and debts. It then recapitalized them as new banks with clean balance sheets and new managements, using a better business model and a streamlined cost structure. In due course, the Icelandic public will earn a profit from selling its stake in the new banks instead of shouldering a huge burden of lingering liabilities. Moreover, Iceland's policy will teach its banks valuable discipline by establishing that *no bank is too big to fail*, thereby preempting a potent source of financial blackmail.

The Icelandic lesson is illuminating for anyone who wants to see. Within four years, unemployment in Iceland was down to 4.5 percent and its economic growth was 3.5 percent, the fastest in Europe. To put the economic efficiency of the Icelandic solution in proper perspective, one only needs to compare it to the Greek muddle.

The Greek crisis began in 2009, about the same time as that of Iceland. Lenders and their governments intimidated the Greek government into abiding by the austerity policies they prescribed. By 2015, the lending banks had pushed Greece into a deep depression, with average unemployment around 25 percent and youth unemployment over 50 percent. With no light at the end of the tunnel, the most talented Greeks are emigrating.

In the absence of morality, the West implemented *schizophrenic capitalism*: gentle socialist policies for the banks and harsh capitalism and economic Darwinism for the rest.[24] For the United States and Greece, anti-societal policies came at a prohibitive cost. By contrast, the Icelandic solution, by letting the losers lose, was consistent with economic morality, efficiency, capitalism, and democracy.

Why Read This Book?

Is the Great Recession a taste of things to come? How does it compare with the Great Depression? Why is the West the epicenter of crises and stagnation? What policies guided the West to this economic quagmire? Why is the West addicted to debt? How did the Western economies become financial casinos? What was the contribution of the powerful banks to all of this? Does corporate income tax—contrary to the claims of public finance textbooks—increase instability, promote inefficiency, and stifle growth? Is personal income tax economically rational? Should we tax interest?

There are many more questions, all left unanswered. Mainstream neoclassical economists are not even considering those problems, never mind proposing solutions. In an interview with Charlie Rose, a noted economist compared the situation to a deer frozen by incoming headlights.[25]

This book will answer these questions and many more besides. It will do so by looking at the big picture as well as the details. It will rely on known facts, common sense and uncompromising economic logic, a modest dose of imagination, and a deliberate focus on the essential and disregard of the nonessential. It seeks to deliver convincing macroeconomic analysis and practical solutions that are readily understandable, using economic terms sparingly and avoiding theoretical niceties that have little real-world significance. Moreover, to explain why defunct macroeconomics is still with us in spite of the evidence of its past failure, I will undertake to sketch the historical and political context of its conception, the interests it serves, and its systematic marketing.

This book has been simmering in my mind for three decades, time enough to learn a few new ideas and to shed many. The crash of 2008 and its aftermath sharpened my focus. Consequently, I have spent a good part of the last five years listening, researching, learning, and intermittently writing but mostly pondering because, like so many things, ideas cannot be hurried;

they take time to ripen. Endless editing and reviewing of this work, intended to make it easier to read, has had the unexpected dividend of sharpening my own understanding of the issues.

I have been fortunate to enjoy a degree of flexibility in arriving at my current conclusions, being free of any baggage of previously published material requiring defending or retracting. I set out knowing what I wanted to say, but at some vague turn the book seemed to take over. What is now before you surprised me; it may surprise you too. Seeing the end of the exercise was like chasing a mirage. I was nudged along by a sense of public service, by my own curiosity, and most of all, by my love for economics that dates back to a chance encounter as a youngster, when I read about why Great Britain devalued the British Pound in 1958 in a book titled *Cyclopedia of World Events*, as I recall.

Advances in technology were my good fortune too; it made my work easier and better. I am grateful to all the programmers and innovators who brought us Microsoft Word, the Internet, BrainyQuote, The Free Dictionary, Amazon, and Google search, but my greatest gratitude goes to Wikipedia. Wikipedia was my brilliant and untiring research assistant; it was a revelation. It permitted me to bring to the attention of the reader little-known facts and half-forgotten truths that are essential for the correct interpretation of economic events. I was also lucky to have learned economics before neoclassical macroeconomics colored the subject in the 1980s. Naturally, all errors in this book are mine.

On the question of style, John Maynard Keynes advised, "Words ought to be a little wild, for they are the assault of thoughts on the unthinking."[26] George Orwell, the author of the frightening futuristic novel 1984, cautioned, "In a time of universal deceit, telling the truth is a revolutionary act."[27] In setting the tone of this book, I took the advice of Keynes and the challenge of Orwell; it is neither hedged nor subtle, because it would have made things easier on the perpetrators of the economic mess in the West. I admit that criticizing past economic theories is unfair because today we have the benefit of more information and hindsight, and because the great thinkers of the past cannot answer back. Still, silence is not a path to economic progress, considering that macroeconomic theory has been in need of rousing for a long time. At the same time, this book seeks to give credit where credit is due, particularly where academic institutions and the economic literature have failed to do so.

This book is a dialogue not just with students of economics but also with students of public finance, banking, investment, political science, and sociology. Most of all, I wanted the general public to see the possibility that good economics, stripped of the fog of political ideologies, can dramatically improve the lives of people. To that end, this book mostly avoids technical terms and uses a wealth of examples to make things clear. Public opinion is possibly the best impediment against the relentless enforcement of flawed economic policies by the political elite. The public needs to become an interested party because it has endured the worst consequences of parasitic economics that has precipitated debt crises, unfair taxation, and misdirected public expenditure.

I have used italics to highlight new or rarely used economic concepts and for emphasis. Economics books repeat the phrase *ceteris paribus*, meaning other things being equal or held constant. In what follows, to avoid boring the reader by repeatedly invoking this phrase, let us agree that it applies wherever it is relevant and it will not be mentioned unless necessary to clarify a particularly delicate shade of meaning. One last point regarding style deserves mentioning. Well-known facts that are well-documented by readily available sources were deemed to render statistical tables unnecessary, unless absolutely required for explaining a particular concept such as the structural transformation of business cycles following 1942. This less encumbered approach permitted a smoother flow of ideas and the covering of vast grounds using a limited space.

Following this introduction, Part I provides an overview of the macroeconomic landscape, the conflicting theories, and their uneven progress. It covers classical, Marxist, Keynesian, and neoclassical theories. It explores their contributions, but especially their oversights and errors that hindered the progress of macroeconomics. Part II introduces *the unified theory of macroeconomic failure*, an alternative framework for explaining and solving economic problems and financial crises. Parts III and IV apply *the unified theory of macroeconomic failure* to diagnose a range of chronic macroeconomic problems, including indebtedness, monetary policy, amplified cyclicality, monopolies, low-quality information, and ailing democracies' failure to make economically efficient public choices.[28] Part V proposes economically efficient and rational financial and tax alternatives that conform to the guidelines of *the unified theory.* Part VI concludes with an economic and political outlook.

The present economic system is demonstrably wobbly, yet no alternative economic architecture has surfaced to replace it. Moreover, if you suspect (as I do) that the financial breakdown in 2008–2009 was not a passing glitch on the economic radar and we ignore its warnings at our peril, then I urge you to read on. A fascinating journey through time with distinctly different perspectives and a world several degrees removed from where you expect it awaits you. Together, we will inspect the very foundations of *parasitic economics* and the roots of economic crises, expose popular economic myths, discard obsolete dogmas, and consider alternatives. It is my sincere hope that the analysis will keep the reader engaged, stimulated, and rewarded to the very end. Because of the abundance of its novel concepts and distinctly different interpretations, this book will likely generate controversy and debate—I hope that debate will spark many creative ideas. Finally, if you decide to read on, kindly take the time to share your reflections and thoughts with your peers because it will enrich economics.

Part I

THE DIALECTIC PATH OF ECONOMIC THEORY

TWO

CLASSICAL ECONOMIC THEORY
(1776–1873)[29]

*It is preoccupation with possessions, more than anything
else, that prevents us from living freely and nobly.*[30]

BERTRAND RUSSELL

Studying the progress of macroeconomics requires segregating economics into its micro and macro components. Briefly, microeconomics
studies the behavior of economic participants as individuals and firms and
the demand and supply they generate for goods and services, which determine market prices. By contrast, macroeconomics looks at the big picture
of the economy as a whole, focusing on aggregate economic variables such
as total demand and supply in an economy, employment, inflation, and
growth. Early economists were infatuated with markets and their apparent
efficiency. However, markets' inability to resolve macroeconomic crises during the first half of the 19th century, prompted Karl Marx (1818–1883) to
label those early theories *classical*, meaning obsolete.

This chapter examines the impact of the classical theory on macroeconomics, particularly its choice of economic driver, its economic

decision-makers, and the conditions surrounding these; appreciation of these early concepts is vital to understanding current macroeconomic problems.

The Pioneers

The pioneering economists contributed a wealth of economic ideas for almost a century between 1776 and 1873, while Europe was transitioning from feudalism to industrialization. Inevitably, the prevailing class structure colored their outlook. They laid the foundations of modern microeconomics, such as demand, supply, price, markets, the division of labor, and factor incomes: wages to labor, rent to land, and profit (interest) to capital. Theirs was individual effort; they did not think of themselves as belonging to a particular school of thought. In contrast to their considerable contribution to microeconomic theory, they had limited success with macroeconomics.

The four distinguished classical economists were:

Adam Smith (1723–1790) was Scottish. In 1776, he published his seminal work, *The Wealth of Nations*, making him the father of classical economics.[31]

David Ricardo (1772–1823) was a British political economist. He developed the concepts of the labor theory of value, comparative advantage, the law of diminishing returns, economic rent, and Ricardian equivalence. His theory of comparative advantage and specialization by nations supported free trade, and consequently he opposed the British Corn Laws. He made a fortune speculating on financial markets, which allowed him, in later life, to purchase a seat in the British Parliament.[32]

Jean-Baptiste Say (1767–1832) was a French businessman and economist. He was a strong advocate of free markets. Say's Law states that supply creates its own demand.[33] As with several classical concepts, it is more valid at the micro level than at the macro level. For instance, the introduction of a new gadget, like a new mobile phone, creates its own demand. However, it would be a mistake to extend this analysis to the macro economy because the demand for the new gadget is likely a demand shift away from older gadgets (e.g., an earlier version of the mobile phone), with little impact on aggregate demand. However, on rare occasions Say's Law could conceivably extend to the macro level if a series of innovations drive large investments at the same time, as suggested by Joseph Schumpeter (1883–1950) in his innovations cycle.[34]

John Stuart Mill (1806–1873) was a British economist, an influential social philosopher and the last and most moral of the pioneers. He was against slavery and supported free speech, individual freedoms, women's suffrage, and proportional representation. In his later years, he advocated economic democracy, labor unions, and farm cooperatives, and opposed unrestrained capitalism.[35]

A fifth "economist," Reverend Thomas Malthus (1766–1834), was an Anglican cleric whose admirers consider him a pillar of classical economics and habitually include him with the pioneers. His often cited contribution to economics was a mistaken impending crisis theory that presumed populations would grow exponentially while agricultural production would only grow linearly, resulting in mass starvation, unless population growth is checked. Malthus had not realized that agricultural production had kept pace with population growth by clearing marshes and forests and increasing agricultural yields through the use of metal-bladed ploughs, crop rotation, etc.[36] His worst transgression on economics was in advancing flawed economic arguments to benefit the British feudal aristocracy by lobbying for the British Corn Laws, which resulted in the deprivation and starvation of millions in Great Britain. Hence, he could hardly belong to the above-mentioned league of pioneers of classical economics.

The other mistake was to exclude the veritable macroeconomics pioneer, Jean Charles Léonard de Sismondi (1773–1842), from the list of pioneers. De Sismondi was a Swiss economist and the father of macroeconomics and business cycle theory. Among his other noteworthy contributions was to refute David Ricardo's general equilibrium theory and its focus on the long run. Instead, he understood markets' inability to self-correct in a reasonable period and called for a larger government role in economic stabilization, which Keynes would later advocate as well.[37] By rejecting de Sismondi's contributions, classical economics remained incomplete and without a viable solution to economic contractions; hence, economic crises continued unabated until the 1940s, providing a foothold for Marxism and all that flowed from it. Curiously, neoclassical economists' rejection of Keynesian macroeconomics in the 1930s mirrored the classical rejection of de Sismondi's theories a century earlier.

Critical Classical Assumptions

Assumptions about the real world are the foundations of economic theory. Their validity, realism, and completeness are prerequisites for a robust theory. Hence, careful examination of those assumptions is equivalent to inspecting the very foundations of a theory to reveal its strengths and weaknesses.

Classical theory adopted heroic, simplistic assumptions such as the idea that markets are perfectly competitive, efficient, and self-regulating. It also assumed that self-interest, sometimes referred to as Adam Smith's hidden hand, is the sole driver of economic participants as consumers, savers, investors, and businesses. Regrettably, capitalist economic theories have adhered to this crucial assumption of a single economic driver.

Let us begin by clarifying the relationship between self-interest and capitalism. Some capitalist enthusiasts have mistakenly attributed self-interest to capitalism. No doubt, capitalism has achieved much, but it could not have implanted self-interest in the mind of the human species. Self-interest and the profit motive permeate the economy and the markets because they are part of our survival instinct. They are hard-wired into our psyche.[38] For countless millennia before capitalism, self-interest was one of our built-in autopilots, helping us survive and adapt. In Mesopotamia, it likely gave rise to the first barter trade—a free market without government interference—marking the birth of capitalism.

Free markets proved an economic wonder, most of the time. However, we should not become infatuated with them the way classical economists were and the neoclassical economists since. We should not lose sight of the fact that markets and capitalism are manmade and, therefore, bound to be imperfect and occasionally disastrous.

Classical economics also makes idealized assumptions about economic man (*homo economicus*), such as the following:[39]

1. He is perfectly rational.
2. He has perfect information, or at least the necessary information, for making rational and correct decisions.
3. His decision-making process rationally weighs and selects alternative outcomes.
4. Self-interest is the sole arbiter between alternative courses of action.
5. His actions, driven by self-interest, are not only beneficial to himself but also to society.

If economic behavior is at least sometimes inconsistent with these assumptions, then it is reasonable to conclude that such assumptions do not fully define economic behavior and it becomes paramount to identify what else drives it and under what conditions.

Self-Interest, Rationality, and Instinct

Classical theory tends to overemphasize logic and rationality in human behavior and to ignore the role of instinct. This is understandable; people hold logical deduction in high esteem because it has cleared the path to many scientific discoveries, while instinct has animal connotations, even irrationality. Yet, humans only began using formal logic recently—a mere few thousand years ago—while instinct has played a vital role in human survival since the beginning of our existence. Instinct is easily mistaken for irrationality because its logic is fuzzy, deep, and more complex than formal logic, arriving at conclusions that frequently challenge those based on formal logic. Carl Jung (1875–1961), the celebrated Swiss psychiatrist, psychotherapist and founder of analytical psychology, once remarked, "We should not pretend to understand the world only by the intellect. The judgement of the intellect is only part of the truth."[40]Once again, since self-interest itself is a consequence of our survival instinct then, instinct necessarily plays a big role in our decision-making, including in economic matters.

Rationality, logic, and other deductive tools work best when we have comprehensive information about a problem and sufficient time to consider it carefully and unemotionally, as in designing a functional and cost-effective building. However, in real life such prerequisites are frequently missing when making important, but time-critical, decisions. Often, it is not just that we do not know everything about an issue, but also that we do not know how much we do not know about it. Scientific advancement is a good illustration, frequently compelling us to revise our scientific knowledge.

By contrast, instinct, vague and complex though it may be, is most effective for processing large, incomplete, and uncertain information and making decisions at lightning speed. Without realizing it, we make such decisions numerous times every day, instinctively. For example, when something happens abruptly on the roadway, the driver has to respond immediately and instinctively. Even in the arts and sciences, an instinctive sixth sense unencumbered by rationality has shepherded our most creative inspirations.

Instinct and logic are frequently so intertwined that it is difficult to draw the line between them. By way of illustration, imagine a herd of gazelles grazing serenely in the wild. A twig breaks. Some gazelles instinctively run; others stop grazing and look about to ascertain the source. Presumably, the latter group is rational because instead of running for no clear reason, they seek a rational explanation for the sound before deciding to run or stay. They could be rationally weighing the cost and benefit of running versus staying: the calories expended in running and the opportunity cost of calories lost by not grazing against the benefit of avoiding an uncertain risk.

Shortly thereafter, a leopard springs and captures one of the "rational" gazelles. Those that stayed behind took a risk to obtain better information, so as to rationally decide whether to stay or run. When they got the information, it was too late for one of them. Thus, the rational gazelles learned the hard way that in the absence of perfect information, pursuing rationality at the expense of instinct proved irrational for one of their lot.

Let us explore the complexity of this situation further. What else might have motivated the gazelles to run or stay? Was it differences in their individual circumstances? Perhaps the gazelles that ran had fuller stomachs, which afforded them the loss of actual and potential calories, while those that stayed behind were hungry (the equivalent of rich versus poor). Alternatively, were the gazelles that ran closer to the source of the sound, permitting them to assess the risk better by virtue of superior information? Perhaps they had survived previous predatory attacks, giving them more experience in assessing risk. Maybe some behaved as a herd, surrendering their will to those closest to them in running or staying, as panicked humans do. This example illustrates how the same stimulus can produce different responses due to differences in circumstance (e.g., biological needs, availability of information, experience, and herd behavior).

A variation on the previous example is a stock market crash that affects a large percentage of the investing public. Again, the same type of stimulus could propel different reactions due to the rational, instinctive, or emotional processing of the stimulus, as well as differences in individual circumstances such as wealth, indebtedness (full vs. hungry gazelles), information, experience, education, psychology, and self-discipline. Moreover, incomplete information can yield bizarre outcomes where, in retrospect, rational behavior could turn out to be irrational and instinctive behavior, rational.

However, even this degree of uncertainty about motives understates the real complexity of the situation. Fear can overwhelm the senses, while a false sense of security and inertia can dull the instinct, with implications for financial and other markets. Another level of complexity applies to the human species because it comprises of both prey and predators. In other words, there are human equivalents to both leopard and gazelles, with diametrically opposite motives.

Clearly, rational self-interest is an inadequate explanation of the broad spectrum of human behavior.

Insufficient Information, Emotion, and Irrationality

Investment is central to economic activity. It entails expending time, effort, and capital resources in the near term in anticipation of a larger, though uncertain and more distant, return. Profits compensate investors for their effort, the risk of loss, the delay in recovering their principal, and the inconvenience of illiquidity. These basic concepts apply whether the investment is a corner grocery store or a multi-billion-dollar petrochemical complex.

People tend to invest when they are optimistic about the future and overinvest when they are overly optimistic. Similarly, they tend to stop investing when they are pessimistic and to liquidate their investments when they are very pessimistic. Moreover, the emotions of optimism and pessimism are often contagious, producing bouts of overinvesting followed by shutting off the investment spigot or even the mass liquidation of investments. Man fears what he does not know and a sudden awareness of the inadequacy of information can trigger a panic.

The foregoing simplified investment and economic cycle mirrors an emotional cycle that does not conform to the classical model of rational self-interest. Indeed, too often, the investing public acts irrationally, without sufficient information and without the foresight to spot market turning points, contrary to the expectations of the classical model. At the same time, the rational self-interest model has some validity. For example, the most successful investors, like Warren Buffett, control their emotions, collect the necessary information, and undertake the required analysis to make rational decisions that yield outstanding returns on their investments—but they are the exception, not the rule.[41]

Positively Sloping Marginal Utility Curves

For the thirsty, the first mouthful of water provides the greatest satisfaction or utility. Successive mouthfuls provide decreasing utility until the thirst is quenched and drinking stops. This illustrates the economic law of diminishing marginal utility of consumption. It is portrayed graphically as a negatively sloping curve, with utility on the vertical axis and quantity consumed on the horizontal. This is the normal and rational consumption pattern.

However, there are also irrational, compulsive, consumption patterns, such as overeating, smoking, gambling, alcoholism, and drug addiction. Such harmful consumptions violate the classical principles of self-interest and rationality.

Indeed, some behaviors appear driven by self-interest and rationality, but are in fact compulsive. The preeminent example is *compulsive wealth gathering*; religions wanted to spare humanity the burden of avarice and its unrestrained adoration of gold, wasting lives in pursuit of an irrational and compulsive urge. Worse still, when money gathering occurs by depriving the disadvantaged, it becomes sadistic; wealth without charity suffocates the humanity of the wealthy, reducing them to gold zombies. Unlike communism, religions did not contemplate wealth confiscation, but rather a path to emancipation from gold bondage through contentment.

Wealth accumulation, as a store of value to provide for future consumption, is very rational. For normal people, the demand for wealth is a derived demand for future consumption; therefore, its underlying utility curve is normal and negatively sloping. Excessive wealth is unnecessary because humans have limited life spans and limited present and future consumption needs, whether it be food, drink, clothing, shelter, security, entertainment, or extravagance. Hence, the need for wealth gathering is finite.

When the urge for more riches is overpowering and exceeds any rational present and future consumption needs, it crosses over from normality to compulsive behavior and irrationality. Future consumption needs are not an adequate explanation for those with an insatiable appetite for wealth because their marginal utility curve for wealth is positively sloping.[42]

The song "Don't Cry for Me Argentina" portrays wealth accumulation as an illusion, not a solution. Abundant wealth makes further accumulation self-defeating and irrational because the ultimate scarce resource is time. The pursuit of a larger treasure wastes the limited time available for enjoying wealth's consumption possibilities; wealth gathering becomes an addiction that makes the addict oblivious to the fact that he or she only has a transit visa on earth and time is ticking. Sadly, the realization that materialism is not a path to contentment, much less happiness, comes late in the game to many wealth-gathering addicts, if it comes at all.

Even the desire of parents to leave an inheritance becomes irrational when the inheritance is excessive. A materialistic upbringing implies that the larger the inheritance, the happier the offspring; thus, loss of one's parents is transformed into a happy occasion that the beneficiaries covertly look forward to, to say nothing of the occasional motive for crime. Hence, for a multitude of reasons, boundless wealth accumulation is counterproductive and irrational. It is a Shakespearean tragedy of the first order: insatiable thirst for wealth is the curse of the chronically thirsty, making them lose sight of the original purpose of the endeavor.

Wealth, Power, and Insecurity

Several hypotheses surround the compulsion for wealth accumulation. Misers evidently have positively sloping marginal utility curves for wealth. They also display traits characterized as obsessive–compulsive personality disorder.

Adam Smith argued that the enjoyment of wealth lay not in its consumption, but in its exhibition. In other words, avarice is an exercise in exhibitionist frivolity. It raises questions about the insecurity of the exhibitionists, compelling them to take from the meager resources of their fellow humans to satisfy a craving for attention. Such subliminal insecurity turns psychopathic when it is associated with criminal acts.

William Shakespeare (1564–1616), the eminent observer of human failings, illustrated this phenomenon in his celebrated play *The Merchant of Venice*. It delivers a vivid picture of Shylock, a pitiless moneylender driven by psychopathic cold-heartedness, demanding *a pound of flesh for a pound of gold* should the borrower default. Shakespeare's Shylock conveys the moral repugnance of predatory finance.

John Maynard Keynes harbored strong reservations about unlimited wealth accumulation. He asserted, "… The love of money as a possession—as distinguished from the love of money as a means to the enjoyments and re-alities of life—will be recognized for what it is, a somewhat disgusting mor-bidity, one of those semi-criminal, semi-pathological propensities which one hands over with a shudder to the specialists in mental disease ... But beware! ... For at least another hundred years we must pretend to ourselves and to everyone that fair is foul and foul is fair; for foul is useful and fair is not. Avarice and usury and precaution must be our gods for a little longer still."[43]

Bertrand Russell, in his incisive work *Power*, explored the problems of government and the thirst for power in its various forms: religious, military, political, and economic.[44] He considered those varied forms of power, like different forms of energy, interchangeable. For example, just as heat energy is convertible into electrical or mechanical energy, similarly, economic pow-er can provide political or military power. Hence, the underlying impulse for excessive wealth may be an urge for greater political power.

Conceivably, in the deepest recesses of the minds of compulsive wealth accumulators, the power of wealth offers better chances of survival and a heightened sense of security. An insatiable hunger for power and survival is compulsive too because with aging there should be a declining marginal utility curve, even for survival itself. In any case, excessive wealth is excessive power and even in the hands of the psychologically sane, it is a threat to the proper functioning of a democratic system and a backdoor to plutocracy, albeit with democratic trappings.

Parasitic Economics and Parasitic Capitalism

In the interest of clarity, it is important to establish the relationship between two related but distinct concepts: *parasitic economics* and *parasitic capitalism*. *Parasitic economics* is the provision of the contrived theoretical economic basis that supports and justifies *Parasitic capitalism*. This can arise by way of an unintentional analytical error but more often as a means of supporting a plutocratic economic agenda that advances the interest of a small minor-ity to the detriment of the rest of society. As a result, it proposes unsound economics that results in economic inefficiency, inferior performance and seeds economic crises and depressions. The flaws in its economic arguments are not always obvious, but flawed nonetheless. The arguments in support of *parasitic economics* have been put forth by classical economics initially and later expanded on by neoclassical economics.

Parasitic capitalism, on the other hand, refers to the immoral and, occasionally, criminal, pursuit of unrestrained parasitic profits in a coercive parasite-host relationship enforced by a plutocratic state apparatus. Such patristic profits have been extorted in a variety of means, including feudalism, serfdom, genocidal imperialism, looting of nations, trafficking in human cargo, racism, torture, political murder, imprisonment, banishment, suppression of political rights, destitution, famines, and more recently, debt-bondage without regard to its consequences, including loss of shelter, break-up of families, and suicides.[45]

Parasitic Capitalism, Plutocracy, and Psychopathy

As previously mentioned, classical economists have built their economic theories around the assumptions of self-interest, rationality, and sanity. Their model has some applicability, but not universality. Its validity weakens further as we move to the extremes of the personality spectrum: those with the highest and lowest moral fibers. People driven by honorable, gallant, and virtuous morality are at one end of the scale. They come from all backgrounds and provide society, and their loved ones, with moral leadership by their acts of selflessness, humanity, charity, bravery, and sacrifice. At the other end of the spectrum are psychopathic individuals whose irrationality propels them to undertake barbaric acts to satisfy their compulsion for wealth gathering by practicing *parasitic capitalism.*

Unchecked *parasitic capitalism* is economic fascism or worse. To protect its drug-trafficking profits, *parasitic capitalism* has waged the *opium wars* in the name of the Motherland, using citizens for cannon fodder.[46] Imperialist *parasitic capitalism* expropriated the surplus out of their colonies, thereby stifling economic development there to spur the development of the imperial powers and forcibly widening the economic gap between the exploiters and their victims. The resultant malnutrition among natives cut their life expectancy by half.[47] Imperialism and *Parasitic capitalism* are vulgar criminalities and not economic endeavors; they have reduced scientific advances, architectural marvels, breathtaking paintings, enchanting music, and captivating literature to the mere paraphernalia of civilization, an outer shell of barbaric regimes. The establishments and aristocracies that sanctioned those crimes, regardless of their fine table manners and pomp and circumstance, are essentially exclusive clubs of criminals that make the Mafia a gathering of angels. Stripped of morality, society has no soul and its claim to civilization is hollow.

The perpetrators of such crimes do so with impunity, fearing no punishment because they are certain of their political cover. The democratic charade does not change the reality that *parasitic capitalism* is institutionalized sadism practiced by a wealthy plutocracy. The question is do plutocrats derive pleasure as well as material gain from committing atrocities? After all, such criminalities require not just moral bankruptcy but also deranged minds. No sane person could commit such crimes. The shocking truth is that psychopaths are among us and they are often the most powerful economic actors, although economics textbooks pretend they do not exist. Clearly, deviant political systems require deviant macroeconomics to support them. Perhaps students of political science can shed more light on the role of plutocratic motives in historical political developments.

The words of Jesus Christ on wealth accumulation are most illuminating: "For what shall it profit a man, if he gain the whole world, and suffer the loss of his soul?"[48] Human history is an inglorious record of parasitic exploitation within and beyond national borders, with the majority of people defenseless against the tons of sin committed against them.

Plutocracies have survived despite the misery they spread because they are manned by talented and formidable individuals, capable of projecting alternate realities like the idea that the poor are to blame for their poverty. The Reverend Thomas Malthus, a Fellow of the Royal Society and intellectually close to David Ricardo, is a case in point. Although an Anglican clergyman, he was against Christ's teachings by rejecting empathy and charity to the poor. Paradoxically, the Anglican Church did not find his anti-Christian values and proposals grounds for expelling him from the Church.

His economic writings reflected a right-wing conservative disposition that supported the plutocratic status quo. It is no coincidence that he was a professor of political economy at a college belonging to the notorious East India Company in Hertfordshire, England. Its shareholders were relatively few and wealthy; their company had obtained license from the imperial British government to do as it pleased with the natives of the British colonies.

The East India Company practiced the nastiest forms of *parasitic capitalism*; it swelled its *parasitic profits* to become Europe's foremost imperialist franchise through gruesome atrocities. Its most profitable line of business was the slave trade and, following the First Opium War of 1839–1842, a monopoly on drug trafficking into China from Afghanistan and its opium plantations in India. To right-wing conservative economists of the day, the East India Company was a model of economic efficiency and rationality by privatizing and outsourcing imperialism and downsizing the government. The economic logic of these arguments has chilling parallels today in the calls for privatizing public monopolies.

During the first half of the 19th century, workers in the "democratic" British Isles were often on the brink of starvation, hardly better off than were the natives in the colonies. By perverse economic logic, Reverend Malthus proposed abolishing the meager assistance that the extremely poor people received under the English Poor Laws, this in a sadistic attempt to prevent them from marrying and multiplying.[49] He maintained this stance for the rest of his life, arguing that shrinking the labor supply was good for labor because it would raise their wages and living standards. However, Malthus failed to mention how many must perish to implement his plan. Like all immoral economic policies, it was shortsighted. He did not foresee that once the standard of living of the poor improved, they would again marry and multiply, driving down their future wages and returning them to poverty. By Malthus's sick logic, the poor people's rebound would have necessitated their periodic culling. His plan bore an uncanny resemblance to Nazi death camps, which used death by starvation almost a century later. The criminality of his plans as well as his flawed logic requires dismissing Malthus as an economist altogether, never mind including him among the pioneers.

The British plutocracy, fearing Malthus's proposals would spark a revolt, decided not to implement the ghoulish scheme. However, he had previously lobbied for another scheme to increase the profits of the wealthy and the hardship of the downtrodden, which the British government adopted and the British Parliament passed. More specifically, in 1815, Reverend Malthus lobbied for putting a tariff on grain imports (the British Corn Laws), which not only impoverished the British working class for decades but also starved about a million of them to death, all to increase the wealth of the British land-owning aristocracy.[50] Any political system that shuns the interests of the vast majority of the people—the poor and underprivileged—is vile and undeserving of the label "democracy." True democracies do not tolerate the dictatorship of money.

Plutocratic atrocities rarely shocked 19th-century economists, making them intellectual servants of morally bankrupt ruling classes. To maintain a modicum of respectability, at some point economists invented "value judgments" to justify violations of the moral code. The gold worshipers used social Darwinism to explain that their wealth and privilege were proof that they were the fittest, entitling them to an alternate morality that permits gold gatherers to starve the underclass at home and massacre the natives abroad. However, like Malthus, their logic was flawed. Authentic social Darwinism, as John Kenneth Galbraith incisively noted, required confiscating the inheritance of the rich to ensure that the next generation was as fit as their parents presumably were.[51] Hypocritical double standards and inconsistency in applying social Darwinism hardly bothered its economic adherents in the 19th century. Hypocrisy masquerading as macroeconomics is still with us.

Plutocratic domination extended to the church; it obliged by appeasing the impoverished with promises of a better afterlife, provided they endured the status quo. Like the economists, many theologians' response to those crimes ranged between support and silence, thereby sacrificing Christian values.[52] The imperialist plutocracy also engaged local plutocracies in the colonies and the periphery as a low cost solution for maintaining control.

The Ramifications of Missing Drivers

A structural flaw of the classical model was its amorality. Its rational self-interest did not seem to conflict with the institutionalized economic criminality at the time. The economic actor it envisioned was a moneymaking machine without moral depth or humanity. It overlooked the full spectrum of human tendencies: egotistic self-interest to the point of psychopathic criminality, nobility of spirit to the point of sainthood, and everything in between. Hence, it cannot properly explain why soldiers volunteer at wartime to defend their country, why mothers spend sleepless nights looking after their sick children, or why parents willingly make great sacrifices to see their children through universities, without any expectation of financial reward. It does not explain our instinct for charity.

More generally, it does not explain our instinct for morality, which drives *societal-interest*. Morality and *societal-interest* have subtle links to our survival instinct, not at the individual level but at the level of collective survival as families, groups, tribes, societies, nations, and species. Perhaps our instinct for morality resides in the deepest recesses of the unconscious, which Carl Jung referred to as the "collective unconscious."[53]

Classical economics' assumption that self-interest is the sole driver of economic behavior is a caricature of economic reality and a disservice to macroeconomics because it projects a plutocratic perspective: a world where humaneness is an inconvenience. Indoctrinating the minds of students of economics and the public at large that self-interest is the sole rational economic driver is to suggest that egotism, greed, and materialism are normal attributes of economic behavior, implying that nobler attributes are irrational and aberrant. This callous indoctrination relegated economic morality, improving income distribution, and welfare programs to mere social and political agendas, treating such moral considerations as outside of the realm of economics because they collide with plutocratic selfishness. Disregard of the majority is one explanation for dire macroeconomic policies. Unfortunately, economic thinking has inherited this error from the classical economists, producing a corrupted, deviant, and grotesque macroeconomics that propelled the rise of Marxism.

A Post-Classical Model of Economic Behavior

The classical model of economic behavior resembles the early, primitive, version of the personal computer Disk Operating System (DOS). DOS permitted running only one computer program at a time. About two decades later, Windows replaced DOS, permitting multitasking in real time. Like the unidimensional DOS, classical economics based economic decisions on a narrow hypothesis: only self-interest for an economic driver, only rational actors, only perfect information, and only perfect markets. Unlike DOS, this highly unrealistic and restrictive theoretical environment has been with us for two centuries. It is high time for the economics profession to throw off this mistaken economic model.

Observation suggests there is not one but at least six economic drivers, two rational and four irrational. These drivers are present in everyone in varying degrees; their relative dominance depends on the personality of the actors concerned, circumstances, *perceived* information, and the decision-making process.

Besides certain established facts such as the dawning of the sun in the east, critical information for decision-making is rarely certain; normally, only partial information is available, bundled with wrong and uncertain facts and it gets progressively less reliable the farther we gaze into the future. A realistic decision-making process is a blend of rationality and instinct with instinct taking a larger role when information is noticeably inadequate and decision-making is time-critical. Instinct also takes on a bigger role in essentially moral issues like charity and love of family, and country. Disregarding morality has given rise to imperfect markets, an imperfect political system, and inefficient tax and public expenditure policies. In addition, emotion can overwhelm the entire decision-making process in moments of extreme excitement or fright. The model proposed here is a better approximation of reality than the classical model, though by no means perfect. It assumes that all people are subject to multiple drivers, and that the relative dominance of certain drivers at different times is what colors behavior.

I. Economic Drivers

A. Instinctually Rational Economic Drivers

Although these drivers, *societal-interest* and self-interest, have been labelled rational to distinguish them from the irrational drivers to follow, they are in fact a blend of logic and instinct. Most significantly, *societal-interest* and self-interest can be complementary, provided they are fairly balanced under an environment of high moral standards such as a genuine representative democracy.

1. *Self-Interest*: This economic driver is hard-wired into the human psyche, a byproduct of the survival instinct of the individual. It is explicit within a market system, driving most people to earn a living, consume, save, and invest. Borrowing loosely from something Abraham Lincoln said, self-interest drives all the people some of the time, and some of the people all the time, but not all the people all the time.[54] Normally, self-interest is conducive to *societal-interest* but it requires restraint when it becomes excessive, immoral, irrational, and, consequently, detrimental to *societal-interest*.

2. *Societal-Interest*: This driver expresses itself through such moral behaviors as win-win strategies; charity; fairness; standing by the weak against the heartless; love and sacrifice for family, country and principles. Like self-interest, it is also hard-wired into the human psyche, a byproduct of the instinct for collective survival of families, tribes, and nations, and as such, even more rational than self-interest. It is implicit in a market framework. It also functions as a check against

36

the destructive power of unrestrained self-interest, and therefore, as an antidote to economic barbarism.

Societal-interest drives the need for public goods: justice, police protection, public health, the welfare state, improving the lot of the downtrodden, environmental protection, and national defense. It is intrinsically linked to the preservation of society, morality, humaneness, religious instincts, and public concerns. Hence, economic morality implies *societal-interest* and is inseparable from economic efficiency. Naturally, *societal-interest* is meaningless if it is not a two-way obligation between society and the individual. Hence, societies are obligated to take on the role of tribes in centuries past, by looking after their members. Economics without concern for *societal-interest* is not just the economics of vampires but also irrational and inefficient. Most seriously, a society that has fading *societal-interest* is itself fading. Typically, plutocracies favor their group or individual interest over *societal-interest*, which requires lowering moral standards.

The chapters and economic arguments to follow will use the current model—particularly the balancing of self-interest and societal interest—for evaluating the economic efficiency of public policy. This balance is only approximately achievable under a centrist political agenda, which is also the most democratic because it is consistent with the desires of the majority of the people by definition. The political agenda of the Left is economically inefficient because it tends to sacrifice self-interest, whereas the political agenda of the Right is economically inefficient because it tends to sacrifice *societal-interest*.

B. Irrational Economic Drivers

These drivers are essentially irrational and, typically, contrary to the self-interest and *societal-interest* drivers cited above.

1. *Emotional Behavior.* This driver sometimes manifests itself as crowd behavior. It is observable as avarice, reckless courage, exuberance, and

infinite optimism when markets are rising spectacularly and as panic and widespread pessimism when markets are crashing. It typically peaks around the turning points of speculative markets, becoming self-destructive and overwhelming rational decision-making and instinct. It produces irrational decisions as well as decision-paralysis. Other than in the marketplace, infatuation, hate, famine, revolution, war, among other stimuli can trigger emotional behavior.

2. *Compulsive Consumption*: This driver is irrational because it has a tendency for self-destruction; it manifests as addictions to food, cigarettes, alcohol, drugs, and gambling.

3. *Compulsive Wealth Gathering*: This driver is irrational because it entails an abnormal, positively sloping, marginal utility curve for wealth accumulation, which is typical of misers and others who stop short of criminality.

4. *Compulsive, Psychopathic Wealth Gathering*: This driver is irrational because it entails an abnormal, positively sloping, marginal utility curve for wealth accumulation; however, it also entails psychopathic behavior, characterized by amorality, absence of empathy for others, and a willingness to commit crimes in pursuit of wealth gathering. Hence, those suffering from this condition behave as human predators, taking other humans for prey. The causes of their psychological ailment may be hereditary, environmental, or both. Many powerful politicians, wealthy individuals, and criminals belong to this group, but not all. Historically, plutocracies have often manifested this disorder as a group as well as individually.

II. Decision-Making

The relative weight of the above drivers provides the impulse that colors a variety of economic behaviors. In addition, the decision-making process uses *perceived* information, however imperfect, to arrive at decisions. The type of decision-making process is itself a function of the availability of information and the time constraint. In theory, under conditions of relatively complete information and enough time to consider that information, rational decision-making is appropriate. However, under conditions of uncertainty, limited information, and time constraints, instinctual decision-making is usually best. Moreover, under extreme emotional conditions, the entire decision-making process breaks down and a form of herd behavior takes over.

A complicating factor regarding the assumption of the classical theory of perfect information is that there are diseconomies associated with the today's abundant information, producing an information overload that can clog our minds causing a state of decision paralysis. Hence, for information to remain manageable and useful it needs filtering in some fashion to retain the essential and discard the non-essential elements. In that case, the quality of the filtering process may well be a more critical factor for arriving at suitable decisions than the availability of voluminous data. Indeed, how to limit information is nowadays an important decision-making tool.

Another complicating factor is that it is frequently difficult to foresee the remote and unintended consequences of decisions, which may be larger and opposite to their immediate effects. Moreover, occasionally a "butterfly effect" can enormously magnify the distant and unexpected consequences, especially as regards moral and immoral acts. *The unified theory of macroeconomic failure* examines these complicating factors.[55]

In conclusion, qualitative and mathematical modeling of realistic economic behavior is more demanding than the present oversimplified version of reality, but it is potentially more rewarding in terms of its explanatory and predictive powers. Economics could also do with statistical methods that are more tolerant of diverse probability distributions.[56]

Behavioral economics can be a great help too, if only it can stop using self-indulgent assumptions such as knowing the probabilities of future outcomes, which requires not just perfect information but also perfect foresight.

Critique of Classical Economics

Classical economics contributed numerous valuable and essential microeconomic concepts. However, its erroneous macroeconomic formulations have held back the progress of that branch of economics.

The previously discussed inadequate assumptions of classical economics need no repeating here, but other shortcomings deserve passing mention.

Classical theory's lack of appreciation of *externalities*, a central theme of this book, was a major oversight with sweeping negative repercussions. In part, that error is understandable because economic knowledge at the time had not advanced sufficiently. Briefly, an externality refers to a market failure where market forces, on their own, cannot internalize all the costs or benefits of a good or service, resulting in a suboptimal market price that is too low or too high, and therefore economically inefficient. This lack of familiarity with externalities led to a grossly inadequate classical macroeconomic model, which could not recognize the causes of market failures and the need for state intervention in the form of public expenditure, tax, monetary and antimonopoly policies, and other measures.

Lack of appreciation of externalities led to another grievous error of the classical theory: overlooking the pivotal role of morality in formulating efficient and rational economic policies. Morality is a difficult concept to grasp as an economic variable, not the least because it is not a tradeable good. The absence of an economics of morality made it easier for classical economists to tolerate and support imperialism and *parasitic capitalism*. Similarly, the lack of an economics of morality facilitated overlooking the downside of unchecked self-interest on markets, permitting psychopathic profit maximizers to gouge consumers and starve workers, producing *chronic underconsumption* and slow economic growth. Thus, without moral restraints, capitalism is relegated to a destructive beast that subverts *societal-interest*.

John Maynard Keynes described the absurdity of unrestrained capitalism succinctly: "Capitalism is the astounding belief that the wickedest of men will do the wickedest of things for the greatest good of everyone."[57] The oversights of classical economics, intentional and otherwise, made it possible for *parasitic economics* to slip between the cracks and we continue to suffer the consequences.

Three

THE RISE AND FALL OF MARXIST ECONOMICS
(1848–1988)[58]

Religion is what keeps the poor from murdering the rich.[59]

Napoleon Bonaparte

The condition of the downtrodden in Western Europe temporarily improved following major upheavals. In the middle of the 14th century, the Black Death decimated half the labor force, making labor scarce relative to land and improving the terms of trade in labor's favor; real wages became higher for about a century.[60] The circumstances of the French working class also became better following the French Revolution in 1789. The condition of the working class and its political rights also improved following the European revolutions of 1848. Alas, from the perspective of the vast majority of people, good times were few and transitory.

In 1819, Jean Charles Léonard de Sismondi published his *Nouveaux principes d'économie politique* (*New Principles of Political Economy*), criticizing economics for making wealth gathering an end in itself (to the detriment of the poor) instead of a means to happiness. The major religions have called for a kinder world in which the wealthy sustain the deprived, but many of the rich disregard those teachings because they presume it detracts from their wealth gathering.

Nineteenth Century Poverty and Plutocracy in Europe

In 19th-century Europe, the economic hardship and unrestrained exploitation of the working class during the Industrial Revolution left workers in graver misery than ever before. By 1829, the life expectancy of industrial workers in Liverpool, England, had shrunk to twenty-eight years.[61] The infamous British Corn Laws were the worst form of feudalism; in 1815, the British Parliament levied a tariff on cereal imports to raise their domestic prices and augment the income of the rentier class of landed aristocracy.[62] The British Parliament was the conduit for income redistribution from the underprivileged to ultra-privileged.[63] The tax on cereal imports continued for three decades, until exceptionally poor harvests in the British Isles precipitated the starvation and death of a million people.

Curiously, the British parliament that passed the Corn Laws prided itself on seven centuries of democratic traditions stretching back to the *Magna Carta*, although its seats were bought and sold for a price. Moreover, members of parliament had to have independent means because they received no salary at all until 1911 and then only a meager one until 1946.[64] The laws it passed mostly served the plutocracy and not the people, therefore, it was a democratic charade, irrespective of its paraphernalia.

The British Parliament repealed its parasitic tax on cereals in 1846 in response to industrialists' demands, because starvation was making labor scarce and pricy and because cheaper food imports would lower wages and increase industrial profits. Hunger was also fanning unrest—a precursor to revolution.

Friedrich Engels, in his book *The Condition of the Working Class in England in 1844*, described the state of workers there as the most unconcealed pinnacle of social misery in that day. Those conditions did not resemble a democracy. However, the British aristocracy was not the only one presiding over miserable poverty in the midst of plenty.

The sorry state of workers across most of Europe was almost as bad. Vilfredo Pareto (1848–1923), the father of Pareto optimality, documented some disturbing findings. He uncovered that for centuries in several European countries, including Italy, 80 percent of all wealth belonged to just 20 percent of the population, with the destitute either on the brink of starvation or starving. He demolished the much-touted concept of an income pyramid because he found that real income distribution was more like a dart atop a vast flat surface.[65] Perpetual poverty had been the faithful companion of the masses for millennia, but 19th-century industrialization shed the last vestiges of humanity; it was the *age of savage economic barbarism*.

Marxist Interpretations

Poverty in 19th-century Europe brewed revolutions; the working classes were becoming aware that they were victims of ruthless plutocratic exploitation. Karl Marx (1818–1883), Fredrick Engels (1820–1895), and others contributed to this class-consciousness. They offered a radically different interpretation of history and a correspondingly radical alternative to classical economic theory.

Marx spent years observing and analyzing the workings of the capitalist system in Western Europe, in which the wealthy classes basked in extreme luxury while squeezing the working class to subsistence levels and occasionally starvation.[66] He saw widespread poverty, a reserve army of the unemployed and underemployed, and underconsumption. He attributed the ruthless income distribution to the nature of capitalism. Ironically, underconsumption was detrimental to economic growth and capitalist profits, but classical economists did not grasp that.

Marx presented materialism as the foundation of his theories, while preaching social moralism and anti-egotism. Oddly, he saw religion as contributing to the exploitation of the masses, hence his statement that religion is the opium of the masses. His conclusion was wrong, although wicked rulers did use religious institutions to deliver social sedatives. The original calls of religions tended to be revolutionary, supporting the masses against the status quo and often calling for a kinder, non-exploitive social order. Why religious institutions deviated subsequently and how the plutocracy hijacked them and subverted their purpose is another matter.

Plutocracies preserved the status quo through laws and brute force. When faced with overpowering rebellions as in 1848, they offered the working class concessions to cool their revolutionary fervor, only to rescind it later once the crises abated. Observing this, Marx and Engels concluded that securing enduring fair wages and reasonable working conditions for the working class was impossible in a market economy because agreements with the double-crossing capitalists were worthless. Hence, in 1848, Marx and Engels published *The Communist Manifesto*, calling for class struggle and revolution to bring down the capitalist system as the only means of ending mass misery. That book became the capitalists' nightmare.

Marx also observed the periodic crises of capitalism and concluded that capitalism was not just unfair, exploitative, and irredeemable, but also inherently unstable and unsustainable. Inspired by Marx, Vladimir Lenin (1870–1924), the balding communist leader of the Russian Revolution in 1917, famously compared production and income distribution under capitalism to his hair: "…. abundant production and bad distribution."

An Unforeseen Revolutionary Springboard

Karl Marx had predicted that the socialist revolutions would begin in the most industrialized European countries, where labor was class-conscious and highly organized. The only truly socialist prototypes that had existed previously were certain faraway indigenous communities, before European settlers disturbed their lifestyles. North America, in particular, was a fortunate continent: vast, fertile, with favorable weather, plentiful game, wild fruits and crops, and sparsely populated. The natives were mostly hunter-gatherers and corn farmers. In the absence of scarcity, everyone was a *de facto* collective owner of nature. Fencing land to register a title deed made little sense because of the sheer abundance of land relative to the population. Reinforcing this was the natives' natural inclination toward nonmaterial contentment. They were in harmony with nature and satisfied with a few essential personal possessions, like simple clothes, a tent, hunting and fishing tools, and a horse or two. With meager personal possessions and de facto communal ownership of nature, they were almost living the communist dream of peaceful contentment, if only they had not occasionally engaged in tribal raids, which sometimes escalated into wars.

It is perhaps more than a coincidence that the first proletarian revolution took place in Russia—the most agrarian country in Europe—instead of England or Germany, the most industrialized, as Marx had predicted. Russia's expansive spaces, abundant natural resources, and sparse population made it Europe's closest approximation of the environment that had sustained a Native American socialist existence. Conceivably, Russia's abundant resources per capita made an economically inefficient communist model more sustainable. However, Vladimir Lenin attributed the first revolution to Russia because the Western imperialists were diffusing the class hatred within their societies by bribing their proletariat with a small share of their imperialist loot.

Like the French Revolution before it, the Russian Bolshevik (communist) Revolution in 1917 frightened Western plutocrats enough to dispatch their armies to Russia to nip its ideas in the bud. As with the French Revolution, the invading armies were eventually defeated. The plutocratic assault solidified the communist home front and made the imperialists the scapegoat for all failings.

The Bolshevik Revolution raised numerous questions. Could communism work? Why did it not materialize before? How would it operate?

Critique of Marxist Economics

Karl Marx's major contribution was as a political philosopher, not as an economist. He was better at spotting the flaws of capitalism than at articulating an economically viable alternative to it. Marx's idyllic dream of *from each according to his ability and to each according to his need* was only partially fulfilled. The economic implementation of various versions of his utopian dream by communist countries became their Achilles heel.

Marx saw no possibility of the capitalist class making an enduring compromise with labor to arrive at a fairer society; his solution was to abolish classes and make the state the sole owner of the means of production, which would also deprive the capitalists of the resources for staging a *counter-revolution*. Nevertheless, he underestimated the need for maintaining self-interest in an economy, with fatal long-term economic consequences. He made several assumptions about the capitalist model, such as a progressively declining rate of return on capital, which proved invalid. More important is why his economic model failed in practice.

The Soviet (Russian) communist party tried indoctrinating the masses with communist ideology to expunge self-interest and replace it with idealism. Instead of market prices, they adopted centrally determined shadow prices based on perceived social needs as determined by a central planning committee, causing widespread economic havoc.

Absent monopolies, monopsonies, and other externalities, market price is an unrivaled decentralized economic planning tool that fosters optimal resource allocation and economic efficiency. It is spontaneous and automatic, simultaneously and seamlessly pricing all final goods (services) in an economy, as well as all their inputs. Thus, it conducts a dynamic and ever-evolving balancing act between supply and demand for all goods. An increase in the price of a good, relative to the prices of other goods, signals a shortage caused by an increase in demand or a reduction in supply, or both.[67] If the price rise persists, it triggers a chain of market reactions and adjustments. A relative price rise of a good, without a corresponding increase in its cost, increases the profitability of supplying it. This induces the employment of more resources in its production, transportation, and distribution. At the same time, if such an increase in demand is sufficiently significant, it could potentially raise the prices of some, or all, of the relevant inputs. That would affect the input prices of a host of other goods and services, potentially reducing their profitability and supply with further supply/demand reverberations and adjustments.

The relative price decline of a good without a corresponding decline in its input costs sends the opposite signal. The price fall reduces the profitability of a good, curtailing its production, transportation, and distribution. If the fall in demand is significant enough, it could potentially lower the prices of some or all of its inputs. That would affect the input costs and prices of a host of other goods and services, potentially increasing their profitability and their supply with further supply/demand reverberations and adjustments.

These multiple synchronized adjustments occur automatically with minimal delay, without the formal coordination between thousands of market participants, and without bureaucratic red tape. The magic of the price mechanism even drives the pace of the introduction of a new technology, based on the price premium of new tech to old, sometimes referred to in marketing circles as *skimming-the-cream pricing*. What could be simpler? [68] No central planning committee, however talented and well-informed, could match that. Genius is simple, indeed.

The main communist states, the Soviet Union and the People's Republic of China, succeeded in rapidly developing heavy industries and undertaking gigantic infrastructure projects. However, in the absence of a market price mechanism, it was difficult to spot shortages and surpluses on a timely basis across these vast countries, especially in consumer goods and agricultural products. Bureaucracy, resource misallocations, and chronic consumer shortages became the norm, with detrimental effects on the long-term growth of most sectors.

Market prices and the profit motive (self-interest) were the critically missing components in the communist economic model, leading to its eventual collapse. Starting in the 1980s, the progressive transition of the Chinese economy to a market economy resulted in three decades of double-digit economic growth. About 1990, the Russian economy, the former bastion of communism, began a slower transition to a market economy. Under communism, despite abundant agricultural lands and water Russia was the world's largest wheat importer for decades; today, it is the world's leading wheat exporter. Its hydrocarbon production, after years of decline, has increased dramatically too. Other countries, like India and Brazil, that had mixed economies but constrained their private sectors, also realized significant economic improvements following economic liberalization.

The error of Marxist economics flowed from its exclusive reliance on *societal-interest* and the marginalization of self-interest. The case for self-interest, as a necessary condition for the efficient operation of an economy, is manifest; however, it is not a sufficient condition. It is worth noting here that the neoclassical macroeconomists, walking in the footsteps of classical economists, make the opposite mistake of putting their full faith in self-interest and markets and downplaying the role of *societal-interest*.

The Demise of Parasitic Capitalism

Marx predicted the collapse of capitalism. His detractors see in capitalism's survival to this day proof of the error of his judgment. That conclusion seems correct on the surface but, in fact, it is too simplistic because what Marx meant and what they are referring to are two different things. Marx predicted that the increasing concentration of wealth, the worsening poverty and the increasing severity of the seven-year capitalist crisis-cycle made capitalism unsustainable and revolutions inevitable. Indeed, communism succeeded in bringing down many capitalist countries around the world, but then it stopped.

Marx assumed that the extremely harsh conditions of 19th-century patristic capitalism would persist; he did not foresee that plutocracies, to survive, would accept a gentler, more moral, capitalism. This is always a complicating factor in making economic predictions: observations, analysis, and feedback influence the future behavior of economic actors, potentially undermining the validity of a forecast. Hence, the very spread of communism seeded the survival of capitalism, albeit a transformed one. More precisely, Marx predicted the demise of extreme *parasitic capitalism*, which he had observed, and (thankfully) it became almost extinct, although, in recent decades it has been making a comeback.

Two Great Communist Legacies

Communism's fatal weakness was economics, but it was also politically repressive, abrogating individual freedoms to the point of banning religious practices. Its demise has granted all those who once dreaded it, including this author, an opportunity to reconsider it from a neutral perspective. Today, we can afford to admit things we never dared confess before. We have this luxury because we no longer worry that it might tip the political scales in favor of communism or that the terrified right might unleash a McCarthy-style inquisition against us. We no longer need to whisper yesterday's taboos. Communism has left enduring marks on numerous countries, but especially on its archenemy: the capitalist West. Of particular interest are two landmark communist legacies.

Following World War II, communism absorbed the whole of Eastern Europe, at a time when the economic suffering in some West European countries was shocking. The "Red Peril" was at the West's doorstep; its highly effective party cadre, already inside the gate, was gaining converts at an alarming rate. In France, Germany, Italy, and Greece, communist parties were winning mass support. These disturbing developments and the memory of the comprehensive losses of the Russian plutocracy following the communist revolution there in 1917 petrified Western plutocracies into adopting countermeasures. Instead of exacting war reparations, as the victors had done at the end of World War I, America rushed economic aid to Germany and Italy under the Marshall Plan, hoping to stem the communist tide. The speed of communist triumphs in Southeast Asia only exacerbated Western fears, prompting America to extend aid to Japan, South Korea, and others.

The scent of upper-class extinction compelled Western plutocracies to take the only insurance policy available to them: improving the conditions of their workers.[69] Overnight, they raised workers' standard of living and adopted welfare programs and economic democratization. Welfare states became a reality and economic morality fashionable, at last.[70] After centuries of ruthless exploitation and neglect, Western plutocracies were treating their workers with dignity, humanity, humility, and morality. Fear of communism radically improved workers' lives in capitalist countries and improved Western economic as well as political democracy—a profound communist economic legacy. Aside from putting an end to hostilities, the end of World

War II marked the end of *the age of economic barbarism*, the greatest moment in history of mass liberation from the yoke of plutocracy and its *parasitic capitalism*. Actually, communism had set out to end that era and it did, albeit in a manner it had not visualized nor intended.

In the aftermath of World War II came the other enduring communist legacy: ending the yoke of *conventional Western imperialism* and its associated economics. Aside from its injustice, racism, and all its other foulness, at its core imperialism was the apex of *parasitic capitalism*. The lure of imperialism to Western plutocracies was its easy loot and parasitic profits, which we could refer to as *the economics of imperialism*. By simultaneously supporting multiple wars of liberation, communism dramatically raised the cost of imperialism to the point that it far exceeded its financial reward, rendering *the economics of imperialism* uneconomical to Western plutocracies.[71] Moreover, if all the potential wars of liberation were to run their full course, there was a real risk that Western plutocracies would end up isolated, confined to Western Europe and North America.

The British Labor governments of 1945–1951 led the decolonization process, but subsequent conservative British governments interrupted it. However, escalating costs, the difficulty of maintaining the colonies, and growing communist support for liberation movements all over the world prompted Conservative Prime Minister Harrold Macmillan to resume decolonization in 1960, despite strong objections from extremist right-wing conservative circles who desperately wanted to hold onto the British Empire.[72] That year, whilst on a visit to Africa, Macmillan delivered a landmark speech in which he declared, "The wind of change is blowing through this continent. Whether we like it or not, this growth of national consciousness is a political fact." The United States supported decolonization as a means of opening new markets for its companies and stemming the spread of communism in Third World countries.[73]

As the largest colonizing power and the epicenter of imperialism, the British position was important in signaling the winds of change for the rest of the imperialist powers. The sustained attrition of liberation wars during the 1960s and 1970s compelled the imperialist West to abandon many of its colonies and protectorates. Moreover, to avoid an impending route and to preempt more wars of liberation and communist victories, Western imperialists declared that their colonies no longer needed imperialist administration because the natives have matured and could assume responsibility for running their own affairs. The dissolution of the British Empire in particular and the rest of the Western empires in general, represented the most rapid in history up to that point, ending centuries of imperialist barbarism. Doubtless, from the victims' perspective, ending imperialism was communism's finest hour.

A Hegelian Interpretation of History

Marx used the Hegelian dialectic to interpret history's twists, forecasting the demise of capitalism and the rise of Marxism to replace it.[74] It deserves revisiting. Using that framework, 19th-century *parasitic capitalism*'s impoverishment of the masses was a *thesis*. Hence, the Russian Bolshevik Revolution in 1917 and the other communist revolutions it inspired were an *antithesis*. Following the end of World War II, almost half of Europe was in communist hands, as was China. As stated in the previous section, the response of the West to the communist threat was to improve its standards of economic and political democracy, marking a Hegelian *synthesis* that completed a full Hegelian cycle.

The faltering Soviet economy in the 1970s marked the start of a new cycle, this time with communism as the *thesis*. About 1980, the West began leaning to the right. It discarded Keynesianism and replaced it with neoclassical macroeconomics, lowered the tax burden of the rich and increased it on the underprivileged, increased military spending and decreased social services, and deregulated markets.[75] The fall of the Soviet Union in 1988 eased residual plutocratic restraints due to fears of communism threatening Western capitalism, accelerating the West's swing to the right. Even left-of-center parties, such as Labor in Britain and Democrat in the US, became right-wing, compared to their traditional positions. The previously communist states in Eastern Europe replaced their single-party systems with multi-parties while, paradoxically, the Anglo-American *democracies* further curtailed the limited political choice of their citizenry from two parties to a single party in everything but name. This rightward transformation constituted a Hegelian *antithesis*.

Finally, the 2008 Great Recession and its aftermath hint at a brewing Hegelian *synthesis*. In less than a century, the political wheel has completed one full circle and two thirds of the second. Given the nature of these political cycles, perhaps the rapid decline in economic and political moral standards in the West offers a clue about tomorrow: a moral revival could be the *synthesis* of the ongoing Hegelian cycle.

———————

Marxism was a romantic dream that flourished under *parasitic capitalism* and perished under *moral capitalism*. Plutocracies' ongoing dismantling of the welfare state and tolerance of a spreading poverty are grave political errors because the masses that had propelled Marxism to power could undoubtedly adopt another doctrine to shake the system again, if from a different direction.

Four

*All truth passes through three stages. First, it is
ridiculed. Second, it is violently opposed. Third,
it is accepted as being self-evident.*[77]

Arthur Schopenhauer

Macroeconomics deals with the economy as a whole. The major parameters of a national economy include aggregate production, consumption, investment, savings, international trade, and employment, government expenditure, taxation, inflation, growth, balance of payments, national debt, and income distribution. Macroeconomics also deals with the effects of economic cycles on these variables and appropriate stabilization policies.

An understanding of macroeconomics began in the early 19th century. However, a broad appreciation of the potential for manipulating a national economy only emerged in the 1930s, when pioneering economists articulated expansionary fiscal and monetary policies to counter the effects of the Great Depression. This paved the way for better handling of unemployment, inflation, balance of payment deficits, and economic growth. It was equivalent to discovering a revolutionary new technology, and its economic consequences were as important, if not more so.

Jean Charles Léonard de Sismondi

Swiss economist Jean Charles Léonard de Sismondi (1773–1842) is, regrettably, the unrecognized father of macroeconomics and economic cycle theory. His work, *Nouveaux principes d'économie politique* (*New Principles of Political Economy*), published in 1819, was the first systematic exposé of periodic economic crises. It challenged the classical general equilibrium theory, which focused on the long run and avoided formal discussion of business cycles, attributing them to transitory exogenous factors, principally wars.

De Sismondi confronted the economic theories of his contemporaries, like David Ricardo, by refuting that the economy could achieve full employment equilibrium quickly and independently. He wrote, "Let us beware of this dangerous theory of equilibrium which is supposed to be automatically established. A certain kind of equilibrium, it is true, is reestablished in the long-run, but it is after a frightful amount of suffering." The Panic of 1825, an international economic crisis that occurred during peacetime, disproved the classical claim that contractions were a consequence of war and confirmed de Sismondi's theory.

De Sismondi observed that industrial producers in England increase production to the point of oversupply, resulting in falling profits, wage reductions, and layoffs. These actions reduced workers' purchasing power, which produced underconsumption. De Sismondi was the first to conclude that raising wages, by increasing labor's purchasing power, would stimulate demand, increase employment, clear markets, and revive the economy. This conclusion was a macroeconomic landmark because it recognized the impact of stimulative economic policies on aggregate demand. It was a concept that was ahead of its time because too few economists understood it.

De Sismondi and a contemporary, Robert Owen (1771–1858), independently identified another cause of underconsumption and economic cycles, namely, extreme wealth inequality. They proposed government intervention instead of *laissez-faire*.

Two Centuries of Parasitic Economics

Charles Dunoyer (1786–1862) extended de Sismondi's periodic crisis theory to a theory of economic cycles and Johann Karl Rodbertus (1805–1875) proposed a similar theory. This research established underconsumption as a branch of economics. Karl Marx popularized the concept in his *Das Kapital*, attributing underconsumption to the worsening periodic crises of capitalism.

Durations and Stages of Economic Cycles[78]

In 1860, French economist Clement Juglar (1819–1905) estimated an economic cycle's duration at between 7 and 11 years. Subsequently, three additional cycles of shorter and longer durations were identified bringing the total to four: the Joseph Kitchin (1861–1932) inventory cycle (3 to 5 years), Clement Juglar fixed investment cycle (7 to 11 years) Simon Kuznets (1901–1985) infrastructural investment cycle (15 to 25 years), and Nikolai Kondratiev (1892–1938) long technological cycle (45 to 60 years).

Austrian American economist Joseph Schumpeter (1883–1950) proposed a novel explanation of the causes of cycles: entrepreneurs, by adopting new inventions and innovations in their products, unleash cycles of creative destruction that produce economic growth. However, he also recognized that increases in aggregate demand increased production, profitability, and prices, bringing about economic recovery and prosperity. He saw cycles as complex waves resulting from the simultaneous influence of all the above-mentioned cycles. He used a nine-year Juglar cycle to divide the business cycle into four stages:

a. Expansion
b. Crisis
c. Recession
d. Recovery

Viscount Takahashi's Macroeconomic Revolution

The English-language economic literature hardly mentions the father of modern Keynesian economics. In the early stages of the Great Depression, Japan began pursuing uncompromising and innovative economic policies that were diametrically opposite to those advocated by neoclassical macroeconomists and accepted at face value in the West. The outstanding economist who was the first to demonstrate the effectiveness of expansionary fiscal policies as a solution to cyclical underconsumption and depression was Japan's finance minister, Viscount Korekiyo Takahashi (1854–1936). That transformation in economic assessment required a profound and courageous thinker to realize the futility of neoclassical macroeconomic passivity and to make the 180-degree policy shift against the then-prevailing economic wisdom.

In 1929–1931, the Great Depression had engulfed the Japanese economy, shrinking it by 8 percent. To counter the depression, Viscount Takahashi articulated and promoted powerful expansionary fiscal and monetary stimuli. Those policies required economic flexibility, which was impossible within the confines of a gold standard; accordingly, Japan abandoned it. It would take the United States another dozen years before abandoning the gold standard.[79] In 1933, Japan set the record as the first industrial nation in the world to recover fully from the Great Depression.[80] Viscount Takahashi's intellectual vision and daring had paid off.

In 1932, before the results of the Japanese policy shift became abundantly evident, Germany's commissioner for employment in the Schleicher government, Günther Gereke (1893–1970), instituted a public works program to relieve unemployment. In 1934, Dr. Hjalmar Schacht (1877–1970), Germany's new economics minister, maintained that public works program. Those expansionary economic policies brought about a rapid recovery in Germany as well. It also inspired President Franklin Roosevelt to undertake an extensive US highway construction program later.

Japan and Germany continued to grow rapidly, while the rest of Europe and the United States lingered in neoclassical macroeconomic depression. Japan, in particular, had performed a remarkable economic feat, four years ahead of Keynes's *General Theory of Employment, Interest, and Money,* and nine years ahead of the full recovery in the United States in 1942 (following America's mobilization in World War II). Japan and Germany's economic recoveries had a profound effect and provided fresh ideas to a stagnant macroeconomic theory. The United States and Great Britain did not benefit from the Japanese and German examples, probably because of the influence of Austrian School, Friedrich von Hayek and Lionel Robbins, who in the 1930s were in London preaching doing nothing, as discussed in the next chapter.

Keynesian Economic Explanations

Neoclassical economics, like its classical predecessor, used static-equilibrium analysis to conclude that full-employment equilibrium was the natural state of the economy. It explained unemployment as a voluntary choice by lazy workers who refuse to work for less pay; hence, government intervention was unnecessary. Yet, business contractions were often painful and protracted affairs; the resultant high unemployment rate was not a collective personal choice of reluctant workers. The neoclassical explanation was unimaginative, lacking in empathy and indifferent to the suffering of workers and businesses alike; at best, it was an intellectually lazy explanation.

Economies are alive, dynamic, and subject to a myriad of disturbances, which makes attaining equilibrium a chancy affair. For instance, exceptionally good weather can cause agricultural production to be greater than planned, the equivalent of a rightward shift in its supply curve, resulting in lower prices. Because agricultural supply is inelastic in the short term, oversupply and lower prices would persist, pending adjustment in the next harvest with the distinct possibility of over adjustment, leading to further market reverberations. Superimposed on this cobweb path in agricultural supply are future weather patterns, making any movement toward a stable equilibrium tentative.[81]

At the other extreme, adjusting supply can require several years, a decade, or longer, as with increasing (or reducing) the global shipping tonnage. For example, the closure of the Suez Canal (1967–1975) following the 1967 Six-Day War was equivalent to a huge reduction in shipping capacity because overnight ships had to travel much longer distances from the North Atlantic shores to East Africa and Asia. The long lead-time required to construct significant additional shipping tonnage prolonged the adjustment process. Generally, the more durable the life of an asset, the longer it takes to increase or decrease its supply. This makes for wider price fluctuations, as cycles move from undersupply to oversupply. These are but two of the many examples that make attaining general equilibrium improbable, yet classical and neoclassical theories cheerfully assume it is the natural state of economic affairs.

John Maynard Keynes (1883–1946) was not just a brilliant economist with compassion and high standards of social morality, but also a shrewd investor. The economic policies he proposed reflected his broad expertise and values. He insisted on making the attainment of full employment a primary objective of economic policy. He held that the economy, on its own, could have a short-run equilibrium at higher or lower than full-employment output, and that full employment was an exceptional state rather than the norm.

Keynes believed underconsumption and underinvestment could persist for prolonged periods, giving rise to chronic unemployment, recession, or depression. Hence, the government's role is to act as an economic stabilizer by managing aggregate demand: increasing public spending and/or reducing taxes to offset a shortfall in private demand, or cutting public spending and raising taxes to curtail excessive aggregate demand and inflation. During contractions, he thought monetary easing was necessary to eliminate restraint but ineffective on its own to bring about economic expansion, while monetary restraint was more effective in curbing demand-pull inflation.

Keynes also observed the market's tendency toward periodic irrationality. This played out as exuberant optimism, resulting in overinvestment, vigorous expansion followed by excess supply, falling profits, despondent pessimism, falling investment and consumption, and recession.[82]

Paul Samuelson successfully depicted the tendency for a Keynesian model to oscillate where an exogenous shock affected investments by using an accelerator, which in turn affected aggregate demand, consumption, and the multiplier.[83]

Neoclassical economists criticized Keynes for emphasizing the short run over the long run, to which Keynes famously replied, "In the long run we are all dead." Paradoxically, Keynesian countercyclical policies, although short-term, tactical, and lacking in long-term strategic measures, had far superior long-run results than the neoclassical policy of passivity. By ignoring the large shortfalls in aggregate demand, waiting for markets to self-correct and the economy miraculously to climb out of depression, the neoclassical policy of inaction was tantamount to an abdication of economic responsibility. Keynes saw no evidence that markets behaved as neoclassical macroeconomists expected. He considered the economy too important to leave unattended. He thought passive *laissez-faire* neoclassical macroeconomic policies were inflicting elective economic hardship on nations by prolonging recessions, depressions, and poverty. He sensed no logic in workers enduring hunger and employers going bankrupt, while economists sit back, observing and wishing. Indeed, such a policy makes the economic profession an impediment to economic stability and redundant.

The Interest Elasticity of Investment

Classical and neoclassical economists assumed that investment demand was interest-elastic, such that a fall in interest rates would discourage savings, encourage investment and employment, stimulate the economy and help bring about general equilibrium and vice versa.[81]

Keynes, on the other hand, saw the relationship between investment and interest rates as asymmetrical: Higher interest rates can curb investment and economic activity during an expansion, but falling interest rates usually coincide with falling investment during a recession. He attributed this to the fall in the marginal efficiency of capital (MEC) during a recession, making the undertaking of new investments unattractive. Thus, when the profit outlook is bleak, businesses turned cautious, preferring to husband their resources as a precaution against continued economic weakness, regardless of low interest rates—hence, Keynes's famous *liquidity trap*.[84]

The Golden Age of Keynesianism (1946–1973)

In the aftermath of World War II, the foresight of Keynesian economic policy prevented military demobilization and cuts in military spending from precipitating a severe post-war recession. In the United States and the United Kingdom, relatively light taxation and shortages in civilian goods during the war left households with plenty of cash, little debt, and a large pent-up demand. Moreover, as mentioned previously, the threat of communism induced Western plutocracies to initiate gentler capitalism by raising labor living standards and promoting welfare programs.

The decades immediately following World War II revealed what Keynesianism was capable of delivering: a golden age of unrivaled economic prosperity. The United States achieved its best economic performance on record: the fastest sustained economic growth, rapidly rising living standards, low unemployment, and subdued inflation. Keynesian countercyclical fiscal and monetary policies made recessions brief and shallow. Remarkably, the Keynesian economic miracle took place while unions were at their strongest, real wages rising, investment in education and welfare high, and tax rates on upper incomes steep, yet inflation remained slight.

The exceedingly high personal income tax rates prompted the landmark Kennedy tax cut in the 1960s, increasing employment and the rate of economic growth and, surprisingly, through the multiplier, augmenting tax revenue to boot.

During those golden decades, the labor movement in Europe and America enjoyed its best conditions, including widespread unionization, collective bargaining, the right to strike, unemployment benefits, pensions, free education, medical care, childcare, and care for the elderly, to name a few. The West moved from parasitic to *moral capitalism*, implementing an economic democracy that rendered political democracy meaningful. The unprecedented success of Keynesian economics exposed the fundamental errors of neoclassical macroeconomic theory.

The Challenge of Stagflation (1973–1982)

By the 1970s, the excessive demands of the Vietnam War were pushing the United States to live beyond its means; rising inflation indicated the economy was overheating.[83]

Two Centuries of Parasitic Economics

In August 1971, the Republican administration of President Richard Nixon terminated the dollar gold convertibility to preserve US gold reserves in the face of deteriorating US trade deficits, thereby unilaterally terminating the Bretton Woods system. This resulted in a dollar devaluation of 8 percent against the major currencies, adding to US inflationary pressures through imported inflation. Shockingly, to curtail inflation, a right-wing US administration borrowed a leaf from the communist command economy by resorting to a broad range of wage and price controls, thereby partially abandoning the capitalist model of supply and demand and Keynesianism.

In 1973, a confluence of negative factors made for an exceptionally difficult year. Poor agricultural harvests resulted in higher food prices, adding cost-push inflation to imported-inflation, following the dollar devaluation, and the already simmering demand-pull inflation. In October the 1973, the fourth Arab-Israeli war (Yom Kippur War) flared, quadrupling oil prices and sending a global shock wave of cost-push inflation and payment imbalances. The oil price escalation was a windfall to oil-exporting countries and Western oil companies, greatly multiplying their revenues and the value of their oil reserves underground.

In the rest of the world, it produced bizarre and contradictory economic effects, generating, at once, stagnation and inflation, hence stagflation. A British Member of Parliament (MP), Iain Macleod, had coined the term "stagflation" to describe a similar condition in Great Britain back in 1965. Payment for a dramatically higher oil bill was a huge financial leakage that drained funds out of the economic cycle of oil-importing countries. Oil-exporting countries could not recycle back to the oil-importing countries their sudden and huge financial surpluses fast enough; they needed time to formulate and implement massively larger national development and expenditure plans before they could significantly increase their imports.

Similarly, although some Western oil companies increased their cash dividends, they continued to hold substantial cash reserves for several years to finance their hugely expanded oil exploration and development plans. This sudden parking of vast funds, pending investment and recirculation, restricted economic activity in oil-importing countries. Thus, the oil price spike was more contractionary than a hefty tax hike because the associated revenue was not recirculating back into the economies of the oil-importers. This powerful economic brake caused the stagnation.[85]

In the United States, inflation peaked in 1974 at 11.03 percent, the contraction in GDP was 3.2 percent, and unemployment peaked in 1975 at 9 percent.[86] Several Eastern European and developing countries faced spiraling national debts denominated in foreign currencies, mostly US dollars, to finance their bulging trade deficits because of the steep oil price rise.

The sudden jump in the oil price produced widespread cost-push inflation because oil and energy went into the production of most goods. Unlike the more familiar demand-pull inflation, controlling cost-push inflation by curtailing demand was ineffective at best because its source was on the supply side of the market equation. Economic policymakers in the United States and Western oil-importing countries faced a schizophrenic economic choice: economic restraint to counter inflation or easing to counter high unemployment. Worst still, neither choice was very effective in achieving its objective.

The oil crisis ushered in the deepest and longest recession since the Great Depression. It was intractable in the short term, given simultaneously high inflation and unemployment. It violated the underlying assumptions of the familiar Keynesian *Phillips curve,* depicting a trade-off between unemployment and inflation because both were rising concurrently. Nixon's price controls followed by the oil crisis disrupted almost three decades of a brilliant Keynesian economic record. There was no quick fix to stagflation.

Keynes had focused on short-term aggregate demand management to counter cyclical swings. Stagflation was not a problem that he encountered, hence, he had not addressed it.

In the early 1970s, economists were unfamiliar with stagflation and unsure how best to tackle it. At first, US policymakers tried applying traditional Keynesian anti-inflationary policies to curb demand by tightening fiscal and monetary policies, but that increased unemployment without resolving inflation. Conceivably, they were hoping a global recession would decrease global oil demand, leading to a breakup of the oil cartel and a quick collapse in the oil price. Indeed, global oil demand did fall but the response of the oil producers was to cut supply instead of lowering price; the oil cartel held. Ironically, had the global recessionary policy succeeded in reducing the oil price quickly, it would have removed the incentive to increase oil supplies, making the global economy prone to repeated oil shortages, crises, and stag-flation following each recovery.

Since the problem was on the supply side, it required long-term supply-side solutions that, on the one hand, augmented oil supply and, on the other, provided new technologies that improved the efficiency of oil consumption. Eventually, effective economic policies evolved to tackle inflation and un-employment by liberalizing the domestic oil price in the United States and granting investment tax credits to encourage oil exploration and develop-ment, as well as encouraging the design and production of energy-efficient cars. The investment tax credits contributed to modest improvements in employment, but were insufficient to offset the large leakage caused by the high oil price.

Fine-tuning that policy to speed up the transition to greater avail-ability and efficient use of oil could have included more generous invest-ment credits, purposely limited to a few years to speed up investment in that sector, and a sharply rising sales tax on new oil-guzzling cars. Another measure should have been the immediate removal of the US price ceiling over old oil, because that resulted in some withholding of cheaper older oil, whereas it was the fastest route to increasing oil sup-plies. Indeed, price controls on natural gas continued for many years. These restrictions decreased the price elasticity of energy supplies and protracted the problem.

Strictly speaking, the oil investment tax-credits and the introduction of better energy-efficiency standards were not traditional Keynesian policies, but rather supply-side microeconomic policies to achieve macroeconomic objectives. The structural adjustments to solve the cost-push inflation re-quired time to increase the supply of oil and improve the efficiency of its use. Normally, it takes about seven years to identify a new oil field, de-velop it, and bring its oil to market. Moreover, developing and marketing fuel-efficient cars in sufficient numbers to dent the fuel consumption of the national car pool needed about a decade.[87]

The persistence of high unemployment, high inflation, and anemic economic growth exasperated the public. In a rare confluence of interests, stagflation managed to unite the capitalists and labor unions, the former opposing high inflation and the latter protesting high unemployment. Keynesianism took the blame for not providing a fast economic solution where none existed. In that confused and despairing economic environment, neoclassical economists claimed to have a solution.

Keynesian Oversight

For almost a century, Anglo-Saxon economics departments and their economic literature have been in violation of international academic standards by not recognizing Viscount Takahashi's landmark contribution to macroeconomics.

At the time, Keynes was a professor of economics at Cambridge University, as well as senior advisor to the British Treasury. Unless British commercial attachés stationed in Tokyo were on an extended holiday during the 1930s, they were bound to notice and report to the British Foreign Office and Treasury the exceptionally rapid Japanese economic recovery, while the rest of the world lingered in depression. Moreover, it was practically impossible not to notice the super-fast German economic recovery across the Channel that followed on the heels of the one in Japan by using similar economic tools.

Although unlikely, it is conceivable that Keynes was unaware of the Japanese and German economic miracles and their tools.[88] It is more plausible that the growing prospects of war in 1936, when Keynes published *The General Theory of Employment, Interest and Money*, dictated not to recognize the stunning macroeconomic revolutions in Japan and Germany so as not to concede a moral advantage to potential adversaries. Or else, British academia did not want to acknowledge that other nations were now better at economics, a disciple in which the British were traditionally leaders. In any case, there is no longer a valid reason for persisting with that charade. Metaphorically, Viscount Takahashi had successfully designed and flown the aircraft; six years later, Keynes masterfully explained to English speakers how it flew and, thus, his was an important contribution too.

Viscount Takahashi's contribution is worthy of special recognition for another reason. Like Keynes, he comes from a rare breed of economists with a solid moral fiber. In his capacity as a minister of finance, Viscount Takahashi insisted, despite threats to his life, on reducing Japanese military spending. His refusal to compromise resulted in his assassination, paradoxically, in 1936.

To a lesser extent, credit should also go to Günther Gereke and Dr. Hjalmar Schacht. Like Viscount Takahashi, Dr. Schacht also opposed German rearmament. His intransigence resulted in his being sacked from the German government in 1937. Subsequently, German authorities arrested him and sent him to a concentration camp.

The academic world expects Cambridge University, that traditional citadel of learning excellence, to observe and maintain the highest and most uncompromising academic standards, particularly giving credit where credit is due. Academic standards require Cambridge to recognize the unparalleled contributions of Viscount Takahashi to macroeconomics, precisely because Keynes was a senior Cambridge faculty member at the time. This oversight has lingered for nearly a century; a correction is long overdue. Indeed, any university that claims to uphold academic standards must insist that the macroeconomics textbooks it uses recognize the contribution of Viscount Takahashi fairly.

Critique of Keynesian Economics

The General Theory was revolutionary; it provided English speakers with the theoretical basis for adopting countercyclical policies, particularly expansionary fiscal policies to counter recessions. Keynes proposed applying effective tactical measures, after the event, once a recession had set in. However, he stopped short of proposing strategic economic measures that could—other things being equal—dampen the tendency for cyclicality, cut the rate of structural unemployment and income inequality, achieve faster economic growth, and improve long-term macroeconomic performance, thereby reducing the need for tactical measures in the first place.

The Great Depression must have exposed Keynes to the flaws of the banking and tax regimes, two important structural destabilizers.[89] Irving Fisher (1867–1947) had been discussing indebtedness extensively and had written about it in 1933. Regrettably, Keynes did not give sufficient thought to the destabilizing impact of financial institutions, debt and inefficient taxes to propose economically efficient alternatives that could improve long-term employment, economic stability, and growth. With his stature, Keynes was ideally positioned to propose those changes, especially since he harbored no ideological bias against making the economic system more efficient and fair, a sorely missed opportunity.

Five

THE FALL AND RISE OF NEOCLASSICAL MACROECONOMICS[90]
(1871–Present)[91]

We had to struggle with the old enemies of peace—business and financial monopoly, speculation, reckless banking, class antagonism, sectionalism, war profiteering.[92]

Franklin Roosevelt

S ignificant advances in microeconomic theory occurred in the early 20th century; Alfred Marshall (1842–1924) revolutionized classical microeconomic theory, justifying the label neoclassical microeconomics. He introduced the concepts of elasticity, marginal utility, marginal cost, and increasing and diminishing returns. Joan Robinson (1903–1983) and Edward Chamberlin (1899–1967) developed the theory of monopolistic competition.

However, there have been no equivalent neoclassical macroeconomic thinkers to justify a neoclassical macroeconomics label. Keynes certainly revolutionized macroeconomic theory; the neoclassical economists should have adopted him as their intellectual leader in macroeconomics to upgrade their obsolete theory. Just as the classical economists rejected the macroeconomic theories of Jean Charles Léonard de Sismondi neoclassical economists rejected Keynes's theories and have remained in a state of denial ever since. Their response to Keynesian macroeconomics has been a patchwork that reflects their desperate search for a coherent macroeconomic theory that can fit with their extreme right-wing political ideology. Neoclassical macroeconomics could not produce anyone of the stature of Alfred Marshall or John Maynard Keynes; hence, it could not break out of its obsolete classical microeconomic mold.

The Fall

For centuries, the world endured, with resignation, the misery of recessions and depressions as inevitable calamities. During the Great Depression, unemployment in several Western countries hovered around 25 percent, with bankruptcies rife, government revenues falling, and budget deficits ballooning.[93]

The prescriptions of the high priests of neoclassical macroeconomics were bizarre. Their most enlightened proposed abdicating economic policy to market forces. The less enlightened proposed raising interest rates and cutting the government deficit by raising taxes and reducing spending, tipping a recession into depression. There are two possible explanations for their economic irrationality. One is the invalidity of their theories that misrepresent the workings of a national economy. The other, more sinister, explanation is that a deeper contraction was useful because it increased the market shares of oligopolistic corporations. Bizarrely, almost a century later, similar policies perpetuate the ongoing economic crises in the West, raising the old question as to why, only more sternly.

The Great Depression and Keynesian theories freed economics from the ramshackle of neoclassical macroeconomics and its noninterventionist *laissez-faire* prescriptions. Unfortunately, for capitalism and the world, the fall of neoclassical macroeconomics from grace proved too short. Its rise from the dead came in the late 1970s. In the intervening decades, its tireless advocates advanced a torrent of misguided and ineffective economic formulations.

The Austrian School

The followers of the Austrian School do not see themselves as neoclassical economists, although both share more common ground than meets the eye. Hence, since the Austrian School following is not wide enough to justify a separate chapter, the practical choice was to include it in the present one.

Professor Friedrich von Hayek (1899–1992) is probably the most celebrated scholar in the Austrian School, and considered by his devotees a pillar of economic thinking. He was anti-Keynesian, supported *laissez-faire*, and strongly opposed government intervention, even for cyclical stabilization.

During the 1930s, the brilliant economic research of Joan Robinson and Edward Chamberlin on the theory of monopolistic competition had demolished the assumption of perfect competition and, with it, the case for *laissez-faire*. As the 20th century wore on, the remnants of perfect competition were fast disappearing, and with it any lingering justification for *laissez-faire*. Yet, von Hayek and others did not acknowledge they needed to revise their theories. The Austrian School and neoclassical macroeconomists stuck to their perceptions of a world that had long disappeared.

John Maynard Keynes did not find Friedrich von Hayek a coherent thinker and his comments on Hayek's book *Prices and Production* were blunt: "The book, as it stands, seems to me to be one of the most frightful muddles I have ever read, with scarcely a sound proposition in it. ... It is an extraordinary example of how, starting with a mistake, a remorseless logician can end up in bedlam."[94]

Milton Friedman was just as blunt, describing the Austrian business-cycle theory as "dangerous nonsense."[95] He wrote, "...back to the 1930s... sitting in London, Hayek and Lionel Robbins, and saying you just have to let the bottom drop out of the world...You can't do anything about it...encouraging that kind of do-nothing policy both in Britain and in the United States, they did harm."[96]

Friedrich von Hayek was an advocate of social Darwinism. In his book, *The Road to Serfdom*, he expressed alarm at the growth of the state, proclaiming it could lead not just to socialism and loss of individual freedoms but also to tyranny and serfdom. These allegations were against countries that were offering welfare to their citizens. The economic justice that those reforms brought to the majority of the people seem to have troubled him but not the centuries of slavery, serfdom, tyranny, imperialism, and piracy that had prevailed under *laissez-faire* and *parasitic capitalism*. His contention that the welfare state, *moral capitalism*, and economic democracy would result in worse crimes than under past plutocracies, was a further demonstration of his incoherence. *The Road to Serfdom* confuses cause with effect. To put matters in their proper perspective, we must ask what drove people to communism. Political and economic oppression under plutocracy's *parasitic capitalism* precipitated extreme income inequality and poverty to the point of despair, which fueled revolutions. Even communist regimes, with voting restricted to party members, had a semblance of democracy, which the plutocratic dictatorships it replaced often lacked.

Professor Hayek's apparent alarm that economic democracy would lead to tyranny is another example of an absurd mind unless it is to promote political ends, using clever counterintuitive logic to confuse a naïve audience. This raises the possibility of interpreting his stance as a quasi-Napoleonic strategy of "attack is the best defense" so as to distract attention away from the growing inequality under economic liberalism. In any case, his use of communism as a bogeyman is now redundant because communism is not about to rise from the ashes. Friedrich von Hayek's call for smaller governments to preserve freedoms hints at a plutocratic agenda to cut welfare for the majority and the taxes of the rich. That such policies result in deteriorating living conditions for the masses, presumably to benefit the wealthy few, was apparently the intended outcome. In many ways, his ideas resemble those of Reverend Thomas Malthus. Despite voicing great concern for democracy, since Hayek's policies ran contrary to the interests of the majority they were in effect anti-democratic.

Von Hayek was even inconsistent as a conservative because he was in favor of comprehensive health care for all. Finally, like neoclassical macroeconomists in general, he was oblivious to the externalities that cause market failures.

Parasitic capitalism, despite temporary right-wing successes in squeezing low-income groups, is politically doomed in modern society. Friedrich von Hayek's pronouncements were political statements and not considered economic analyses—and universities and economic departments ought to classify them accordingly.

Remarkably, despite his demonstrable incoherence, Professor Friedrich von Hayek, like many neoclassical economists, earned the admiration of a Nobel Prize granting committee.

The Monetarist School

Professor Milton Friedman (1912–2006) is the father of the monetarist school, a neoclassical macroeconomic fringe school based on the classical quantity theory of money. His followers consider him a leader of modern economic thought. His biggest economic impact was in providing neoclassical arguments supporting the Thatcher-Reagan economic policies.

In the 1930s, Friedman began his career as a Keynesian. However, over the following decades, he drifted to free markets, *laissez-faire*, and neoclassical macroeconomics. He encapsulated his philosophy in a lecture at the Pontifical Catholic University of Chile (*Universidad Católica de Chile*), in which he claimed that *free markets would undermine political centralization and political control*. In time, those views would encourage deregulation in the United States, with disastrous economic consequences. Those prescriptions were political because the economic history of the United States demonstrated that the opposite is true: lack of regulation resulted in monopolies and cartels, necessitating antitrust statutes in 1890 and 1914 to promote fair competition and to protect consumers.[97]

Professor Friedman also believed an easy monetary policy was sufficient to bring about an economic recovery, without fiscal stimulus. Ironically, he was also against using a proactive monetary policy because he saw a difficulty in forecasting economic activity and proposed a steady growth in the money supply instead. Hence, his policy prescription reduces to the very kind of *laissez-faire* for which he had previously criticized Professor von Hayek.

Applying steady growth in the money supply hinged on a stable velocity of money in circulation and an absence of a Keynesian *liquidity trap*. Yet, economic common sense suggests, a priori, that the velocity of money is bound to fluctuate, rising with higher interest rates during an expansion and falling with falling interest rates during a contraction. In addition, the ineffectiveness of expansionary monetary policy during severe contractions confirms the presence of a liquidity trap. Other than that, it is a nice little theory. For a while in the 1980s, Professor Friedman's prescriptions were tested and abandoned because they proved ineffective.

Professor Friedman also articulated a curious inflation theory. He hypothesized that inflation occurs via a "transmission mechanism." He saw excessive money supply as disturbing the optimal asset allocations of portfolios held by the public by involuntarily increasing the cash component of their holdings. This compels excessive cash holders to rebalance their portfolios by reducing their cash in exchange for other assets. That, in turn, causes the value of cash relative to other assets to fall, producing inflation.

In practice, the majority of the public, under the influence of what Irving Fisher termed "monetary illusion," is pleased with an increase in the money supply—before becoming aware of the loss of its purchasing power. At first, only a few alert people notice and successfully adapt to inflation. Others observe them and follow their lead. Ultimately, cash holders adapt according to their individual circumstances.

The underclasses, to the extent that they can, tend to decrease their cash balances by moving forward their future purchases of necessities, like nonperishable foods, to avoid paying higher prices later. The rich tend to cut their cash holdings by acquiring various assets that act as inflation hedges, like real estate. They also borrow for the purpose, provided the interest rate is lower than the expected rate of asset price inflation plus the rental yield.

Professor Friedman's inflation hypothesis necessitated some farfetched and unnecessary assumptions. People have dealt with inflation for hundreds of years, long before the recent advent of the concept of *portfolios*. Even today, apart from financial experts, most people are unfamiliar with the concept—never mind using it to rebalance their portfolios to precipitate inflation. Friedman's inflation mechanism and portfolio adjustment imply that people everywhere have always been instinctive portfolio managers, periodically conducting portfolio rebalancing. This level of sophistication is not normally observed, and his idealized version of reality is characteristic of many neoclassical theories.

By comparison, traditional demand-supply analysis suggests that, other things being equal, excess supply (a supply curve shift to the right) of anything lowers its price. Thus, an excessive money supply reduces the value (purchasing power) of money, which is inflation. Hence, it is economically intuitive that an excessive money supply leads, eventually, to inflation or even hyperinflation. If two theories arrive at the same conclusion, the scientific approach endorses the simpler explanation, reaffirming that genius is simple. In other words, an elaborate new economic theory is redundant when a good old supply-and-demand analysis is sufficient.

Moreover, Professor Friedman's explanation of inflation is restricted to the demand-pull variety. It is a consequence of the excessive use of the printing press; stopping it stops inflation. However, a restrictive monetary policy is less effective in the case of cost-push or imported inflation, as the mid-1970s demonstrated. His theory did not touch on how to handle these more intricate types of inflation. Hence, to the extent that his theories influenced the Fed in using a tight monetary policy to fight cost-push inflation in the late 1970s and early 1980s, they inflicted inestimable damage on the US economy.

Predictably, Professor Milton Friedman received a Nobel Prize in economics, like many other neoclassical economists, for his work on monetary history and theory and for identifying a positive correlation between wealth and consumption (besides the stronger and already established Keynesian correlation between disposable income and consumption).[98]

Revival

Logic suggests that the disastrous performance of neoclassical macroeconomics during the Great Depression, followed by the severe recession of 1937–1938, would have been sufficient to convince its adherents that it had no economic foundation and it was time to abandon it for good. Instead, they held onto it like a religion, circling their intellectual wagons—resorting to subsidiary theories, abstractions, contrived complexity, redundant mathematics, and economic nuances, waiting for an opportunity to rehabilitate their precious Humpty Dumpty. Four decades later and with stagflation for a Trojan horse, the Thatcher-Reagan "revolution" elevated neoclassical macroeconomics to the status of mainstream macroeconomics.

Misdiagnosis of Stagflation (1979–1982)

In 1979, President Jimmy Carter appointed Paul Volcker to be the Federal Reserve chairman. President Ronald Reagan reappointed him for a second term in 1983. Paul Volcker, a neoclassical monetary economist, is widely credited with curing the US economy from the inflation of the late 1970s and early 1980s. His inflation medicine was recessions.

This raises a fundamental macroeconomic question: are recessions a valid remedy for curing cost-push inflation? The inflation rate rose between 1979 and 1981, because of a sharp rise in the price of oil in 1979. The cause was the disruption of oil supplies from Iran and Iraq, following Saddam Hussein's invasion of Iran, with US blessings, to subdue the recent revolution there. To counter inflation, Volker engineered two recessions in quick succession, in 1980 and 1981–1982, through interest rate shocks that saw fed funds spike to 20 percent by 1981. He precipitated the worst financial crises since the 1930s, causing contractions in GDP of 2.2 percent and 2.7 percent, respectively. Unemployment peaked at 10.4 percent in 1982, higher than the 9 percent peak unemployment rate reached during the harsh 1973–1975 recession.[99]

Tight monetary policy had already proved ineffective against cost-push inflation following the first oil crisis of the mid-1970s: It neither increased oil supplies nor lowered oil prices, the root cause of that cost-push inflation, yielding only a marginal reduction in the international demand for oil and hardly affecting the OPEC oil cartel. Therefore, there was no tangible economic reason for repeating the same medicine a few years later expecting a different outcome. The two elective Volker recessions came at a huge cost to the US economy, squandering vast economic resources for no constructive purpose.

More specifically, there are compelling reasons why the Volker recessions did not cure US inflation, as follows:

1. The inflation was not of the demand-pull variety and therefore its source was not monetary; hence, the ultra-tight monetary policy was inappropriate and ineffective.

2. The source of the cost-push inflation was on the supply-side, due to a constrained oil supply. Curing that problem required increasing the supply of oil and improving energy efficiency, which took time. By late 1982, nine years had elapsed since the first major oil price spike in 1973. This was time enough for new oil to begin flowing in sufficient quantities from all over the world to moderate oil prices and with it the cost-push inflation.

3. Nine years' time was also enough for a marked global improvement in fuel efficiency to materialize, in response to a variety of measures including high oil prices, higher petrol taxes, and higher fuel-efficiency standards for cars and energy use. Improved energy efficiency restrained the global demand for oil.

4. These developments stabilized the oil price by 1982, and thereafter it began to slide. The price of oil crashed in 1985 due to a glut in supply. The US inflation rate broadly mirrored the price of oil.

5. Inflation did not return following the recovery in 1983. The oil price remained depressed up to Saddam Hussein's invasion of Kuwait in August 1990, when a brief spike appeared in 1990–1991.

6. Thereafter, a weak oil price continued for another decade due to the structural increase in supply coupled with slower growth in demand

due to improved fuel efficiency—monetary policy had no role in these effects.

7. More challenging than the oil price rise from the mid-1970s to the early1980s, was the fourteen-fold oil price increase between the late 1990s and 2007, yet it did not trigger inflation. The chief reason was the flood of exceedingly cheap imports, particularly from China, which were sufficiently deflationary on the supply side to absorb the inflationary impact of a higher oil price.

8. Between 2008 and 2015, the money supply has been more bloated than ever before, but inflation has remained tame, tempered by a flood of cheap imports, including oil. Thus, the relationship between money supply and inflation is neither as tight nor as simple as the naïve monetarist model presumes.

The foregoing shows that tight monetary policy was counterproductive and likely delayed the satisfactory resolution of the cost-push inflation. Restrictive neoclassical monetary policy operating on the demand side is no more effective than a Keynesian curtailment of aggregate demand. Volker was simply lucky; his recessions coincided with the increase in oil supplies and the improvement in fuel efficiency. A neutral monetary policy would have been economically far less costly; still, it would have required an ability to withstand public pressure, while waiting for developments in the oil sector to run their course.

By contrast, the economists who devised the targeted measures such as investment tax credits that augmented oil supplies and improved fuel-efficiency are the unknown soldiers that contributed to curing the cost-push inflation. Those economists ought to be recognized publicly for their solid contributions.

Less generally appreciated is that Volcker's extremely high interest rate regime launched the dismantling of Regulation Q, which a decade later culminated in wiping out the savings and loan industry. Volcker's other not so obvious influence is that his outrageously high interest rates initiated banking deregulation, which, two Fed chairs later, brought about the Great Recession and the present financial difficulties.[100]

Two Centuries of Parasitic Economics

Neoclassical Supply-Side Economics

Supply side economic policies helped solve the oil crisis, principally, oil-investment tax credits, liberalization of the price of old oil, and higher car mileage standards. Contrary to neoclassical claims, supply-side policies did not diminish the relevance of Keynesian policies, which operate on the demand side. Rather, the two complement each other.

For a time, in the 1980s, neoclassical "supply-side economics" became all the rage. Unlike the above-mentioned genuine version of supply-side policies, the focus of the neoclassical version was to cut the taxation of the rich. They claimed lower taxes for the rich was good for the poor because it incentivized the rich to get richer, resulting in a trickle-down of new jobs and better wages to the underclasses, whereas cutting social security tax and sales taxes was more certain to improve the lot of the underclass with some trickle-up for the rich.

The politically astute neoclassical supply-siders then used the fall in tax revenue that resulted from cutting the taxes of the rich to justify raising the indirect taxes on the underclass and cutting welfare programs; the tangible trickle-down from their policies was worsening inequality, *chronic underconsumption*, hardship, and slower growth. Neoclassical supply-side economics, like the rest of the "neo" labels, was against the interest of the majority and, therefore, anti-democracy.

Like all reverse–Robin Hood ploys, it had distinct Malthusian resonance: abolishing relief to the poor to help them. More worrisome was the media's willingness to market such claims, reminiscent of the Soviet state-controlled media. Neoclassical doctrine, supported by the media, proved once again that red is green and anyone who disagrees is colorblind.

MPT versus Dynamic Portfolio Theory

Modern portfolio theory (MPT) first appeared in the 1950s and developed thereafter. Its primary focus is the securities markets, which have considerable influence over the real economy. Like the followers of the Austrian School, the developers and advocates of MPT have traditionally presented it as distinct from neoclassical theory; however, it swims, walks, and quakes like it is part of it, as the following demonstrates:

- MPT uses the traditional assumptions of neoclassical theory such as perfect markets, perfect information, and rational actors.
- The macroeconomic policy recommendations of both are identical, centering on deregulating markets, with equally disastrous consequences.
- Applying *rational expectations hypothesis* (REH), an extension of neoclassical theory, to securities markets yields similar results as MPT.
- Both use elaborate mathematics as a substitute for common sense.
- Like neoclassical macroeconomic theories, MPT is intellectually seductive but short on realism.
- The relation between neoclassical economics and MPT is also incestuous. The same academic institutions have fostered both theories. For example, the University of Chicago, the bastion of neoclassical economics, has been the bastion of MPT also. Thus, Professor Eugene Fama (b. 1939), the father of the *efficient market hypothesis* and MPT, spent his teaching career at the University of Chicago. Harry Markowitz (b. 1927), best known for his efficient frontier in portfolio selection, studied at the University of Chicago. Fischer Black (1938–1995) and Myron Scholes (b. 1941), best known for their Black-Scholes model, both worked at the University of Chicago. Moreover, the originator of the *rational expectations hypothesis*, Robert Lucas (b. 1937), also studied at the University of Chicago.[101]
- Most remarkable, all the aforementioned MPT scholars, like many of their celebrated neoclassical peers, have received Nobel Prizes.

The literature provides elaborate formal criticisms of MPT.[102] Our task here is more modest, limited to analyzing some core premises of MPT, using qualitative analysis, namely:

1. The reward for assuming greater risk is higher return and vice versa.
2. Securities markets and investors are rational.
3. Given market and investor rationality, expected risk and return are valid proxies for the same.
4. Standard deviation and variance are valid measures of risk.
5. Diversification per se provides a satisfactory means of risk-reduction.

Let us begin by considering MPT's central premise: the risk-return tradeoff. Like so much of neoclassical macroeconomic theory, any measure of validity of this central premise of MPT is limited to static, stationary, analysis, but it breaks down in a dynamic setting. Admittedly, it seems counter intuitive that securities markets have a negatively correlated risk-return trade-off, such that the reward for assuming less risk is greater return and the reward for assuming greater risk is lower return, but this is precisely what is on offer in a dynamic investment process, as we shall demonstrate.

Let us illustrate by using the stock market cycle, starting with its turning points. Near a market bottom, potential risk approaches its nadir while potential return approaches its zenith. In other words, the risk-return trade-off near a market bottom is minimum potential risk for maximum potential return. Hence, the risk-return tradeoff is negatively correlated near a market bottom, contrary to MPT's expectation.

The opposite is true near a market top; risk approaches its zenith while return approaches maximum potential loss. Stated differently, the risk-return trade-off near a market top is maximum potential risk for maximum negative return. Thus, the risk-return tradeoff is negatively correlated near a market top, again contrary to MPT's expectation.

For the analysis to cover a full stock market cycle, we must also consider the regions between the market turning points. During a bull market, realized return is positive. However, as prices rise, risk rises and potential return falls (the potential of more profit gets smaller). Accordingly, during a bull market, risk and return are negatively correlated, also contrary to MPT's expectation.

During a bear market, realized return is negative. However, as prices fall, risk also falls, while potential return improves (or at least the potential loss falls). In other words, during a bear market, risk and return are negatively correlated, again contrary to MPT's expectation.

For ease of reference, let us label the preceding analysis of the relationship between risk and return in a dynamic investment setting as the *dynamic portfolio theory (DPT)* to distinguish from MPT.

DPT shows that contrary to the central premise of MPT, risk and return is not positively, but rather negatively, correlated. In other words, the reward for assuming less risk is greater return while the reward for assuming greater risk is lower return. Granted, the precise market turning points only become known with certainty after the event, but experienced investors have an expectation, a sense, of when the market is approaching one or the other extreme. To that end, skilled investors use a battery of indicators including the stage and duration of the business cycle, economic outlook, stock valuations such as price to earnings, price to cash flow, and price to book value ratios, the trend in sales, earnings momentum, and the absolute level of the stock market but above all their instinct.

The central premise of MPT of a positively correlated risk-return tradeoff fails because markets are misinformed and irrational, reaching the height of their irrationality near market turning points. Thus, near a market top, greed and optimism overwhelm rationality while near a market bottom fear and pessimism take over. In other words, near a market top, the market is very optimistic, its perception of expected risk is too low, and its expected return is too high. On the other hand, near a market bottom, the market is very pessimistic and its perception of expected risk is too high, and its expected return is too low. This in fact is the central premise of a contrarian investment strategy, which has a better chance of achieving an above average rate of return than MPT. Contrarian investing also provides a dampening effect on the market through its tendency to sell an overpriced market, thereby limiting its excessive rise and, once liquid, it has a tendency to buy into an overly discounted market, thereby limiting its fall. MPT, on the other hand, is happy to follow the market passively, not unlike the passivity of neoclassical economics with regard to the economy.

Thus, MPT's second premise that markets are rational fails, particularly near market turning points. But, what drives markets to irrationality? First, the investing public has a tendency to extrapolate the present into the future, instead of anticipating turning points. Another factor is the poor advice provided by the financial media, investment advisors, and various experts. The financial media are very good at providing explanations of what happened yesterday, but hopeless when it comes to predicting what will happen tomorrow or the day after. This is not to say that there is necessarily intentional or coordinated disinformation, although there is some systematic disinformation; the sub-prime credit rating fiasco demonstrated as much. Moreover, it is not only difficult to tell good from bad advice ahead of time but also, good advice is rare by definition (like true excellence), hence it can easily get lost in a sea of mediocrity. The section titled "In Search of Reliable Signposts" in Chapter 1 alluded to this problem. Moreover, are those with superior analysis interested in sharing their market outlook? Lao Tzu's sage advice has cautionary implications for investors: those who know do not speak and those who speak do not know.[103]

The third premise of MPT is using expected risk and expected return as proxies for true risk and return. In this MPT has miss specified risk and return, because given that markets are irrational then so are their expectations. The better approximation is to use an estimate of potential risk and return, based on how far the market can potentially fall as a proxy for risk and how much higher it can potentially rise as a proxy for return.

The fourth premise of MPT is that standard deviation and variance are valid measures of risk. These blunt mechanical tools measure fluctuations not risk; fluctuation and risk are very different. Two stocks can theoretically have a similar degree of fluctuation (variance) while one is rising like a rocket, as happens with many good stocks, while the other is falling like a rock to its ultimate demise, as happened with Enron. Variance makes no distinction between the risks associated with the two situations. To claim that fluctuation without regard to the direction of travel of various stocks can measure risk is gross simplification of reality; it gives rise to absurd conclusions and theories.

The fifth premise of MPT is diversification and, to that end, it devotes a battery of equations. Sadly, by overlooking the dynamics of the investment process, MPT's attempt to reduce risk by measuring the covariance of securities is hardly satisfactory. The brilliance of its fine mathematics blinds it to the simple reality. On its own, the capacity of diversification for reducing risk is very marginal because when the tide of the stock market ebbs all investment boats go down with it, including diversified portfolios. Whether to invest or not to invest—that is the question. Only after answering it does the question of diversification arise. Those who find that question too formidable and duck it by staying fully invested over the full cycle should not engage in making investment decisions.

Having explained MPT's limitations, we can turn to how to use it. MPT is useful as a static, tactical, investment tool, without a forward vision. Let us illustrate, using the bond market. At any point in time, rational investors naturally prefer less risk to more and, therefore, to induce them to assume more risk requires inducing them with a higher return; hence, corporate bond yields are normally higher than Treasury yields. Thus, in a static setting, MPT's risk-return trade-off is valid because choosing between investments at a moment in time disregards the future. Within this very narrow context, MPT is rational. In other words, once the decision to invest has been taken then MPT can help in making bond selections, assuming credit ratings are reliable these days.

In essence, DPT and MPT yield different results because their respective decisions take place over different time horizons and attempt to answer different questions. DPT is concerned with investment strategy over time, particularly the central question of whether to invest or not to invest. On the other hand, MPT is a tactical tool appropriate for the more limited task of choosing between investments at a point in time. Furthermore, MPT, even in a static context, is too naïve for making superior stock selections, because stock investing is intrinsically more complex than bond investing.

MPT's premise that risk and return are positively correlated in a dynamic investment setting, markets are efficient, and investors are rational has resulted in unfortunate public policies. Multiple versions of the *efficient market hypothesis* have evolved overtime.[104] The most efficient version presumes that markets are so efficient that they discount all available information about securities prices fairly, objectively, and quickly. Accordingly, securities research is unnecessary and throwing darts, randomly, at lists of stocks appearing in daily newspapers can replace stock selection. This implies that we operate in a zone of economic nirvana and financial bliss, where corporate surprises, market crashes, and financial crises are highly unlikely, if not impossible. The inference is clear enough: extend neoclassical *laissez-fair* to the securities and other financial markets through deregulation.

One consequence of this seemingly harmless academic exercise has been to justify curbing the budgets for supervising securities markets such as that of the Securities and Exchange Commission (SEC), which has diminished securities markets efficiency and increased the potential for securities fraud, as evidenced by the collapse of Enron and the protracted operations of Ponzi schemes à la Madoff.[105] Doubtless, reducing market efficiency provides greater opportunity for profit by the better informed at the expense of the less well informed, namely, the investing public; hence, the primary loser from the *efficient market hypothesis* has been the investing public because curtailed budgets for market supervision have decreased market efficiency while deregulation has increased the scope of institutional speculation.[106]

In tandem with this assertion of market efficiency, a growing phenomenon of systematically massaging and overstating earnings has surfaced.[107] Other grim consequences have been the justifications it has provided for deregulating banking and keeping derivatives over the counter and unregulated.

A crucial test of the relevance of the *rational expectations hypothesis* and market efficiency came in 2008. Given rational expectations, why did the believers in neoclassical macroeconomic theory fail to anticipate the 2008 crisis while the skeptics did?[108]

Wisely, the investment superstars have doubted the utility of MPT. For example, Warren Buffet, probably the best-known successful investor, flatly shuns it. The old saying that those who know invest, and those who do not know teach, is particularly pertinent to MPT. Indeed, the most prominent MPT scholars have ventured to apply their sophisticated investment theories to the real world with disastrous results. Clearly, if using MPT yields disastrous results to those who articulated it (as Long-Term Capital Management (LTCM) has demonstrated), then it is not very wise for anyone else to use it.[109]

Critique of Neoclassical Macroeconomics

To protect consumers against gouging by trusts, cartels, monopolies, and oligopolies, the United States Congress passed three landmark acts—the Sherman Act in 1890, the Clayton Antitrust Act in 1914, and the Federal Trade Commission Act, also in 1914. These were measures to repair and limit the economic damage caused by the then prevailing policies of *laissez-faire* and "free markets." Furthermore, in the 1930s, two neoclassical economists, Joan Robinson and Edward Chamberlin, independently developed the theory of monopolistic competition, which essentially confirmed the economic rationale of the aforementioned congressional resolutions. Yet, since the 1980s, on the advice of some neoclassical economists, there has been a reversion to deregulating markets and increasing the market shares of oligopolies. The consequence of dismantling the Glass–Steagall Act is no different. Neoclassical macroeconomists have been busy dismantling the US economic infrastructure, which had taken more than a century of hard work to build.

The presence of market externalities refutes the neoclassical belief that markets are sufficiently efficient to drive the economy to a full-employment general equilibrium.[110] Thus, in several European Union countries, *chronic underconsumption* is rampant and youth unemployment exceeds 50 percent. The lingering European economic contraction is comprehensive evidence of the errors of neoclassical macroeconomics, a tragic repeat of the failed *laissez-faire* policy during the Great Depression.

Another critique of neoclassical *laissez-faire* policies is its subliminal call for war. By not using civilian expenditures to bring about economic recovery, in effect policymakers make military spending and war the only option available for improving economic conditions. Voltaire once remarked, "Those who can make you believe absurdities can make you commit atrocities."[111] Indeed, wars of choice are the worst war crime. An often-cited justification for using wars to solve economic problems is that the US economy only came out of depression after entering World War II.[112] This raises the question whether the urge to shake off the Great Depression through military instead of civilian expenditure was a factor in imposing the US oil embargo on Japan, which, predictably, drove the Japanese to attack the United States. Making room for military expenditure also explains why current US infrastructure, which is in bad need of extensive repairs and upgrading, has been starved of investment.

Another neoclassical dogma, with implications for using monetary instead of fiscal policy for cyclical stabilization, is that investment and interest rate are negatively correlated and the former is elastic with respect to the latter, such that investment rises in response to a fall in interest rate and falls in response to a rise in interest rate. However, casual observation shows that investment tends to fall rather than rise when interest rate is falling, typically during the onset of economic contractions. On the other hand, during an expansion, investment and interest rate both tend to rise together. In other words, the sign of the coefficient of correlations between investment and interest rate tends to be mostly positive, not negative as neoclassical theory stipulates, although it tends to flip briefly around cyclical turning points.

In any case, lowering the interest on Treasury paper does not readily translate into lower interest for most corporate credits, because the interest spread between Treasuries and nonprime credits tends to peak during a recession to compensate lenders for a perceived increase in the credit risk. Credit also tends to dry up during contractions because banks become risk-averse in the face of mounting bad debts.

A more reasonable macroeconomic model would be to assume that, subject to certain constraints, investment demand is profit-elastic instead of interest-elastic—with profit meaning expected profit over the life of an investment. Hence, low interest rates cannot stimulate investment while the profit outlook is dim. Indeed, a reduction in interest is no more than a minor cost reduction, insufficient to induce investment. During a contraction, the fall in costs, including interest, does not offset the effect on profit of falling sales and sales prices. Hence, profits fall and losses may develop, eliminating the stimulus for investing. In addition, economic contractions change entrepreneurs' priority from profit maximization to loss minimization, liquidity preservation, and sheer survival. In any case, investment in a new plant and equipment makes little sense during contractions while there is excess idle capacity available at a fraction of the cost of "new investment."

These crucial factors block the rise of investment in response to a fall in interest rate. Thus, monetary policy is often compared to an elastic band; pulling on it can restrain an expansion through high interest rates, but pushing on it through low interest rates has little effect in stimulating a contraction. Hence, Keynes warned against a *liquidity trap* where falling interest could not stimulate investment, which has been observed repeatedly.

In choosing between increasing public expenditure and cutting taxes to stimulate the economy, neoclassical economists prefer cutting taxes, which is the wrong choice for three reasons. It tends to benefit the rich more than the poor. Moreover, if a tax cut includes the rich then that portion of the tax cut has little stimulative effect, because the rich have a low marginal propensity to consume. Stated simply, the rich already have enough money to buy what they want; hence, giving them more money does not induce them to spend more, and the richer they are the more valid this observation becomes. Infrastructure expenditure is also more stimulative because it tends to have a larger domestic purchases component in the form of building materials and wages instead of imports. In addition, infrastructure spending improves and adds to public assets, with benefits accruing to the public over extended periods, long after its stimulative effects have subsided. By comparison, the benefits from a tax cut are fleeting, swelling the national debt without an offsetting increase in national assets. The current US policy of resorting to tax cuts instead of increasing public expenditure is in part because the proponents of tax cuts block the planning budgets for infrastructure projects during normal economic times, thereby thwarting the timely implementation of public investment in infrastructure during contractions.

Most of the failings of the neoclassical macroeconomic theory are traceable to its failure to incorporate *societal-interest* (morality) as a critical economic driver.[113] Hence, the most serious critique of neoclassical macroeconomics is its promotion of the interest of the very rich and big business at the expense of the majority of the people—be they workers, consumers, investors, taxpayers, or welfare recipients. This extremist right-wing political agenda has colored much of its macroeconomics, which may help explain its persistence in adopting irrational theories and policies. Neoclassical macroeconomics, by promoting the interest of the rich instead of the majority, it undermines democracy.

The foregoing is but a sampling of the criticisms of neoclassical macroeconomics; nevertheless, it rings the alarm that, as with Marxist economics before it, it lacks scientific validity. Neoclassical macroeconomic policies have failed repeatedly in the past but neoclassical macroeconomists are determined to repeat them. It is irrational to repeat previously failed policies and expect a different outcome. Albert Einstein described such behavior succinctly by saying, "Insanity: doing the same thing over and over again and expecting different results."[114]

Finally, philosophy is the ultimate arbiter of controversies. Philosophy classifies conjunctures that use flawed logic as formal fallacies (e.g., deregulation results in more competitive markets and economic efficiency, *laissez-faire* can clear markets). Philosophy also classifies the use of false premises in arguments as informal fallacies (e.g., general equilibrium is the natural state of the economy, self-interest is the sole economic driver, economic behavior is always rational). Thus, philosophy drives us to conclude that neoclassical macroeconomic theory is both a formal and an informal fallacy.

Hence, persisting with an obviously defunct, indeed, baseless economic model is the antithesis of wisdom and sheer folly. Neoclassical macroeconomics has been used to disseminate a version of *parasitic economics* that furthers *patristic capitalism*. It is essentially a political ideology with an economics label attached to it and universities have an obligation to reclassify it and alert their students accordingly.

———

Part I reviewed the meandering dialectic path of the development of macroeconomic thought. Part II offers an alternative macroeconomic framework.

Part II

An Alternative Macroeconomic Framework

Six

THE UNIFIED THEORY OF MACROECONOMIC FAILURE

The difficulty lies not so much in developing
new ideas as in escaping from old ones.[115]

John Maynard Keynes

Sir Thomas Gresham (1519–1579) was a financier in Tudor England. He articulated a law with further reaching implications than he probably anticipated; Gresham's Law states, *"Bad money drives out good money."*[116] The law describes what happens to coinage when moral laxity numbs society into accepting the theft of gold and silver from the coinage in circulation through scrapping until the lowest common moral denominator triumphs, and more individuals join in debasing their currency to extract a selfish, short-term advantage. Thus, Gresham's law implicitly points to immorality as a negative externality whose cost is not internalized by the market, resulting in market failure. Similarly, the classical and neoclassical economists' acceptance of the validity of this law was an implicit, if unconscious, admission of the economics of morality. In fact, Gresham's Law as it relates to coinage is a special case of a more general law, which *the unified theory of macroeconomic failure* seeks to bring to the attention of the reader.

Morality and Economic Efficiency

Morality is subtle. Hence, it is easy to underrate its far-reaching economic influences. Perhaps it helps to think of it as an environment. Like the natural environment, morality is a public good that we take for granted until it is contaminated. Invariably, the principal cause of a failing society is a failing morality.

What constitutes morality?

Jesus Christ decreed, "Do unto others as you would have them do unto you." [117] This call for moral reciprocity sums up the Ten Commandments; it is sometimes referred to as the "Golden Rule" or the "Golden Law." No doubt, Christ wanted morality to have a civilizing influence, to give society a soul and a conscience, and to shed egotism, injustice, depravity, and barbarism. Hence, technical advancement without parallel moral advancement reduces to advanced barbarism, not civilization.

Remarkably, sixteen religions have shared a similar moral message. It is also present in non-religious, ethical traditions since the early beginnings of man. [118] It is a universal moral code for determining the appropriateness of actions; it has withstood the test of time across religions, beliefs, cultures, and the immoralities and brainwashing of plutocracies.

What is the social utility of this universal moral code? In essence, it is a means for distinguishing, instinctively, between what is good and helpful to societies and what is harmful to them. The social value of morality derives from its promotion of the well-being of societies, hence, its durability. In contrast, its nemesis, immorality, is evil because it furthers the interest of an individual or a small group to the detriment of the rest of society. Thus, economic policies that serve the public interest are, by definition, moral, whereas economic policies that serve the interests of a narrow group by sacrificing the public interest are immoral. Moreover, discarding economic morality is equivalent to discarding the economic compass that guides societies' public policy with inevitable and significant economic and social costs.

Implementing morally correct economic policies provides added value even to small everyday transactions, because it improves economic efficiency. For example, most religions demand that their adherents practice honesty, the gateway to morality, and fair dealings. Compliance with this basic moral guideline in the marketplace requires the provision of accurate information on prices, weights, measures, descriptions, and specifications of tradeable goods and services, fair competition, and transparent intentions. Those measures improve the quality of information available to market participants and markets' efficiency. Hence, the functions of a consumer protection agency include insuring that the information on the label of a product for example, such as its volume or weight, is correct, in effect acting as a watchdog of honesty. It is also tantamount to an informal official recognition of the link between morality and economic efficiency. In the public sector, compliance requires governments to provide accurate economic statistics on unemployment, inflation, and other economic data, which improves economic decision-making. These are everyday examples of how morality fosters economic efficiency and the well-being of societies, while dishonesty and amoral practices detract from the same.

Value Judgments

Value judgment is a much-touted economic concept. Its lack of constancy makes it prone to manipulation. It is not feasible to use it for assessing the appropriateness of economic policies because it is morally ambiguous. The principal function of *value judgments* is to bypass moral values—*value judgments* usher in a Trojan horse of amoral economics, marginalizing morality as a mere personal preference, like a fashion, and presenting good and evil as relative values, not absolutes. Value judgments has been sanitizing amoral economic policies, making them politically acceptable despite their conflict with *societal-interest*.

Thus, major religions make the rich responsible for supporting the poor, while value judgments justify shunning this responsibility, thus, perpetuating poverty under the guise of economic efficiency.[119] Hence, the only conceivable economic utility of value judgments is limited to choosing between equally moral alternatives, not promoting immoral ones.

Plutocracies and Psychopaths

Immoral wealth-gathering methods and lack of compassion for the poor, both characteristics of plutocracy, prompted Jesus Christ to declare, "It is easier for a camel to go through the eye of a needle than for a rich man to enter the kingdom of Heaven."[120] Plutocracies hate everything that Christ loved and they seek all that he warned against.

President Theodore Roosevelt (1858–1919) was known as the trust-buster for his efforts to break up monopolies and cartels. He was concerned about the effect of great wealth on democracy. In his autobiography, he recounted, "...and of all forms of tyranny the least attractive and the most vulgar is the tyranny of mere wealth, the tyranny of a plutocracy."[121]

The subject of plutocracy came up in the context of classical economics in Chapter 2; however, its influence is still strong today, deserving further elaboration. The evidence suggests that throughout history, plutocracy's tyrannical rule has been humanity's worst enemy. It employs *parasitic capitalism* for its wealth gathering and plunders with impunity when it is the law. Thus, plutocracies have trapped the bulk of humanity in a vortex of poverty. The few interludes when poverty was not the constant companion of man coincided with the decline or demise of plutocratic power due to epidemics, religion, revolution, an enlightened ruler, and, recently, the threat of communism. *This does not mean that all the wealthy are plutocrats, but only those that use their wealth to gain political or economic advantage to the detriment of the rest of society.*

Plutocracies have been indestructible hydras despite their intense social disutility, a remarkable feat. Even when a plutocratic regime falls, its replacement soon tends to regress to plutocracy, making this characteristic *plutocratic persistence* almost a law of the physical world. At various times, their well-honed political skills have subverted religious institutions, academia, and the press. Another measure of its versatility is that it has penetrated, overtly or covertly, all forms of government. Even communist regimes have not escaped plutocratic creep; hence, we find corrupt communist dictators, like the late Nicolae Ceaușescu of Romania and unending trials of corrupt communist party members in China.

Plutocracies are vulnerable to the ascent of morality. It fears and silences its moral critics to prevent them from alerting the world to injustice. Thus, to maintain its patristic existence it has condemned some of the noblest and the best: compelling Socrates to drink poison, crucifying Jesus Christ, and martyring Al-Hussein, to name a few. [122] Such is the calculus of plutocracy. Plutocracy and crime are inseparable, like a thing and its shadow.

Psychopaths are the worst plutocratic strain. Sadly, the percentage of humanity that is psychopathic is not so small.[123] With the indifference of predators toward their prey, psychopaths feel no empathy or compassion toward those in pain, grief, or hunger. Perched atop the food chain, they are the ultimate predators, but, unlike those in the wild, nothing satisfies their hunger for more riches, regardless how many people suffer or perish.[124] They tend to reach elevated positions in criminality, wealth, politics, and form the backbone of plutocracies, often holding ultimate power, irrespective of the political exterior of a regime—whether autocracy, monarchy, republic, democracy, or some blended version.

What proof is there that psychopaths are politically powerful? Chapter 2 gave examples of their crimes against humanity, which require ultimate political power to escape punishment. Those acts entailed sadistic criminality, regardless of any justification such as serving the greater good.

Science is a powerful tool which plutocracies have abused for their ends. How would they misuse it in future? Perhaps within two decades, advances in automation would make it possible to create robotic armies. Robots, devoid of morality or restraint, can use limitless brutality to suppress rebellious populations and wage ceaseless wars of aggression. The other risk of an amoral transition to intense automation is that it could lead to technological dualism, mass unemployment, and depressed wages.[125] We can only speculate on how powerful psychopaths might exploit such vulnerabilities, or can we? Would they reintroduce slavery? How would they exploit the hungry and vulnerable? For example, in the war zones of the Middle East, terrorists have developed a lucrative niche market, supplying organs of enslaved children to use as spare parts for wealthy psychopaths.[126]

The call for *morality in politics and economics* is not trivial—the destiny of hundreds of millions is at stake, perhaps all of humanity, including the psychopaths, though they cannot realize it. We are at the gates of new technologies and new barbarism; humanity's only shield is morality because it can suffocate plutocracy and the evil it generates.

Academia's Failings

The quality of learning is critical for the future of nations generally and a high standard of economics education, in particular, is essential for guiding vigorous economies. Yet, the economic policies pursued by prominent graduates of the West's most renowned universities have inflicted terrible economic damage on their countries. What does that tell us about the value and relevance of the economics taught by those eminent universities?

The deterioration in the standards of economic education since the 1980s is a consequence of plutocratic meddling in academic affairs and academia's subservience to power, best demonstrated by its support of right-wing neoclassical macroeconomics, a major culprit behind the economic crises facing the West. Indeed, academia has been a willing promoter of parasitic economics. This lack of academic backbone has prompted Professor Noam Chomsky to conclude that the "intellectual tradition is one of servility to power...."

With rare exceptions, the celebrated centers of Western economic learning have been teaching inadequate, irrelevant, and flawed curricula of which the following is but a sample, in no particular order:

- Deafening silence on the economics of morality
- Lack of examination of *societal-interest* versus self-interest
- Lack of concern for the inefficiency of the presently regressive tax regime
- Teaching economic dogmas such as neoclassical macroeconomics as core subject matter

- Support for deregulation of markets without regard to its empowerment of monopolies
- Acceptance of modern portfolio theory
- Acceptance of usury and *usurious capitalism*
- Support for the downgrading of the role of fiscal policy
- Lack of serious criticism of the Federal Reserve or its boom-bust policies
- Non-objection to plutocracies' progressive hijacking of the political process
- Silence on the role of psychopaths in setting the economic agenda
- Allowing political agendas instead of objective science to set their macroeconomic curriculum

These and other failings have undermined the quality of economic learning. There have been knowledge revolutions in all fields, but not in economics because academia has been a formidable obstacle to economic progress. The economics it teaches should pass the tests of realism, relevance, utility, and common sense; instead, it delights in redundant complexity and layered irrationality. It breeds conformity and tunnel vision. Despite harsh economic problems, it has not engaged in vigorous debates about the root causes of these crises; instead, it has settled for reiterating defunct solutions.

Academia teaches a long list of economics specialties, including the economics of industry, agriculture, fisheries, mining, petroleum, transportation, the environment, trade, finance, money and banking, and many more besides; strikingly absent is *the economics of morality*, although the link between the two is organic. Economics textbooks treat morality as a taboo, shunning discussion of its impact on economic activity.[127] They overlook that morality is an externality with wide economic spillover effects and that it is fundamental to understanding the causes of numerous economic problems such as *chronic underconsumption*, financial fragility, the debt burden, inefficient taxation, anemic growth, worsening income inequality, and waning democracy, among others.

Moreover, academia does not teach subjects that are essential for under-standing the workings of macroeconomics like politics, economic history, morality, sociology, and psychology; without bridges of knowledge to these vital subjects, economics has been an isolated island, unable to explain, for example, what is driving irrational economic policies, which are seeding conditions that could spark revolutions. The present curriculum is about as adequate as teaching medicine without chemistry, physics, biology, or physiology.

Furthermore, the tone of the economics it teaches is without a moral stance regarding human problems, as though a natural science dealing with substances like hydrogen and nitrogen. The claim that morality renders economics unscientific is false because morality is the social compass of public policy; in its absence, special interests determine economic policy instead of *societal-interest*.

Poverty is the world's foremost economic problem, yet economics textbooks hardly give it the attention it deserves. Eradicating it is a moral, as well as an economic, priority. To appreciate what it does to its victims, students of economics need to observe it at close range, in its natural surroundings. Academia's aloofness towards the poor is not unlike Marie Antoinette's, the French queen; when the royal courtiers explained to her that the peasants are revolting because they have no bread, she inquired why don't they eat cakes instead. A good dose of social awareness of the suffering of the underclasses would improve future economists' sense of public priorities. It can refocus their attention toward the economic challenges that really matter—like poverty, homelessness, education, health services, and the cost-effectiveness of public services—instead of wasting their lives and talent researching issues of marginal relevance.

Leading economics professors have championed neoclassical macroeconomics and the plutocratic agendas, spawning the present Western economic malaise. Would anyone consult a physician who gives wrong advice? Yet eminent universities keep their misguided professors to play the same old records for fresh students, year after year.

The West's high-flying economics schools suffer from an ancient affliction; Plato described the merchants of knowledge as Sophists, selling their wares to wealthy students, insincerely repeating what is popular instead of what is reasoned and wise.[128] Despite their prestige, Sophists schools, as well as average for profit universities, deliver inferior education in economics and possibly other social sciences. The 2008 meltdown startled their economics professors and flagged their lack of expertise. Professors cannot teach what they do not know. It raises an interesting question: Does this imply that those Sophist universities do not know how to choose their professors or is it proof that they do? Either way, the Sophists' systematic dissemination of redundant economics makes them wellsprings of economic crises, gravely damaging national economies. Paradoxically, the Consumer Protection Agency does not protect the consumers of economics education, the students, from the flawed economics products of the Sophists.

The other characteristic of Sophist schools is exorbitant fees, pushing students with limited means into the financial slavery of indebtedness. The irony is that those schools earn huge surpluses yet they are registered charities and, therefore, tax exempt. Where is the charity in the fees they charge? In Britain too, under the present conservative government, public universities, which used to be free before the Thatcher-Reagan *counter-revolution*, are now charging students nine thousand pounds a year. Education no longer caters for merit but money. Learning is rationed so the have-nots remain ignorant, which expedites the perpetuation of plutocracy and the deterioration of democracy. It also means that a major part of the Anglo-Saxon world is steadily falling behind countries with relatively generous education budgets like China, India, Japan, and Russia.

Sophists are also conformists of the first order, unable to withstand controversy. Does knowledge flourish in a culture of conformity or intellectual challenge? For example, communism failed decades ago and no longer poses a threat to capitalism, yet academia has not fostered an objective reevaluation of communism's enduring impact. Thus, it does not recognize its effect on the West in propelling labor unions, the welfare state, economic and political democracy, improving income distribution, curbing *parasitic capitalism*, the defeat of imperialism, never mind the economic development and industrialization of the communist states. Granted, many of these were unintended consequences of communism, but its consequences, all the same.

Sophist conformity—and the intellectual fences protecting it—reflect an insecurity emanating from the inferior product it delivers. Academia implements conformity imperceptibly, through a regime of intellectual censorship. Its most effective tool is academic journals, using editorial committees populated by orthodox economists to weed out intellectually adventurous articles. For an economist to prosper in academia, he or she must publish frequently in those very journals and, with few exceptions, the price he or she must accept is conformity. In the words of Albert Einstein, "Great spirits have always encountered violent opposition from mediocre minds."[129]

Enforcing present-day conformity on economics departments is in the tradition of the anxious and narrow-minded Inquisition that threatened and silenced a non-conforming Galileo Galilei (1564–1642) for declaring that the earth rotated around the sun and not the other way around.[130] By one measure, matters are worse today because silencing those of a different mind no longer requires threatening their lives when rejecting publication of their articles in academic journals suffices. Still, academia's ultimate coercive tool is always there, in the background. It is not above dismissing non-conformists, as when Trinity College (Cambridge) dismissed the intellectually gifted Bertrand Russell in 1916, to its undying shame.[131]

Certain celebrated institutions, dedicated to promoting knowledge and excellence, are jointly responsible with universities for the present state of economic mediocrity. For example, the Nobel Foundation's committees award the most prestigious prizes and have done a reasonably good job in assessing scientific contributions, but some of their economic and political awards are indefensible, showing the Nobel Foundation to be siding with extremist right-wing political agendas. The award of Nobel Peace Prize offers unfortunate demonstrations for this inclination. Let us cite three outrageous decisions from different periods. It considered Mahatma Gandhi (1869–1948) of India, the ultimate lover of peace, undeserving of their Nobel "Peace Prize," presumably to indulge a waning and embittered British imperialist plutocracy. However, it found Henry Kissinger (b. 1923) deserving of a Peace Prize, despite his roles in prolonging the Vietnam War, initiating war on Laos and Cambodia, and the military coup against the democratically elected government of Chile, which resulted in the murder of President Salvador Allende and tens of thousands of Chileans? It also found President Barack Obama (b. 1961) deserving of the Peace Prize before he had time as a president to demonstrate his love for war, consenting to the aerial destruction of Libya by NATO members, the global terrorist war on Syria, and numerous mistaken drone killings. By these standards, one day a Stalin of the extreme right will be eligible for the Nobel Peace Prize too.

An independent review of Nobel Prizes in the social sciences would reveal a similarly misguided pattern. In recent decades, the Nobel committees have exhibited a distinct partiality for right-wing neoclassical economists, even though two centuries ago Jean Charles Léonard de Sismondi revealed the error and menace of classical macroeconomic theories, which continues to this day in the neoclassical format. Improving the standards that govern the Nobel Prize in economics will require excluding from the award committees those who presume that neoclassical macroeconomics is a valid branch of economics, because the massive damage it has inflicted on the world economy is testimony enough of its redundancy. By awarding the purveyors of bad economics, the Nobel Foundation has inflicted irreparable damage on the economies of the West. This must stop and until it does all earnest economists need to reject this debased prize. Similarly, the Swedish government and parliament have a moral obligation to demand that the Nobel Foundation reform itself or risk losing its status as a charity. It is far better for the world to end these awards altogether than to continue handing them to the undeserving.

Friedrich Nietzsche (1844–1900), the German philosopher, expressed the precariousness and vulnerability of the truth by observing, "All things are subject to interpretation [and] whichever interpretation prevails at a given time is a function of power and not truth."[132] McCarthyism, long before McCarthy, has etched Pavlovian conditioning on economic minds, making economics a stagnant pond: infertile and dismal.[133] Academia's servility to political masters and its subtle inquisition culture too often result in a trampling of the truth. It is time academia stopped churning out rationalizations in support of the defective economic policies of the establishment.

A repeat of 2008 with perplexed professors proposing Band-Aid solutions will exhaust any residual credibility of those eminent economics departments. Academia does not have infinite time to update its curricula; its window of opportunity is probably limited to the time available between now and the next crisis. Its role should change from a conformist implementer of political agendas (seeding economic disasters) to a defender of creativity that can only flourish by not penalizing originality and alternate ideas.

Academia cannot hold back the march of knowledge forever. Perhaps the Magnificent Dozen, who predicted the 2008 meltdown, can help academia transition to relevant economics.[134] Alternatively, new centers of learning will spring, perhaps in China, India, or elsewhere, to fill the knowledge void by teaching valid economics. The subservience of academia and its scholars to the plutocratic establishment is very similar to the communist economic theoreticians' subservience to the Politburo in the Soviet Union, with predictably similar catastrophic results. Academia, by propagating *parasitic economics*, is unwittingly enfeebling the West, a weighty responsibility to bear before history.

The Nature of Externalities

In an ideal world, market participants are well informed and rational, markets are competitive and efficient, and supply expands or contracts to the point where marginal revenue (the revenue from the last unit sold) equals the marginal cost (the cost of the last unit produced). Furthermore, resource allocation is optimal and prices are fair, adjusting upward or downward quickly in response to changes in demand and supply. Such an idealized environment needs no government intervention.

Unfortunately, such stringent conditions are not satisfied in the real world; among other things, stealthy externalities block the efficient functioning of markets. Private and public (social) benefits often diverge, as do private and public costs; hence, market prices fail to internalize all public benefits and costs, resulting in sub-optimal prices and resource allocation, economic inefficiencies, and market failures.[135]

Since most markets are imperfect, suitable government intervention can improve their efficiency. This can take diverse forms: establishing quality standards, measures, labels, inspections, consumer protection, regulations to prevent predatory competition and monopolies, subsidies and excise taxes to encourage beneficial consumption or discourage harmful consumption, etc.

Public finance textbooks explain that when the public benefit from consuming a good exceeds its private benefit, it has positive spillover effects in the form of additional benefits accruing to third parties that are not party to the transaction, giving rise to a positive externality.[136] For example, education is a positive externality because besides benefiting the students concerned, also benefits society by improving the skills of the work force, resulting in better employment prospects with higher pay and, potentially, requiring less income support and contributing more tax revenue. Some educated individuals become successful entrepreneurs, develop new industries, provide employment opportunities for others, and spur economic growth. Moreover, an educated society tends to make better political and economic decisions and enjoys a better quality of life, higher living standards, and less crime. These additional benefits to society make education a *merit good* because its widespread public benefits exceed its private benefits; hence, pricing it based on its private benefits would result in less than optimal consumption from society's perspective. Accordingly, society reaps more benefits from education than realized by the individual, necessitating its encouragement by reducing its cost to consumers through subsidies or by offering it free of charge.

On the other hand, a negative externality implies a negative spillover affecting third parties, who are not party to the transaction, thereby raising the public (social) cost of a good over and above its market price, giving rise to a negative externality.[137] Environmental pollution is the most frequently cited example of a negative externality; it carries a near-zero private cost to the polluter, but a large public (social) cost to society. Air and water pollution poison the air and drinking water, damage public health, increase medical bills, damage buildings, and harm forests, crops, fish, and animal herds.[138]

Thus, relevant laws, regulations, penalties, and taxes deter chemical companies from polluting the air, water and soil at prohibitive cost to society. Similarly, a petrol tax attempts to raise the private cost of petrol consumption closer to its social cost to curtail consumption and its associated air pollution—the negative externality. The additional tax revenue also helps pay for the health bills consequent to inhaling noxious gases.

Likewise, consuming *demerit goods*, such as cigarettes and alcohol, results in spillover costs not included in their price, such as health costs, car accidents, and social problems. Thus, responsible governments resort to excise taxes to raise the cost of consuming demerit goods, thereby helping to restrain their consumption.

More generally, the presence of externalities requires government intervention to improve market efficiency, resource allocation, income distribution, and economic stability, to name a few. This framework is helpful in identifying other nontraditional externalities, which economics and public finance have not classified as such. Categorizing these as part of an extended family of negative externalities contributes to a better understanding of their nature. It also assists in identifying suitable tools for tackling them to improve economic efficiency.

Intriguingly, all positive externalities entail positive morality and all negative externalities entail negative morality (immorality). Equally intriguing, morality is itself an externality and a public good and improving morality improves the general well-being of society and vice versa. Moreover, invariably moral policies are consistent with *societal-interest*, economically rational, and efficient while immoral policies are detrimental to *societal-interest*, economically irrational, and inefficient from the perspective of society.

The Unified Theory of Macroeconomic Failure

Early economists might have avoided tackling the economics of morality not just because the ruling plutocracies were practicing grossly immoral policies but also because it is intangible and elusive. Morality is not a tradeable good and lacks an explicit price; its economic influence is diffused and, unless treated as a market externality, immeasurable. This might partially explain why morality was a blind spot in classical theory, because the concept of externalities had not yet crystalized. Economists have since developed cost-benefit analysis, which can measure the economic impact of externalities, including that of morality and its nemesis, immorality. These concepts of externalities, cost-benefit analysis, and morality provide a fresh approach and a logical framework for identifying, investigating, and understanding economic problems, with the prospect of more efficient solutions.

One possible economic definition of morality is the positive spillover effect of a positive externality and immorality is the negative spillover effect of a negative externality. Thus, the economic contribution of morality is measurable as the excess of public benefits over private benefits associated with an activity. Similarly, the impact of immorality (negative morality) is measurable as the excess of public costs over private costs that is associated with a given activity.

Furthermore, positive and negative moralities constitute a common thread to all positive and negative externalities, respectively. Thus, theft is immoral and, therefore, a negative externality. On the other hand, vaccination is a moral act because it cuts the risk of infection to the public at large, giving rise to a positive externality. It would be laborious to go through every known positive and negative externality to identify its moral or immoral dimension.

Since negative externalities are a consequence of immorality, then the yardstick of morality can be utilized to identify and resolve economic problems. Furthermore, since what constitutes the essence of morality is unambiguous, this yardstick is a surprisingly incisive economic tool, a shortcut for spotting negative and positive externalities, followed by remedial action to curtail or encourage such activities.

Thus, moral policies are inevitably economically efficient and immoral ones inefficient; any counter indication is because a policy has been wrongly classified as to its morality or its efficiency and a thorough analysis would resolve any inconsistency. Much of the uncertainty surrounding the economic efficiency of morality is attributable to a complicating factor, which we might term *the fog of decision-making*, because of the opaqueness and uncertainty of the long-term consequences of *economic decisions* (where the *fog of war* is a special case that applies to military matters).[139] Sir Winston Churchill recognized the problem, generally, by saying, "…difficult to look further than you can see."[140]

The fog arises because moral and immoral macroeconomic policies have visible and identifiable short-term results, but their distant outcomes are less discernable, although far larger and in the opposite direction to their short-term effects. Thus, education, a moral act and a positive externality, entails an immediate and visible cost in the form of school fees, but yields distant, though far larger, benefits (an educated population). Similarly, theft, an immoral act and a negative externality, provides an immediate and visible advantage to the thief at a prohibitive long-term cost to society and sometimes the thief (e.g., alarms, police, court cases, prisons).

This *fog of economic decisions* has plagued neoclassical macroeconomics, because it has stuck to static analysis and shunned dynamic analysis; hence, it has not properly recognized the dynamic benefits of Keynesian expansionary policies, which accrue over time. Specifically, it does not see through the *fog* of *an economic chain reaction*: a rise in government expenditure has a multiplier effect on aggregate consumption, leading to improving the economies of scale, increasing business profits, causing an increase in private investment and higher stock prices, which increase wealth and consumption, and so on. Perhaps the cause of this myopic neoclassical vision is that it focuses solely on the cost side of the economic equation and ignores the demand side. This would explain the tendency for making matters worse by resorting to austerity during economic contractions. However, this is not the only possible explanation. Deeper contractions expedite greater market concentrations, which serve oligopolistic interests. Prolonged contractions also aid the political marketing of war as an economic solution. Not understanding all the motives of all the economic players adds yet more layers to the fog of decision-making.

Incomplete information and complexity also add to the density of the fog of decision-making, making the full benefits of moral policies nearly impossible to foresee far in advance, with fascinating consequences. On the other hand, the fog of ill intentions and immorality is also the cause of terrible unintended consequences and, occasionally, devastating butterfly effects. Later in this chapter, several examples will illustrate some of the profound riddles of economic morality and immorality.

Chapter 2 alluded to instinct as a superior decision-making tool relative to rational deduction when there is a time constraint and limited information. It is also superior when the range of possible outcomes is too wide, making it beyond our mental capacity to assess the diverse effects of truly complex matters except perhaps in retrospect. Accordingly, adopting moral economic policies instinctively is the most efficient economic strategy because it avoids many of the long-term negative surprises associated with immoral policies due to the fog of decision-making. Hence, the instinctive moral choice is invariably the better choice.

The foregoing has important macroeconomic policy implications. For instance, since usury (interest) was banned on moral grounds, then we can expect, *a priori,* that interest-bearing debt to entail a significant negative externality and to cause macroeconomic failure. Similarly, we can expect the economy of a country to perform better during periods when it follows morally superior economic policies than when adopting morally inferior ones. *The unified theory* also suggests that the root cause of the ongoing Western economic decline is a moral decay.

The traditional tools of solving economic crises have been limited to tactical, short-term, measures. These typically consist of increasing public expenditure, reducing taxes and lowering interest rates to counter recessions, and the opposite measures to curtail inflation; occasionally they extend to tinkering with financial and other regulations. On their own, such responses are of transitory benefit because they act on the symptoms without curing the underlying causes of financial crises, exaggerated cyclicality, *chronic underconsumption*, high and persistent unemployment, and anemic growth. Hence, the economic malaise in the West has continued to advance from one cycle to the next.

In contrast, by viewing macroeconomic challenges as externalities, *the unified theory* provides a general framework for their effective handling. It seeks to pinpoint the structural causes of externalities followed by strategic solutions to permanently lessen their negative effects or enhance their positive effects, through government intervention.

Specifically, *the unified theory of macroeconomic failure* considers immoral macroeconomic policy inefficient and irrational because:

- It ignores or sacrifices *societal-interest* and therefore serves narrow self-interests to the detriment of the interest of society.
- It invariably entails negative externalities, and therefore is inefficient, irrational and unintelligent.
- Typically, its focus is short-term because of selfish motives and because the fog of decision-making obscures its long-term unintended consequences, which are opposite and significantly greater than its short-term effects.
- It views macroeconomic policy as a static zero-sum (win-lose) game instead of a dynamic win-win game. As a result, it tends to underestimate the dynamics of the macro economy such as the multiplier effect, economies of scale, and so on.
- The adoption of immoral macroeconomic policies puts a nation at a competitive disadvantage relative to competitor nations that pursue moral economic policies.

More specifically, negative externalities provide a unified explanation of macroeconomic problems. The term "unified" also refers to the implicit union between morality and economic efficiency, rendering them synonymous, two sides of the same coin. Accordingly, a primary cause of the current macroeconomic problems facing the West is moral failure, which precipitates democratic failure and self-interest to overwhelm societal-interest in setting public policy, thus, triggering macroeconomic problems.

On occasion, a natural factor causes a macroeconomic problem, as when excessive volcanic activity produces a drought and famine; nevertheless, not acting to mitigate its negative impact is a moral failure.

Macroeconomic efficiency requires maximizing the benefit from positive externalities and minimizing the damage from negative externalities through the balancing of self-interest and societal-interest, which is only achievable under an environment of high moral standards and a political system that promotes valid and efficient public choice, such as a genuinely representative democracy. Satisfying this condition gives rise to a moral capitalism that is economically superior to both parasitic capitalism and Marxist socialism.

Thus, we can summarize *the unified theory of macroeconomic failure* as:

A moral deficit, typically driven by irrational plutocratic greed for wealth gathering, causes a democratic deficit, inferior public choice, immoral policies, economic inefficiency, and negative externalities, culminating in macroeconomic failure. Immoral policies are necessarily inefficient and vice versa, and not just in economic matters; any counter indication is because a policy has been wrongly classified as to its morality, efficiency or both.

Chronic Negative Externalities

Negative macroeconomic externalities share three common ingredients: irrationality, inefficiency, and immorality. They become chronic because attempts to solve them, if any, only treat their symptoms, rather than their causes. The following are some of the most acute and chronic negative macroeconomic externalities plaguing Western economies today:

1. Immorality Eclipsing Morality
2. Failing Democratic Process: Plutocracy Dominates Democracy
   a. Neoclassical Macroeconomics
   b. Political Contributions
   c. The Media
   d. Corporate Democracy
   e. Poverty

    f.   Crime

    g.   Wars of Aggression

    h.   Excessive Plutocratic Wealth

3. Self-Interest Eclipses *Societal-Interest*: Inefficient Public Expenditure

4. Self-Interest Eclipses *Societal-Interest*: Inefficient and Irrational Taxes

    a.   Indirect Taxes

    b.   Corporate Taxes

    c.   Personal Taxes

5. *Banking Plutocracy*: Usury Dominates the Economy

    a.   Banks

    b.   The Federal Reserve

    c.   Usurious Products

    d.   *Usurious capitalism*: Immoral, Contradictory, and Irreconcilable Economics

6. Amplified Business Cycles

7. Inefficient Markets: The Ascent of Monopolies

    a.   Monopolies in the Goods Markets

    b.   Monopsonies in the Labor Markets

    c.   Chronic Underconsumption

8. Inefficient Markets: Quality of Information

    a.   Government Reporting

    b.   Credit Rating Agencies

    c.   Corporate Reporting

    d.   Regulators and Supervisors

    e.   Economic Counseling

The above externalities are sources of pronounced economic inefficiencies and loss of economic potential. The above list does not purport to be comprehensive but rather a reasonable starting point. Purposely missing from the list are environmental pollution and climate change because the literature already provides a wealth of coverage of these topics. Climate change, caused by the continued rise in the level of carbon dioxide in the atmosphere, is a potential threat to human existence on planet earth; bad economic policies have played a major role in perpetuating its rise, which in turn is a consequence of deteriorating democratic standards. Other negative externalities, such as gambling, are missing due to time constraints.

The order of the above negative externalities attempts to reflect the typical direction of causation of one negative externality on another. Briefly, deteriorating morality is a prerequisite for a waning democracy and the rise of plutocracy. In turn, deteriorating democratic standards have led to self-interest progressively displacing *societal-interest*, resulting in inefficient and inappropriate public expenditure and tax policies. Furthermore, the rising power of the *banking plutocracy* has led to a variety of public policies favoring the big banks, including favorable tax treatment of usury, a privately owned central bank, banking deregulation, the facilitation of the dominance of usury and derivatives over the real economy, and colossal funds to save the big banks from failing. Furthermore, those influences resulted in extreme indebtedness in the economy, which amplified economic cycles and increased instability. The dominance of self-interest over *societal-interest* has also resulted in deteriorating market efficiency due to the rise of monopolies and a decline in the quality of information. These conditions contributed to a wide range of ills including anemic growth.

Overcoming these massive negative externalities requires working in the same sequence, starting with improving public morality followed by reforming the political process and then appropriate economic measures can follow. For instance, an effective democratic process is a prerequisite for enacting efficient tax legislation, which in turn is necessary for increasing equity financing and reducing indebtedness to achieve milder cyclicality.

In this regard, it is important to note that the presentation of the subject matter to follow deviates from the above sequence to ensure a smoother flow. Specifically, some major negative externalities appear first, followed by their proposed solutions. Thus, improving democratic standards, solving the problem of indebtedness, and adopting economically more rational and efficient public expenditure and tax policies appear later because they are the natural route for solving the rest of the negative externalities.

Unintended Spillover Effects of an Incomes Policy

This section and the one to follow illustrate the effects of the fog of decision-making, particularly the difficult-to-foresee unintended consequences of moral and immoral economic policies referred to in the section titled "The Unified Theory of Macroeconomic Failure." In the absence of government intervention and regulations, parasitic capitalism relegates the economy to a zero-sum game, where labor gains become synonymous with business losses, and vice versa. Hence, wage minimization to subsistence level or lower becomes a business objective, whereas a public policy supporting a higher wage can benefit labor as well as business, at once changing the economic game from win-lose to win-win.

Most plutocracies have an immoral zero-sum game (win-lose) mentality ingrained in their egotistic psyche; hence, they tend to adopt policies that generate negative externalities and macroeconomic failure. Accordingly, plutocrats are inclined to shun policies that improve labor conditions, naively believing that doing so is detrimental to their business interests. Accordingly, they cannot grasp that the moral policies in the West in the aftermath of World War II, which materially increased the cost of labor and welfare, also launched an unprecedented economic boom that was very favorable to the growth of corporate profits, stock prices, and the economy.[141] Indeed, favorable economic results have been consistently associated with the implementation of moral economic policies before and since.

Present economic theory has no appreciation that morality is a necessary, if insufficient condition, for economic efficiency. This is perhaps part of a broader misconception—especially in politics, economics and business—that only the dull can afford to be moral, not the talented. Nothing is further from the truth. In fact, without implying that all those who are moral are gifted, there is an almost observable proportionality between intelligence and morality. Indeed, the immoral only tend to succeed against an otherwise matched adversary that is less moral and, inevitably, less shrewd. Let us illustrate.

Otto von Bismarck (1815–1898), the long-serving German chancellor who masterminded German unification—against the interests and desires of all major European powers—is a recognized political genius. A Machiavellian quote, *might is right,* has been attributed to Bismarck, which he never said. Moreover, few appreciate that his success drives from his superior morality, especially compared to his contemporaries.[142] Less obvious is that he used might sparingly, mainly to bring about German unification, which otherwise was impossible to achieve. Where might was clearly not right, he did not use it. Thus, he did not exercise his might where it was easiest to apply, in Africa and Asia, as the imperialist powers of his day did. He resisted pressures at home to expand the tiny overseas German empire and shunned spilling African and Asian blood in imperialist pursuits.[143] In stark contrast, between 1885 and 1908, the genocidal imperialism of King Leopold II of tiny neighboring Belgium applied limitless terror against the helpless civilians of the Congo, butchering half the population, an estimated 10 million victims, in pursuit of personal gains.[144] Equally obscure are Bismarck's moral economic policies, which laid the foundations of German industrial might.

In the closing decades of the 19th century, Great Britain held a considerable industrial lead over Germany and, to a lesser degree, so did France. The British and French empires enjoyed seemingly insurmountable advantages over Germany; they were the largest empires, providing their industries with captive markets, and cheap natural resources, while their respective plutocracies enforced low wages, ostensibly ideal conditions for their continued industrial supremacy. Remarkably, Germany managed to overtake them both in a few short decades, by practicing higher moral standards.

Regardless of what we might think of Bismarck's innate morality, his instinctive genius was so profound as to sense the economic brilliance of morality, cutting through the fog of the elaborate classical economic arguments of the time and beyond the grasp of most economists even today. At the same time, his deep self-confidence and immense courage empowered him to swim against the prevailing egotistic intellectual tide. His economic policies initiated a process that culminated in ending *the age of economic barbarism* in Germany, which would take the rest of the West another three quarters of a century to complete.

German plutocracy had a softer grip on the German economy and enjoyed fewer privileges than its British and French counterparts did. Bismarck used that to Germany's economic advantage. Despite Germany's inferior industry, he pursued a seemingly irrational industrial incomes policy that increased the cost of German labor relative to that of Britain and France. He not only offered German workers higher wages and better working conditions but also launched the German welfare state by passing a health insurance bill in 1883, an accident insurance bill in 1884, and an old age and disability insurance bill in 1889. The social contract he established was moral, humane, and treated German workers with dignity.

Despite the increased cost of German labor and contrary to the expectations of zero-sum gamers, German industrial production surpassed that of France, and shortly after the turn of the century, it outstripped that of Great Britain as well. To the unimaginative monopsony-minded, cost-and-wage minimizers, this outcome is inexplicable. Anglo-French economists simplistically attribute the German industrial miracle to the industriousness of German labor, unwilling to fathom all the complex effects of Bismarck's superior moral incomes policy as the source of Germany's industrial might.

No doubt, Bismarck's policy improved German industrial relations and contributed to a more satisfied, loyal, and industrious work force. As a result, German industrial productivity increased, but that was hardly the only effect. More important, his measures increased the purchasing power of German labor and, with the multiplier effect, substantially expanded the German home market; in turn, that permitted German industry to realize economies of scale, which lowered the cost of German industrial products, making German exports competitive and feasible. By contrast, low wages in Great Britain and France caused *chronic underconsumption,* which limited the size of their home markets and prevented them from realizing similar economies of scale. Clearly, British and French plutocracies could not see through the fog of decision-making, whereas Otto von Bismarck did in some fashion.

It is safe to assume that Otto von Bismarck did not possess economic knowledge of the multiplier effect, economies of scale and the like, which only became generally recognized decades later. Yet these effects were critical to the success of his policy. Why would someone of his genius pursue a policy without understanding its intricate logic? This throws further light on the discussion in Chapter 2 concerning rationality versus instinct in economic decision-making. Bismarck understood what was at stake instinctively. He instinctively made the moral choice, which is consistently the better choice. On the other hand, the classical economists that guided Great Britain and France recognized neither instinct, nor morality, nor instinctively moral decisions that are superior even if we do not know why they are superior when we make them. Bismarck's moral policies also demonstrated that *right was might*, not the other way around.

Decades later, Henry Ford achieved something similar in the United States. Paying his workers higher wages turned them into customers and helped create a mass car market, while his large-scale production techniques cut the production cost per car.

Strikingly, the traditions of moral economic policies and immoral economic policies have persisted for generations. Car manufacturing is the centerpiece of modern industry. Germany lost World War I and World War II while Great Britain was a victor. Yet today, Germany is the lead car manufacturer in Europe, while Great Britain, aside from some minor workshops, has lost all its indigenous car industry to foreign manufacturers. Other British industries have experienced serious decline too. British politicians and economists, generally, have persistently blamed the failure of British industry on the low productivity and the strife of British labor.

I found the demise of British industry puzzling, but I was skeptical about the customary British explanations. In the early 1980s, a Japanese investment bank kindly invited me to visit Japan. While there, I met with a senior executive of a leading Japanese car company that had large car manufacturing plants in Great Britain. I took the opportunity to ask him about the quality of British labor. His answer startled me. He said British labor was more productive than Japanese labor in their Tokyo plants. The implication was clear: British labor was not the cause of the demise of British Industry, but rather British management.

This raises a subsidiary question regarding the effect of differences in plutocratic perceptions on industrial performance. German and Japanese history during the first half of the 20th century does not suggest that their plutocracies were more benevolent than their British equivalent. There is also no reason to suspect that the German and Japanese people are more intelligent than the British are. This leaves one possible explanation: the difference in performance is attributable to a shortsighted and less intelligent British plutocratic establishment compared to its German and Japanese counterparts. All plutocracies are profit maximizers; however, some are long-term maximizers, while others focus on immediate, short-term gains. Clearly, Japanese and German plutocracies are of the former type, while the British plutocracy is of the latter. Moreover, the arrogance and snobbery of the British upper class and the managements it appoints are world-famous, looking down on labor as an inferior species. This lack of empathy for labor has been a longstanding British social problem; it permitted the passage of the Corn Laws that starved a million people.[145] These factors explain why today Great Britain is the only major Western economy without an indigenous car industry.

It seems that intelligent plutocracies maximize long-run profits and pursue benevolent policies, even if they are not innately benevolent. In contrast, the dullest plutocracies pursue very short-term profits without empathy, precipitating, for example, the French and Bolshevik revolutions and becoming extinct in the process. Between these extremes are politically clever but economically dull plutocracies, such as the British, that have survived, but their economies have suffered. Perhaps it is high time the West replaced it plutocracies with a wiser breed that sees the logic of pursuing benevolent policies to further their own interest, thereby changing the economic game to win-win. The currently powerful but shortsighted Western banking plutocracies do not fit the bill.

The Butterfly Effect of Reparations

The section titled the "The Unified Theory of Macroeconomic Failure" alluded to the butterfly effect of immoral policies. The following illustrates the severity of one such effect that has transpired in the sphere of political economy.

The mathematics of chaos theory demonstrates a phenomenon referred to as the butterfly effect, where a slight action precipitates a huge and unanticipated outcome. The metaphorical example is that of a butterfly flapping it wings in the African jungle, only to unleash a hurricane in the Caribbean a few weeks later.

It seems farfetched that the application of a seemingly minor economic policy could, among other things, change the world map and spell the end of empires. Yet, those were precisely the negative spillover effects of imposing immoral and exuberant reparations on a defeated Germany following World War I, which shortsighted politicians in Great Britain and France, the victors, demanded against the instinctive advice of John Maynard Keynes.

In 1923, the French occupied the Ruhr, the German industrial heartland, to enforce payment of the reparations, producing grave German economic hardship. The reparations pushed Germany into *hyper-stagflation*, an economically lethal combination of hyperinflation in the midst of depression and mass unemployment. Hard times swelled the ranks of the German Communist Party, making a communist takeover seem imminent. The one party with sufficient mass support to challenge the communists was the National Socialist Party (Nazi Party); hence, the German plutocracy decided to provide it with the financial backing it needed to check the communist threat. The ascent of the Nazis resulted in a German dictatorship and a world war followed by the redrawing of the map of Europe, the spread of communism, and the beginning of the end of the British and French empires.

British and French policymakers certainly did not imagine that an economic straw could have such profound effects, including breaking the backs of their empires. The desperate situation in Germany produced more than demonstrations, something to remember amid the current economic conditions in Europe. Indeed, harsh periods, often the consequence of immoral policies, have hatched revolutions, Napoleons, and endless wars across continents. The thing to remember is that the fog of decision-making blurs the vision of those who implement amoral economics; they cannot see the potentially devastating negative butterfly effects of their policies, or else they would not adopt them in the first place. Hence, moral economic policies are instinctively superior and safer bets.

———

A better understanding of the causes of economic and historic failures requires in-depth analysis of the contribution of immorality to such disasters; a moral interpretation of history is long overdue. A similar analysis is also required for current failures.

Parts III and IV to follow, use the framework of *the unified theory of macroeconomic failure* to diagnose the root causes of the current economic malaise.

Part III

USURIOUS PRODUCTS AND INSTITUTIONS

Seven

Man is born free, and everywhere he is in chains.[146]

Jean Jacques Rousseau

Interest-bearing debt is a negative externality because, as this and the chapters to follow show, its social cost far exceeds its private cost, making it equivalent to a financial pollutant. Hence, its preponderance is baffling. Understanding this economic irrationality requires tracking the rise of usury, a spellbinding story of how lenders succeeded in putting the world in financial bondage. It also hints at the difficulty of freeing the world from its awful grip.

Religion and Usury[147]
Usury was vile long before there was a word for it in the English language; the Latin meaning of mortgage is death, a stark reminder of its looming tragedy. Some loan sharks, driven by avarice, specialize in lending to the powerless and charging them excruciating interest rates. Their enforcers solve bad debts by turning nonperforming borrowers into financial slaves. The ethics

of "A pound of flesh for a pound of gold" has never left us. Paradoxically, lenders and enforces too are victims of usury's sadism because it strips away their residual humanity.

The UN's Supplementary Convention on the Abolition of Slavery (1956) specifically prohibits *debt bondage* (Article 1a).[148] Despite that, in some countries, defaulting on debt carries a prison sentence, which reinforces debt bondage. Permitting usury entails accepting its immorality, economic irrationality, and worsening financial crises in the West.

Incredibly, two millennia ago, long before any financial crisis, a modest man from Nazareth wanted to spare the world the misery of usury by banning it. Doubtless, Christ was guiding humanity to a gentler and better world. Six centuries later, the Quran affirmed Christ's teachings by prohibiting usury too. Both Christianity and Islam encouraged interest-free charitable lending in support of the financially distressed, with flexible and lenient repayment.[149] Judaism also forbade Jews from lending to one another with interest, but it allowed them to do so to a foreigner (perhaps implying a pagan).[150]

To understand how and why the West stopped heeding Christ's command requires going back in time. Original Christians accepted the prohibition of usury as an integral part of their faith. In the intervening centuries, a profound misunderstanding has emerged that banning usury was morally correct, but economically wrong. This entailed an error in logic because morality is always consistent with *societal-interest*, economic and otherwise. Hence, it is a logical absurdity for usury to be both morally flawed and economically correct.[151]

Despite usury's unequivocal condemnation, three factors contributed to its revival. First, there was no concerted effort to develop morally correct and viable alternatives to usury. Second, while the degree of indebtedness in the economy remained modest, if increasing, the economic damage from usury remained limited and isolated. Hardly anyone foresaw the cancerous growth of usury or the severity and range of hardships that it would inflict. Third, given the church ban on usury, moneylenders resorted to obscuring their usurious practices. All three factors contributed to usury's eventual acceptance as a *fait accompli*.

Two Centuries of Parasitic Economics

The spread of usury was foremost a failing of those who did not see the need to provide alternative financing and, in the name of religion, stifled science and, perhaps, equity innovations too. Indeed, in the name of religion grievous misdeeds have been committed such as the burning of witches and scientists, religious wars, and imperialist pursuits. However, these were the failings of men, not religion, just as cars are useful, but drunk drivers cause accidents. The great religions do not stray, but their institutions, leaders, and followers do.

Usury can never claim the high moral ground; hence, its only justification is economic. Doubtless, the spread of usury is a challenge to the great religions. Its preponderance today implicitly suggests that banning it was economically wrong. Yet, the periodic banking crises tell a different story, testimony to an impaired usurious system. Hence, the unequivocal banning of usury that long ago entailed extraordinary vision.

The lack of incisive economic examinations of usury has worked in its favor. By enforcing conformity, Western centers of learning have constrained economic thinking, mostly to topics of marginal value. Hence, we find no profound economic debate or exhaustive research on why Jesus Christ, no less, categorically forbade interest. Conceivably, university administrators avoided such examinations for political reasons; perhaps, they feared the results of such analysis would give the church cause for intervening in economic life, thereby challenging the power of the plutocracy and their financiers. In any case, the decision not to study the economics of banning usury reeks of subservience to authority or intellectual arrogance and in any case, it is a dereliction of academic duty.

It is time that the economics profession remedied this major lapse in responsibility. This blind spot has plagued macroeconomic theory since the days of Adam Smith; the West has been bumping into grave financial accidents ever since. Today, with deepening financial crises, economists need to make a choice: defend usury, sit on the sidelines, or expose usury's economic faults and articulate viable alternatives to end the grief of perpetual debt crises.

All church denominations and their associated universities have an unambiguous moral obligation to dedicate the necessary resources to investigate the economic significance of Christ's ban on usury and to research viable, non-usurious financial alternatives. Islamic institutions have a similar obligation to mobilize the best economic minds to investigate the economic rationale for the ban on usury and to seek alternatives to usury. The latter have also neglected to investigate several other religious directives that have economic bearings.

Exposing the profound economic logic of banning usury is all the more surreal precisely because Jesus did not devote his life to the study of economics at elitist universities. Indeed, for the best economic minds not to have fathomed the economic significance of Christ's command could be an unforeseen gift to the church, serene proof of the living miracle of Christ, precisely because his moral order promotes economic efficiency and not just kindness.

Christ's economic miracle will become self-evident for the world to witness when the first vibrant, fair, and non-usurious economy replaces a sickly debt-ridden one. The church today has an extraordinary opportunity to become the catalyst in crystalizing ideas and unveiling institutions to realize Christ's vision.

Disguising Usury

The Catholic Church in Rome has upheld usury as a deadly sin. For centuries, it punished unrepentant usurers, and the princes who failed to curb them, with excommunication and even death. Circumventing and eroding this uncompromising edict required cunning. Usury stealthily tiptoed in on a lack of understanding, lies, and deception. Its rehabilitation during the Renaissance inched forward in diverse places.[152]

At the School of Salamanca—a Spanish school of theologians and jurists—instead of devoting their energies to developing non-usurious alternatives, its scholars began advocating charging interest on non-consumption business loans, without comprehensive assessment of the long-term economic consequences of this course, to say nothing of violating Christ's prohibition. In due course, this paved the way for other church denominations to repeat this mistake.

In 15th-century Florence, Bank de Medici began skirting the ban on usury by covering it with opaqueness and complexity, not unlike the exaggerated intricacies of today's financial products. Medici's clever financial charade made usurious lending appear as trade, concealing the interest by inflating the selling price of the merchandise in return for delayed payment (financing), without mention of usury or interest. Another technique to mask the interest was to lend in one currency and accept repayment later in another at an inflated exchange rate.

The Evolution of a Ponzi Scheme

Centuries ago, goldsmiths had to acquire safes, build strong rooms, and hire guards to protect their precious wares. Merchants and wealthy individuals also needed safekeeping for their gold and silver coinage. To recover some of the operational costs associated with their facilities, goldsmiths began to offer custody services for a fee and issue receipts for the deposits in their safes. Merchants quickly discovered that, instead of carrying gold and silver coins to settle payments, it was safer and more convenient to endorse and surrender goldsmiths' receipts to counterparties. These receipts evolved into promissory notes payable on demand to the bearer and later into bank notes or paper currency.

Because endorsing deposit receipts became an accepted means of settling accounts, the gold and silver that these receipts represented, instead of changing hands, remained mostly in the safes of the goldsmiths. Steadily, it dawned on goldsmiths that their receipts were circulating on sheer trust because third parties did not know the actual amount of precious coinage on deposit. This realization launched moneylending. As a side business, goldsmiths began to grant loans and charge interest by issuing deposit receipts without corresponding coinage or gold bullion to back their lending. They expected most of these receipts, and their replacements, to continue circulating indefinitely, along with the rest of the float of the deposit receipts, with no one ever calling their bluff.

This process created a virtual gold stock that increased the effective money supply. The goldsmiths had accidentally initiated fractional reserve banking, a clever feat of financial sorcery that created currency out of thin air. The easy profit of earning interest on nonexistent gold was tempting, inducing lenders to lend more, thereby creating ever more virtual currency. This dishonesty was profitable until the day when there were too many withdrawals, and the lender could not honor them all. Thus, whenever a rumor circulated that a big merchant had lost his ships in a storm, the depositors—fearing the loss would bankrupt the lender—rushed to withdraw their money, triggering a run on the lending goldsmith (the bank). Thus, the survival of lending goldsmiths rested on continued public confidence, an elusive and volatile foundation. At the same time, avarice drove banking to ever more leverage until it failed.

The high risk of failure stemmed from the intrinsically crooked and insolvent business model because the goldsmiths were lending and risking money that they did not have. This remains the natural fate of all financial sorcery, tempered by government rescue packages and central banks acting as lenders of last resort. Still, in good times, moneylending was sufficiently enticing that some goldsmiths dropped their jewelry trade to focus exclusively on lending, thereby propelling banking as a separate business.

This development had several moral and economic implications. It was more immoral than usury, on its own, because it entailed two additional immoralities. First, it was dishonest because it loaned nonexistent gold and silver. Second, it betrayed the public trust by putting depositors' funds at risk. These three immoralities are the sources of the intrinsic structural weakness of banking and the cause of its periodic crises. Despite appearances to the contrary, in essence, banking is an elaborate Ponzi pyramiding scheme and, like all Ponzi schemes, it is inherently unstable.

More generally, *the unified theory of macroeconomic failure* expects banking to fail because its basis is immoral and represents a negative externality. Moreover, as the immoralities of banking have increased over time, as will become clear in due course, the effect of the negative banking externality has become progressively larger, making it impossible for banking to survive without heavy overt and covert subsidies to the detriment of taxpayers.

Two Centuries of Parasitic Economics

The Rehabilitation of Usury

To gain public acceptance, the business of usurious lending exploited every means, including a new vocabulary, to give it the respectability it lacked. Interest, a morally neutral-sounding term, replaced the morally repugnant usury, although the two are precisely the same. Bankers and banks, terms with prestigious and dignified rings, replaced moneylenders and pawnshops. The marketing spin has radically reversed the status of usury and its practitioners, transforming yesterday's taboo into today's golden calf. Today moneylenders occupy the highest social pedestals, and their financial powerhouses decree the usurious macroeconomic culture, ideology, and policy. Terminology aside, underneath the veneer, banking remains a ruthless moneylending business as portrayed by William Shakespeare in *The Merchant of Venice*.

Islamist Banking

For those interested in developing genuine interest-free financing, they need to be alert to the pitfalls they face. Like Christianity, Islam prohibits usury. The past few decades saw the introduction of "Islamist banking" to provide "non-usurious," interest-free banking as an alternative to conventional banking. Despite excellent intentions, "Islamist" banking was unfortunate in that its founders came from conventional banking backgrounds; they understood interest-bearing debt and its instruments, but they were not versed in equity investments, the only mode capable of providing interest-free financing. In other words, the founders of "Islamist banking" lacked the requisite expertise for setting up an interest-free financing model and as such, their efforts were doomed. Hence, their focus was on relabeling and repackaging conventional banking transactions, unaware that they were mimicking the techniques used by Bank de Medici centuries earlier to obscure usury from the eyes of the church. Like Bank de Medici, they also earned a predetermined profit for financing, wrapped in fictitious trade deals. Most significantly, like Bank de Medici, they refused any business risk, requiring full repayment with "profit," regardless of whether their counterparties lost or profited from the underlying transactions.

Thus, current "Islamist" finance sets a predetermined "profit" (interest). "Islamist" banks routinely fix their short-term "Islamist" profit with reference to the London inter-bank offered rate (LIBOR) and their long-term "profit" targets with reference to long-term bond yields. As with conventional lending, the nonpayment of a principal amount or "profit" bankrupts the borrower.

"Islamist" banks execute financing deals by creating synthetic merchandise trades. The bank makes a cash purchase of a virtual commodity from a client and simultaneously sells it back to the same client for delivery at a future date and a higher price to secure the bank's "profit." Typically, the client does not intend to purchase the commodity in question. In any case, the commodity only changes hands on paper, recording phantom purchase and sale transactions. Not surprising, numerous conventional banks have found it easy to engage in "Islamist" banking, dedicating special departments and subsidiaries to that end. The changes they needed to make to their regular operations were superficial, consisting mostly of relabeling and repackaging their conventional banking business.

Unlike conventional banks, in the event of a default, "Islamist" banks do not charge a "profit" for late payment. The downside, however, is that they rush delinquent borrowers to court to minimize lost time and lost income, giving borrowers even less breathing space to solve their problems than conventional banks permit. The ultimate irony, based on a personal experience, was that one "Islamist" investment company charged a significantly higher rate of "profit" than a conventional bank did—at 10 percent and 8 percent, respectively. Worse still, a year later, the "Islamist" rollover offer was prohibitive at 15 percent, claiming they wanted to discontinue personal finance.

Still, "Islamist" banks, like most non-Western financial institutions, coped well with the 2008 debt crisis, requiring relatively modest assistance from their respective governments. In large part, this was because non-Western economies have a lower degree of financial deepening and leverage than that prevailing in the West.

In addition, the guidance of religious committees that oversee the operations of "Islamist" banks proved helpful. First, the religious committees consider it unlawful, based on Islamic law, to trade debt, which barred

"Islamist" banks from participating in "Islamist" versions of securitized sub-prime toxic products. Second, Islamic law also prohibits selling anything one does not own. This prohibition spared "Islamist" banks from engaging in short selling. Third, Islamist religious committees suspected that derivatives entailed debt and, therefore, usury. Thus, despite the determined efforts by Western "Islamist" economics and finance scholars to convince them otherwise, the religious committees remained unconvinced. This disallowed the "Islamist" banks from diving into the derivatives swamp. These restrictions have limited the leverage of "Islamist" banks—so far.

Genuine non-usurious financing must be in the form of equity, which requires accepting the loss of profit and principal as a business risk, instead of treating it as an event of default. Perhaps one day, religious committees will ban cleverly disguised usurious lending too, once they see through it, and insist on replacing it with religiously correct equity alternatives.[153] Perhaps organizing competitions to innovate non-usurious financial products could transform the financing business, especially if enticing prizes were on offer.

A Greek philosopher once said, "Endings are defined by their beginnings." In other words, if we take the wrong path, we will arrive at the wrong destination. Economists set economics on the wrong path the day they assigned factor incomes as wages to labor, rent to land, and interest, instead of profit, to capital.

Eight

The Ascent of Banking

*We cannot solve our problems with the same
thinking we used when we created them.*[154]

Albert Einstein

Six economic revolutions mark the milestones of economic history. With
each revolution, a new sector became the engine of growth that re-
shaped the economy; it disrupted the existing economic relationships and
propelled new stakeholders, increasing their wealth and political power relative to the rest but always within the plutocratic framework. Monopolies,
cartels, oligopolies, and monopsonies restricted competition through privileges, dispensations, laws, regulations, and licenses—plutocracies' vehicles
for gouging consumers and exploiting workers to satisfy their addiction to
wealth gathering through parasitic profits.

Plutocracies evolved with the economic revolutions, with the center of
gravity of their economic and political power shifting accordingly. For example, within the industrial revolution, economic change precipitated the
rise of steel, railway, oil, and military plutocracies.

Economic Revolutions

The first economic revolution was in agriculture, approximately eight thousand years ago. Prior to that, humans were engaged in hunting, gathering, and relocating. The invention of agriculture provided greater food security and allowed humans to settle down in farming villages, which provided some safety against predators. It also gave them—when not planting, harvesting, or tending to farm animals—the luxury of a little free time to think.

The need for protection gave rise to feudalism. Feudal lords became the local dictators and monopsonists, earning patristic profits by exploiting the farmers. They evolved to become the backbone of regional and central plutocratic power, offering the sovereign tribute money and, during times of war, provided farmers to serve as foot soldiers in his army. [155] In return, the sovereign protected his lords against foreign invaders, resolved their disputes, helped them suppress farm rebellions, and gave them license to treat their farmers as serfs. Feudalism, in its various forms, proved the longest lasting politico-economic arrangement because economic change came slowly at first, then accelerated.

The second revolution was in trade. Mercantilism bestowed privileges, wealth, and power on the merchant class, which paid tribute to the sovereign and used its plutocratic influence to obtain trading privileges. In many cases, the merchant class also had feudal roots. Mercantilism promoted *laissez-faire* to overcome local trade barriers often to the detriment of feudal lords, while seeking trade barriers against foreign competitors. Mercantilist classes practiced their version of *parasitic capitalism* by restricting competition and securing monopolies over certain trades. During the mercantilist-imperialist era, the slave trade and opium trafficking were its most profitable enterprises.

The third revolution was in industry, giving rise to numerous new technologies and their associated industrial products. The industrial plutocracy too sought to increase its parasitic profits by restricting competition, gouging consumers and exploiting workers. It supported protectionism to the detriment of consumers and, sometimes, the mercantilists. The powerful industrial plutocracy lobbied for laws that freed farmers from serfdom and attachment to the soil to the detriment of the feudal plutocracy, resulting in an abundant labor supply in the cities, which drove industrial wages lower, aggravating the condition of labor.

The fourth revolution was in finance. It paralleled and expedited the Industrial Revolution. Remarkably, scientific and technological progress drove all economic revolutions, save the financial revolution.

The fifth economic revolution was in transportation. It flowed from the Industrial Revolution. The steam engine gave rise to larger ships and railways that lowered transportation costs, expanding the markets for industrial products and trade generally.

Most recently, the sixth economic revolution has been in electronics and digital technology with sweeping effects on economic life, particularly in computers, information, and communications.

The Equity Finance Revolution

Prior to the Industrial Revolution, investments were modest and short-lived. In a typical joint venture, small investors participated in the capital needed for a shipload of cargo, the arrangement lasting until its delivery and sale. Any borrowing or amount owed by the venture was an unlimited—joint and several—liability of all the partners.

The Industrial Revolution opened up immense opportunities for investing in factories, mines, ports, transportation canals, and railways. Some projects were huge. For example, developing a giant overseas mine often required not just capital for the mine, but also for constructing a seaport and a rail link between the mine and the port. Such projects required colossal sums. They were lumpy because it was not meaningful to build a fraction of a project, taking years to complete and decades to utilize fully. Few investors, if any, had the means or inclination to assume such enormous undertakings on their own and for protracted periods. Traditional modes of finance could not provide the gigantic sums necessary for the major projects of the Industrial Revolution.

Financial innovators came to the rescue, revolutionizing equity financing by making it flexible and impersonal. They devised the limited liability company, which limited the risk assumed by investors to their capital participations, instead of extending to all their personal wealth when a project failed (a major limitation of traditional partnerships).

To facilitate the financing of very large projects, the financial innovators developed fractional ownership by splitting the capital of a limited liability company into numerous shares to tap broader sources of capital and to mobilize smaller savings.

There remained, however, the problem of exceedingly long time horizons of investing in the giant projects because investors could not predict their need for liquidity over very protracted periods. Financial engineers overcame this problem by devising over-the-counter stock trading, which evolved into organized stock exchanges. It permitted shareholders to liquidate their investments at will without disrupting the investments of the underlying venture.

These legal and financial adaptations created a corporate buffer between a venture's investments and its shareholders. It allowed enterprises to invest the proceeds of their share subscriptions in illiquid, long-lived, and lumpy fixed assets with unlimited liability, while their shareholders invested smaller sums with limited risk for flexible periods. Less obvious, but no less significant, these financial novelties also opened the gates of more aggressive risk taking in new technologies, which spurred the pace of the Industrial Revolution. Thus, the equity revolution became the catalyst of the Industrial Revolution.

Equity capital provided the financial infrastructure for economic growth, but two factors continued to hinder it. The first was debt, which caused periodic financial crises, recessions, and depressions. When it was not the immediate cause of economic disturbances, it amplified them. For centuries, debt crises have been a common occurrence across Europe, the United States, and the rest of the world, interrupting economic growth and making the pitiful conditions of the masses worse.

The second constraint on economic growth was *chronic underconsumption*. Plutocratic avarice tended to constrain wages to subsistence levels using a variety of means, but especially by prohibiting trade unions. This policy was shortsighted because low wages kept markets small, thereby preventing the realization of economies of scale, and setting an artificially low limit on the size of economies and economic growth.

The Usurious Revolution

The financial revolution in equity finance made equity the undisputed financial backbone of the economy. In parallel, debt innovations produced a revolution in banking by making traditionally illiquid bank loans tradeable and liquid as bonds. This dramatically expanded the scope of bank lending and profits by overcoming the capacity constraints of banks' balance sheets. However, by selling the bonds to third parties, the banks transferred the credit risk to them, thereby adding a fourth immorality to the business of banking—this time through the conflict of interest between the banks and the bond investors, with the 2008 subprime crisis for a recent illustration.[156]

Usurious debt innovations continued unabated, providing short-term advantage to the lenders while increasing the risk of financial instability to themselves and the economy. For example, banking innovations included stock margin lending and short selling, which considerably amplified the volatility of securities markets.[157] However, the most menacing innovations of the usurious revolution have been futures and derivatives because these greatly exaggerated leverage and, therefore, risk. Today, the estimated size of the derivatives market is in the hundreds of trillions of dollars and growing. These financial instruments represent concentrated financial power and the greatest threat to global financial and economic stability.

Unlike any other economic revolution, the products of the usurious revolution entail an intrinsic negative externality that grows like a cancer. In other words, if equity products were to replace usurious products, a large net economic gain would certainly result.

The Incurable Defects of a Ponzi Scheme

Hyman Minsky (1919–1996), the celebrated post-Keynesian economist, revived and extended Fisher's theories on credit crises and their effect on economic cycles.[158] Minsky identified three types of borrowers that could potentially become insolvent: hedge, speculative, and Ponzi borrowers. Of these, he classified Ponzi borrowers as the most speculative and, therefore, the weakest link in the financial chain and at greatest risk of insolvency; their collapse typically sets off a domino effect that culminates in a financial fiasco.[159]

Minsky's analysis is compelling. Banks fit his description of "Ponzi units" because they are the most leveraged borrowers—as well as the largest lenders—and, therefore, the weakest link in the financial chain. Regrettably, Minsky stopped short of explicitly identifying his "Ponzi units." He also did not propose an alternative to debt to cut the risk of financial disasters.

No doubt, banking is the most intriguing of all Ponzi schemes, working like magic for years or decades until it abruptly fails. In part, the problem lies with bankers' chronic shortsightedness. Instead of strategically rethinking their flawed business model, with its ever-present risk of failure, bankers have sought tactical solutions to improve the odds of surviving crises. Initially, they tried guaranteeing each other during panics, which helped banks weather mild financial storms, until the public lost confidence in the lot and withdrew its deposits from all of them at once, triggering a tsunami of banking failures.

The instability of their business model drove the big banks to lobby for government crutches. The United States established the Federal Reserve to act as a lender of last resort to banks and the Federal Deposit Insurance Corporation to assure small depositors that their bank deposits are safe. The government also introduced discipline to banking through regulations, supervision, and financial ratios to contain bankers' periodic fits of speculative folly. However, as soon as the regulators plugged one defect, another appeared. Perversely, these crutches relaxed bankers' discipline and increased their financial adventurism, making crises less frequent but graver. Unlike any other business, banking needs progressively more government help to survive.

Decades of experimenting with bank crutches have solved nothing. The only dependable solution is for governments to stop licensing Ponzi schemes and to insist on rational, moral, and stable financing models. Unlike the days of the Renaissance, today the tables are turned: equity could easily replace usury because numerous equity alternatives are readily available now or require only slight modification to make them tailor-made for specific financing needs. Usury is without economic justification; its products are inferior and its social cost is prohibitive. Today, the continued survival of Western banking is contingent upon Western governments' favor, through central banks acting as lenders of last resort and lending trillions of dollars in taxpayers' money at subsidized interest rates to sustain the zombie banks, and a flawed tax system that encourages interest and discriminates against profits and dividends. All these measures are necessary to postpone the natural demise of Western banking, which is on the critical list, permanently; it can only survive in an intensive care environment because it cannot sustain its social cost as a polluter of the financial environment.

The Democratic Revolution

One can detect a ring of pride when the mainstream media speak of the West's "democratic traditions." The reality is that Western democracy is barely decades old; it is still in its infancy and more vulnerable to a relapse than is generally appreciated. A prerequisite to political democracy is economic democracy; the two go hand in hand. It is meaningless to claim one without the other.

The West began putting on the trappings of political democracy in the 19th century, but without economic democracy, and with voting often restricted to landowners, it was hollow. Real Western political democracy began hesitantly, a century later—following Russia's communist revolution. President Franklin Roosevelt's New Deal in the midst of the Great Depression was the tentative beginning of economic democracy in the United States. It became much more earnest after communism engulfed Eastern Europe in the aftermath of World War II, pressuring Western plutocracies to accept economic democracy and the welfare state. Labor unions negotiated better labor pay and living conditions. The consequences were nothing short of an economic miracle. The rise in labor's purchasing power and the welfare state eliminated *chronic underconsumption*, expanded markets, improved economies of scale, and increased profits, resulting in rapid economic growth, low unemployment, mild recessions, and mild inflation, leading to further improvements in the living standards of the masses. Only then did the journey to genuine political democracy begin. The destination was still far. It accomplished a transition to a benevolent plutocracy, but not democracy.

By the summer of 1963, workers under capitalism were enjoying markedly higher living standards than those under communism. It was against this backdrop of an idealized economic and political democracy that President Kennedy delivered his challenge to communism from West Berlin. His memorable speech "*Ich bin ein Berliner*" (I am a Berliner) projected the spirit and confidence of a *moral capitalism*. Communism's promise of a workers' paradise was falling far short of workers' expectations on the other side of the Berlin wall. Paradoxically, *chronic underconsumption*, a shortfall in aggregate demand, which Marx had predicted would bring about the downfall of capitalism, had become a critical problem in East Berlin and beyond; subsequent events would show that communism could not overcome it.

The Counter-Revolution

Genuine democracy is not easily reversible, but a benevolent plutocracy is. Following the aforementioned democratization and its associated economic gains, Margaret Thatcher and Ronald Reagan launched their widely hailed "revolution" in the 1980s. In its early days, the fervent slogans and elaborate neoclassical arguments of the "revolution" concerning the common good and national economic efficiency confused the issues and obscured the destination of its conservative rightward march. Like most of its political and economic slogans, the label "revolution" was a misnomer. Revolutions are populist movements that seek to topple a patristic class to improve the lot of the masses. The Thatcher-Reagan revolution was the precise opposite: a movement propelled by a *parasitic* plutocracy led by banking to grab a larger slice of the economic pie and greater political and economic control.

It attempted and succeeded in gradually shrinking the economic share of the rest of society and stripping away their political rights. Hence, a precise description of the Thatcher-Reagan revolution is *counter-revolution*; its objective was to revive plutocratic power and privileges by changing the Republican and the Conservative parties in the United States and Britain, respectively, from centrist to elitist parties of the extreme right, contrary to the interests of the majority of the supporters of both parties.[160]

What prompted the *counter-revolution*? Sometimes success breeds failure. Following World War II, economic democracy in the West launched an economic miracle that left communist economies in the dust. The social justice it provided rendered the calls for communist revolution redundant. As a result, the communist threat receded. Regrettably, from the perspective of the ruling money elites this meant economic and political democracy was no longer necessary to assure their own survival. The Thatcher-Reagan *counter-revolution* was a reactionary rearguard action to reinstate the plutocratic privileges lost to the masses, starting with Roosevelt's New Deal, an attempt to turn back the clock to plutocracies' glory days in the 19th century.

Financial Feudalism

As stated previously, each economic revolution produced its own plutocratic type: feudal, mercantilist-imperialist, industrialist, and banking. These plutocracies evolved over decades and centuries but they retained certain predispositions, especially for *parasitic capitalism*. Strikingly, the *banking plutocracy*, the most recent, shares more similarities with the earliest, the feudal plutocracy.

Feudalism is essentially a parasitic monopsony, which used farmers for parasitic hosts. At the height of its tyrannical power, it relegated farm laborers to mere serfs without pay, and sold them with the land they ploughed. Feudalism used its privileges and the power of the state to perpetuate those vile conditions, until the upcoming plutocratic powers—namely, mercantilists and then industrialists—degraded its power base. A little before the American Civil War (1861–1865), the last of the feudal lords in Europe lost their privilege of treating farm hands as serfs.

Like the feudal lords, the *banking plutocracy* is rentier. Its parasitic hosts are the borrowers. Its profit medium is lending and covert debt bondage instead of land ownership and overt serfdom. Unlike the feudal lords' treatment of their serfs, the usurious lords are civil with borrowers while they comply with the terms of their financial bondage; the ruthlessness is reserved for the violators, squeezing them for the last grain of gold owed and depriving them, in the tens of millions, of their possessions, including their shelters. However, unlike racial slavery, usurious bondage is "racially correct" because it is equally hard-nosed with violators, regardless of race.

Today, the big banks are at the zenith of their power. They have eclipsed the power of old money—the once-proud owners of steel mills, railroads, automotive, oil, and military industries. To the envy of the rest, they have used their immense political power to exploit the public purse with impunity and without bounds.

Neocons, Neoclassical Economics, Neo-Feudalism, and Neo-Imperialism

The reactionary ideology of the *counter-revolution* spread across the West in varying degrees, resuscitating failed concepts. It used four chariots to launch its reactionary era: neo-conservatism (neocons), neoclassical macroeconomics, neo-feudalism, and neo-imperialism. Feudal banking became the plutocracy to lead the charge of the *counter-revolution*; the neocons implemented political control; neoclassical economics provided the economic ideology and policy; neo-imperialism became the new framework for exploiting the Third World.

The big banks emerged as the most powerful of the West's plutocratic class. Discussion of their rise to power appears in the sections and chapters to follow.

The neocons' political strategy at home relied on fear to mobilize support. It framed everything that was not right-wing as leftist, socialist, and communist threats to national economic interest and national security, with nothing in between. They left no room for centrist policies that balanced the interests of all segments of society, the primary function of democracy. They systematically undermined all rival sources of political power by weakening unions, taking control of rival media and pushing the Democratic Party in the United States and the Labor Party in Britain to adopt right-wing ideologies.[161]

In the economic sphere, neoclassical economic policies lowered the taxes of the super-rich and financed the resultant revenue deficit by raising the taxes of the rest, reducing social welfare, and increasing the national debt. This led to an immense transfer of income and wealth from the poor to the rich. Income disparity hit levels not seen since the 1920s. It enabled labor exploitation by tolerating high unemployment, which undermined the power of unions and decreased real wages. In parallel, under the guise of free markets, it promoted monopolies through the deregulation of markets, which opened the gates for predatory competition and larger market shares for oligopolies. It privatized natural monopolies and quasi-monopolies such as stock exchanges, airports, railways, national health services, prisons, etc. The rise in market concentration and extensive privatization significantly increased the cost to consumers and the public sector.

Neo-imperialism ensnared Third World countries mostly using exploitive financing arrangements and, occasionally, imperialist wars, although this was proving increasingly less cost effective. It extended loans, often to unrepresentative governments, to gain a say in their economic and political affairs. When borrowers failed to meet their obligations, the financial feudal lords demanded the surrender of valuable natural resources and state monopolies for a pittance. Enforcing the neo-imperialist policies sometimes required instigating military coupes or popular uprisings in the name of freedom, democracy, and human rights. Sometimes it resorted to trade sanctions to ferment political turmoil to compel governments to succumb to its pressures, but when all else failed, it resorted to imperialist wars of aggression.

The apparent success of the *counter-revolution* over the past three decades is more illusionary than real. It has been running on the economic momentum created prior to its takeover. It is destined to collapse because its four pillars—namely, banking, neocons, neoclassical economics, and neo-imperialism—stand on erratic foundations. Banking is essentially a Ponzi scheme in perpetual crisis. Neocons deny the majority centrist agendas; therefore, the neocons' course will be unsustainable. Neoclassical macroeconomics is a defunct economic theory, as the Great Depression demonstrated and comprehensive economic failure is looming across the West. Lastly, neo-imperialism will fail for the same reasons that imperialism failed in the first place.

Ascent of the Banking Plutocracy

The transition to a *banking plutocracy* has been underway for centuries. Its progress has been mostly faint, save for two periods when it was manifest: from 1913 to 1933, and since 1979.[162] The following milestones chronicle its rise to dominance:

- Its first steps were in 15th-century Florence when Bank de Medici launched opaque lending to circumvent the church ban on usury.
- The ban on usury withered over time. Goldsmiths evolved safekeeping into moneylending and banking.
- In the United States, on December 23, 1913, following intense lobbying by the big banks, Congress approved the creation of the Federal Reserve System, a privately owned central bank controlled by its shareholders, the banks. The period of 1913–1933 marked a surge in the power of big banks in America.
- The *banking plutocracy* suffered a major setback in 1933 when Congress passed certain provisions of the Glass–Steagall Act that forced the segregation of investment banking from commercial banking and restrained banks in various ways.
- The Glass–Steagall Act aside, the Great Depression had a silver lining for the strongest banks because thousands of smaller banks failed, reducing competition and increasing the market share of those that survived.

- The *banking plutocracy* bore another reversal in 1936 with the publication of *The General Theory*, which introduced Keynesian economics. Keynesianism undermined the *banking plutocracy's* preferred version of economics, neoclassical macroeconomics, which among other things preached *laissez-faire* and deregulation.
- The *banking plutocracy* endured a third setback following World War II; Keynesianism gained momentum, and the strong impetus toward benevolent and *moral capitalism* in the West further marginalized the role of neoclassical macroeconomics and its policies.
- Neoclassical macroeconomics and the *banking plutocracy* used the stagflation of the mid-1970s to make a comeback by blaming Keynesianism for failing to provide a quick solution to a supply-side problem.
- In the 1980s, the Thatcher-Reagan *counter-revolution* reinstated neoclassical macroeconomics, increased reliance on monetary policy, and marginalized Keynesian fiscal policies.
- During the 1980s and 1990s, the systematic dismantling of banking regulations and the blocking of derivatives regulation were landmark victories for big banking.
- The fruit of a highly leveraged usurious economy, guided by neoclassical ideology, was an overly inflated speculative credit bubble in Internet stocks; it finally burst, precipitating the recession in 2000.
- The 2008 Great Recession followed the burst of another speculative bubble, this time in housing and sub-prime mortgages. The wide use of derivatives made matters worse. The subsequent colossal government bailout of the big banks—even more than the creation of the Federal Reserve—demonstrated the big banks' absolute control over the government.

Nine

Blessed are the young for they shall
inherit the national debt.[163]

Herbert Hoover

The section titled "The Evolution of a Ponzi Scheme" in Chapter 7 pointed that *the unified theory of macroeconomic failure* predicts that banking, without government aid, would fail because its immorality represents a large negative externality. Chapter 8 exposed additional immoralities, and, therefore, negative externalities of banking. This chapter will shed more light on how usury, its institutions, products, and economics constitute a mushrooming and economically cancerous negative externality.

Among other things, credit inflates asset bubbles that ultimately burst to precipitate bankruptcies, bank failures, recessions, and depressions. Today, the West is battling multiple credit crises, but the media underplay those problems. Granted, the West has weathered economic storms before, but this time it is worrying because, for many countries, the debt load has become excessive and unmanageable, made worse by eurozone inflexibilities, a neoclassical ideology preaching austerity in the midst of recessions, and fierce international competition. These factors have suffocated economic growth; without growth, the ratio of indebtedness to gross domestic product (GDP) continues to rise. Yet, the banks seem unperturbed about rising indebtedness. They have been loading sinking ships.

Irving Fisher is all the wiser today for his early warnings against indebtedness. That the West, the most sophisticated, is also the most financially troubled, is no coincidence. "Learned" neoclassical economists have been advising that indebtedness is a mark of financial sophistication and advancement. The West, ambivalent to the peril, went along, gulping large doses of that poisonous prescription.

Banking in Perpetual Crisis[164]

Banks, debt, and crises are inseparable. *This Time Is Different* is an illuminating book; its title hints at the characteristic reluctance to see emerging crises as endless replays of the past. It documents debt crises since 1258, providing numerous illuminating and alarming tables.[165] For example, in the last two centuries alone, between 1800 and 2008, the world has endured 268 debt crises, averaging about 1.29 crises per year. Since World War II, advanced economies have experienced 19 banking crises.[166]

Curiously, although developing countries have less financial sophistication, poor planning, and less discipline than advanced economies, nevertheless, they have had less frequent and shallower debt crises, and affecting fewer countries.[167]

One likely explanation is that the development of the financial sector in the West has increased the integration of usury into the tax, legal, economic, and political arrangements, facilitating more indebtedness relative to GDP and, consequently, deeper and more frequent crises. This suggests that the West will not be able to halt its deepening crises while its thinking remains locked inside the usury box.

The Banking Model

Many factors contribute to making banking a precarious business not least the usurious banking model itself, bankers' decision-making process, their ethics, their political influence, their usurious innovations, and the economics of debt. This section discusses the first of these factors.

As explained previously, banking is a Ponzi scheme and, therefore, chronically vulnerable. Banking is also a highly cyclical business, which greatly adds to its susceptibility. During a cyclical recovery, loan portfolios expand and banking profits rise.[168] However, during the crisis phase, short-term interest rates, including the cost of short-term deposits, rise much faster than long-term rates on fixed-income loan and bond portfolios, squeezing banks' interest-spread and precipitating a fall in profits or even losses.[169] Simultaneously, rising interest rates shrink the realizable value of banks' substantial fixed-income portfolios at a time when bad debts are rising due to deteriorating business conditions.

Yet another banking vulnerability is the structural mismatch in the maturities between banking assets and liabilities. The principal assets of commercial banks are loans and bonds, with maturities extending for several years, while their principal liability is deposits, with maturities in months or less; this mismatch, coupled with high leverage makes banking—more than any other business—vulnerable to adverse rumors, which can simultaneously trigger large deposit withdrawals and the drying up of lines of credit. To meet such liquidity crises, especially during the cyclical crisis phase, banks are compelled to liquidate their loan and bond portfolios at deep discounts in the face of rising interest rates, which shrink the value of fixed income portfolios, causing banking losses and failures.[170]

Adding to the absurdity of the banking model is the banks' insane leverage. During the 2008 meltdown, the debt ratios of several aggressive investment banks were 40 to 50 times their equities (debt-to-equity ratios). In other words, their equity represented as little as 2 percent of their balance sheet; thus, a mere 2 percent drop in the value of their assets was sufficient to wipe out their entire equity capital. Giant investment banks like Lehman Brothers failed abruptly and big banks took over others on the verge of failure like Bear Stearns (at the behest of the Federal Reserve and the Treasury), to prevent the crisis of confidence from spreading. Even "conservative" banks rarely have debt-to-equity ratios of less than 12.5 times (i.e., equity to total assets of 8 percent). This means that even a mild drop of 3 percent in the value of their assets would wipe out 37.5 percent of their equity capital, potentially triggering deposit withdrawals on a scale sufficient to sink a bank.

High leverage magnifies the effect of correct and wrong decisions on banks' profitability and solvency, making first-rate forecasting a banking necessity. However, forecasting human behavior is not an exact science. Even the most sophisticated and dedicated forecasters, using the most elaborate mathematics, are not immune to disastrous errors, as the case of Long-Term Capital Management (LTCM), briefly referred to earlier, demonstrated. Strictly speaking, LTCM was a hedge fund and not a bank; nevertheless, it illustrates the absolute necessity of precise forecasting for highly leveraged balance sheets.[171]

Founded in 1994, LTCM had an exceptional investment team headed by three outstanding experts in finance. Two were Nobel laureates: Robert C. Merton, a leading Harvard University finance scholar and, to many experts, a financial genius, and Myron Scholes, who helped devise the Black-Scholes mathematical model for pricing options, no less. The third was David Mullins, steeped in high finance and the former vice chair of the US Federal Reserve, second only to Fed Chairman Alan Greenspan. In addition, a team of first-rate mathematicians and financial experts assisted those celebrated scholars.

Predictably, LTCM employed state-of-the-art statistical models for its investment decisions and it was amazingly profitable for several years. However, in 1998, it abruptly folded despite Fed-orchestrated bank lines of credit to keep it afloat. LTCM's experts discovered the hard way that their models malfunctioned during financial crises, while its high leverage left little margin for error. Shortly before its collapse, LTCM had capital funds of $4.18 billion, which it had leveraged 30 times, bringing its total assets to $125 billion; these were mostly bond arbitrage derivatives (equity volatility and swap spreads) financed by banks. The Federal Reserve oversaw its shutdown to avoid a forced liquidation of its sizable portfolio and a general financial meltdown. Still, its creditor banks lost billions.

Banks' other vulnerability is their abuse of their political power. Their feverish lobbying for deregulation has relaxed the restraints on their gambling instincts, making their business riskier still. The odds are that bankers are not wise enough to desist from making ever-larger bets and triggering ever-larger economic disasters.

Bankers' Decision-Making

Impeccable headquarters in soaring office towers, pinstriped suits, clever conversations, disarming smiles, and attentive staff radiate confidence and hint at bankers' mastery of their craft. They employ advanced credit-screening and forecasting models and credit committees that are well versed in the alchemy of high finance. Top bankers earn much more than top mathematicians, astrophysicists, and chess grandmasters. Yet, they are incapable of developing credit policies that factor in the effect of their collective actions; they act like a herd, stumbling from one credit black hole to the next, always with good reason for doing the wrong thing.

To their misfortunate, bankers do not go about their business quietly. When they finance a significant transaction, they publicize it in newspaper ads and commemorate it with tombstones. This attracts the lethal attention of the rest of the horde, who then try to pull similar, but bigger, deals, with ads and tombstones to match. Instead of becoming alarmed, the banking crowd draws comfort from other bankers chasing similar credits. They persevere with more financing for fashionable sectors until excess capacity leads to losses; only then do their credit committees shut their credit spigots, albeit too late. This boom-bust credit policy has ruined many highly profitable economic sectors through its unrestrained finance. A few examples can illustrate bankers' "Midas touch."

The 1967 Arab-Israeli War (a.k.a. Six-Day War) shut the Suez Canal, significantly stretching shipping routes between the North Atlantic and Asia. Consequently, freight rates rose steeply and bankers could scarcely resist financing an unrestrained ship-construction boom. Within a few years, excessive new shipping tonnage resulted in large losses for shipping companies and their bankers.

The October 1973 Arab-Israeli War (a.k.a. Yom Kippur War) quadrupled oil prices, causing large trade deficits for many countries. Enticed by wide credit spreads, bankers aggressively competed to finance the balance of payment deficits of struggling countries, which the oil crisis had placed on the critical list. About a decade later, countries ranging from Argentina to Poland were defaulting, and new governments sometimes repudiated old debts. US bank credit losses mounted in Latin America, prompting the US government to intervene by guaranteeing the so-called Brady bonds, in an effort to save the lending banks by reducing the interest cost to certain Latin American borrowers.

In 1980, Iraq invaded Iran, sparking a second oil boom in six years. As expected, the banks rushed en masse to finance this second, and more speculative, round of oil exploration, drilling, and production.[172] By 1985, excessive oil financing turned the boom to bust, crashing oil prices and triggering major banking losses.

In the early 1990s, following a construction boom in shopping malls and office towers, the financing banks suffered grave losses, leaving Citibank and several others teetering on the brink.[173]

Similarly, excessive financing precipitated the crash of the dot-coms in the 1990s, the sub-prime mortgages in 2008, and the oil fracking in 2015. Banking has a history littered with fiascos, unmatched by any surviving industry.[174]

Bankers' Ethical Failures

In the epic film *Wall Street,* lead actor Michael Douglas declares, "Greed is good," reflecting a pervasive money culture unfettered by moral values. This highly entertaining, bold, and candid movie is also disturbing in its depiction of shameless amorality. Greed, like medicine, is useful in modest doses, but can turn deadly in excess.

Avarice is a factor in every crash. It drives bankers to commit frauds on a massive scale. The savings and loan debacle in the late 1980s exposed the worst fraud in decades, costing taxpayers tens of billions of dollars. Fraud also laced the dot-com fiasco in 2000 and the sub-prime mortgage meltdown in 2008, at great cost to taxpayers.

On July 5, 2012, Richard Quest of CNN reported, "There is something smelly in the London financial world." He was referring to the exposure of a new and substantial banking fraud that has been going on for years: the fraudulent fixing of the London interbank offered rate (LIBOR).[175] Shortly after, on July 10, 2012, HSBC admitted to and apologized for laundering drug money. Union Bank of Switzerland agreed to disclose the names of its American clients who might have been evading US taxes. Numerous banks have paid billions in fines for committing securities fraud. Banking fraud is endemic.

Bankers also engage in little recognized, but numerous, breaches of ethics. For instance, bankers circulate buy recommendations of the stocks of their corporate-finance clients, but they rarely circulate recommendations to sell them. They also circulate forecasts to their clients, without providing an impartial evaluation of their previous forecasts.

The Seduction of National Indebtedness

Debt has sapped the vitality of many once-proud nations, accelerated their decline and reduced them to houses of cards. Easy credit entices governments to spend beyond their means; it is easy and addictive and, like all addictions, difficult to rein in.

National debt violates the principles of democracy, morality, and sound economics. In a properly functioning democracy, taxes are the price of public goods (including public services). Hence, voting for increased public goods implies accepting higher taxation. When national indebtedness is constitutionally permissible, democracies are prone to become increasingly indebted over time because cunning politicians can entice voters with a seemingly free lunch—increasing public goods without a corresponding increase in taxes—for a decade or more.

Politicians who initiate big budget deficits know that sharp increases in taxes must follow, hopefully, after they depart the political scene. They bequeath future generations a debt burden, particularly if they used the debt to pay for current expenditures instead of financing long-lived infrastructure that benefits future generations. Taxing future generations without giving them corresponding benefits swindles future taxpayers. It is an inter-generational inequity because it increases the benefits to and cuts the tax burden of mature citizens today, while increasing the tax without corresponding benefits on the young and yet-to-be-born. Moreover, deferring the tax increases its ultimate amount by the cumulative interest on the debt it represents until its full repayment.[176] National debt also encourages nations to live beyond their means, loosens fiscal discipline, lowers future living standards, inhibits economic growth, distorts public choice, and undermines the foundations of democracy.

Admiral Mike Mullen, a former chair of the US Joint Chiefs of Staff, is well qualified to assess threats to national security. In an interview with *Fortune* magazine, he commented on national debt by saying, "It's the single biggest threat to our national security."[177] Niall Ferguson published an article in *Foreign Affairs* entitled "Complexity and Collapse," in which he predicted that by 2019, interest payments on the federal debt would rise to 17 percent of the federal revenue, which would limit US military spending and US international power projection.[178] Moreover, a significant credit downgrading of the United States could result in a sudden spike in the cost of federal debt.

The problem of servicing national debt in the West is acute, but it will become worse for three reasons. First, the interest rate has been at record lows, which is unsustainable over long periods; hence, the inevitable rise in the interest rate will radically increase the debt burden. In 2012, the interest rate on a ten-year US Treasury bond was about 1.7 percent, yet the US federal government spent $225 billion on interest payments on a national debt of $16 trillion. In 2000, the interest rate on a ten-year US Treasury bond was about 6.5 percent. A return to that interest environment would increase the federal interest cost to about $1 trillion per year.[179]

Second, given the ongoing large budget deficits and slow economic growth, the national debt will continue to rise much faster than the GDP.

Third, longevity and an aging population will add another growing financial burden, particularly if emigration rates fall.

These factors will affect all Western countries in some degree. Thus, it is a matter of math and time before interest payments on Western national debts, without corresponding benefits, become unbearable for taxpayers and politically impossible to sustain. At that point, Western governments must choose from among higher taxes on the ultra-rich, inflation where the bulk of the debt is denominated in a national currency, repudiation of the debt, or a combination of these.

Almost eight decades ago, Keynes's general theory explained that climbing out of a contraction required an expansionary fiscal policy, meaning significantly increasing expenditure on public works and not austerity. Yet, heavily indebted Western countries have yielded to bankers' perplexing lobbying for austerity, which suffocates growth, produces recessions, and increases the debt-to-GDP ratio, making the debt problem more intractable. Pleading economic ignorance is not credible today. This raises the question whether the *banking plutocracy* is aggravating the economic conditions of indebted countries to compel them to surrender their valuable national assets at deep discounts through privatizations, as observed in Greece and elsewhere. Hence, banking and heavy indebtedness are now the gravest threats to the future of the West.

Odious Debt and International Institutions

In 1927, Aleksandr Naumovich Zak (1890–1955) initiated the call to renounce odious (illegitimate) national debts.[180] More recently, Patricia Adams put forth powerful arguments for renouncing some Third World debt.[181] In a paper to the Cato Institute, she argued that Iraqi debts incurred by Saddam Hussein are illegitimate because it did not benefit the Iraqi people.

Economists Seema Jayachandran and Michael Kremer proposed loan sanctions to stop international bank lending to dictators.[182]

International debt has been extending the lifespans of dictatorships, thereby prolonging the oppression of their subjects. Logically, once a dictator falls, international lenders have no claim on the victims to repay a debt that contributed to their hardship. Indeed, justice demands that the lenders compensate the victims for any suffering they endured because of such lending. Moreover, the illegal wealth accumulated by the corrupt dictators and their entourages is typically channeled back to the West as properties, stocks, investments, and deposits in Swiss banks; therefore, the West should return it to its rightful owners.

Even more concerning, foreign debt is a potential backdoor to neo-imperialism. The stated purpose of the World Bank, the International Monetary Fund, the US Agency for International Development (USAID), and foreign-aid organizations is egalitarian: to improve the economic conditions of developing countries. However, John Perkins, the best-selling author of *Confessions of an Economic Hit Man,* tells a different story. His firsthand assessment is that these institutions are neo-imperialist tools; their real purpose is to facilitate the exploitation of developing countries by foreign corporations.[183] Drawing on his experience in implementing their policies and observing their operations all over the world, he warns that they use aid and debt to ensnare Third World countries economically. Their financial dictates follow, typically demanding that recipients cut aid to the underprivileged, raise indirect taxes, and sell prime public assets to American corporations at favorable prices. Perkins warns that several countries have suffered loss of sovereignty, deteriorating balance-of-payments, and worsening economic conditions pursuant to receiving such "aid" and credits.

The handovers of natural resources to foreign entities makes matters worse for developing countries because the profit passes to foreign entities. Moreover, parasitic multinational corporations that take over natural monopolies have no qualms about gouging Third World consumers to increase their profits and dividends, accentuating the balance-of-payment difficulties of their host countries. As conditions worsen, the pressure increases on those countries to surrender more choice public assets to predatory foreign investors at deep discounts. The net result is a self-feeding vicious cycle of deteriorating living standards in the debtor nations to pay for the swelling profits of predatory foreign investors. Imperialism left the Third World by the door, but has sneaked backed in through the window. The Third World needs to stop this neo-imperialist wave as it did the original version.

The media labelled Perkins's observations a "conspiracy theory" providing plausible deniability to deflect criticism of the West.[184] The term "conspiracy theory" first appeared following the assassination of President Kennedy, although neither his assassination nor the subsequent mystery surrounding it was a "theory."[185] Through excessive use, it now has the opposite effect on public perception. The published statistics indicate that the cumulative budgets of US intelligence services since World War II amounted to trillions in current dollars; even a small fraction of such an astronomical sum is sufficient to finance boundless conspiracies. For instance, *The Game of Nations*, a widely read book by Kermit Roosevelt, proudly describes how, while working for the Central Intelligence Agency (CIA) in the 1950s, he toppled Iran's democratic Prime Minster Musadaq to further Anglo-American oil interests. He also explains his involvement in toppling the Syrian and other governments. Hence, it is misleading to deny the existence of conspiracies by pretending they are theories.[186]

Predatory debt is no longer restricted to Third World countries; American cities and European countries have become victims too, using debt to pressure public borrowers to part with their valuable public assets. The city of Detroit, Michigan, in the United States, is a recent example. It is one of the victims of flawed monetary policies and a chronically overvalued dollar, which contributed to its deindustrialization, exceptionally high unemployment, and shrinking tax base. To meet its debt obligations, Detroit has had to surrender ownership of its water utility to private investors. Shortly thereafter, the cost of water doubled, while big swathes of Detroit—the city with the greatest abundance of fresh water on earth—have become, intermittently, without water. This raises the question of why the Federal Reserve did not step in to revive Detroit with near-zero interest rate loans instead of subsidizing the banks that suffocate American cities with their usury. The simple answer is that the Fed's empathy extends only to some banks and some international corporations, but not to their victims.

Greece, Portugal, Spain, and other heavily indebted European countries, like American cities, now face the same bleak prospects as Third World countries. Their lenders require them to surrender prime assets in return for some debt relief. The avarice of the Western *banking plutocracy* has reached a new, higher threshold, expecting those countries and cities to remain calm while being devoured.

International Financial Institutions

Since World War II, Western dominated international lending institutions like the World Bank have had the field to themselves but now they have a new competitor. The BRICS countries (Brazil, Russia, India, China and South Africa) are establishing the New Development Bank (NBD), with $100 billion in capital. BRICS countries will own 55 percent, developing countries 25 percent, and developed countries 20 percent of its capital; unlike the World Bank, all shareholding countries will have an equal vote, regardless of their ownership. The New Development Bank, with fresh capital and fairer policies, will likely marginalize the World Bank, unless it revises its policies toward the Third World.[187]

In 1974, the governors of the central banks of the ten largest economies established the Basel Committee on Banking Supervision. It has since developed banking guidelines and regulations, aptly labeled Basel I, Basel II, and—most recently, in 2010–2011—Basel III, to improve bank survivability. In reality, these guidelines have been no more than desperate tinkering with a broken banking model; it has neither prevented periodic banking crises nor individual banks from failing. It has provided, however, the illusion of a solution. By offering a false hope to the world that banks can, one-day, stand on their own feet, it has prolonged the agonies of the world and the banks, instead of declaring banking defunct and mercifully hastening its demise (the only useful service it can offer to the world).

Debt and Hyperinflation

Annual inflation is the rate of increase of a price index over a twelve-month period. It measures the loss of the purchasing power of a currency using indexes based on consumer, wholesale, and producer prices, among others. There are several distinct inflation types, with correspondingly different economic policy implications.

Frictional or sectoral shift inflation is a consequence of uneven economic growth across sectors, with some growing fast and others slowly or declining.[188] Where input prices are inflexible downward, higher input prices in the faster-growing sectors facilitate bidding resources away from the stagnant sectors. Hence, a modest sectoral shift inflation of 1 percent to 3 percent, depending on the growth rate, helps lubricate the growth process.

Cost-push inflation and wage-push inflation are rooted in rising supply costs.

Also rooted in the supply side is imported inflation, the result of rising international prices, currency devaluation, or both.

Finally, demand-pull inflation, our primary concern here, is rooted in excessive growth in the money supply, often in response to an unsustainable debt burden. In extreme cases, it can degenerate into runaway inflation or even hyperinflation.

The multiple incidents of hyperinflation in South America and Europe during the 20th century were a direct consequence of excessive government indebtedness. Fiscally irresponsible governments do not balance their budgets by increasing their tax revenues, reducing their expenditures, or both, not even during economic expansions.

When the burden of national debt becomes excessive, governments are tempted to resort to the printing press, precipitating demand-pull inflation. A conscious inflationary policy to lighten the debt burden is most effective when a substantial part of the debt is denominated in the domestic currency, and carries a fixed interest rate and a long maturity. Once the debt burden, in real terms, falls to a manageable level, the challenge facing central authority becomes how to wean itself off the printing press.

A high rate of inflation decreases economic efficiency because it increases uncertainty about the input costs and sales prices, making corporate decisions prone to errors; it also induces corporations to shorten their planning horizons and to lessen the capital intensity of their investments.

Inflation is a de facto tax on cash balances and fixed-rate debt. To the extent that short-term interest rates do not fully compensate for the rate of inflation, it becomes a partial tax on the floating-rate debt as well. It transfers income and wealth away from those on fixed incomes, such as pensioners, wage earners, lessors, and holders of fixed-income instruments to fixed-interest borrowers and those who can readily increase the prices they charge as inflation accelerates.

Inflation elicits social tension when various segments of society struggle to maintain or increase their slice of the national economic pie by raising their incomes faster than the rest. Thus, workers, civil servants, and even the military tend to suffer as their incomes fail to keep pace with an escalating cost of living, resulting in social turmoil, labor unrest, strikes, and occasionally mutiny. It could also unleash political polarization and radical political parties. For example, the German hyperinflation in the 1920s played a role in undermining democracy and facilitating the emergence of a dictatorship.

Atypically, from 2008 to 2015, reported inflation in the United States has remained mild, despite trillions of dollars in federal deficits and the Federal Reserve's potentially massive debasement of the currency through colossal overt and covert quantitative easing.[189] There are at least three explanations for this. First, the inflation indexes, particularly the consumer price index, understate the real inflation rate. Second, a liquidity trap has prevented the excess money supply from stimulating the economy. Third, the overvalued dollar permitted the flood of cheap imports to continue to suppress and postpone domestic inflation. An important question is how much longer this simmering potential inflation will remain on hold. Indeed, Western central banks, including the Fed, have not only planted the seeds of future hyperinflation but also its associated political turmoil as well.

Derivatives and Warrants

Derivatives are the most lethal innovation of the debt revolution. The outward attraction of derivatives is their great capacity for leverage, permitting limited capital to control huge investments since their prices are a fraction of the market value of the underlying asset they represent. Their primary building blocks are call and put options. A call option (a call) is the right to buy a security (or asset) at a specified strike price within a specified time. The price of a call tends to rise as the price of the underlying security rises, and vice versa. The premium it commands over and above its intrinsic value tends to evaporate as its final maturity draws closer.

A put option (a put) is the right to sell a security (or asset) at a specified strike price within a specified time. The price of a put tends to rise as the price of the underlying security falls, and vice versa. As with calls, the premium that a put commands, over and above its intrinsic value, dissipates as its final maturity approaches. In addition to these two primary building blocks, the range and structure of derivative cocktails are limited only by the imagination of the punters.

Warrants, attached to preferred shares and bonds, give their holders the right to acquire the common stock of the issuers at a preset strike price. Warrants can be detached from the aforementioned securities to trade on their own, making them similar to call options, but with an extended life and a less active market.

These and synthetic derivatives have greatly increased the odds of bankrupting banks, financial institutions, and nations. Their risk emanates from several sources. Foremost is their powerful leverage, which is similar to that of debt, only far more potent per dollar of outlay.

Their second source of risk is their complexity.[190] Derivative valuation models assume that future probabilities will be the same as in the past. However, past data do not accurately portray all possible future outcomes, particularly the outliers triggered by infrequent events, such as debt crises, wars, or climate change.[191] Hence, derivative pricing models tend to fail at the most critical junctures.

The near-instantaneous collapse of several once-prominent institutions built over decades, or even centuries, after meddling in complex derivatives is testimony to derivatives' considerable negative externality. Complex derivative cocktails have increased many fold the diverse combinations of bets on and hedges against a multitude of financial and investment outcomes. Most worrisome is that the directors and chief executive officers (CEOs) of some major banks that create or meddle in derivatives often do not fathom their full impact on their firm's balance sheet under every possible scenario.[192]

A third source of risk—and the scariest—is derivatives' overwhelming volume. Moderate estimates put total derivatives at over $500 trillion, a huge multiple of the underlying assets, making the global economy highly speculative, unstable, and liable to horrific crises. Moreover, there appears to be no limit to the growth of this financial cancer. Hence, Warren Buffet, a financial genius and probably the most successful investor in the world, labeled derivatives as financial weapons of mass destruction (FWMD).

The size of the derivative arsenal is already more than sufficient for the total financial annihilation of the West. In other words, if those making monstrously large financial bets should fail at any time between now and the infinite future, then they will bring everybody down with them. Hence, we live in the shadow of a colossal financial blackmail that will necessitate limitless quantitative easing because the financial wizards have strapped the West to FWMD. The lack of regulation has made this problem worse. The Commodities Futures Modernization Act of December 2000 permitted derivatives to continue trading, unregulated, in over-the-counter markets, where their amounts, risk, and trades are without government supervision.

In addition, selling calls and puts short has the same problems associated with short selling, which the next section explores. The only exception to this rule is when the short seller of a call owns the underlying security, or covered, rather than naked, short selling. Still, covered short selling suggests that the seller is without a clear strategy because if the seller liked the security he (she) held, he (she) should not risk losing it for an insignificant call premium, while if he (she) did not, then he (she) should sell it without further ado. As with most things, simplicity is the best policy. In this case, it can spare an investor the insanity of not wanting the stock to appreciate, lest he (she) lose it, and, at the same time, not wanting the stock to fall, lest he (she) incur a loss. A familiar argument of stockbrokers is that covered option writing is a valid investment strategy if we expect the market to move sideways. This argument stimulates brokerage commissions, but it is without merit because no one knows if the market will move sideways and the minor extra yield does not justify the risk of loss should the stock fall without an offsetting potential profit if the stock should rise.

Short Selling

Short selling is another destabilizing innovation of the debt revolution. Unlike ordinary selling, a short seller sells an asset (e.g., security, commodity, currency) that he (she) does not own. In the case of a security, a broker—acting on behalf of the short seller—borrows the security from someone holding it, sells it, and credits the proceeds to the account of the short seller. The short seller is required to buy back the shorted security at an unspecified future date to return it to its rightful owner. Hence, the short seller makes a profit by buying it back at a cheaper price than he (she) had sold it for, but incurs a loss if the price rises. Thus, short selling is equivalent to a cash advance equal to the sale proceeds and a variable loan corresponding to the fluctuating market value of the sold security. The indebtedness it entails is one source of its negative externality, among others.

Institutional advocates of short selling make three claims for preserving it. First, short selling provides liquidity to securities markets when there are insufficient sellers, thereby enhancing price stability. This line of reasoning has some merit in bull markets; the problem, however, is that short selling peaks during bear markets, making it the equivalent of throwing a wrench into the market engine. In a down market, trend-following software can generate tidal waves of short sell orders, artificially augmenting the supply of falling stocks without a corresponding increase in demand, thereby reducing liquidity, increasing volatility, inducing panics, and triggering stock crashes in individual securities or whole markets.

Indeed, computerized trend-following software triggered the market crash in October 1987, and has crashed countless individual securities since that time. Institutional short selling displaces legitimate sell orders, compelling the investing public to accept lower prices, smaller profits, or bigger losses than it would otherwise, while the institutional short sellers earn parasitic profits. Such contrived profits ought to be banned because they are immoral and, consequently, are contrary to the public interest and market efficiency. Accordingly, in addition to the implicit debt it embodies, the other reason why short selling constitutes a negative externality is that it precipitates market failure.

The second claim by institutional advocates of short selling is that it improves market efficiency by bringing down the prices of overpriced securities quickly. Indeed, institutional short sellers use their super-fast automated reaction times and short selling to bring prices down abruptly. Short selling also creates selling momentums that result in unfair and excessive price falls, thereby reducing market efficiency. In addition, such contrived price falls attract negative press coverage, which distorts prices further. Furthermore, the profitability of short selling is a direct function of price instability, providing short sellers with a powerful motive for instigating crashes to the detriment of the economy, listed companies, and the investing public.

To preserve short selling in the face of public outrage in the aftermath of the 1987 crash, American regulators reintroduced circuit breakers (the rational policy would have been to eliminate the cause of the crash by banning short selling altogether). That measure cooled public anger but solved nothing; short sellers helped crash the market in 2008–2009. Hence, in 2010, Germany and Italy banned short selling; their market analysis indicated that short selling increased market volatility and risk, without offsetting benefits to the investing public. Regrettably, Anglo-Saxon securities regulations continue to serve the interest of the institutions instead of protecting the investing public.

The final claim by the proponents of short selling is that the regulators would catch the abusers. This argument is hollow because regulators have not stopped short sellers from crashing individual stocks, whole markets, or the whole economy, as the Great Recession of 2008 demonstrated. This argument is no more valid than claiming that locks, security cameras, police officers, courts, and prisons stop crime. The logical solution is to eliminate the incentive for abuse by banning short selling.

It is noteworthy that Islamic scholars have banned short selling on moral grounds; they consider it immoral for any party to sell assets that it does not own. This principle is imperative because it removes the conflict of interest, a motive for fraud and immoral acts, from the securities markets. It is consistent with the policies of prudent insurance companies not to insure property other than to its beneficial owner; otherwise, it would give an incentive for the unscrupulous to insure and then damage the properties of third parties.

In the same vein, banning short selling removes the incentive for unscrupulous short sellers to harm companies by circulating negative rumors, issuing and distributing biased stock research, and creating problems for companies to bring down their stocks, or worse.

Two examples should suffice to illustrate these additional risks of short selling. Destroying a company from the inside is easier, faster, and more certain than building it, and it requires less talent to boot. Greedy but incompetent managers cannot profit from generous corporate stock options and bonus incentives because they are incapable of improving the performance and profitability of the companies they run. The illegal, but easier alternative is to engineer problems for the companies entrusted to them and to use offshore accounts to sell their stock short and buy stock puts. They maximize their profit by driving the company to the wall. This is not far-fetched because the incentive is clearly there. Hence, banning short selling removes a powerful motive for harming corporations and the economy.

Short selling also damages the national economy in other ways. Prior to the 2008 meltdown, several banks packaged and marketed defective sub-prime loans, while making big bets against those very loans by buying credit default swaps from insurance companies. In fact, the insurance companies were violating their sacred principle of not offering insurance except to the beneficial owners. Those banks were shorting the very loans they had marketed to their clients, without alerting them to this fundamental conflict of interest. The banks made giant profits when those loans subsequently defaulted. Thus, short selling provides an incentive for immoral and economically harmful transactions. It is not unlike selling a fire insurance policy to an arsonist on properties he (she) does not own and liable to set on fire.

Finally, institutions that are sincere about improving market liquidity must trade against the direction of the market, not with it. This requires them to sell securities from their inventories on stock upticks and to buy on downticks. Such a strategy, without short selling, could indeed improve liquidity if that is their intention.

Usurious Capitalism[193]

In recent decades, parasitic economics has produced a deviant form of capitalism best described as *usurious capitalism, entailing* extreme violations of economic principles. If it were not a product of the *banking plutocracy,* a more appropriate description would be *Machiavellian, hypocritical,* or *schizophrenic capitalism.* In fact, each of these terms describes a facet of *usurious capitalism,* and taken together, they provide a more complete picture. *Usurious capitalism* is *parasitic capitalism* at its worst; it has expunged any residual credibility of the neoclassical macroeconomists who justified it. It reeks of flagrant inconsistencies, contradictions, gross unfairness, selectivity, and tailor-made solutions that would be hilarious if only they did not hurt tens of millions of people and damage economies, to say nothing of its blatant disrespect for public intelligence.

In essence, *usurious capitalism* is a moral failure, the root of all market failures discussed herein. Its greatest feat has been the rationalization of irrationality. The Federal Reserve and Western central banks have perfected *usurious capitalism,* as the following examples make clear.

Two Centuries of Parasitic Economics

The arguments of America's big banks and the Federal Reserve for deregulating banking centered on *laissez-faire*, free markets, economic Darwinism, and survival of the fittest, insisting that government intervention interfered with, and diminished, the economic efficiency of a capitalist economy. It specifically required governments never to bail out sickly enterprises.

However, in 2008, when the big banks were on the verge of collapse en masse, they together with the Federal Reserve and the Treasury reversed their policy prescriptions in the blink of an eye, dropping all past arguments of free markets, economic Darwinism, and survival of the fittest, and feverishly lobbied to rescue the insolvent banks. Their European counterparts quickly followed suit. Such spineless policy reversals demonstrate the application of *usurious capitalism*.

That sudden policy reversal was in fact economically more schizophrenic, immoral, and absurd than it seemed. Western governments used taxpayers' money to bail out the big banks instead of the tens of millions of taxpayers who were left at the mercy of those callous institutions. Thus, *usurious capitalism* decreed different economic policies for different economic actors: gentle socialism for the big banks and merciless capitalist Darwinism for the taxpayers.

Another consequence of *usurious economic* policies is its absurd allocation of return: big banks retained their speculative profits when their bets came through, but taxpayers paid for banks losses when their bets did not. Hence, *usurious capitalism* is a dual, indeed, *schizophrenic capitalism*: capitalism for banking profits and socialism for banking losses.

The ingenuity of the Federal Reserve found other applications for *usurious capitalism*. Fed Chairman Ben Bernanke professed great respect for the theories of Milton Friedman, monetarism, *laissez-faire*, and neoclassical economics to attain Pareto optimal resource allocation and economic efficiency.[194] In monetary policy terms this implied free, market-determined, interest rates as the correct price of money. In practice, the Federal Reserve has been a blatant violator of Pareto optimality. For example, quantitative easing is an acute form of interest rate rigging. It tramples on a vaunted neoclassical economic concept: the time value of money. By setting shadow

163

interest rates outside the market mechanism, the Federal Reserve was mimicking the practices of communist central planning committees but as applied to the capital market instead of setting prices for goods and services. Nevertheless, this gross violation of Pareto optimality is permissible under the ad hoc rules of *usurious capitalism*.

The illusive rules of *usurious capitalism* permitted the Fed to operate as a central planning committee for the capital market of the foremost capitalist economy, with inestimable negative consequences. For example, by artificially setting the risk-free rate of return, instead of the market, it has made, in a stroke, all the sophisticated financial models and the investments decision that emanate from them misleading. Fed interest rate rigging, by distorting the whole term structure of interest rates, has introduced major error to all discounted cash-flow calculations for evaluating investment projects, undermining an important yardstick for making rational investment decisions in a market economy.

Since 1979, one of the worst perversions of the free market system has been the Fed's wild interest-rate manipulations, first setting them too high, then, since the 1990s, too low. These protracted periods of gross interest rate distortions were large deviations from the free market rate that must have caused grave misallocation of US economic resources and loss of efficiency. The Fed's current economic distortions are the most extreme: allotting humongous funds to zombie banks has been the ultimate misallocation of resources, a final trampling on any residual Pareto optimality.

The litany of dislocations of *usurious capitalism* is long. Interest is a major negative externality because its private (nominal) cost vastly understates its social cost. Quantitative easing has artificially lowered the private cost of interest, further widening the gap between its private and social cost, thereby accentuating its negative externality by causing asset bubbles and economic crises. To the extent that the de facto interest rate subsidy has been extreme, so will be the social cost of the forthcoming bubble, when it bursts. The epicenter of the next crash will likely be the bond market, with aftershocks affecting the stock market, property, banks, financial services, and the economy at large.

Ten

THE FEDERAL RESERVE AS AN
EXTENSION OF BANKING POWER

*We the people are the rightful masters of both Congress
and the courts, not to overthrow the Constitution but to
overthrow the men who pervert the Constitution.*[195]

Abraham Lincoln

Chapter 8 explained that the economic revolutions resulted in shifts in plutocratic economic power. Moreover, each one of these powers, whether feudal, mercantilist, industrial, transport or technological, sought in some fashion and to some degree to increase its power so as to restrict competition in order to earn an incrementally higher return than obtainable by a competitive market, thereby earning an incremental parasitic profit. However, aside from their attempts to restrict competition, those plutocracies operated essentially sound business models. The banking plutocracy has had similar motives with a difference.

The banking plutocracy, although it provided a service required by the market place, financing, it used a defunct and chronically unstable financing model to do so, based on usury instead of equity financing. Hence, for the big banks gaining political power was not a just matter of earning an incremental parasitic profit as with the rest of the plutocracies, but a question of survival. *The unified theory of macroeconomic failure* diagnosed the intrinsic negative externality of banking as the prime cause of periodic waves of bank failures and economic crises. A large negative externality meant that banking was not economically viable and, therefore, could not survive on purely economic grounds; therefore, it needed a high degree of communist style government support to prop it up, which in turn required a correspondingly high degree of banking political power to enforce the absurd economic policies it called for. In other words, banking demanded large government subsidies to maintain its flawed and parasitic banking superstructure, which necessitated considerable banking power to enforce it. Moreover, as the usurious revolution developed and its range of usurious products expanded, the indebtedness of banking and the economy and with it the negative externality of usury grew exponentially, requiring the banks to have ever more power to ensure the ready availability of ever larger government bailouts. Extending this trend further, one must inevitably conclude that at some point, the subsidy would become so massive that the big banks must assume absolute political power, making a banking dictatorship an absolute necessity for their continued survival. Indeed, many Western countries have already passed this mark. It is in this context that we must understand the birth of the Federal Reserve, its growing power, and its progressive assumption of the economic powers of the executive and legislative branches of government. This perspective also sheds additional light on the motives behind the *counter-revolution* discussed earlier.

The Birth of the Federal Reserve

The big banks orchestrated an intense lobbying effort, led by J. P. Morgan Bank, to establish a private central bank. They succeeded in getting a bill through the House of Representatives, but a majority of the senators repeatedly rejected it. Its advocates saw their opportunity on December 23, 1913, as the ranks of the opposing senators thinned, departing from Washington, DC, to join their far-flung families for Christmas celebrations. Thus, the resolution to establish the Federal Reserve passed on Christmas Eve. Establishing a safe harbor for usurious banks on the most sacred of nights was beyond ominous.

The Federal Reserve is a mediaeval concept. It mimicked the Bank of England, a privately owned central bank established centuries earlier in 1694. Back then, government and private interests overlapped, but times had changed. In 1858, the British Parliament passed the Government of India Act, which among other things, nationalized the operations of the East India Company, marking the beginning of the formal separation between private interests and the affairs of state in Great Britain. Alas, the formal divorce between the British government and its private central bank would take a while longer. Hence, for powerful American bankers to seek to encroach on and meddle in the economic affairs of the American state in the 20th century through a private central bank was a march against time toward a feudal past. It has been the most detrimental act to public interest.

The Bank of England used gold for its currency, with silver playing an auxiliary role. Hence, it could not create physical currency. By the late 19th century, the inflexibility of managing national economies under a gold standard was becoming clear. The Great Depression provided the impetus to make the switch to fiat currencies. Several countries, including Great Britain, abandoned the gold standard by 1931, but the United States only devalued the gold content of the dollar.

In July 1944, in the midst of World War II, forty-four allied countries held feverish talks in Bretton Woods, New Hampshire, in the United States, culminating in the signing of the Bretton Woods Agreement. It established a new international monetary system based on the US dollar, initially with fixed exchange rates; the US government promised member central banks dollar-gold convertibility if they so desired. The abandonment of the gold standard, despite a slender link remaining, was a game-changer because the dollar became a fiat currency. Money creation and monetary policy became key tools in conducting national economic policy, making it more essential than ever for central bank ownership and control to be in government hands—particularly in the United States, the center of the new international monetary order.

In 1946, after 252 years of private ownership, a British labor government nationalized the politically and economically powerful Bank of England. The new fiat currency regime dictated this measure to uphold the sovereignty of the British state by preventing the bankers from assuming economic powers of the state in violation of democratic principles.

There was another critical reason for nationalizing the Bank of England: to preempt conflicts between fiscal and monetary policies. The ease of creating and destroying fiat currency required monetary policy synchronization with fiscal policy to avoid catastrophic policy contradictions and to ensure maximum economic effectiveness. For the same reason no responsible insurance company insures an airplane or ship with two captains: two minds at the helm cause accidents. Hence, economic sanity requires one authority in charge of fiscal and monetary policies to avoid schizophrenic economic policies.

In the early 1970s, the US government discarded the last remaining straw of the gold standard by suspending the dollar-gold convertibility, which ended Bretton Woods. It was another opportunity to synchronize America's fiscal and monetary policies under one roof. Alas, it was lost in the distractions of the Vietnam War, a Nixon presidency in crisis, and the oil shock of 1973. Banking interests saw the confusion as an opportunity to expand their authority by stripping away more powers from the government. They lobbied for and obtained complete Federal Reserve independence from the government. One consequence is today's *usurious capitalism*.[196]

The Riddle of the Federal Reserve

The Federal Reserve is an enigma. Many things about it are confusing. Most people presume the US federal government owns the Federal Reserve System, disbelieving that it is a private entity. To most people a privately owned central bank is a contradiction of terms—no less absurd than a square circle. Remarkably, more than a century after its establishment, the American public is still in the dark about the most basic facts concerning their private central bank.

This is principally the fault of the Fed itself and the confusing information it circulates. Let us take an example. On November 2, 2014, the Federal Reserve website carried a publication titled "Who Owns the Federal Reserve?"[197] It states, "...the Federal Reserve System fulfills its public mission as an independent entity within government. It is not owned by anyone and is not a private, profit-making institution." The statement "not owned by anyone" is absurd because all corporations must have owners.

The same publication goes on to state that "dividends are, by law, 6 percent per year." This refutes the earlier statement that "It is not owned by anyone..." because dividends are distributed to the owners (i.e., the shareholders). If the Fed is in fact "not owned by anyone," then who has been receiving the billions of dollars in annual dividends?

By law, the shareholders of the twelve regional Federal Reserve Banks are banks; this means the statement "the Federal Reserve System...[is] not...a private [entity]" is misleading, because it is a private corporation owned by banks.

The statement "[it] is not a private, profit-making institution" is another yarn. Clearly, dividends are profit distributions; therefore, it takes "profit-making" to distribute dividends, whereas "not a private, profit-making institution" gives the impression that it is a charity, but charities do not distribute dividends to their shareholders.

In this age, high standards of transparency are expected, whereas this Fed publication is baffling and misleading. The Fed would serve public information better by withdrawing all such confusing publications and replacing them with ones that accurately present the facts, without a shade of vagueness. We will have more to say about this publication later.

Another riddle of the Federal Reserve—a private entity—is that it holds a monopoly over the creation of money and the conduct of monetary policy, despite the prevailing US antitrust statutes in 1913 specifically enacted to prevent and to break up monopolies and cartels. Moreover, bank representatives sit on the boards of the Regional Reserve Banks, with the power to decide which competitive bank to save or sink, entailing unbound conflict of interest—a flagrant violation of the principles of fair competition and a level playing field.

The complex structure of the Federal Reserve System is a yet another riddle. The mission of the twelve regional Federal Reserve Banks has no rational parallel in the annals of modern management because they are charged with supervising their shareholders. This is no less absurd than tasking a child with responsibility for supervising his (her) parents. More precisely, a regional Federal Reserve Bank must supervise the banks in its region, which are not only its shareholders but also appoint its board of directors with ultimate power for setting policy and appointing the top management. In other words, the management structure of a regional Federal Reserve Bank represents an infinite loop, whereby the member banks within a region supervise the operations of the regional Federal Reserve Bank and the latter in turn supervises the operations of those banks. This type of management structure is not common for good reason: it is preposterous. The failure of thousands of banks, despite Fed supervision, testifies to its absurdity. The way to cut this weird loop and improve the survival rate of the banks is to have government ownership of the Regional Reserve Banks, as in the rest of the world.

The Direct Cost of the Federal Reserve

Another riddle of the Federal Reserve is its direct cost to taxpayers. The previously cited Fed publication "Who Owns the Federal Reserve?" gives the dividends as 6 percent of capital, but it makes no mention of a larger sum: "Net Transfers to Surplus." The 2013 Annual Report of the Board of Governors of the Federal Reserve System coincided with the Fed's centennial; hence, it contains interesting facts about the financial history of the Fed.[198] The annual report shows that, since its inception, "Net Transfers to Surplus" have totaled more than $27,506.8 million compared to total dividends at $18,796.2 million, bringing the total direct cost to $46,303.1 million. In other words, "Net Transfers to Surplus" have averaged approximately 146.34

percent of dividends. Thus, a full disclosure of the direct cost of the Federal Reserve is 14.78 percent of the capital, not just 6 percent in dividends. The Federal Reserve does not distribute the "Net Transfers to Surplus" but uses it to increase its capital, which increases the dollar amount of its 6 percent dividend (see Table 10.1).

Table 10.1 provides a partial summary of Table 11 titled "Income and Expenses of the Federal Reserve Banks" in the Fed 2013 annual report. It shows that between 1917 and 2013, dividends increased from $1.7 million to $1,649.3 million, a 242-fold increase. The Federal Reserve's direct cost to taxpayers has been rising much faster than the growth in gross domestic product (GDP) and it has accelerated following the dismantling of the banking regulations.

To assess the effect of the political shift to the right of the *counter-revolution* on the Fed's dividend growth rate, we considered three periods: 1917–1982 (pre-deregulation), 1982–1999 (a period of progressive deregulation), and 1999–2013 (post-deregulation). Up to 1982, dividend growth was generous at 6.05 percent per annum. It accelerated to 9.54 percent per annum between 1983 and 1999. After 1999, dividend growth accelerated further to 11.19 percent per annum. Remarkably, dividends growth accelerated as inflation was falling. One possible explanation of the accelerating growth in dividends is the growing political power of the banks, making them unconcerned about any public outcry.

TABLE 10.1

Dividends Paid by Federal Reserve Banks

(U.S. $ Millions)

Year	Dividends	Period	Dividend Growth Rate	Transfers to Surplus	Dividends +Transfers
1917	$ 1.7				
1982	$ 79.4	1917-1982	6.05%		
1999	$ 373.6	1982-1999	9.54%		
2013	$ 1,649.3	1999-2013	11.19%		
Total	$ 18,796.2	1917-2013	7.40%	$ 27,506.8	$ 46,303.1

Source: Table 11, "Income and expenses of the Federal Reserve Banks," the 2013 Annual Report of the Board of Governors of the Federal Reserve System.

Thus, the total cost of the Federal Reserve is 14.78 percent of capital (6 percent dividends + 8.78 percent Net Transfers to Surplus). Some financial scholars might dispute the theoretical basis for this calculation because the Net Transfers to Surplus are not distributed to the shareholders. The generally accepted alternative calculation is the total return to the shareholders, representing the dividend yield plus its growth rate. Post-deregulation, the dividend growth rate reached 11.19 percent per annum, bringing the total returns to the shareholders to 17.19 percent (6 percent dividends + 11.19 percent growth). This is a phenomenally high reward for assuming practically no risk. Compared to the return on long-term Treasuries, a total return of 17.19 percent represents great extravagance with taxpayers' money.

To grasp this degree of extravagance, one needs to project it into the future, say to 2030. Table 10.2 assumes dividends will continue to grow at 11.19 percent per annum and "Net Transfers to Surplus" continue to average 146.34 percent of dividends. Table 10.2 projects the cumulative direct cost of the Federal Reserve for the period 2014–2030 at $204,602.3 million, a prohibitive cost to taxpayers and tax exempt to boot.

Doubtless, the impoverished in America deserve this money more than the banks. Earmarking it for the needy is not only a moral choice, but also economically rational. The financial burden of supporting a private Federal Reserve System for the benefit of its shareholding banks and their wealthy shareholders is too onerous for a democracy. It is clearly more cost-effective to nationalize the Federal Reserve System. Alas, this is hardly the full economic cost of the Federal Reserve.

TABLE 10.2

Projected Cost of the Federal Reserve Banks, 2014-2030

(U.S. $ Millions)

2013 Dividends	Dividend Growth Rate	Transfers to Surplus as % of Dividends	Dividends+Transfers as % of Capital
$ 1,649.0	11.19%	146.34%	14.78%

Year	Dividends	Transfers to Surplus	Dividends + Transfers
2014	$ 1,833.5	$ 2,683.2	$ 4,516.7
2015	$ 2,038.7	$ 2,983.5	$ 5,022.2
2016	$ 2,266.8	$ 3,317.3	$ 5,584.1
2017	$ 2,520.5	$ 3,688.5	$ 6,209.0
2018	$ 2,802.5	$ 4,101.2	$ 6,903.8
2019	$ 3,116.1	$ 4,560.2	$ 7,676.3
2020	$ 3,464.8	$ 5,070.4	$ 8,535.2
2021	$ 3,852.5	$ 5,637.8	$ 9,490.3
2022	$ 4,283.6	$ 6,268.7	$ 10,552.3
2023	$ 4,762.9	$ 6,970.1	$ 11,733.0
2024	$ 5,295.9	$ 7,750.1	$ 13,045.9
2025	$ 5,888.5	$ 8,617.3	$ 14,505.8
2026	$ 6,547.4	$ 9,581.6	$ 16,128.9
2027	$ 7,280.0	$ 10,653.7	$ 17,933.7
2028	$ 8,094.6	$ 11,845.9	$ 19,940.5
2029	$ 9,000.4	$ 13,171.4	$ 22,171.8
2030	$ 10,007.5	$ 14,645.3	$ 24,652.8
Total	$ 83,056.1	$ 121,546.2	$ 204,602.3

Source: Table 11, "Income and expenses of the Federal Reserve Banks," the 2013 Annual Report of the Board of Governors of the Federal Reserve System.

Fed Monetary Policy

Theoretically, timely countercyclical monetary policies can smooth economic cycles; however, what are the odds of its success? Given a time lag of about one year between a monetary policy action and its effects taking hold, a central bank needs to forecast changes in the direction of the economy about a year in advance. Moreover, economic data, the raw material for decision-making, are only available several months in arears and are subject to several revisions, further extending the time horizon of the required forecast. Furthermore, forecasts are notoriously inaccurate, and forecasting economic turning points, although most useful, is also the most challenging. Monetary authorities' use of a wrong or inaccurate forecast risks increasing instead of dampening cyclical fluctuations.

In addition to the requisite economic and forecasting skills, central bankers must be immune to the influence of third parties, especially the big banks, holding the prospect of future employment with lavish pay. Prolonging an expansion also requires walking a tightrope of applying monetary brakes early enough to abort speculative bubbles and to prevent the economy from overheating, yet lightly enough to avoid tipping it into a recession; this also demands psychological immunity from the pressures of the media and the public.

Thus, correct monetary policy requires the foresight of a sage, the nobility of an angel, and the courage of a lion. These are rare qualities indeed, and not just among central bankers. Hence, even under the most favorable assumptions, there can be no assurance a priori that monetary policy will be countercyclical and stabilizing, instead of pro-cyclical and destabilizing. In other words, we are expecting central bankers to perform feats that are beyond the abilities of most humans.

Professor Friedman understood the difficulties of implementing an effective countercyclical monetary policy.[199] Hence, he advised limiting monetary policy to a steady growth in the money supply throughout the cycle to achieve the more modest objective of accommodating economic growth and its associated frictional inflation. Such a policy is less demanding, but not without its own problems. It presumes that the velocity of the circulation of money is stable over an economic cycle, even though the evidence suggests that it fluctuates—widely.

Intuitively, one would expect the velocity of circulation to pick up during an economic expansion and to fall during a contraction. For example, rising interest rate during an expansion increases the opportunity cost of holding cash, inducing a reduction in idle balances and a corresponding increase in the velocity of circulation, and vice versa. Thus, a steady expansion in the money supply would be doubly expansionary during an expansion and ineffective during a contraction. Furthermore, the introduction of new technologies (e.g., credit cards, Internet transfers) tends to increase the velocity of circulation, further complicating the analysis.

Finally, the behavior of the economic actors can reinforce or neutralize a monetary policy. Thus, the Fed's gigantic quantitative easing has had a minimal stimulative effect because many banks, fearing a rise in credit risk, have used the near-zero cost of funds to earn a spread on Treasury bonds instead of expanding credit.

The difficulties of conducting an effective monetary policy are clear. Yet, even allowing for this factor, the Federal Reserve monetary policy is an inexplicably consistent failure, unmitigated by any randomness. As a result, the cost of the Federal Reserve monetary policy to the US economy is phenomenally greater than its direct cost, as estimated in the previous section.

We can only speculate on the reasons behind the appalling performance of the Federal Reserve. For one thing, the representatives of the member banks sit on the boards of the Federal Reserve's regional banks and participate in setting monetary policy. Yet, banks' past performance demonstrates that they are incompetent in managing the affairs of their own banks, requiring constant Fed support and periodic government bailouts to survive. Hence, it is economically suicidal to have those same economic "wizards" responsible for running the monetary affairs of the United States, the largest economy in the world.

In 1963, Professor Milton Friedman and Anna Schwartz published their treatise, *A Monetary History of the United States*. Their study showed that the Federal Reserve had pushed the US economy into the Great Depression by tightening monetary policy during a contraction—an unfathomable error. In a 2002 speech, Fed Chairman Ben Bernanke stated, "Let me end my talk by abusing slightly my status as an official representative of the Federal Reserve. I would like to say to Milton and Anna: Regarding the Great Depression. *You're right, we did it.* We're very sorry. But thanks to you, we won't do it again."[200] Based on his examination of the record of Fed monetary policy, Professor Friedman recommended abolishing the Federal Reserve altogether.

Fed Chairman Ben Bernanke stopped short of explaining why they "did it." Neither did Professor Friedman dwell on other possible reasons for the Fed's peculiar actions, besides gross incompetence. The Fed's actions would seem to be perplexing to say the least. But it is even spookier to realize that the Fed has consistently repeated an irrational policy.

Table 11.1 in Chapter 11 presents the seven economic contractions in the twenty-nine years following the creation of the Fed in 1913 until 1942, the start of American mobilization for World War II. Of these, three major contractions in 1920–1921, 1929–1933 (the Great Depression), and 1937–1938 appear to have been caused by tight monetary policy. The Fed appears incapable of learning from the economic crises it seeds, but is that a plausible explanation?

We could speculate about other possible causes for Fed policy during the Great Depression for example. Did the Communist Party USA want the US economy to plunge in depression as a prelude to revolution? They almost certainly did, but it is unthinkable that the Fed had communist leanings, swelling the armies of the unemployed to bring about a communist takeover of America, even if the Fed's actions increased that risk.

That aside, every US recession and depression thinned the number of US banks. The Great Depression alone bankrupted more than nine thousand banks.[201] The huge reduction in competition increased the market shares of the banks that survived. Conflict of interest was present then as now, but we have no evidence that the Fed purposely engineered those contractions to increase the market share of the big banks by shrinking their competition.

The Fed went back to its tight monetary policies during the recessions in 1973–1975, 1980, and 1981–1982.[202] In all three instances, a tight monetary policy was inappropriate for containing cost-push inflation and a neutral stance would have been more appropriate.

The Federal Reserve shifted its monetary policy from overly restrictive to overly expansionary in the 1990s. What prompted that dramatic reversal is a mystery. Artificially low interest rates launched an era of speculative bubbles and crashes. By the late 1990s, easy monetary policy helped lift NASDAQ to a highly inflated level. The Fed then reversed course, precipitating a recession. The dot-com crash of 2000, as measured by NASDAQ, was comparable to the Dow's crash during the Great Depression, only sharper.

Following that crash, the Fed went back to lowering interest rates; its effect on the United States was modest growth, while fueling another speculative bubble—this time in housing. With the Fed's oversight, banks raised hundreds of billions of dollars in collateralized mortgage debt (CMD), pumping the housing bubble further. In the face of public concern over a housing bubble, Fed Chairman Ben Bernanke assured the public that a crash in housing had never happened across the United States, overlooking the fact that there is always a first time. The Fed kept pumping cheap money and inflating housing prices to exhilarating heights. It then abruptly reversed course by raising interest rates, which helped precipitate the housing crash in late 2007. The stock market crashed in sympathy, falling by almost as much as it did during the 1973–1975 recession.

In the fourth quarter of 2008, the Fed dramatically reversed course yet again, this time to save the big banks from bankruptcy. Its monetary policy was far easier than ever before. US growth remained anemic; however, by 2015, the Fed succeeded in inflating a gargantuan bond bubble—far bigger than any past stock market or real estate bubbles. Thus, before the debris from the previous crash had settled, the Fed was back to priming the American economy for another cataclysm.

At best, the Fed's monetary policy appears naïve: fast forward followed by sharp braking and reversing, then fast forward again. Nothing could be simpler. In less than two decades, two renowned Fed chairs with superb academic credentials used easy monetary policies to inflate giant asset bubbles in all three major asset classes: stocks, real estate, and bonds, respectively.

Alan Greenspan's reign as Fed chair lasted almost two decades, from August 11, 1987, until January 31, 2006. He is credited with overseeing the comprehensive dismantling of banking regulations in America. His other major accomplishments included pumping the Internet bubble then bursting it, followed by pumping the housing bubble. His term ended before he could burst the second bubble.

The bubble baton passed to his successor, Ben Bernanke, whose reign as Fed chairman lasted eight years, from February 1, 2006, to January 31, 2014. Bernanke's monetary policy was a continuation of his predecessor's: pumping two asset bubbles and bursting one in nearly as many years. After fully inflating and bursting the housing bubble, he proceeded to pump the bond bubble, which he too could not finish pumping it before the end of his term. Both men were great bubble makers and blasters—perhaps the most outstanding in history. The bubble baton passed to the current Fed Chair Janet Yellen. The odds are that this pattern in Fed monetary policy of bubble pumping and bursting will continue.

Reasonable men, armed with common sense, must conclude that the Fed monetary policies are harmful to American prosperity. It will puzzle researchers for decades to come, as it has puzzled many economists for almost a century. When the next bubble bursts, it will reconfirm that the Federal Reserve's policies are damaging to the US economy. This concern prompted Congressman Ron Paul, chair of the House of Representatives Monetary Policy Subcommittee in 2011, to propose nationalizing the Federal Reserve, which too few politicians have dared to support so far.

Dismantling Glass–Steagall

After four decades of relative banking sanity imposed by the Glass–Steagall Act, the big banks were eager to go back to their old ways of doing as they pleased. Stagflation in the 1970s presented the opportunity. The opening gambit began with the Federal Reserve raising interest rates, prompting the big banks to circumvent Regulation Q, which had placed a ceiling on interest rates following Glass–Steagall; they did so by establishing and expanding the so-called euro banks in offshore banking centers without limit on interest rates. In 1974, higher interest rates abroad began draining liquidity out of the United States, aggravating the US recession. Thus, the scrapping of

Regulation Q began tentatively in New England in 1974, the first step in the progressive dismantling of Glass–Steagall.

The sweeping blow to Regulation Q came when the Federal Reserve, under Paul Volker, raised interest rates to absurd levels, with fed funds peaking at 20 percent and the prime rate at 21.5 percent in June 1981.[203] Even before March 1981 when President Carter signed into law the liberalization of interest rates, Volker's high interest rate policy already made Regulation Q unsustainable. At a minimum, the Federal Reserve should have asked Congress for a temporary lifting of the interest rate ceiling, pending the return to interest rate normality. Today, one consequence of the scrapping of Regulation Q is that it legalized the punitive interest rates charged by payday loan sharks and credit card issuers.[204]

Between 1981 and 1986, the Depository Institutions Deregulation and Monetary Control Act of 1980 phased out the interest rate ceiling on all bank accounts, save demand deposits. This resulted in commercial banks biding funds away from savings and loan institutions (S&Ls), which had traditionally provided low-cost mortgage financing to the real estate sector. It precipitated a liquidity crisis for S&Ls, prompting them to call for extending the lifting of Regulation Q to them as well. However, the subsequent lifting of the interest rate ceiling was a death blow to S&Ls because it also removed the restrictions on commercial banks engaging in the mortgage business, permitting the big banks, with their lower costs of funds, to enjoy a decisive competitive advantage.

These measures produced the S&L crisis in the early 1990s, which wiped out the whole of the S&L sector, permanently extinguishing this source of competition to commercial banks.

Between 1984 and 1991, 1,400 S&Ls and 1,300 banks failed, mostly due to high interest rates and the progressive dismantling of banking regulations.[205] This rate of bank failure was alarming given it occurred in the absence of a depression and the number of banks was a fraction of their number in the 1930s. The Federal Reserve, despite playing a key role in the S&L debacle, did not extend a hand to the victims of its policies.

This bad experiment demonstrated that banking deregulation dramatically increased competition at first, followed by extensive bank failures and, ultimately, less competition and greater market concentration. Yet, the loss of all those financial institutions hardly dented the Federal Reserve's enthusiasm for more deregulation with predicable results: smaller banks folded while the big banks increased their market shares.

By 1999, a quarter-century of lobbying by the big banks and Fed support, culminated in Congress repealing what was left of Glass–Steagall. That same year, the Federal Reserve supported the passage of the Commodities Futures Modernization Act, ensuring that derivatives remained unregulated and setting the stage for devastating future predicaments.

Democracy and the Federal Reserve

As the elected representatives of the people, members of Congress are entrusted with powers that they should not surrender to private interests. Abraham Lincoln echoed this in his famous Gettysburg Address by saying "government of the people, by the people, for the people."[206] It is the foundation of democracy. Congress probably did not intend to break Lincoln's promise to the people by abdicating its financial powers to the Fed, but lost those powers gradually and covertly. The colossal monetary size of this congressional oversight and its constitutional violation is manifest proof that it should not continue.

The Federal Reserve System today, supported by the big banks, is sure of its economic supremacy. The Fed publication cited earlier spells out its powers: "It is considered an independent central bank because its monetary policy decisions do not have to be approved by the President or anyone else in the executive or legislative branches of government."[207] It does not take a constitutional lawyer to conclude this is a violation of democratic principles because it implies the Fed has unlimited powers and operates without democratic oversight. The Fed's mission statement, as it were, also circumvents the much-touted system of checks and balances in American democracy.

Ashvin Pandurangi warns about the Fed's considerable powers in his *Business Insider* article, "How Did a Single Unconstitutional Agency Become the Most Powerful Organization in America." Pandurangi notes that the President appoints the Fed's Board of Governors by choosing from a list of candidates provided by banks; the banks also get to choose the remaining five members of the Board of Governors.[208] He notes that "the members of the Fed's Board of Governors cannot be impeached by Congress" whereas even the President of the United States can be impeached for "high crimes and misdemeanors."[209] In effect, the Fed's Board of Governors have been given supreme immunity above everybody in the land. Without legal consequences, there is no legal assurance of the reliability of their testimonies before Congress, eliminating any residual effectiveness of congressional oversight of Federal Reserve activities.

Moreover, the Federal Reserve has blatantly kept Congress in the dark, making even any presumption of oversight hollow. An accident revealed the extent of Congressional marginalization. An amendment by Senator Bernie Sanders to the Wall Street reform law directed the Government Accountability Office (GAO) to conduct an audit of the Federal Reserve for the first time ever.[210]

A year later, Senator Sanders' exceptional dedication and diligence paid off. On July 21, 2011, Senator Sanders published a landmark article titled "The Fed Audit." It stated that the first top-to-bottom audit of the Federal Reserve "uncovered eye-popping new details about how the United States provided a whopping $16 trillion in secret loans to bail out American and foreign banks and businesses during the worst economic crisis since the Great Depression."[211]

Senator Sanders cited a July 2011 "Report to Congressional Addressees" by the GAO: "Among the investigation's key findings is that the Fed unilaterally provided trillions of dollars in financial assistance to foreign banks and corporations…"[212]

Senator Sanders further cited that the investigative arm of Congress determined, "…that the Fed lacks a comprehensive system to deal with conflicts of interest, despite the serious potential for abuse…. For example, the

CEO (chief executive officer) of JP Morgan Chase served on the New York Fed's board of directors at the same time that his bank received more than $390 billion in financial assistance from the Fed."

Senator Sanders further stated, "JP Morgan Chase, Morgan Stanley, and Wells Fargo also received trillions of dollars in Fed loans at near-zero interest rates." Senator Sanders further declared, "The Federal Reserve must be reformed to serve the needs of working families, not just CEOs on Wall Street."

This astronomical sum, $16 trillion in secret loans, is bewildering. It makes one wonder whether the Fed dwells in a world of alternative reality, where it presumes there is no government, or whether we are the dwellers of that world by presuming there is. Sixteen trillion dollars in 2011 is equivalent to several years of US government tax revenue; it is more than the output of the entire United States economy. It raises important questions, such as:

- Is this gargantuan sum recoverable?
- Will Congress pass an act to recover this money?
- Has any of this money been repaid and how much?

Lending $16 trillion at a negligible interest rate—below the interest that the Fed charges the Treasury on its bonds—is a colossal subsidy to the recipients and, as such, falls within the jurisdiction of fiscal policy, which, presumably, is still outside the scope of the Federal Reserve. Giant subsidies to foreign entities are tantamount to enormous gifts, allowing them to earn trillions of dollars effortlessly, without attracting US corporate income taxes. This is extraordinary Fed generosity with US taxpayers' money without the knowledge of Congress, the President, or the people.

A fraction of this sum would have been sufficient to solve all the problems of the mortgage borrowers and homelessness in the United States; but alas, critical social issues are not on the agenda of the Federal Reserve.

Prior to this government audit, the Federal Reserve's annual reports had made no mention of any $16 trillion, bringing into question the relevance of the Federal Reserve annual reports and the dependability of its auditors. Predictably, the new Fed Chair Janet Yellen has reportedly objected to a new audit of the Fed.[213]

Those covert subsidies aside, the Federal Reserve's charter does not authorize it to grant subsidies, however small, to anyone, yet it has been openly providing giant subsidies to its shareholders, the banks. The trillions of dollars in so-called "quantitative easing" are, in reality, hundreds of billions of dollars in annual interest subsidies to the big banks, without the requisite congressional vote on the matter, thereby bypassing Congress altogether. Yet, fiscal matters such as subsidies are still the responsibility of Congress, at least in appearance.

The banks, not satisfied that the Federal Reserve has acquired unlimited monetary powers, have stealthily crossed the Rubicon to assume unlimited powers over the fiscal purse strings as well. Congress, having lost its monetary powers, has discovered by sheer chance that a private central bank, controlled by the banks, has been exercising sweeping fiscal powers. Unelected bankers in charge of the Federal Reserve have been appropriating the economic powers of Congress, dwarfing the power of the state to become the supreme economic power in the United States, a problem compounded by their demonstrable economic incompetence and extreme egotism. In other words, the banks, through the Fed, are now more powerful than the combined power of the President and Congress, a sad development for democracy. The future may yet hold worse surprises.

Thus, the independence of the Federal Reserve, in addition to the damage it has been inflicting on the US economy, has been undermining democracy in the United States of America. Clearly, democracy and a private central bank cannot coexist. The prime threat to democracy is no longer the military-industrial complex, as President Eisenhower famously warned, but rather the Federal Reserve–banking complex. Senator Bernie Sanders's conclusion that "[the] Federal Reserve must be reformed" is a watershed. As the epicenter of usury, it is remarkable how what started as a usurious immorality has initiated a chain of immoral finance, immoral economics, and immoral politics, culminating in the hijacking of democracy itself. It is high time Congress heeded the advice of Professor Milton Friedman by abolishing the Federal Reserve. The alternative is to accept the current political system of the United States: a banking dictatorship with democratic paraphernalia. The United States desperately needs a revitalized economy, which is not going to happen without reforming its democracy, which in turn requires restricting the power of the ultra-rich to the economic sphere.

Looking back, we realize that the birth of the Federal Reserve on Christmas Eve, 1913, was more ominous than anyone could have imagined.

Part IV

CYCLICALITY, MARKET AND PUBLIC SECTOR
INEFFICIENCY, AND DEMOCRACY

Eleven

AMPLIFIED BUSINESS CYCLES

Long run is a misleading guide to current affairs. In the long run we are all dead.[214]

John Maynard Keynes

Chapter 4 already discussed certain aspects of economic cycles, making it unnecessary to repeat it here. Economic cycles are a natural phenomenon, occurring even in the absence of pro-cyclical human intervention. Consider sunspots. Their intensity on the sun's surface fluctuates over an approximately eleven-year cycle.[215] Peak sunspot activity increases the gravitational pull of the sun and disturbs the fragile gravitational balance on the earth's crust, sparking an increase in volcanic activity. The increased spewing of millions of tons of volcanic ash, smog, and dust into the stratosphere slightly blocks the sun's rays for a year or two. The haze cools the earth's atmosphere, perhaps by as much as 1°C, thereby reducing water evaporation and rainfall.[216] The drop in precipitation can range from mild, with only a slight decline in agricultural yields, to drastic, resulting in droughts and even famines. Consequently, agricultural prices could rise moderately or sharply.

Indeed, severe droughts can propel more than spirited inflation. History is replete with examples of droughts causing famines, wars, and

187

mass migrations, including one that reportedly thrusted the Mongol Empire onto the world, to become the largest empire in history.[217] Apparently, a major volcanic eruption in Iceland also preceded the French Revolution; the drought that ensued drove the hungry French farmers to rebel.

In addition, there are manmade cycles. Joseph Schumpeter's creative destruction theory attributed major economic cycles to entrepreneurs undertaking large investments to supply products that incorporate new inventions and innovations, thereby spurring economic growth. In addition, changes in tastes, optimism, and pessimism can affect private consumption and investment, and therefore economic cycles. Regrettably, inappropriate government fiscal, monetary, and foreign policies are probably the largest factor in amplifying economic cyclicality, such as a restrictive monetary policy during a contraction, an abrupt cut in military spending at the end of a war without a compensating expansion in civilian public expenditure, or a distant war spiking oil prices.

Economic Cycles as Externalities

The unified theory of macroeconomic failure considers economic contractions negative externalities requiring government intervention. Keynes also treated the Great Depression as a negative externality, but without labeling it as such. The cause of recession or depression is frequently a shortfall in aggregate demand, which the private sector, on its own, cannot offset in a reasonable time, if at all. Given the slack in the economy during a contraction, government expenditure on infrastructure, for example, is much more stimulative than the actual amount spent due to the feedback from the so-called multiplier effect in stimulating consumption, employment, and aggregate demand. Consumption in particular has a large impact on economic activity, given that in the United States, for example, it represents about two thirds of the gross domestic product (GDP). The increase in aggregate demand also improves capacity utilization, and with economies of scale, improves profitability, business confidence, and, therefore, the prospects for new private investments, which together spur the economy to further expansion. A recovery in asset prices also has a wealth effect that prompts a mild increase in consumption.

The public benefits from the fiscal stimulus of investing in infrastructure include the new infrastructure itself, the reduction in unemployment and social security disbursements due to increased employment, the increase in tax revenue due to increased economic activity, as well as all the benefits accruing to the private sector from the economic expansion. Taken together, these far exceed the social cost of the new infrastructure. Accordingly, the slack in the economy during a contraction makes the public benefits from public expenditure, on say infrastructure, exceed its cost, hence, the existence of an externality during a contraction.

The critical element in the foregoing analysis is the presence of economic slack, which implies public expenditure is not displacing or competing with private expenditure but rather stimulating it. It also implies that temporary stimulation that is limited to taking up some of the slack in the economy does not cause the economy to overheat, with only mild inflationary effects, if any. The foregoing also implies that the stimulative element of public expenditure must taper off as the economy recovers, to avoid displacing the private sector and forestalling the potential inflationary effects of excessive aggregate demand. Thus, as the economic slack disappears, so does the cyclical externality.

Similarly, an inflationary expansion is a negative cyclical externality too because excessive aggregate demand exceeds the capacity of the economy to deliver, calling for demand restraint by curtailing monetary expansion and postponing noncritical infrastructure to avoid displacing the private sector.

Given the foregoing, by implication, any measure that causes or amplifies cyclicality is itself a negative externality, as in the case of debt.[218] The other factors that amplify cyclicality include the withholding of fiscal stimulus during a down turn and the non-curtailment of stimulative measures during an expansion.

War as an Endogenous Variable

Given the present decisive influence of business over government decisions, it is inappropriate to classify government decisions as exogenous. Therefore, to pin down the role of economic actors, including governments, in precipitating or smoothing economic cycles, one needs to define endogenous variables as those generated within a political and economic system, and the truly exogenous as those generated outside that system.

Accordingly, war is an endogenous variable for the country that initiates it, but exogenous for the defending country and the rest of the world. This is a stricter definition than the prevalent one. Economists have traditionally classified all wars and threats of war as exogenous variables, disregarding that it is an endogenous decision to the party that initiates it. Similarly, if a country initiates economic sanctions, boycotts, or other measures that threaten the vital interests of another country, compelling the latter to respond militarily, then war in that case is an endogenous variable for the initiator of such measures, rather than the initiator of actual hostilities.

Thus, war can be either exogenous or endogenous, depending on the initiator of the chain reaction that leads to war. In most cases, making this classification is easy enough, although, at times, as with World War I, the sequence of events is complex, making a clear distinction difficult.

Surges in oil prices since the 1970s have all been associated with war, or the threat of war, in the Middle East.[219] Thus, the Arab-Israeli War (1973), the Iraq-Iran War (1980–1988), the First Gulf War (1990–1991), the September 11 events in 2001 followed by the War on Afghanistan (2001–present), the War on Iraq (2003–2011), and the perceived threat of an American attack on Iran in 2007 all resulted in spikes in oil prices. Since the 1970s, spikes in the oil price have preceded and contributed to all recessions. Thus, the 2007 oil price spike slowed the economy, while the rise in interest rates brought forward the simmering crisis in sub-mortgages, tipping the economy into the Great Recession of 2008. Hence, for most countries around the world, the recessions they experienced were frequently the result of exogenous variables. However, to the extent that the United States encouraged, facilitated, waged, or threatened war, resulting in an oil spike followed by a US recession, it was the result of an endogenous US policy variable. This approach has the advantage of illuminating the impact of foreign policy decisions on economic activity and assigning economic responsibility for its consequences.

Credit Cycles

The Wall Street crash in 1929 followed by the Great Depression, surprised Irving Fisher (1867–1947) because he had expected the boom to continue.

Two Centuries of Parasitic Economics

Although Fisher was a neoclassical economist, the Great Depression convinced him that debt creation induces economic expansion and fuels asset bubbles, while credit contraction bursts them, followed by recession or depression. Regrettably, Fisher had not foreseen the Great Depression and, for a while, continued to doubt it was underway although it was becoming self-evident. This undermined his credibility and limited the attention given to his seminal work *Debt-deflation theory*, published in 1933.[220]

However, since the 1980s, Fisher's theory has enjoyed a comeback among mainstream post-Keynesian economists like Hyman Minsky, who developed it further, while Steve Keen (b. 1953) modeled Minsky's financial instability mathematically.[221] Alas, Fisher offered no structural solution to the problem of credit and indebtedness, such as replacing usurious financing to dampen the amplitude of economic cycles.

Clearly, heavy doses of credit expansion fuel speculative asset price bubbles, which ultimately burst to trigger financial crises and painful contractions. Cycles with markedly different degrees of indebtedness have occurred since 1929. The best-publicized debt-driven contractions include the Great Depression, the twin Volker recessions in the early 1980s, the Internet bubble in 2000, and the sub-prime crisis in 2008. It is economically less disruptive and more efficient to have longer and gentler expansions and shallower contractions, along with smoother instead of violent fluctuations in asset prices (e.g., stocks, bonds, properties).

The following presents aspects of Fisher's credit expansion-contraction cycle with some elaboration:

1. Excessive expansion of housing credit fuels higher house prices. This attracts speculative demand and expands housing construction, employment, and consumption. Ultimately, an excess in housing inventory builds, followed by tumbling house prices, housing credit, housing construction, employment, and consumption.

2. Credit expansion also amplifies the cycle in stock prices. For example, a 50 percent margin policy permits the doubling of the size of stock portfolios on credit, lifting stock prices. Higher stock prices increase the equity of stock accounts with brokers, providing more

margin borrowing and purchasing power, which feeds the cycle of stock purchases followed by higher stock prices and a further boost to margin availability. At some point, the market tops and begins to decline, inducing the cycle to work in reverse as a price-credit contraction cycle. Lower stock prices diminish the market value of the stock portfolios, triggering margin maintenance calls, which require investors to liquidate stocks to maintain credit margins, pushing prices lower and so on. Thus, borrowing on margin exaggerates the rise and fall of stock prices.

3. The availability of credit induces speculative, herd behavior, which exacerbates investment performance. Credit availability increases as stock prices rise, facilitating more purchases at higher prices. As a result, margin availability and maximum portfolio positions peak near market tops. On the other hand, credit availability contracts as stock prices fall, inducing stock selling at lower prices. Hence, minimum stock positions coincide with minimum credit availability near market bottoms.

In other words, margin finance results in the worst investment strategy imaginable because it violates the cardinal rule of shrewd investing: buy low and sell high. Instead, it finances and, subsequently, enforces an irrational investment strategy: buy high and sell low. Record stock turnover around market peaks and bottoms supports this conclusion. Moreover, this naïve investment strategy, enforced by credit availability, gives astute investors the opportunity to act as counterparties, by selling at high prices and buying at low prices, thereby significantly increasing their return. The credit cycle has a similar negative effect on the performance of many investors in other asset classes as well.

To protect the investing public, regulators should ban margin credit for stocks. Failing that, regulators should require margin availability to peak at say 50 percent after a market correction of 40 percent or more and for the margin availability to decline gradually to zero as the market recovers to say 90 percent of its previous high. This mechanical rule would permit purchasing more stocks at lower prices and enforce credit repayment and progressive selling at higher prices, thereby harnessing the markets' speculative tendency to rise and fall to improve the public's investment performance. Such a policy also has the added advantage of making stock cycles gentler.

4. Debt artificially inflates asset prices and investors' wealth, inducing them to boost their consumption as markets rise. When the bubble bursts, debt works in reverse, excessively reducing wealth and consumption. Thus, the credit cycle amplifies the wealth effect on consumption, thereby indirectly amplifying cyclical fluctuation.

5. Bankers tend to relax credit standards during an expansion, thereby accelerating the pace of expansion, as well as its premature end. In contrast, during a recession, when credit is dear, bankers become cautious and raise their credit standards, making a recession deeper than it would be otherwise. These pro-cyclical credit policies increase the amplitude of cycles.

6. Easy credit finances excessive business investment during the expansion phase, resulting—during the contraction phase—in greater excess capacity, larger investment cutbacks, heavy indebtedness, and increased business failures.

7. Monetary authorities tend to misjudge the state of the economy. During an upturn, they tend to delay raising interest rates and then raise it too high and too fast. During a downturn, they tend to delay cutting interest rates and then cut them but not enough. Both effects tend to amplify cyclical swings.

8. National debt is also pro-cyclical. During an expansion, national debt facilitates more government spending than is available based on its tax revenue, thereby exaggerating the expansion. During a recession, the deficit becomes too big, inducing banks to lobby the government to adopt austerity, consequently making the recession deeper.

The heavy indebtedness of other countries further amplifies this effect. Thus, after decades of debt-financed overspending, excessive national debts have prompted the governments of Greece, Italy, Portugal, Spain, Ireland, Hungary, Britain, France, and other nations to cut their budgets in the depth of contractions. As a result,

they are facing widespread unemployment, unrest, deteriorating social services, and larger budget deficits, while their national debts
continue to spiral out of control.

9. When the debt burden becomes too heavy, it seeds public unrest
and prompts governments to resort to the printing press. Inflation
torches debt denominated in domestic currencies, which adds another source of economic and political instability. On the other
hand, the repudiation of debt denominated in foreign currencies
can reduce the debt burden as well as potentially trigger threats to
national sovereignty by powerful foreign creditor nations.

Stages of a Business Cycle

The progressive replacement of Keynesianism by neoclassical macroeconomics made monetary policy the primary macroeconomic instrument
and relegated fiscal policy to a secondary role. Hence, business cycles
have undergone significant changes since the early 1980s. Cycles share
many common characteristics, nevertheless, each has its own unique fin-
gerprints. In practice, the stages of a cycle tend to overlap, blurring the
transition from one stage to the next and only becoming clear in retrospect. Moreover, depending on the cycle, some developments might appear sooner and others later than usual. On average, the recovery and
expansion phases last approximately four times as long as the crisis and
recession phases, although this too varies considerably from one cycle to
the next. The following is a general outline of the stages of a business cycle
that is not overwhelmed by a dramatic event such as an oil crisis, a financial crisis, or war:

(a) *Recovery*: The stock market, consumer confidence, production,
profits, and investments rise while inventory-to-sales ratio, unemployment, and bankruptcies fall, and inflation and interest rates remain low.

(b) *Expansion*: The stock market, consumer confidence, production, investments, profits, and employment peak while inventory-to-sales ratio, inflation, and interest rates continue to rise and bankruptcies hit bottom.

(c) *Crisis*: The stock market crashes and consumer confidence, production, investments, and profits fall while unemployment and bankruptcies rise and inventory-to-sales ratio, inflation, and interest rates peak.

(d) *Recession*: The stock prices, consumer confidence, production, investment, profits, inflation, and interest rates hit bottom, inventory-to-sales ratio stops deteriorating while unemployment and bankruptcies peak.

The following paragraphs provide a more detailed presentation of the stages of a business cycle, starting with the recovery phase.

The impetus to a recovery could be a fiscal stimulus. The private sector begins to feel it when inventories prove too low to meet demand, with the loss of sales inducing managements to expand production to raise their inventory-to-sales ratio to a more customary level. Incremental expansions in production encourage managements to increase working hours, followed by rehiring. Exogenous stimulative factors may also come into play, such as falling prices of imported raw materials, including oil, due to a fall in international demand or an increase in supply.[222]

As sales improve, a sense that the worst of the economic crisis is past gradually replaces the gloom, followed by guarded optimism and then a budding cheerfulness. Previously cautious consumers, who worried about becoming unemployed and postponed the purchase of durable goods, begin to spend, taking advantage of discounted prices and low interest rates. Revived business confidence encourages businesses that had earmarked funds for fixed investments, but had been waiting for a sign of an uptick in the economy, to begin replacing obsolete plants and equipment. In parallel, the multiplier effect generates a virtuous cycle, whereby rising consumption prompts production expansion, increasing employment, incomes, profits, and business investments, leading to further increases in consumption.

Gradually, the economy moves to the second stage of the cycle, the expansion phase. Certainty about a brighter tomorrow replaces hesitancy. Cheerful sentiments become contagious. Stock prices register big jumps, delighting investors, and they begin to throw caution to the wind. Margin borrowing provides further fuel to the rise in the stock market. In turn, higher stock prices make more margin debt possible, driving stock prices higher still, in euphoric cycles of self-realized expectations that sow the seeds of a speculative bubble. At the same time, rising asset prices increase wealth, which stimulates consumption (the wealth effect). Firm demand develops for housing and durable goods, such as furniture, white goods, and cars. The economic expansion gathers momentum and continues for two to three years, or longer. Plant utilization approaches its capacity limits, prompting new investments; unemployment falls, the labor market tightens, and wages rise.

With the faster tempo of the economy, inflation picks up, prompting the central bank to tighten monetary policy and raise interest rates. As monetary policy becomes tighter, the business outlook dims. Stock prices peak and then begin to slide.

When the economy slides into the third stage of a cycle, the crisis phase, doubt steadily replaces optimism, until the public mood turns cautious. Some enterprises, in anticipation of a slowing economy, begin to conserve cash by postponing investments and hiring, and reducing inventories. The rise in interest rates produces crashes in asset prices, including stocks, bonds, houses, and commercial property. Falling asset prices and shrinking wealth induce cutbacks in consumption. The sale of houses and durable goods falters. A generalized weakness in demand triggers falls in production, profits, and employment. In parallel, the multiplier works in reverse, turning the initial fall in economic activity into a self-feeding process.

During the recession phase, pessimism, gloom, and negative business news dominate. Corporate profits shrink or turn to losses, unemployment peaks, bankruptcies abound, and mortgage repossessions become commonplace. Lower interest rates fail to stimulate new investment. Oddly, in the midst of the deep gloom, and before any noticeable recovery in economic activity, stock prices stabilize and begin to crawl higher.

United States Cyclical Contractions (1785–2009)

With the proviso that early statistical data was less reliable and less detailed, in the 224 years between 1785 and 2009, the United States experienced forty-nine economic cycles. The data shows that US cycles underwent major change after 1941. Accordingly, it was logical to split US economic cycles into two groups, with January 1, 1942, for a cutoff date, as follows:

1. Table 11.1 covers the period from 1785 to 1941
2. Table 11.2 covers the period from 1942 to 2009

The final row of each table is important because it provides a summary about the cycles and their contractions during the period concerned. Table 11.1 shows that during the first period there were thirty-seven cycles. Of these, twenty-three were credit crises, with at least some of the following characteristics: rising interest rate, credit contraction, the burst of a speculative bubble, a market crash, panic, bank failures, and deflation. This confirms Fisher's diagnosis that credit contractions were a major cause of recessions and depressions. The remaining fourteen contractions had various causes including falls in aggregate demand, peace recessions following the end of hostilities, and trade restrictions imposed by Great Britain. The final row of Table 11.1 also reveals that during the era of classical and neoclassical macroeconomics and *laissez-faire,* cycles were shorter and contractions were longer and deeper.

TABLE 11.1

U.S. Contractions under Classical & Neoclassical Macroeconomics, 1785-1941

Contraction Years	Primary Cause	Duration in Years	Economic Contraction	Unemployment Peak	Year	Inflation Peak	Year	Inflation Low	Year
1785-1788	Debt Contraction	4.0							
1789-1793	Coinage Debasement	4.0							
1796-1799	Property Bubble, Panic	3.0							
1802-1804	Peace Recession	2.0							
1807-1810	U.K. Embargo	3.0							
1812	Mild Recession	0.5							
1815-1821	Bank Failures, Bubble	6.0							
1822-1823	Commodity Deflation	1.0							
1825-1826	Bank Failures, Bubble	1.0							
1828-1829	U.K. Trade Prohibition	1.0							
1833-1834	Mild Recession	1.0							
1836-1838	Bank Failures, Deflation	2.0	-32.8%						
1839-1843	Massive Deflation	4.0	-34.3%						
1845-1846	Mild Recession	1.0	-5.9%						
1847-1848	Financial Crisis, Bubble	1.0	-19.7%						
1853-1854	Rise in Interest Rates	1.0	-18.4%						
1857-1858	Bank Failures, Bubble	1.5	-23.1%						
1860-1861	Recession	0.7	-14.5%						
1865-1867	Post Civil War Deflation	2.7	-23.8%						
1869-1870	Bank Panic	1.6	-9.7%						
1873-1879	Bank Failures, Deflation	5.4	-30.5%						
1882-1885	Fall in Rail Invest., Panic	3.2	-32.8%						
1887-1888	Fall in Rail Investment	1.1	-14.6%						
1890-1891	Bank Panic	0.8	-22.1%						
1893-1894	Railway Failure, Panic	1.4	-37.3%						
1895-1897	Bank Panic, Deflation	1.5	-25.2%						
1899-1900	Recession	1.5	-15.5%						
1902-1904	Stock Market Crash	1.9	-16.2%						
1907-1908	Bank Panic	1.1	-29.2%						
1910-1911	Deflation	2.0	-14.7%						
1913-1814	Aggregate Demand Fall	1.9	-25.9%						
1918-1919	Post WWI Recession	0.6	-24.5%			17.8%	1917	0.9%	1915
1920-1921	Inflation Then Deflation	1.5	-38.1%			15.9%	1920	-10.9%	1921
1923-1924	Aggregate Demand Fall	1.2	-25.4%			1.8%	1923	-6.1%	1922
1926-1927	Ford Model T Switch	1.1	-12.2%			2.4%	1925	-1.9%	1927
1929-1933	Bubble, Panic, Trade	3.6	-26.7%	24.9%	1933	0.0%	1929	-10.3%	1932
1937-1938	Tight Economic Policies	1.1	-18.2%	19.0%	1938	3.7%	1937	-2.1%	1938
37 Cycles	Avg. Duration 4.2 Yrs.	2.0	-22.7%	-	-	-	-	-	-

U.S. recessions data source (Excl. inflation): http://en.wikipedia.org/wiki/List_of_recessions_in_the_United_States

Inflation data source: http://inflationdata.com/Inflation/Inflation_Rate/HistoricalInflation.aspx#table

Table 11.2 (1942 to 2009) illustrates the structural change to the US economy, starting in 1942. The final row of Table 11.2 shows that on average cycles became longer, lasting 5.7 years compared to 4.2 years, contractions became shorter, lasting only 0.9 years compared to 2.0 years, and shallower at -2.2 percent instead of -22.7 percent of GDP.

TABLE 11.2

U.S. Contractions under Keynesian and Neoclassical Macroeconomics, 1942-2009

Contraction Years	Primary Cause	Duration in Years	Economic Contraction	Unemployment Peak	Unemployment Year	Inflation Peak	Inflation Year	Inflation Low	Inflation Year
1945	WWII Peace Recession	0.7	-1.7%	5.2%	1946	6.0%	1943	1.6%	1944
1949	Monetary Tightening	0.9	-1.7%	7.9%	1949	14.7%	1947	-1.0%	1949
1953	Monetary Tightening	0.8	-2.6%	6.1%	1954	7.9%	1951	82.0%	1953
1958	Monetary Tightening	0.7	-3.7%	7.5%	1958	3.3%	1957	-0.3%	1955
1960-1961	Monetary Tightening	0.8	-1.6%	7.1%	1961	1.5%	1960	1.0%	1959
1969-1970	Monetary Tightening	0.9	-0.6%	6.1%	1970	5.8%	1970	1.2%	1962
1973-1975	Oil Crisis, Stagflation	1.3	-3.2%	9.0%	1975	11.0%	1974	3.3%	1972
1980	Interest Rates	0.5	-2.2%	7.8%	1980	13.6%	1980	5.8%	1976
1981-1982	Oil Prices, Interest Rates	1.3	-2.7%	10.8%	1982	10.4%	1981	6.2%	1982
1990-1991	Oil Prices	0.7	-1.4%	7.8%	1992	5.4%	1990	1.9%	1986
2001	Dot.Com Bubble, 9/11	0.7	-0.3%	6.3%	2003	3.4%	2000	1.6%	1998
2007-2009	Credit-Housing Bubbles	1.5	-4.3%	10.0%	2009	3.4%	2005	3.9%	2008
12 Cycles	Avg. Duration 5.7 Yrs.	0.9	-2.2%	7.6%	-	-	-	-	-

U.S. recessions data source (Excl. inflation): http://en.wikipedia.org/wiki/List_of_recessions_in_the_United_States

Inflation data source: http://inflationdata.com/Inflation/Inflation_Rate/HistoricalInflation.aspx#table

The interesting question is what brought about this structural change in the business cycle? The Federal Reserve was not the reason because between its establishment in 1913 and 1942, there were three very severe financial crises, including the Great Depression, as Table 1.1 reveals. Moreover, since 1942, there have been twelve contractions. Nine resulted from tight monetary policy (including the Great Recession in 2008, brought about by monetary tightening and a spike in the oil price); a sharp spike in the oil price triggered two recessions, and one was due to the end of World War II hostilities. Thus, the roots of most economic contractions remained monetary, despite the Federal Reserve. Therefore, we can safely conclude that the Federal Reserve did not engineer the milder cycles.

Indeed, the structural change points to two factors. The adoption of Keynesian countercyclical aggregate demand management made contractions briefer and shallower. The other factor was the increased share of US government in GDP, following the adoption of the welfare state. This diminished the effect of the cyclical fluctuations in private demand on the overall economy, thereby dampening overall cyclical fluctuations. Hence, the neoclassical rallying cry for a smaller government is misplaced and inconsistent with economic facts because shrinking the public sector would increase economic volatility, prolong and deepen contractions, and make them more frequent; the severity and frequency of the pre-1942 cycles attest to this.

Moreover, the reversion to neoclassical policies since 1979 shrank the role of fiscal policy and increased the role of monetary policy. Predictably, it amplified economic fluctuations. This countertrend began with the launch of very tight monetary policy of Fed Chairman Paul Volker, producing two grim recessions in quick succession. During the second recession in 1981–1982, peak unemployment exceeded that reached in the first oil crises of 1973–1975. This tendency for magnified cyclicality culminated in the Great Recession.

Neoclassical economic policies increased economic instability further by deregulating banking, spawning financial bubbles and financial crises, including the savings-and-loan debacle in the early 1990s, the Internet bubble in 2001, and the sub-prime crisis in 2007–2009, with unemployment rising to very high levels in the latest contraction. In fact, these crises were probably far worse than the official statistics suggest because in the 1980s the US government changed the statistical definitions of unemployment and inflation, thereby understating their levels compared to earlier definitions.

In conclusion, for one-and-a-half centuries, until 1942, economic contractions—particularly financial crises—gravely disrupted US economic life. The situation improved markedly following the adoption of Keynesian economics and the welfare state. Economic cycles and the state of Western economies began to deteriorate again starting in 1980, mirroring the progressive reintroduction of neoclassical policies.

Twelve

PRIVATE SECTOR INEFFICIENCY: COMPETITION
AND INFORMATION QUALITY

*...a purely capitalistic society, without any type of
regulation at all, you will get one monopoly that
will eat all of the smaller fish and own everything,
and then you'll have zero capitalism...*[223]

Serj Tankian

The unified theory of macroeconomic failure considers monopolies and poor quality information negative externalities requiring government intervention and correction. This chapter discusses the negative externalities that cause market failures in the private sector. In the first part, it considers two negative market externalities: monopolies and monopsonies and *chronic underconsumption*, a negative externality that is a consequence of monopsony. The rest of the chapter focuses on the impact of other negative externalities on economic efficiency, mostly the result of moral failures causing poor quality of information. The next chapter looks at the economic failure of public policy, typically traceable to the failure of the political marketplace.

In addition, efficient markets require rational and efficient financing and taxation, which Part V explores.

Monopolies and Oligopolies

Let us begin by clarifying that the term 'monopolies' here and subsequently refers to all forms of restriction of trade including monopoly, duopoly, oligopoly, cartels, and trusts on the demand side and monopsony on the supply side.

Adam Smith, in his seminal *Wealth of Nations,* recognized that self-interest, free markets, and competition would lower prices and benefit society. However, he also anticipated that businesses would prefer monopolies to maximize prices and profits and that they would conspire to sway politicians and legislation accordingly. His analysis was on the mark.

The quotation at the beginning of this chapter provides interesting insight into monopoly; it is all the more remarkable because its author is a musician, not a professional economist. It hints at a theoretical similarity between parasitic capitalism and communism because the absence of regulation fosters monopoly with a theoretical limit of a single monopolist encompassing the whole economy and, therefore, the state—precisely the communist model. Thus, at some abstract level, both systems have the potential to arrive at the same ultimate destination despite starting from opposite directions. Incidentally, this also provides a conceptual explanation of why the capitalist system becomes less efficient as the share of monopoly elements in GDP increases because its similarity to the inefficient nonmarket Marxist model increases.

Parasitic capitalism seeks to earn above average, parasitic, profit by restricting competition, through monopolies on the sales side and monopsonies on the purchases side of the market equation. Monopolies, our focus in this section, maximize their profit by restricting supply and raising prices. Lack of competition permits the gouging of consumers and the government, artificially their costs. The difference between the price charged by a monopolist and a normal competitive price represents a negative externality caused by this market failure, which is typically irreparable without government intervention. Government intervention could take the form of increasing competition by breaking up monopolies, duopolies, oligopolies and cartels. In the case of natural monopolies such as utilities, railways, ports, airports, stock exchanges, central banks, and the like, increasing competition is not an economically viable option; in such cases government intervention could take the form of price regulation or outright nationalization.

Thus, the United States Congress passed three landmark antitrust laws to promote fair competition and stop the gouging of consumers by regulating markets and breaking up and preventing monopolies. These laws were the Sherman Act in 1890, the Clayton Act in 1914, and the Federal Trade Commission Act in 1914. Congress recognized the economic inefficiency of unregulated markets and these acts were a capitalist solution to a capitalist problem.

However, since the 1980s the *counter-revolution* has been dismantling the barriers to bigger oligopolies in many industries, including banking.[224] It claimed market deregulations promoted competition and efficiency, whereas in reality it unleashed predatory competition, which eliminated weaker and smaller competitors through insolvencies, mergers, and acquisitions, increasing the market share of parasitic oligopolies in the US economy.[225] In addition, the *counter-revolution* in several Western countries privatized natural monopolies such as stock exchanges, airports, ports, and railways, as well as the progressive privatization of national health and education, resulting in far costlier services, among other negative developments.

In many sectors, oligopolies are now drawing billions of dollars through wasteful and overpriced government contracts. The US military budget exceeds the combined military spending of the next eight countries.[226] However, it is not nearly as effective as the combined forces of those countries. American agricultural oligopolies in fertilizers and seeds and wasteful federal subsidies to biofuels from corn increase the cost of food and contribute to world hunger. Big banks have increased their market shares and their operations now encompass all financial services, at significant explicit and implicit costs to the public.

Let us illustrate the social cost of uncompetitive markets with an example. American medical services are far costlier, but deliver inferior outcomes, compared to those of Japan. In 2008, US per capita healthcare costs averaged $7,437—about three times that of Japan at $2,750, yet infant mortality in the United States was about 2.7 times that of Japan.[227] This result is typical of many industries, which is symptomatic of a lack of competition and parasitic pricing.

Greed and price gouging by the US pharmaceutical industry recently triggered a public outcry, as one company attempted to hike the price of its drug, Daraprim, used by AIDS patients by 5000 percent. Hillary Clinton, a democratic presidential candidate, strongly complained about the price gouging. Soon after, on September 22, 2015, Forbes magazine published an article indicating that this extreme price hike is not unique to this drug company, providing other examples of price gouging by US pharmaceutical companies: [228]

- Fentanyl Citrate, a generic painkiller, jumped 6,500 percent between 2010 and 2015
- Doxycycline, an antibiotic, jumped 6,300 percent
- Albuterol Sulfate, an asthma drug, jumped more than 3,400 percent
- Captopril, a generic blood pressure medication, jumped 2,700 percent

These examples are dramatic demonstrations of the rise in social and private costs because of lack of competition, frequently the result of deregulation of markets and increased market concentration, mostly through mergers and acquisitions.

Monopsony in the Labor Market

Like monopolies, monopsony is a means of earning parasitic profits, but on the supply side of the market equation. Monopsony is a market situation where there is a single buyer for a product or service and many sellers. It is most noticeable in the labor market. It is a market failure and negative externality for the same reason that monopoly is, except that wages are too low instead of the prices of goods too high. Lack of competition among employers permits them to underpay labor. The difference between the wages paid by monopsonists and normal competitive wages in a balanced competitive setting indicates the extent of the negative externality.

Although formal monopsony in the labor market does not exist with multiple employers hiring workers, nevertheless, capitalists, acting together, formally or informally, can exploit labor by minimizing wages, resulting in mass poverty. To realize patristic profits, most firms have no qualms about paying labor a small fraction of its marginal product. Fair wages require business and labor to have comparable bargaining powers. Even under perfect competition, never mind imperfect or oligopolistic competition, there are too few employers in relation to the number of workers. Hence, labor's inherently weak negotiating position makes it imperative to have strong labor unions and a reasonable minimum wage for a more level playing field. Without strong labor unions, labor income will continue to deteriorate due to a weak negotiating position, immigration, and the social security tax; the latter favors the systematic displacement of labor by automation and robotics.[229] Businesses who welcome rapid and extensive automation overlook the fact that robots are not consumers.

In the 1930s, wages were meager and poverty was widespread. This prompted some Western countries to support more balanced and fairer wage negotiations by licensing trade unions. President Roosevelt's New Deal legalized unions, but in the midst of the Great Depression, its benefit to labor was marginal. Business interests fiercely attacked unionization on economic grounds and when that failed to convince labor, it resorted to a range of illegal union-busting methods, including outright violence.[230]

Following World War II, unionization, higher wages, better working conditions, and welfare significantly curtailed labor exploitation; the rise in labor purchasing power helped bring about the business boom in the 1950s and 1960s, faster growth, and political stability.

The Thatcher-Reagan *counter-revolution* tweaked labor laws, undermined unions, increased immigration despite rising unemployment thereby obstructing the growth in real wages, diminished competition in the goods and services markets, and permitted the minimum wage in real terms to fall below the subsistence level. This is in contravention of what President Franklin Roosevelt wanted the minimum wage to mean, namely, a living wage. The high interest rate policy in the 1980s accentuated the chronic dollar overvaluation, thereby eroding US industrial competitiveness and the best paying labor jobs.

An example of monopsony practices is that of a giant retailer with billions in annual profits yet it only pays a minimum wage and flouts labor laws by classifying a large percentage of its work force as temporary workers to avoid paying them the benefits they are entitled to by law, without objection from the Department of Labor. This subnormal cost structure saddles local authorities with the cost of bringing the incomes of those employees to the poverty line, in effect compelling hardworking taxpayers to subsidize the operations and profits of the giant retailer. It also drives small competitors out of business for miles around its new outlets.

Moreover, game theory suggests that if large and unscrupulous employers only pay a meager wage, then even moral employers become compelled to follow suit to avoid becoming uncompetitive. Hence, unchecked immoral practices, like debasing the currency, become the norm.

The law has defined the poverty line as the minimum income necessary to cover living essentials. Hence, a minimum wage below the poverty line should be illegal because of its inhumanity; it also constitutes a drain on the public purse at a time when local, state, and federal authorities are incurring large deficits.

The official unemployment figures understate real unemployment and disregard underemployment. It excludes millions of potential job seekers who have lost all hope of finding decent-paying jobs commensurate with their skills. High unemployment has weakened labor's negotiating position. Hence, to curtail labor exploitation, improve labor purchasing power, and limit the drain on the public purse, the federal government needs to raise the minimum wage and support unions in order to have balanced labor negotiations.

Two Centuries of Parasitic Economics

A 2013 study by the Center for Economic and Policy Research suggested that, if the minimum wage had kept pace with productivity gains, by 2013, it would have reached $21.72 per hour.[231] Such a major revision to the minimum wage would be a positive development, but it should be gradual—to permit the economy to adjust smoothly. The expected benefits include a reduction in unemployment, faster economic growth, a rise in corporate profits, a fall in crime, and a major reduction in deficits.

One argument against a higher minimum wage is that it could trigger profit-push inflation by oligopolies. The way to counter this is to increase competition by breaking up oligopolies.

Another argument presented by the media against raising the minimum wage is that it would be detrimental to small businesses. This argument is baseless because it looks at one side of the equation only, namely, the cost side. To the extent that the resultant increase in labor's purchasing power increases the demand for products and services supplied by small businesses relative to large businesses, then on balance, small businesses will enjoy a rise in their profit; moreover, the multiplier effect would significantly increase the benefits to all businesses.

Yet another argument is that a higher minimum wage would hurt exporters and import-substituting industries. To the extent that the wages of the industrial sector engaged in exports and import substitution are more than the minimum wage then the effect of raising the minimum wage on these sectors is negligible to positive (by increasing domestic demand). Moreover, as stated previously, the main problem facing these sectors is an overvalued dollar, as evidenced by the chronic US trade deficits. Hence, reviving those sectors requires a competitive dollar exchange rate. The alternative, the present policy of reducing real wages, requires matching the labor cost in China, a futile solution that is predestined to fail. A falling dollar will inevitably entail some imported inflation, given decades of de facto import subsidies, but this side effect can be curtailed by adopting a gradual currency devaluation to give domestic producers sufficient time to expand their production to match the growing demand.

Another dimension of labor exploitation since the 1980s has been the shrinking welfare state. The relatively few enjoying high incomes and comfortable financial cushions can afford to do without the government's provision of healthcare, unemployment benefits, pensions, education, and other welfare services. These, however, are beyond the reach of most people who receive low wages and risk periodic unemployment and austerity.

For the majority of people, the welfare state supplements the inadequacy of their incomes due to the failure of economic policy to deliver sufficient employment opportunities and a reasonable income level. For those, welfare provides some insulation against the vagaries of periodic economic shocks perpetrated by flawed economic policies. Even for those receiving a decent wage, employment is not sufficiently secure given an economy driven by financial bubbles that periodically burst, causing catastrophic job losses for the victims. Hence, for most people, dependable and comprehensive welfare benefits are critical. The market's inability to provide a fair and secure income is a market failure perpetuated by monopsony power and inadequate and inappropriate state intervention.

The long-run harmonization of the interests of labor and capital requires a better mechanism for conflict resolution. The Germans developed a creative solution to bring the interests of labor and capital closer by offering labor a share in business profits and stock ownership, making labor an interested stakeholder. In addition to reducing conflict, profit sharing has an added advantage to business by transforming part of their fixed labor cost to a variable cost, giving them downward cost flexibility during recessions, thereby increasing business robustness and its chances of surviving sharp contractions.

Chronic Underconsumption

A more severe consequence of monopsony is *chronic underconsumption*. A good indicator of strong monopsony elements in the labor market is that labor has insufficient aggregate consumption demand to induce full-employment, resulting in unemployment, underemployment, and underconsumption. Both Jean Charles Léonard de Sismondi in the early 19th century and Keynes in the 1930s viewed underconsumption as a cyclical phenomenon, a demand deficiency causing recessions and depressions.

Chronic underconsumption is a harsher version because it persists in some degree even during the recovery and expansion phases of an economic cycle, preventing an economy from ever realizing its full potential. It is an ancient problem, which Barthélemy de Laffemas identified back in 1598.[232] Numerous economists have considered *chronic underconsumption* since. Let us illustrate with two examples.

Chronic underconsumption represents slack in the economy and, as with cyclical contractions, the benefits derived from public expenditure, on say infrastructure, exceed the cost, hence, the existence of an externality.

Despite the significant improvement in standards of living since the mid-1940s, by the 1960s there were still indications of residual *chronic underconsumption* limiting economic growth. Hence, the 1964 Kennedy personal income tax cut increased disposable incomes, unleashing a sustained growth rate of 5.5 percent until 1969.

Chronic underconsumption began reappearing with the rise in monopsony power in the early 1980s. Unfavorable changes to the labor laws diminished labor's negotiating power and expedited the fall in real wages and together with changes to the tax code, it reduced the share of labor in the gross domestic product (GDP) and increased that of the rich. This curtailed the growth in labor income, and given rich people's low marginal propensity to consume, *chronic underconsumption* remerged along with slower economic growth.

Between the mid-1990s up to the Great Recession, the banks extended consumer credit to spur consumption. They also provided credit against the rise in house prices. Both proved to be temporary measures, only delaying the full onset of *chronic underconsumption*. Those debt-based consumption stimuli were shortsighted because indebtedness soon piled beyond labor's income capacity to service it and the collapse in house prices ended labor's solvency, deepening the recession in 2008.

This *chronic underconsumption* problem becomes more acute where fiscal authorities attempt to balance their budgets by cutting the standard of living of the working class through reducing welfare payments and increasing the direct and indirect taxation of lower income groups. It is most evident in Greece, Portugal, and Spain, with austerity producing very high rates of unemployment.

Elimination of *chronic underconsumption* requires increasing the purchasing power of labor by curtailing monopsony power, upgrading and expanding the infrastructure to spur employment, repealing sales taxes on essentials, and generally eliminating or lowering direct and indirect taxes on low-income groups.

Keynes made the case for a fairer income distribution as a win-win strategy. Unlike the wealthy, the poor are quick to spend the extra money they receive, and with the multiplier, the rise in their consumption has positive repercussions on the economy. Ultimately, it also benefits the rich as asset holders because as spending increases, so does capacity utilization, corporate profits, and share prices, creating a win-win outcome for all.

Quality of Information

Accurate and timely information makes markets more efficient because it improves economic decisions with widespread benefits, making it a positive externality and vice versa.[233] Joseph Stiglitz, the economics Nobel laureate, has remarked, "I recognized that information was, in many respects, like a public good, and it was this insight that made it clear to me that it was unlikely that the private market would provide efficient resource allocations whenever information was endogenous."[234]

Thus, an important government function is to enhance the quality and timeliness of information to improve economic efficiency. Unfortunately, today the slanting of some important economic statistics reminds us of how a failing Soviet economy routinely manipulated data to hide worsening economic problems and to exaggerate the health of the economy; denying instead of solving the problems made them incurable, making the ultimate collapse of the Soviet Union certain and swift.

The prerequisite for honest, reliable, and accurate information is morality.

Government Reporting

Accurate and timely government reporting on economic activity permits business to fine-tune its production and investment decisions. It helps business curtail the buildup of excessive inventories earlier, thereby avoiding drastic inventory liquidations later, which cause deeper recessions. It also assists business in synchronizing its investments with the early signs of a recovery, while costs are still low, enabling briefer contractions and faster recoveries.

Unfortunately, since the 1980s, political expediency has taken precedence over economic efficiency, compelling revision of the statistical basis of economic data to improve the economic picture. Consequently, today's statistics is less reliable because it understates inflation and unemployment rates. It has had a negative impact on economic decisions that is hard to quantify.

The present statistical definition of unemployment substantially understates the real figure. For instance, the statistics remove a specialist medical doctor from the pool of the unemployed for refusing to work as a junior general practitioner; this is grossly misleading because it pretends that a fall in unemployment has occurred. In the aftermath of the Great Recession, Professor Nouriel Roubini (b. 1958), commenting on official unemployment statistics during an interview on Bloomberg TV, estimated that the true unemployment rate was closer to 17 percent, or about double the official figure at the time. About the same time, surveys by Gallup estimated the unemployment rate at close to 20 percent.[235]

Moreover, the quality of information provided by certain quasi-government organizations is deteriorating, providing increasingly misleading and incomplete information. The most blatant example is the Federal Reserve; it has been misinforming the government and the public about the state of the economy and the true amount of credit it has extended to various parties.[236]

More fundamentally, national income statistics should be conceptual, instead of mechanical as they have been since their inception. It is economically irrational to treat repairing the effects of negative externalities as a positive contribution to national income (NI), as though a normal economic activity. For example, the cost of maintaining a huge prison population, the environmental cleanup following a major oil spill, and engaging in wars of aggression all entail huge negative externalities and therefore should not be presented as positive contributions to national income. In other words, it is statistically misleading to claim that the economy is better off after jailing someone than it was before a crime was committed, or the environment is better after a cleanup than it was before an oil spill occurred, or starting a war of aggression is better than maintaining peace. Clearly, such expenditures represent the cost of negative externalities, which is distinctly different from expenditures that raise the standard of living and improve the quality of life such as improving infrastructure, education, and social services, or buying a new car. More plainly, it is misleading to pretend that the breaking of a window and its subsequent repair is equivalent to installing a new window in a new building, which is what current statistics claim.

Thus, national income statisticians ought to separate the cost of handling negative externalities from the figures that make up national income. They should not presume that the repairs of car accidents are the same as the manufacture and purchase of new cars. Fine-tuning the statistical definition of national income is likely to induce politicians to adopt rational economic choices that improve real economic performance and the well-being of the population, instead of policies that simply bloat negative externalities, such as extending jail sentencing or waging wars of aggression.

Credit-Rating Agencies

Credit-rating agencies are in a bind. Corporate borrowers, to minimize their borrowing costs, shop around for the credit agency that offers them the highest credit rating. The rating agencies need to please their clients, the borrowers, and simultaneously offer accurate credit assessments to bond investors. This irreconcilable conflict of interest requires that credit agencies accomplish an impossible feat, yet another demonstration of *usurious capitalism* at work.

The problem begins with the term *credit-rating agency*, a misnomer. These agencies are, in essence, public relations firms specializing in credit promotion and they should be labelled accordingly.

Aside from credit agencies' built-in bias to overrate credits, their methodology is flawed. Their credit-rating process does not assess a borrower's ability to remain solvent until the full discharge of the debt. A more meaningful credit-rating model would consider the incremental financial stress on a borrower due to the combined effect and timing of potential recessions, concentrations of debt principal repayments, expiration of profitable contracts, loss of competitiveness, and the financing of plant replacements or expansions, among others.[237] This lack of a sensible and formal credit standard has given rating agencies undue flexibility with their ratings, permitting them to elevate junk debt to AAA, which deepened the 2008 crisis. Still, without resolving the inherent conflict of interest, the problem is bound to reemerge, with the fading of the memory of recent misdeeds. Amazingly, the ownership of those credit agencies did not pass to the investors to compensate them for their huge losses resulting from flagrantly poor-quality ratings.

Corporate Reporting

The strong adherents of the efficient market hypothesis (EMH) claim that stock prices reflect all available information and, therefore, obtaining additional information and conducting stock research provides no incremental benefit to investors. On the other hand, common sense suggests that improving corporate reporting standards and providing better analysis of corporate performance is essential for improving capital market efficiency. Regrettably, the skirting of common sense in the EMH culture has encouraged a lack of concern for the quality of corporate information. Moreover, the deterioration in moral business standards, a growing negative externality, has induced a parallel decline in corporate disclosure standards, as the following makes clear.

Enron, a blue chip company with $101 billion in reported revenues, was the darling of the financial media, until it disappeared like a puff of smoke in 2001. The prestigious *Fortune* magazine hailed it as America's most innovative company for six years in a row.[238] Enron's bankruptcy was the largest in history; it surprised investors, despite months of insider selling, which plunged the stock from more than $90 a share to pennies.[239] It must have startled the chairman of the Federal Reserve, Alan Greenspan, too because he accepted an Enron prize barely nineteen days before it folded.

Like most financial disasters, Enron's collapse was the result of multiple failures. Foremost, it was a colossal moral failure, starting with its management and auditors. Enron's management—supported by its public auditors, Arthur Andersen—ventured beyond creative accounting. The accounting charade began in the 1990s, using offshore entities to report billions in illusionary profits and conceal losses, obligations, and debts. Its accounting standards were scandalous. The Enron debacle signaled a still wider professional failure; investment bankers, advisors, funds, and the financial media did not disseminate accurate advice about the company. It was also a supervisory failure because the Securities and Exchange Commission (SEC) did not spot the major discrepancies in the profit figures that Enron was reporting to its shareholders, the SEC, and the tax authorities.[240]

Enron was not an obscure little company. Hence, its sudden disappearance demonstrated the gross inefficiency of capital markets and, therefore, the fundamental fallacy of the modern portfolio theory and the efficient market hypothesis, which encouraged laxity. Indeed, deteriorating accounting standards greatly increased the inefficiency of capital markets but the efficient market hypothesis theorists hardly noticed, perhaps because it invalidated their theory.

In 1998, *Business Week* surveyed 160 chief financial officers; 55 percent indicated that their colleagues had at least suggested cooking the books, while another 12 percent admitted to yielding to such requests. Between 1997 and 2002, approximately 1,000 enterprises were compelled to admit that their reported earnings were not correct.[241]

In 1998, SEC Commissioner Arthur Levitt delivered a blunt speech to the corporate sector, "In the zeal to satisfy consensus earnings estimates and project a smooth earnings path, wishful thinking may be winning the day over faithful representation. The fear is there is *a progressive erosion of the quality of financial reporting* and, consequently, the quality of reported earnings, as management gives way to manipulation."

In 2001, the Jerome Levy Forecasting Center published an alarming report on S&P 500 earnings titled "Two Decades of Overstated Corporate Earnings: The Surprisingly Large Exaggeration of Aggregate Profit." The report identified a systemic problem that was eroding the stock market's efficiency. It reported that in two decades, earnings exaggerations, using creative accounting, doubled from about 10 percent to 20 percent, if not more. Manipulating corporate earnings consisted of understating costs for several years followed by taking a one-time extraordinary write-off as an exceptional, non-operating, expense. The accounting profession has enabled such manipulations by decreeing that those exceptional costs are not regular expenses, which they were, but their occurrence is irregular or their recognition has been delayed. S&P expected these irregularities to constitute 38 percent of earnings by 2004.

Gail Dudack, chief market strategist at SunGard at the time, also observed that, until the mid-1980s, extraordinary items represented a tiny percentage of S&P earnings. Remarkably, the rise in overstated earnings coincided with the gathering pace of the Thatcher-Reagan *counter-revolution*.

These hefty manipulations have rendered corporate reporting misleading, thereby reducing market efficiency. Accounting standards must stop facilitating the massaging of earnings. The investing public needs a separate supervisory body to rein in fictitious accounting.

Public corporations should be required to replace their auditors every two years, without rehiring past auditors for twenty years, and large corporations need to have two auditors at a time. This will effectively break up the present auditing oligopoly, broaden the choice of auditors, cut the inflated auditing fees, and improve accounting standards and market efficiency. Increasing competition among auditing firms and more frequent loss of licenses for lax senior auditors are necessary to discourage violations and improve the standards of practice. The incremental cost of an additional auditor is marginal, given more competitive pricing; in return, it will improve market efficiency and save investors billions in potential fraud.

Regulators and Supervisors

As moral restraint has waned, the incidence of abuse has multiplied, making government supervision the last hope of retaining a reasonable degree of reliable information, compliance, and fairness. This required increasing the budgets of watchdogs, but the lobbyists constrained those budgets, thereby undercutting market efficiency.

In March 2009, Bernie (Bernard) Madoff, a former nonexecutive chair of NASDAQ, pleaded guilty to 11 federal felonies. He admitted to defrauding thousands of investors and that his asset management business had been a Ponzi scheme since the early 1990s, although some analysts suspect it had been a fraud since the 1970s. The market crash of 2008 prompted many of his clients to withdraw their money, unraveling the largest financial fraud in US history, with almost $65 billion missing from clients' accounts.

No one detected Madoff's glaring fraud for decades, casting doubt on the reliability of auditors, the SEC, and investment managers generally. Oddly, the SEC had investigated Madoff's operations in 2003, but did not spot the swindle. Madoff later commented, "They never even looked at my stock records. If investigators had checked with the Depository Trust Company…it would have been easy for them to see."[242]

The SEC and its apologists attribute decades of gross negligence to insufficient budgets. However, insufficient budgets are not a blanket excuse for all wrongdoings. True, the auditor did not report any fraud, but why did the SEC—given the size of Madoff's operations—not require two auditors with a maximum term of two years each, without rehiring of past auditors for twenty years, to minimize the odds of complicity? This would have improved the odds of an early detection of fraud at no cost to the SEC, thereby saving investors billions. More worrisome, even with the benefit of hindsight, there is still no such requirement.

The SEC's line of defense is feeble, validating the saying: There is always a good reason for doing the wrong thing. If Madoff's Ponzi scheme could fool investors for decades, how many more undetected Ponzi schemes are out there? Most puzzling, the SEC could neither recover, nor trace the billions that Madoff looted. Perhaps it is high time that public servants became personally liable when they are chronically negligent.

Economic Counseling

When economists act as hired pens for lobbyists instead of retaining independent opinions, it spells a moral and professional failure. Another disturbing problem arises when economists in the employment of government advise it and Congress to adopt economic policies that favor their past or future employers in a variety of industries, particularly banking. These conflicts of interest have damaged the credibility of the economics profession.

To improve the independence and objectivity of economists, the profession should adopt a code of ethical conduct that requires economists to declare who has paid for their opinions, how much, and what they have been promised in future employment and otherwise. They should also satisfactorily explain why they are willing to leave their high-paying posts in the private sector for the much smaller salaries offered by the government. Various observers have also called for a long cooling-off period between employment in government and a return to the private sector, so as to curb revolving-door employment between government and business.

Thirteen

PUBLIC SECTOR INEFFICIENCY: PLUTOCRACY VS DEMOCRACY

*America will never be destroyed from the
outside. If we falter and lose our freedoms, it
will be because we destroyed ourselves.*[243]

Abraham Lincoln

Self-interest drives the provision of goods and services in the market-place. The previous chapter discussed some of the requisite conditions for the efficient operation of markets, namely, vigorous competition and accurate information. Just as critical, efficient markets require an efficient public sector. In a democracy that implies an efficient political process to ensure valid public choice. As such, democracy itself is a public good; hence, deteriorating democratic standards represent a negative externality, reflecting a failing political marketplace.

When self-interest, instead of *societal-interest*, drives the decisions of the public sector, it leads to a corruption of the decision-making process, resulting in inefficient public expenditure and taxation policies. Efficient public choice requires morally correct and fair decisions driven by *societal-interest*.

Nondemocratic societies sometimes have mechanisms that point to *societal-interest* in some fashion, such as the communist party in China. However, in democratic societies that function rests squarely on the shoulders of the democratic process itself. Hence, promoting *societal-interest* requires a high standard of democracy, which is not to be confused with its trappings. In other words, improving the economic efficiency of the public sector requires, as a first step, raising the democratic standards that govern the political marketplace. In recent decades, self-interest has encroached on the public sector decisions in Western democracies, resulting in loss of public sector efficiency. Hence, it is imperative to identify some of the characteristics of a waning democracy.

Neoclassical Macroeconomics

Chapter 5 explained why neoclassical macroeconomics is a dogma and not a valid economic theory. Its adoption by the *counter-revolution* as its mainstream economic theory has reaffirmed its invalidity. Its purpose has been to justify a wide range of economic policies that culminated in the marginalization of fiscal policy, regressive taxation, debt preponderance, amplified cyclicality, market deregulation, and the rise of monopolies, among other negative consequences. Moreover, neoclassical macroeconomics, by providing justifications for these and other policies, has facilitated the ascent of the *banking plutocracy* and the waning of democracy. Thus, the ascent of neoclassical macroeconomics is not just a symptom of a fading democracy, but also a major negative externality in its own right.

Political Contributions

Political parties that represent the underprivileged necessarily have fewer resources than those that represent the rich. To ensure a level political playing field and prevent the rich from purchasing democracy, limits must be set on political campaign contributions. To create a multiparty system, the five largest political parties should receive government funding of some $200 million each per election, with private funding capped at half the government contribution.

The Media

Leonardo da Vinci understood the implications of silence; he remarked, "Nothing strengthens authority so much as silence."[244] When the media intimidates dissenting voices into silence it suppresses democracy and furthers totalitarianism.

An efficient democratic political market place needs the media to deliver fair coverage of all political and economic views. Hence, in 1949, the US Federal Communications Commission (FCC) adopted the Fairness Doctrine, requiring the holders of broadcast licenses to cover important but controversial public issues in an honest, equitable, and balanced manner.[245]

The *counter-revolution* scrapped this important democratic protection during the watch of President Ronald Reagan. Starting in 1985, the FCC released a report stating that the Fairness Doctrine hurt the public interest and violated free speech. By 1987 the Fairness Doctrine was dead and buried. The US media lost its independence further when the *counter-revolution,* as part of its general policy of deregulation, relaxed the antitrust statutes, paving the way for the media to become an oligopoly.[246] Today, a handful of corporations control the bulk of the news media.[247] As a result, the media oligopoly now exercises self-censorship on topics that are contrary to the interests of the establishment.[248] This is a consequence of its ownership as well as the phenomenal advertising budgets of large corporations and gigantic political campaigns.[249]

The past three decades saw a gradual but large shift to the extreme conservative right in the position of the mainstream media away from centrist positions. Instead of reflecting the views of the full political spectrum and the interests of the majority, today it essentially projects the views of the plutocracy, a microscopic minority. The space available for alternative views has largely disappeared. This explains why, for example, the US media has supported wars of aggression, big subsidies to the big banks, tax cuts for the rich, increases in indirect taxes, relaxing constraints on political campaign contributions, regressive taxation, welfare cuts, and little concern for income inequality, poverty, and homelessness. Before and during the War on Iraq, the news media acted as a propaganda appendage of the US government instead of providing fact-based information and fair opinions to better guide the public and the government about the issues at hand. Until recently, when the terrorists paralyzed Paris in early 2015, the media considered the war on Syria a civil war, overlooking that the vast majority of the fighters arrived via Istanbul airport, Turkey, from as far away as Africa, China, Europe, Russia, and the United States. The near total news blackout on a popular 2016 Democratic presidential candidate, Bernie Sanders, demonstrates plutocratic media censorship and interference in the democratic process of the United States. Media violations of the Constitution are constant and pervasive. The Western news media generally is walking in the footsteps of the defunct Soviet media: a dull propaganda machine, dedicated to promoting the agenda of the establishment. Today, the media machine, run by the plutocracy, is a serious impediment to democracy instead of aiding it.

As broadly discussed in Chapter 6, *the unified theory of macroeconomic failure* considers the efficiency of the political marketplace in a democracy a prerequisite for the efficiency of all other markets. Moreover, the conditions necessary for the operation of an efficient market apply to the political market place too. Thus, the role of the media is important by providing objective and factual information to the public for making correct political and economic decisions. Therefore, just as consumers of goods need a consumer protection agency to insure, among other things, the validity of the information on product labels, so do political consumers need a *Democracy Protection Agency* to insure, among other things, that the media is truthful and provides the necessary and relevant information for the voters to make efficient political and economic choices. An efficient political market place also requires that there is fierce competition amongst the providers of political information rather than a restrained oligopolistic competition.

To restore the media's democratic role, balanced news coverage should be a condition of their continued licensing. It also requires breaking up the news media conglomerates to ensure competition in delivering information and opinions. Finally, protecting the interests of the have-nots, instead of the wrongdoings of the powerful, requires that a good part of the media to become publicly funded and directly supervised by the public.

Corporate Democracy

Today, corporate managements nominate the boards of directors presumably to supervise the very managements that appointed them. This absurd circular management structure is similar to that of the Federal Reserve. Just as worrying, it appropriates corporate democracy, transforming managements from servants of the shareholders to their masters. The shareholders should be the only party entitled to nominate corporate board members and anything to the contrary weakens their ownership rights.

More serious, current regulations have given banks, acting as stockbrokers and custodians of the shares of the investing public, immense additional power over the corporate sector by voting the shares of a mostly passive investing public. The voting of shares is a sacred privilege of the shareholders; as such, custodians should be restricted to voting shares based on shareholders' written instructions on a case-by-case basis and for one time only.

The argument against restricting the banks from voting third party shares in their custody is that it is detrimental to the corporate sector. This argument assumes that the banks are saintly creatures and will vote such shares in a manner that serves the best interest of the shareholders instead of to obtain privileges for the banks in the form of favorable board representations, corporate finance deals, and corporate political support on issues that are detrimental to workers, investors, and economic democracy. On balance, it is far preferable to leave the effect, if any, of not voting some shares to the market place than to tilt the voting scales in favor of the banks and the managements they appoint through the board members they help elect. For one thing, ending the corporate voting power of the banks increases the relative voting power of everybody else, including the pension funds. Moreover, some passive investors many vote their shares when the situation calls for it. On the other hand, a company that is badly managed, whether due to lack of sufficient supervision from the voters or otherwise, its share price will suffer and that will attract new shareholders that are driven to improve its performance by taking partial or full control, usually by paying a premium over its market price. Finally, the banks voting of the shares in their custody has not prevented the deluge of corporate failures, to say nothing of the deteriorating corporate performance and disclosure standards.

This loss of corporate democracy has contributed to the loss of economic and political democracy.

Poverty

The 19th century and the first forty years of the 20th century were part of the *age of economic barbarism* because mass poverty, hunger, and homelessness were commonplace. Mahatma Gandhi considered poverty the worst form of violence. In his 1941 State of the Union Address, President Franklin Roosevelt declared freedom from poverty one of his four essential human rights.[250] A rich democracy shields its citizenry against the evils of unemployment and poverty because the have-nots are voters and, in a real democracy, they can compel their government to look after them. Fortunately, poverty dissipated with the rise of economic democracy in the aftermath of World War II.

Originally founded by Quakers, social activists and Oxford academics, Oxfam today is an international confederation of 17 organizations that seeks to alleviate poverty and instill justice around the world [251]It has called for the ending of extreme wealth concentration to ameliorate global poverty. The group stated that in 2012 the $240 billion increase in the fortunes of the world's richest billionaires was enough to end extreme poverty on earth four times over. It has maintained that wealth concentration amongst the richest one percent has been depressing economic activity and making life harder for everyone else, particularly the poorest.[252]

In recent decades, the Thatcher-Reagan *counter-revolution* has been beating a path back to the *age of economic barbarism* across the West: increasing wealth concentration and spreading poverty to tens of millions on an increasing scale. This undemocratic policy has required the degrading of democracy itself. When the political process offers no democratic option to the underprivileged, such as political parties that represent their interests in parliament, then the vote of the underprivileged is downgraded to political irrelevance, making it a waste of time and effort and the poor become subjects instead of citizens.

Hence, boycotting voting and falling voter participation are tantamount to a protest vote against the plutocratic hijacking of democracy. However, a failing democracy is hardly the only consequence of poverty. Although formal slavery has been abolished a long time ago, nevertheless, the tyranny of poverty, by eliminating economic choice, has perpetuated an *economic slavery*, most evident in human trafficking, prostitution, and the compelling of millions into a life of crime.

Crime

As of the end of 2011, 6.978 million American adults were in prisons, jails, on parole, or on probation—accounting for a shocking quarter (23.4 percent) of the world prison population and six times China's. The United States has the highest rate of detention in the world, at 741 per 100,000, compared to 71 per 100,000 in Norway, 94 per 100,000 in Germany, 155 per 100,000 in England and Wales, and even worse than Rwanda's 561 per 100,000. It also has the worst rate of serious crimes.[253] These ghastly US statistics relative to the rest of the world suggests that the economic system for the poorest Americans borders on economic slavery and, in desperation, it is driving them to crime. Emperor Marcus Aurelius (121–180) was a philosopher and one of the Five Good Emperors of Rome. He noted, "Poverty is the mother of crime."[254] Several studies have substantiated this view, demonstrating a strong link between the rates of homicide and income inequality.[255] Poverty also increases suicides, a self-inflicted crime, everywhere but the statistics don't show it as such.

Two articles in *The Economist* comparing the United States prison population with that of other nations supported this disturbing reality.[256] *The Economist* stated, "If those on parole or probation are included, one adult in thirty is under "correctional supervision." This implies a population of more than ten million. *The Economist* also reported that the per capita prison population has quadrupled since 1970 because crime has increased and prison sentences for trivial offenses have become longer, describing it as, "a characteristic of police states, not democracies."

Prisons use inmates as slave labor, paying them pennies for the work they perform, thereby violating labor laws. Moreover, this is a violation of prisoners' human rights. This extreme monopsony also violates laws on fair trading by giving prisons a huge and unfair competitive advantage over all other businesses. Thus, these multiple violations demand the intervention of the Departments of Labor, Justice, and Commerce, without further ado.

An online article titled "Crime in America," by Kerby Anderson, warned of the mounting costs of crime, which he estimated at a stunning $675 billion a year.[257] This comprises $78 billion for criminal justice, $64 billion for private protection, $202 billion in the loss of life and work, $120 billion in crimes against business, $60 billion in stolen goods and fraud, $40 billion in drug abuse, and $110 billion in drunk driving. Crime is a huge negative externality that is not recognized as such. Its social cost already exceeds that of military spending.

Fareed Zakaria, on CNN, advised that a more normal crime rate would easily save tens of billions of dollars per year. The cost to the states is exorbitant at $50,000 per inmate per year, compared to $8,667 for a student; the states' prison costs have increased six times faster than the cost of education. Private prisons are bankrupting states while producing the wrong graduates.[258]

Still, the preceding costs hardly include the social cost of jailing the innocent in numbers. The statement "*The accused is innocent until proven guilty*" is a reassuring and essential democratic principle, until we learn the odds of *proven innocent*. An article in the *Cornell Law Review* titled "Why Grand Juries Do Not (and Cannot) Protect the Accused" disclosed an alarming statistic: During fiscal 1984, federal grand juries returned an astounding 99.6 percent success rate.[259] In other words, the chance of being proven innocent was a mere 0.4 percent, or practically nonexistent. This statistic has turned a proud democratic principle on its head: *Citizens are innocent until accused by the state.* The near certainty of guilt is frightening for anyone the state decides to prosecute; the forgone conclusion has eliminated any suspense in fighting a government prosecution. Fairness, common sense, and democratic principles require that the accused have a fair chance of proving their innocence, a chance that is at least comparable to that in Third World countries, dictatorships and communist regimes, never mind Europe and Japan. That this finding was in 1984 makes it all the more ominous, with obvious overtones of George Orwell's *1984* and Big Brother.

What is causing this crime epidemic?

Today, it costs a fortune to study medicine, engineering, or management, while prisons teach crime to millions gratis. Naturally, the degree of proficiency attained is a function of time-spent training. Long sentencing improves criminal skills; amateurs receive intensive training by hardy professionals, with state-of-the-art expertise on how to conduct more intricate and financially rewarding crimes. Economics indicates that increasing the subsidy to an activity increases its consumption. Hence, subsidized criminal training has become a lead vocation in America. Prisons also facilitate crime by providing recruiters with a pool of specialist skills in a wide range of criminal undertakings.

In addition, two internationally atypical US judicial attributes have contributed to this prisons abnormality: exceedingly long sentencing and plea-bargaining. Do the innocent plea-bargain and admit guilt to diminish an exceedingly long and near certain sentence? Definitely. Shorter, European standard sentencing would yield less plea-bargaining and higher standards of justice. Furthermore, an excessively high conviction rate by a prosecutor ought to trigger an investigation instead of reward.

The prison industry is the prime lobbyist for long jail sentencing for minor offenses, maximizing prisons' profits and seriously undermining democracy. Long sentencing (without rehabilitation) and repeat crimes sustain prison profitability in the same way that repeat lodgers improve the profitability of hotels, whereas short sentencing, extensive rehabilitation, and a fall in the crime rate would spell the financial ruin of private prisons. The prison industry has also lobbied for disbarring anyone sentenced from ever voting again; in other words, disbarring those who know the inside story of jails, firsthand, which helps perpetuate the status quo with all its faults, a multiple breach of democratic principles.

Evidently, the interest of prison owners and *societal-interest* are in conflict. Accordingly, a prerequisite for solving the crime problem in the United States and its associated prohibitive cost is to nationalize the prisons, the norm in Europe and elsewhere. Once again, the US private sector overstepped its bounds by running prisons, clearly an essential government function.

The philosophy in Europe toward prisoners is markedly different. In the United States, prisons are for exacting punishment, instead of rehabilitating prisoners. Releasing prisoners without changing their circumstances puts society at risk. Indeed, without a job or adequate welfare, those released are practically compelled to return to a life of crime. Similarly, paying inmates a fair wage would encourage them to reform, giving them hope for a fresh start, and a nest egg upon leaving prison. It would also raise the cost of maintaining the huge prison population, which would encourage fairer and shorter sentencing.

To summarize, several reforms are necessary to diminish crime to more normal levels as follows:

1. Prisons must revert to state ownership, to reduce the cost of prisons and eliminate the incessant lobbying that is subverting fair sentencing.
2. Job training must replace jail sentences for minor offenses. Upon the successful completion of such training, decent-paying jobs must be available in infrastructure projects; a condition to that effect needs to be included in government contracts because democratic governments provide their citizens with opportunities for decent living.[260]
3. The present international judicial anomalies of long sentencing and plea bargaining need to be replaced by normal sentencing and an end to plea bargaining.
4. Economic life in prisons need to as normal as possible and mimics real economic life outside to smooth the transition of prisoners to regular members of society upon completing their sentencing.

By promoting fairness, freedom from want, economic democracy, and higher moral standards, a society can lower the incidence of crime and realize abundant cost savings. A high crime rate is symptomatic of an eroding democracy.

Wars of Aggression as Foreign Policy

As with immorality in the market place, immoral foreign policies come at a hefty price for the countries that practice them, though the disciples of Machiavelli may not realize it. The immorality of imperialism and wars of aggression are profound negative externalities, causing macroeconomic failures and corrupting democracy. President Dwight D. Eisenhower was a senior general during World War II; his assessment of wars is particularly instructive: "[e]very gun that is made, every warship launched, every rocket fired, signifies in the final sense a theft from those who hunger and are not fed, those who are cold and are not clothed."[261] The mainstream media has failed to alert the American people about all the subsequent *thefts* that have been going on in the decades following President Eisenhower. Similarly, Major General Smedley Butler, with a long military service, including World War I, criticized wars and the profits that businesses reap from military spending and war profiteering.[262]

Wars of aggression are fascism in everything but name. The Nuremberg trials of Nazi leaders, in the aftermath of World War II, classified wars of aggression as the worst war crimes. Since then the United States has initiated more wars of aggression than any nation on earth, typically without legitimate cause. Thus, the Gulf of Tonkin incident, in which the North Vietnamese allegedly attacked an American naval vessel, is recognized today as a fabrication to provide a pretext for attacking North Vietnam. The pro–Vietnam War lobby claimed it wanted to prevent South Vietnam from becoming communist. After killing millions of Vietnamese, the United States withdrew its forces and today Vietnam has a mixed economy. So what purpose did that war serve?

After fifteen years of war on Afghanistan, there is still no evidence that the Afghan government knew the nineteen perpetrators of 9/11, or of their plans, never mind dispatching them —and, most extraordinarily, not one of them was from Afghanistan, or from Iraq or Syria for that matter, suggesting that that war was incompetently contrived. This is all the more concerning given the investigation of the 9/11 events, like the Kennedy assassination before it, has left too many loose ends. For example, could the onboard flight computers have been programed to shut all communications, disable the captains' flight controls, and direct the incredibly precise navigation of the flights? What are the odds that the Twin Towers were brought down by internal explosions? What brought down the solid building next door? Most amazing, fifty-one minutes after the first at-tack on the World Trade Center, which should have triggered the highest secu-rity alert, the Pentagon remained defenseless against a phantom civilian airliner that managed to evade the mighty American Airforce, batteries of antiaircraft missiles, and hundreds of cameras, then slammed into the Pentagon structure without leaving wing marks on the Pentagon walls.[263] Why did the investigation leave these questions unanswered? Why have those pointing to the gaps in the investigation been summarily dismissed as conspiracy theorists?

In the final years of his presidency, President Clinton achieved a splendid fiscal feat; for the first time in decades, the US budget shifted from deficit to surplus. The hope of eventual freedom from debt held the promise of an American economic revival. This was the state of America's finances when President Bush assumed office. Instead of avoiding past mistakes, Secretary of State Colin Powell testified before the United Nations that Iraq possessed weapons of mass destruction requiring their removal through invasion. After destroying Iraq, the US government admitted that Iraq had no weapons of mass destruction (i.e. that war was without cause).[264]Eight years and two costly wars later, President Bush handed back a wrecked American economy. What is the financial cost of war? In 2008, American economists and Nobel Prize laureate Joseph Stiglitz and Harvard Professor Linda Bilmes estimated the cost of the War on Iraq at three trillion dollars.[265] For generations to come, Americans must pay taxes to repay the cost of that war with interest.

Baghdad Burning is an interesting and beautifully written book that de-scribes the Anglo-American war on Iraq from the perspective of a young Iraqi woman.[266] It has been the worst calamity to befall Iraq since the Mongol hordes ravaged Baghdad in 1258. As a result, over one million Iraqis lost their lives, to say nothing of those who lost limbs, homes, schools, hopes, etc. The first unambiguous indication of neocons malicious intent towards Iraq was in disbanding the army, the border guards, the police, and the security forces, leaving the population at the mercy of criminal gangs and terrorists. This was followed by the plunder of the Iraqi museum in broad daylight in sight of the US military and observed live on TV by millions.

To govern by proxy, the neocons handed the government of Iraq to crooks holding American and British passports of Iraqi origin.[267] A banker, who previously had been convicted and sentenced for embezzling and bankrupting a bank in the region, became in charge of Iraq's economic affairs. Hundreds of billions of dollars have been looted from Iraq. Still, transferring such vast sums to Western banks required the complicity of powerful Western politicians to wave the stringent money-laundering regulations and otherwise, raising the inescapable question what motivated them to facilitate the loot of Iraq?[268] These neo-imperialist practices resemble traditional imperialism, using private vehicles, as with the East India Company, to plunder nations but more covertly than in the 19th century. Moreover, on the rare occasions that looters lost their political cover in Iraq and were on the verge of prosecution by Iraqi courts the United States and Great Britain promptly gave them, together with their loot, safe refuge in their countries. Thus, twelve years after America's mighty air force needlessly destroyed Iraq's power stations, water utilities, sewage treatment plants, and telephone network, Iraqis are still without electricity in a scorching hot country, without clean drinking water, the sewage is still polluting the rivers, and no fixed telephone lines.[269] Equally telling, the thievery hardly spared the budgets which the US had allotted for rebuilding Iraq. Like Afghanistan before it, Iraq. has been a windfall to *parasitic capitalism*. Less obvious is the terrible chain of unintended consequences that war has unleashed on the aggressors.

The plunder of Iraq was financially rewarding to some but a strategy failure for the United States. The neocons try to impart to their American audiences the demeanor of Bismarck, worldly chess players who can see through all the moves and counter moves. They populate think tanks and collect fat salaries to lend their talent to devise plans that can steer the planet and history to a direction of their choosing. Alas, they plan with the foresight of naïve children who are appalled by the unintended consequences of their ill-advised plots. Just as worrisome is the sinister indifference of America's adversaries to neocon's adventurism. They seem to heed Napoleon Bonaparte's advice, "Never interrupt your enemy when he is making a mistake."[270]

The neocons naively misinterpreted America's powerful adversaries lack of objection to the invasion of Iraq as proof of her overwhelming international hegemony. Only after bringing down Saddam did the neocons realize they had committed a strategic blunder of horrific proportions. Saddam was the mortal enemy of Iran and Syria, the presumed enemies of the United States;

by eliminating him, the neocons inadvertently did these countries a great service by ridding them of their enemy, linking them overland, and making them more influential in Iraq and across the region. When this reality dawned on the neocons at a very late hour, they tried to fix their mistake but only succeeded in dragging the United States deeper into the reginal quick sands.

For devising their "Plan B", the neocons committed another blunder by seeking the assistance of the presumed "experts" on Iraq, the British Foreign Office; devoid of morality and intellectually sterile, it has yet to adapt to post-imperialism, with nothing in its bag of tricks other than *divide and rule* from three centuries ago. Indeed, the conceited British Foreign Office has never publicly confessed its role in inadvertently abolishing the British Empire, its numerous futile scheming, disrespect for international law, and, occasionally, humiliating miscalculations as in Suez.[271] Spurred on by a reinvigorated imperialist spirit, the British establishment was ready to repeat past embarrassments.

A short digression is useful here to provide background to the events to follow. As an imperialist power, Great Britain has a long history of pursuing harmful parasitic capitalism and despotic imperialism against Iraq, as well as other vulnerable Third World countries. It began with the invasion of Iraq during World War I. To suppress rebellious Iraqis, it resorted to unrestrained violence, including the use of poison gas and hanging, imprisonment, and banishment of populist leaders. It plundered Iraq's archeological marvels, which it unashamedly displays to this day in the British Museum. It paid the puppet government that it installed pittance for the oil it extracted. And once oil was discovered further south in the Gulf, it curtailed the expansion of Iraq's oil production, although Iraq was more populous and desperately needed additional oil revenue for its development. Finally, when the Iraqi government became extremely unpopular as a result of siding with Great Britain against Egypt during the Suez Crisis, Britain covertly delivered the coup de grace to Iraq's monarchy in 1958 through a coup d'état.[272] Ten years later, in 1968, the Americans displaced the British in running the affairs of Iraq through another coup, paving the way for Saddam to assume total power.

To reinstate the barrier between Syria and Iran, the Neocon-British plan was to create a hostile Sunni state on Iraq's western border with Syria. (Later, they would try the same thing in Syria by facilitating the establishment of ISIL's terrorist state straddling the border region of Syria and Iraq). To this end, they did everything imaginable to promote sectarian violence in the hope of precipitating a civil war to culminate in the breakup of Iraq along sectarian lines. Among the litany of shameful terrorist acts, two British SAS officers dressed in Arab clothes were caught red handed in Basra planting bombs in a Shia mosque to murder innocent civilians, as one of the triggers for the much yearned for civil war. This and other acts of terrorism drove the Iraqis, who were initially docile, to fight American and British occupation. Badly shaken by the ferocity of the resistance in Basra, the British forces retreated away from the urban areas to the relative safety of Shuaiba, a remote desert base, before pulling out of Iraq entirely, leaving their American allies to fend for themselves. Divide and rule backfired royally on its perpetrators. Subsequent events would show that the British Foreign Office, handicapped by a lack of fresh ideas, a dull memory, and absent a learning process, is destined to repeat its past mistakes with tedious predictability. The alternative posture never crossed their minds: better not meddle and be suspected a fool than to do so and remove all doubts.[273]

The resistance resulted in tens of thousands of American casualities, which deterred prospective volunteers from joining the US military.[274] The neocons made up for the shortfall in men by hiring disturbed mercenaries, who thought nothing of using Iraqi civilians, including women, for target practice from helicopters, thereby fanning the flames of Iraqi resistance further.

Even after the American military withdrawal from Iraq, the neocons, with Vice President Joe Biden's support, did not stop trying to break up Iraq. In 2014, the instantaneous melting of reportedly three fully armed Iraqi divisions—American trained and CIA infiltrated—without firing a bullet to a mere 1,400 Daesh (ISIL) terrorists and the subsequent capture of Mosul, a regional Iraqi capital, confirmed that the plan to breakup Iraq is ongoing. However, the odds are that the Neocon-British plan will fail because the planners, despite their pretentions, are in fact clueless about the nature of Iraqi society. All major Iraqi tribes are made up of both the Shia and Sunni religious sects and they cannot be split. Iraqi families, almost without exception, have extensive intermarriages across religious sects. Finally, there is absolutely no difference between the Sunni and Shia sects on core religious matters. The real difference between them is in the interpretation of religious law and it is slight, no more than the differences within the four sections of the Sunni sect and less than, for example, any differences between Catholics, Protestant and Orthodox Christians. Indeed, the four founders of the Sunni schools of jurisprudence, without exception, were students of the founders of the Shia jurisprudence. The differences have intellectually and legally arguable basis, but none of it is fundamental.

On the other hand, with typical lack of foresight, the neocon could not see the potential unintended consequence of their "cunning" plan: strengthening Iraqi unity, weakening the American puppet government in Baghdad, cleansing the Iraqi military from officers run by the CIA, driving Iraq closer to Syria, Iran, and the Russian Federation, and eroding American influence in Iraq. America's generous gift to its adversaries has been its willing consent to a handicap: having the neocons and the British Foreign Office for advisors.

Most serious, the unintended consequences of the wars of aggression have undermined American military capabilities. The disastrous Vietnam War ended military conscription (the draft), transforming the military to an all-volunteer force.[275] Among the unintended consequences of the Iraq War is that it exposed the Achilles heel of a volunteer army: Americans are unwilling to volunteer to fight unjust wars. Falling volunteers, the hopelessness of winning in Iraq, and the mounting economic cost prompted a top-level bipartisan reassessment of America's foreign policy, which produced the Baker-Hamilton report, advising an American withdrawal from Iraq.[276]

As a stopgap measure until military robots can take over in a decade or two and with customary lack of vision as to the unintended consequences, the neocons responded by outsourcing wars to branches of Al-Qaeda terrorists and mercenaries. Hence, they have been against a United Nations definition of international terrorism because that would have restricted their flexibility in assigning and withholding that label. They also supported the "Arab Spring" and the Islamist Brotherhood—the mother organization of Al-Qaeda—to orchestrate political strife and proxy wars to topple Arab republics. The pro-Western governments of Tunisia, Egypt and Yemen soon collapsed, while a terrorist war is still raging in Libya and spilling over to European NATO members.

In 2009 and again 2011, Western governments, supported by their compliant media, zealously backed the protests in Iran, hoping to bring about an Iranian Spring. However, unlike the Arab protests, the ones in Iran lacked mass support and quickly fizzled.

In late 2010, the Turkish government of the Justice and Development Party, an offshoot of the Islamist Brotherhood the spiritual fountain of jihadist terror, began preparing refugee camps for fleeing Syrians months before there was any hint of trouble.

The neocons longed to replicate in Syria Al-Qaeda's success against the Soviet Union in Afghanistan. The *Axis of Imperialism*—the United States, Great Britain and France—worked feverishly to assemble a coalition of "Friends of Syria" of over one hundred countries. To persuade hesitant governments, the British Foreign Office claimed to have reliable intelligence, which it generously shared with potential allies. Its steadfast assessment was that the Syrian government would fall shortly, within a few months at the latest, without mentioning its other similarly optimistic predictions for the disastrous Anglo-American and Anglo-French interventions in Iraq and Libya, respectively. Experience shows that the better odds are in betting against the prophecies of the British Foreign Office. The *Axis of Imperialism* required the "Friends of Syria" to demonstrate their "friendship" to Syria by cutting their diplomatic ties with the Syrian government, imposing an economic embargo on the Syrian people, and supporting terrorists that were about to invade and liberate Syria to establish democracy there.

In compliance with the directions of the United States, its vassals allotted tens of billions of dollars to recruit, train, and arm hundreds of thousands of Syrian-opposition *Freedom Fighters* drawn from about 100 countries. They also bankrolled a colossal media campaign; its strategy was simplicity itself: lie incessantly until the lies become undisputed truths. Soon, it was outdoing Joseph Goebbels—the gifted Nazi minister of propaganda. Media lies, a negative externality, not only mislead the Syrians but also mislead Western voters, thereby undermining democracy in the West, a prime cause of macroeconomic failure.

The *Axis of Imperialism* supplied the *Freedom Fighters* with antiaircraft and TOW antitank missiles, state of the art sniper rifles, and other top-notch NATO weaponry, satellite communications, and intelligence. By mid-2011, the stage was set for the global war on Syria. Turkey, a NATO member, played a critical role. After receiving the waves of *Freedom Fighters* arriving in Ataturk Airport in Istanbul from all over the world, Turkey trained them, transported them to the Syrian border, handed them their allotted NATO weapons, and, subsequently, Turkish hospitals treated their casualties.

At first, the powerful disinformation machine confused the Syrians until they brushed with the *moderate opposition*. They then voted with their feet, fleeing their *liberators* to the relative safety of areas still under the control of their government or abroad with no discernable movement in the opposite direction, exposing the falsehood of the assertion of the *Axis of Imperialism* that the Syrian people are against their government.

The West's vaunted *Free Syrian Army* and other *moderate terrorists* proved to be heart-eating cannibals, as documented by the cannibals themselves and reported by the news channels including CNN.[277] The *Free Syrian Army* was also passing its NATO weapons to Al-Qaeda and its offshoots. The litany of genocidal crimes of what Western leaders and news media warmly label as *moderate opposition* include car and suicide bombings of civilians, and beheadings of Syrian military prisoners, civil servants, and civilians who refuse to join their ranks. Mass graves dote the Syrian countryside. Their lighter sentences consist of cutting tongues, noses, ears, and limbs. They reserve their worst brutality for the Syrian Christians: slaughtering the men and selling their wives and daughters into sexual slavery, and their sons as human spare parts for organ transplants abroad. Kidnappings for ransom and slave markets flourished. Different terrorist factions are also busy butchering each other to gain dominance and a larger slice of the billions of dollars provided by the CIA and America's vassals. The subject of democracy never came up. The neocon elders were disillusioned by the terrorists' lack of success in winning the hearts and minds of the Syrian people. The other disappointment was that Syrian diplomats and military officers specifically, and government officials generally, with rare exceptions and despite their meagre salaries, could not be bribed into switching sides.

The passionate pleas of the Vatican to spare the innocent noncombatants fell on the deaf ears of the facilitators of the *moderate opposition*—the leaders of the *Axis of Imperialism*, their Western conformist media, and their "human rights" organizations. The sole protector of the Christians and the rest of the Syrian civilians was the Syrian army, suffering eighty-five thousand deaths in the process. Estimates of the people killed in Syria exceeded the number killed in Hiroshima by five times.

The *moderate opposition* tried to eradicate the future as well as the past of Syria and Iraq through comprehensive plunder or else destruction of factories, plants, oil wells, and ancient archeological sites representing world heritage; their booty passed through Turkey; private auctions in the West conducted the sale of the priceless archeological trophies, which went to finance the terrorists. The leaders of the *Axis of Imperialism* facilitated the huge bank transfers to the terrorists and their massive oil smuggling via Turkey, a NATO member.

Doubtless, only psychopaths dare argue this global barbarity serves a national interest. In this 21st century, the *Axis of Imperialism* has chosen serial killers and rapists for partners. The stench of the crimes committed in Syria is worse than during Iraq's occupation under President George W. Bush and PM Tony Blair and the torture they sanctioned in Abu Ghraib Prison and elsewhere.[278] Paradoxically, democracies put dictators that commit crimes against humanity on trial but not "democratic" leaders who commit similar crimes. Is there justification for this double standard or is it simply the hypocrisy of plutocracy posing as "democracy"?[279]The widespread crimes raise another question: can a plutocracy afford to permit a return to genuine democracy that would question plutocracy's latest rein, or has it already crossed the Rubicon?

Western opinion surveys and the latest Syrian election results showed that President Bashar Al Assad is much more popular among his constituents than any Western leader among his or hers. He also belongs to a rare breed of world leaders who have not used their power to accumulate a personal fortune, refusing to handover Syria in return for billions of dollars. Moreover, the Syrian state, despite its meagre resources and prolonged state of siege continued to offer all its citizens free education covering all levels, free medication, subsidized food, and cheap housing. Indeed, most American and British voters wish their far richer and ostensibly more *democratic* governments would offer them similar welfare programs. Instead, the *Axis of Imperialism* insists on trampling international law and forcing the handover of the Syrian government to dubious individuals who are unknown to the Syrian public, many in the pay of various intelligence services and holding foreign passports, to create yet another failed state as they did in Iraq, Libya, Somalia, and elsewhere. On the other hand, the height of hypocrisy is that the *Axis of Imperialism* considers any instigators of attempts to depose its governments as traitors.

Two Centuries of Parasitic Economics

The retaking of Palmyra in Syria in late March 2016 by the Syrian army was a major defeat for ISIL, the international terrorist organization, but it did not please David Cameron, the Conservative British Prime Minister, as Robert Fisk observed in an article in the Independent newspaper. [280] The Axis of Imperialism, a presumed coalition against terrorism, had allowed ISIL to take Palmyra a year earlier by not bombing its long attack convoys as it moved across hundreds of miles of desert for hours. The incestuous relationship between the terrorists and several NATO members raises questions about the possibility of a double meaning to the "T" in NATO. [281]

The Axis of Imperialism was stripped of its last fig leaf in a recent landmark Financial Times interview; the former Prime Minister of Qatar, Sheikh Hamad Bin Jassim Bin Jabr Al Thani, for a long time a central figure in the War on Syria, admitted that what has happened in Syria is not a 'revolution', rather an 'international gameplay' whereby the United States has given 'the green light' to both Saudi Arabia and Qatar to intervene in Syria's affairs. [282] He was indirectly confirming earlier statements by the former French Foreign Minister Roland Dumas to the French TV station LCP in 2013. Dumas had stated, "I was in England two years before the violence in Syria on other business. I met with top British officials, who confessed to me that they were preparing something in Syria…Britain was organizing an invasion of rebels into Syria." These confirmations show that the war on Syria was years in the making and should alert conspirators, as against conspiracy theorists, that there are no secrets. The only thing secret is what has not happened yet.

After five years of a global terrorist war, it is all but certain that the *Axis of Imperialism* must swallow the bitter pill of defeat in Syria, all the more remarkable because for the first time the army of a small nation prevails against a massive guerrilla force that is fanatically motivated, well equipped, amply funded, and fiercely supported by the *Axis of Imperialism* and all its vassals. Neither the Soviet Union nor the United States could withstand a force that is a fraction of the size that Syria faced. Unlike Francis Fukuyama's prediction that was a little too soon, this war promises to bring about the real *End of History*, closing the final chapter on the *Axis of Imperialism*.[283] Paradoxically, the longer the *Axis of Imperialism* denies this outcome the more decisive will be the final capitulation, reminiscent of the Vietnam War.

Did the wars since Korea benefit the United States or did they serve a hidden craving? Besides profiteering, were these wars driven by subliminal racism against the rest of the world, given they essentially targeted nonwhite nations? Is the *Axis of Imperialism* the outward expression of an *Axis of Racism*? Does anyone still believe the *Axis of Imperialism* loves nation building, human rights, free speech, democracy, and peace? Will terrorist wars (with "Islamist" labels) against Muslim countries, drive 1.6 billion Muslims—almost a quarter of the world population—to the Russo-Chinese camp?[284] Did any US think tank consider how much longer Russia would tolerate an overly depressed oil price and the unintended consequences of driving Russia into a corner? Was the advice of the think tanks to encourage China and Russia to adopt market economies in America's best interest? Did anyone do a cost-benefit analysis of an alternative policy: America acting as a reliable, trusted, benevolent, and moral partner?

Fools see glory in war. Dwight D. Eisenhower did not; he declared, "I hate war as only a soldier who has lived it can, only as one who has seen its brutality, its futility, its stupidity."[285] Such Machiavellian policies as *the ends justify the means,* and *divide and rule* are immoral and stupid, but their advocates are blind to their negative externalities, spillover effects, and unintended consequences, even in hindsight.[286] For example, consider some of the unintended consequences of America's neo-imperialist policies in Southwest Asia, as follows:

- America encouraged Saddam to invade Iran in 1980; it precipitated a spike in oil prices, resulting in a major US recession (in 1981–1982) of incalculable cost to the US economy. It also launched a chain of events that culminated in the dismantling of Glass–Steagall and the Great Recession of 2008, as explained previously.
- The Taliban government had succeeded in nearly eradicating the cultivation of the opium poppy in Afghanistan. Ousting Taliban reinstated Afghanistan as the cheapest source of cocaine to the West, increasing drug traffickers' profits, and making that war, in effect, the Third Opium War, a grand coup for parasitic capitalism with negative consequences to the West for generations to come.
- The prohibitive cost of the latest War on Iraq has debilitated the US economy with ongoing repercussions that could last decades.

- Western meddling toppled its puppets in Tunisia, Egypt, Yemen, and Iraq (Saddam).
- The misadventures of the *Axis of Imperialism* in the region have seriously weakened the stability of its regional vassals. For example, Turkey, under the pro-neocon Justice and Development Party, as a result of supporting the War on Syria, is now suffering civil strife, terrorist attacks on its cities, a full-fledged civil war, collapse of tourism, a deteriorating economy, tense relations with all its neighbors, and becoming increasingly repressive and fascist. Ironically, Turkey has also become the launching point of attacks by the previously NATO supported Syrian moderate opposition against European NATO members.
- Pursuant to NATO members facilitating the recruitment of terrorists in Europe to send to Syria, some security experts estimate that the number of sleeper terrorists in Europe has mushroomed to over fifty thousand. This represents fifty thousand potential suicide bombs, an unprecedented security blunder.[287]
- The neocons have saddled the world with an indescribable security headache, which will become worse as Syria and Iraq defeat their *moderate oppositions* and thousands of them begin to trickle back to their home countries in Europe, the United States, and elsewhere. This will happen even if the *Axis of Imperialism* channels some of them to some unfortunate Third World countries like Libya, Yemen, and Africa to seed mayhem there.
- By repeatedly projecting naïvely favorable outcomes for their misadventures, the neocons have deceived themselves and everyone who listens to them, rendering the entire "intelligence" apparatus ineffective and an expensive exercise in back patting.
- Given that the US government declared Al-Qaeda to be the perpetrator of the 9/11 attacks, the neocons' covert support of Al Qaeda's in recent proxy wars represents the worst subversion of American democracy, a desperate measure that is tantamount to a declaration of moral bankruptcy.
- Following the Arab Spring and the associated terrorist wars, a mass exodus from Southwest Asia, Afghanistan, and Africa into Europe

has ensued, a demographic and political nightmare for the European Union that threatens its fracture and possibly NATO as well.

- The Syrian economy is in shambles at this time, but contrary to the hopes of the *Axis of Imperialism*, their hated Syrian army is now battle hardened, better equipped, better trained, and a ferocious fighting force.
- Future neocon misadventures will likely meet with more rapid and more dramatic failure because the international vacuum they exploited after the fall of the Soviet Union has vanished.

What is the singular lesson to learn from all this? The neocons are no Bismarck, not mentally and certainly not morally. Among other things, their wars violate Napoleon Bonaparte's cardinal military advice, "You must not fight too often with one enemy, or you will teach him all your art of war."[288] America's adversaries have been observing its tactics. This provides a partial explanation of its diminishing military effectiveness and that of its vassals. The net result of neocons' frantic attempts to extend US hegemony has been a rapid loss of such hegemony and the seeding of a multi-polar world. Across the world, the influence of China, Russia, India, Iran, and others is steadily expanding economically, politically, and militarily while American influence is receding.

Was there any factor the United States did not have in its favor in its wars on Vietnam, Cambodia, Laos, Afghanistan, Iraq, Syria, etc.?[289] Morality was the decisive factor that it lacked in every case. Immorality is tantamount to irrationality, inefficiency, and a dull strategy, and not just in economics, hence, the repeated failures. Generally, these wars are reminiscent of the collapse of the *economics of imperialism* in the 1960s, but since then forgotten by the *Axis of Imperialism* at considerable cost.

The neocons' gift to the world has been to reinstate an age of barbarism. Their high priests presume they can repeatedly navigate the world to the brink of the void and back, oblivious that even a small incident can have a *butterfly effect*, as the one in Sarajevo illustrated a century ago.[290] Plutocrats who support neocon adventurism need to be aware that, ultimately, they are risking an unintended nuclear confrontation, which would reduce their vast wealth to dust in a blink followed by a relentless global hunt down of all the warmongers and their supporters by the enraged survivors. Indeed, the shooting down of a Russian bomber by Turkey, a NATO-member and presumably with the blessing of the *Axis of Imperialism*, could yet prove to be the opening salvo of World War III.[291] Those who cannot imagine how these things can easily get out of hand need to watch the 1960s movie Dr. Strangelove, at once hilarious and dead serious. Making the world safer must begin by completely cleansing governments, think tanks, and the news media of hazardous warmongers.

Excessive Plutocratic Wealth

In August 1936, President Franklin Roosevelt gave a memorable speech in Madison Square Garden, describing the politico-economic state of affairs. "We had to struggle with the old enemies of peace in business and financial monopolies, speculation, reckless banking, class antagonism, sectionalism, war profiteering," FDR said. "They had begun to consider the government of the United States a mere appendage to their own affairs. And we know now that government by organized money is just as dangerous as government by organized mob. Never before, in all our history have these forces so united against our candidate as they stand today. They are unanimous in their hate for me and I welcome their hatred."[292] Today seems so much like yesterday, except there is no Roosevelt to shield American democracy from the encroachment of organized money.

Wealth is power, and excessive wealth gives excessive power to a few extremely wealthy individuals, which undermines democracy. There is also the added risk that some of the extremely wealthy are psychopaths, making excessive wealth a threat to humanity and not just to democracy.[293]

A popular notion suggests that democracy and capitalism go hand in hand. Nothing could be further from the truth. Self-interest and various forms of capitalism have been with us from the very beginning, but not democracy. Indeed, most dictators are capitalists and support capitalism. China today is politically communist, but economically capitalist. In fact, there is an intrinsic conflict between capitalism and democracy because unrestrained capitalism produces wealthy ruling elites, plutocracies, who mostly prefer wealth gathering that is unhindered and unencumbered by democracy.

In a democracy, the social contract between society and its citizens requires that *societal-interest* take precedence over self-interest. Beyond a certain point, wealth stops being a private matter and becomes a public concern. The parting point is when wealth begins to direct public policy to serve plutocratic interests to the detriment of *societal-interest*. Hence, wealth is a privilege and not a right. Indeed, great wealth requires great moral and social responsibilities to match. In the same vein, a driver's license is a privilege that society bestows on responsible drivers, but it is not a right. When drivers act irresponsibly by driving while intoxicated, a responsible society rescinds their licenses to protect the public. The section titled "Democracy Tax" in Chapter 19 explores this subject further.

———

The foregoing sections exposed the deterioration in democratic standards. Given that an efficient democratic process is a prerequisite for an efficient economy, it is imperative that concerned individuals and organizations evaluate the state of Western democracies today.

Fourteen

Measuring Democracy

The people who cast the votes decide nothing.
The people who count the votes decide everything.[294]

Joseph Stalin

President Franklin Roosevelt saw the fragility of democracy. "The liberty of a democracy is not safe if the people tolerate the growth of private power to a point where it becomes stronger than their democratic state," he said. "That, in its essence, is fascism."[295] Democracy is valuable, delicate, and, throughout history, the rarest form of government. It is conceivable that a democratic ruler could implement the wishes of his people without holding elections, but that would be rarer still. In any case, voting and elections do not a democracy make; they are merely its trappings.

Today, most Western democracies are again at a critical juncture of improving their democracies or regressing further toward plutocratic fascism, as President Franklin Roosevelt had warned. Monopolies and oligopolies already dominate many industries and economic sectors, with the big banks visibly stronger than the state, the result of an insidious and sustained plutocratic encroachment on democracy. Restraining plutocratic power requires an acute public awareness of the need for regulating the political power of excessive plutocratic wealth.

Regardless of whether a system is tribal, autocratic, aristocratic, pluto-cratic, elitist, feudalist, monarchist, republican, or constitutional, it is typically a blend of democracy and autocracy, with all countries standing somewhere between the theoretical extremes of absolute democracy and autocracy. Even a country like Switzerland, where citizens are obligated to vote and decide important matters directly through frequent referendums, is not a perfect de-mocracy. The most that any democracy can hope for is to strive to get closer to the democratic ideal. Similarly, there is no pure dictatorship; there are only relative ones. Even the most absolute dictators consult with their entourage, advisors, or astrologers. The main sources of autocratic power are military, religious, political, and economic, or a combination thereof.

In Western democracies, the blend between democracy and autocracy var-ies, with the latter taking the form of economic power or plutocracy. An intrigu-ing question is the relative position of the various Western countries on the democracy-plutocracy scale. As the influence of plutocracy in the political pro-cess increases, economic policies tend to serve private interests instead of public interest and the economy becomes less efficient. Assessing the relative position of a country requires calibration of its democratization relative to a benchmark. It is also possible to calibrate the democratization of a country relative to itself over time, to assess whether it is drifting toward democracy or plutocracy.

Measuring Western Democratization

In a democracy, citizens exercise their collective free will in a competitive political marketplace, where voters act as political consumers, using their votes to purchase the promises of politicians and parties.[296] *The unified theory of macroeconomic fail-ure* considers the erosion of democracy symptomatic of a failure of the political marketplace, due to dwindling political competition and increasing dominance by political monopolies, duopolies, or oligopolies. It also considers a failure of the political marketplace a negative externality that is rooted in moral failure.

As with other market failures, measures such as the adoption of political *lais-sez-faire* and deregulation of the political marketplace result in predatory political competition, providing a decisive advantage to political parties with abundant financial resources that serve the plutocratic establishment, permitting them to purchase democratic leadership and control. The result is an increase in the market share of the political parties representing the wealthy and loss of representation to everybody else, a negative externality that reflects a failing political marketplace, mirrored by a corresponding deterioration in the choice of public goods and taxes. Indeed, dismantling democratic checks is a path that culminates in the dismantling of democracy itself. To check this tendency, mass consciousness and political will are required to enforce regulation of the political marketplace.

Several notable research organizations have constructed freedom and democracy indexes, including the Fraser Institute in Canada, Reporters without Borders in France, Freedom House in the United States, and the Economist Intelligence Unit in Great Britain. They conduct annual country surveys to update their ratings. Each organization has adopted a set of criteria that it judged important for the evaluation of freedom and democracy, with their primary focus being emerging democracies. For instance, the Economist Intelligence Unit computes a democracy index based on an examination of civil liberties, the conduct of elections, media freedom, the functioning of the government, voter participation, public opinion, corruption, and stability.[297]

Those surveys use a broad-brush approach to compare emerging democracies relative to Western democracies. Such an approach does not serve our purpose because one needs to detect democratic trends within Western democracies relative to one another, rather than relative to emerging democracies, requiring a finer set of criteria and the construction of an index for Western democracies specifically.

Finally, the aforementioned organizations receive direct or indirect assistance from their respective governments, making them interested parties, inclined to elevate democratic ratings of their respective countries as well as those that are similar.

An analysis of the Western democracies revealed nine factors that seemed pertinent for inclusion in a *Western Democratization Index*, as follows:

1. Number of Representative Political Parties—a proxy for democratic choice
2. Voter Participation—a proxy for voters' confidence in the political process

3. Economic Policy Determination—a proxy for democratically determined economic policies
4. Economic Inequality—a proxy for lack of economic democracy
5. Inclination for War—a proxy for corruption
6. Prison Population—a proxy for social tension
7. Concentration of Media Ownership—a proxy for press coverage of alternative political views
8. Limits on Political Contributions—a proxy for the fairness of the democratic process
9. Corporate Democracy—a proxy for economic democracy in the corporate sector

The resultant index has some similarities with the ones currently in use but also some distinct differences. For example, freedom of the press, a criterion used in the present indexes, is relevant for identifying an explicit autocracy. On the other hand, a free press is available in all Western democracies, making this factor redundant and the concentration of media ownership more relevant as a proxy for coverage of diverse political views. Similarly, although the pursuit of neoclassical macroeconomic policies suggests a failing democratic process, however, its near universal adoption by Western democracies has rendered it an undiscriminating indicator of relative democracy.

On further consideration, the last three factors (Concentration of Media Ownership, Limits on Political Contributions, and Corporate Democracy), although relevant, were excluded from the computation of the *Western Democratization Index*, because they did not seem as crucial as the first six factors. Hence, the factors actually used in the computation of the *Western Democratization Index* are the following:

1. Number of Representative Political Parties
2. Voters' Participation
3. Democratically Determined Economic Policy
4. Wealth Concentration
5. Inclination for War
6. Prison Population

Reference Country

As stated previously, it is possible to use a democratization index in one of two ways: to compare a country's democracy relative to that of another that serves as a benchmark, or relative to itself over time, measured in decades. Time constraint has restricted the current analysis to the benchmark version only. Thus, it is up to interested students of political science and other researchers to apply the concept more broadly.

As the largest Western democracy, the United States was a natural choice for illustrating the democratization index. There remained choosing a suitable benchmark.

Switzerland probably enjoys the highest democratic standards, but it was judged unsuitable as a benchmark for three reasons. First, it is too small relative to the United States. Second, unlike most countries, it is neutral and does not engage in wars. Third, its democratic standards are probably too lofty for most countries. On the other hand, some political science researchers might prefer it as a benchmark precisely because it has the highest democratic standards.

Canada is another candidate, but it is also small relative to the United States.

The final choice for a democratic benchmark was Germany because it is the second largest Western democracy and enjoys good democratic credentials. Specifically, in the aftermath of World War II, Germany adopted a constitution that protects individual liberties and civil rights. In addition, it distributes political power effectively between the different branches of the government as well as the federal and state levels, thereby making it a satisfactory reference country.[298]

Political Choice

Democracy is just a slogan if voters have no real political choice; hence, it deserves special attention. One proxy for political choice is the number of political parties. For instance, the Soviet Union's Communist Party included millions of members from all over the country who elected the leadership of the party and the state, but it was not a democracy because it lacked political choice with voting restricted to party members. Having just one party is tantamount to a political monopoly and, therefore, undemocratic.

247

Generations ago, the political plutocracies of Great Britain and the United States devised voting systems that restricted political choice to just two political parties in their respective countries. As a result, contrary to democratic norms, these two countries have been ruled by one of two parties for centuries. Occasionally, the names of those parties changed, but never their number. A two-party system offers more choice than a political monopoly, but not by much, because it is a political duopoly. Economic theory tells us that a duopoly is very similar to a monopoly, giving consumers, political and otherwise, only marginally more choice than under a monopoly.

However, in the decades before the onset of the *counter-revolution*, the US two-party system was providing a reasonable level of political choice. Historically, political choice in the United States has been between centrist and right-wing economic agendas. The United States has never had a left-wing socialist leader and neither party has had a socialist agenda, although conservatives on the extreme right habitually accuse centrists of being left-wing socialists or communist. Moreover, both parties have had centrists and right-wing conservative leaders, and significant leaders have had a big role in setting the economic agendas of their parties.

Thus, Republican president Theodore Roosevelt was a reformer, trust-buster, centrist, and predictably hated by the conservative establishment of the Republican Party. Democratic president Franklin Roosevelt, the most popular American leader in history and elected four times, also had a centrist economic agenda and was just as hated by the conservative establishment of the Democratic Party. Republican president Dwight Eisenhower, elected twice and very popular, also had a centrist economic agenda. Similarly, Democratic president John F. Kennedy, who became extremely popular after his narrow election, also had a centrist economic agenda. His assassination indicated he was hated by some quarters. All four presidents supported the average person and opposed the agendas of large oligopolies and monopolies; hence, the conservative establishment on both sides opposed them. Their economic policies were the best available in their time, improving the environment for competition, business profits, economic growth and democracy.

Political choice in both the United States and Great Britain has suffered following the Thatcher-Reagan *counter-revolution*. It succeeded in shifting the

Two Centuries of Parasitic Economics

Republican Party in the United States and the Conservative Party in Great Britain from right of center to the extreme right. Paradoxically, Bill Clinton, the leader of the Democratic Party in the United States, and Tony Blair, the leader of the Labor Party in Great Britain, instead of positioning their parties in the vacant political center, mimicked their competition by moving their parties to the far right as well. Thus, in both countries, the political agendas of the competing parties became almost identical, in effect, reducing political choice to the wings of extremist right-wing parties. This is reminiscent of a customer complaining about Ford cars having a limited choice of color, to which Henry Ford famously replied, "You can have any color you like, as long as it is black." Indeed, when two parties dominate the political scene of a country and both adopt similar economic and political agendas their tiny number grossly overstates the extent of political choice available to voters.

President Ronald Reagan was very popular and elected twice in large measure because voters wrongly credited his conservative neoclassical economic policies with solving the problem of stagflation, whereas stagflation actually ended due to the collapse of the oil price, as discussed previously. The other popular leader with a distinct right-wing agenda was Democratic president Bill Clinton; his neoclassical policies sustained the Thatcher-Reagan *counter-revolution* in the economic sphere; he oversaw the dismantling of market regulations and the abolition of Glass–Steagall, expediting the rise of the *banking* plutocracy to supreme power. Right-wing Republican president George W. Bush was a disciple of President Ronald Reagan; he did his best to further the *counter-revolution* economically, domestically, and internationally. Democratic president Barack Obama ran on a platform of change but his most significant policies supported the *counter-revolution*. The test came early, in 2008-2009. He proved his allegiance to the banking plutocracy by his massive rescue package of the big zombie banks without extending aid to the millions of troubled mortgage borrowers, as detailed in the section titled "The Economic Efficiency of Morality" in Chapter 1. Slogans aside, his policies have been essentially a continuation of those of the Bush presidency by, for example, not repealing the Bush tax cuts for the ultra-rich. Less obvious is the right-wing economic policy of Democratic President Jimmy Carter, who was the first president to adopt extremist neoclassical monetary policy, by not blocking the Fed's violation of the interest rate ceiling set by Glass–Steagall—an action which culminated in the abolition of that law two decades later.

Worse than the limited choice, the political process in United States has ceased producing leaders with profound minds and a moral authority to match. The Republican Party has not produced a leader comparable to Eisenhower in six decades. Similarly, the Democratic Party has not produced anyone of the stature of Franklin Roosevelt or John F. Kennedy. The assassinations of President John Kennedy and his brother, Democratic presidential candidate Robert Kennedy, seem to have shut off the spigot for great American leadership. Perhaps those two assassinations signaled that henceforth the US presidency is a mortal career choice for real leaders. There have also been notable assassinations of popular centrist European political leaders who were against extreme rightwing policies such as former Italian Prime Minister Aldo Moro in 1978 and Swedish Prime Minister Olof Palme in 1986.

After President Kennedy, American leaders, despite their memorable speech making, have stayed clear of implementing a moral and centrist agenda. Indeed, most presidential candidates for the 2016 election present themselves as supporters of extreme right-wing policies to get the backing of the mainstream media and Wall Street. For example, Hillary Clinton, the favorite Democratic presidential hopeful as of early 2016, is positioning herself to the right of the Republican Party by backing Wall Street and the policies of the neocons and the *counter-revolution*. She is supported by the big banks, the media empire, and big business. Her past decisions of backing wars on Iraq, Libya, and Syria indicate she is a female version of George W. Bush under a Democratic label. It also shows that the Democratic Party elders supporting her, including union leaders, are continuing with the *counter-revolution* agenda, which her husband, President Bill Clinton, instituted in the Democratic Party two decades ago.

Meanwhile, the political center, holding the vast majority of voters is ready for the taking by a leader with a moral and centrist economic vision. Senator Bernie Sanders, a Democratic candidate, is offering economic and democratic reforms as a Social Democrat in the European meaning of the term (i.e. a centrist in American terminology). However, his reform agenda has allied the deep pockets, the media empires, and the Democratic Party establishment against him despite his mass popularity, thereby reducing his chances as the Democratic Party candidate.

In the other camp, Donald Trump, the most popular Republican Party presidential candidate is also rejected by his party establishment because he is against certain core economic and foreign policies of the neocons and the *counter-revolution*.

The popularity of Sanders among the Democrats and Trump among the Republicans marks the continued transformation in American public opinion: a large segment of American voters now recognizes that the policies of the *counter-revolution* have served the interests of a microscopic minority of billionaires and sacrificed the interests of the vast majority of Americans. Indeed, President Obama owes his success to capitalizing on this change in public mood and used "change" as his campaign slogan to gain popular support, but he reneged on his promises once he was in the Whitehouse, by supporting the big banks instead of homeowners, pursuing neocon's foreign policy, not repealing Bush's tax cuts for the rich, and generally, implementing the *counter-revolution*. It also shows that Hillary Clinton, several Republican candidates, and the political establishments of both parties are out of touch with the mood of American voters. The establishments running both parties are relying on party delegates to tilt primary elections and, therefore, the democratic process.

It would be misleading to leave the reader with the impression that the Republicans and Democrats are the only political parties in the United States. Indeed, there are approximately thirty other political parties, but, as of January 2015, not one was represented in the House of Representatives or the Senate.[299] To improve the democratic representation in both America and Great Britain, the present electoral system needs scrapping and replacing by proportional representation to permit the emergence of multi-party democracies. Indeed, as far back as the 19th century, John Stuart Mill, the last of the classical economists, advocated proportional representation to improve the standards of British democracy. Germany and Italy adopted proportional representation following World War II to prevent an autocratic concentration of political power in the hands of a single party and to curb their tendency for wars of aggression. For the same reasons, the overhaul of the obsolete and unfair voting systems in the United States and Great Britain would likely have the added benefit of putting an end to their wars of aggression.

The risk of not having a resilient multi-party political process in the lead countries of the West is that Western democracy will progressively degenerate into a parasitic capitalist version of the enfeebled Soviet Union in its final years. Yet reform in the shadow of the *counter-revolution* and the still rising power of the banking plutocracy has meagre chances. Granted that plutocracies desire to perpetuate and extend their economic and political powers, but the present path of Western plutocracies is leading to their demise and the economies they govern. Puzzlingly, they seem unaware of the economic, social, and political ills they are seeding. One possible explanation is that the aging Western plutocracies, are losing their mental prowess. Napoleon Bonaparte had observed that, "In politics stupidity is not a handicap," nevertheless, extreme stupidity is.[300]

Voter Participation

Voter participation reflects the public's perception of the responsiveness of the democratic process to their needs. To protect its democracy, Switzerland made voting mandatory to ensure 100 percent participation. Where it is not mandatory, democracies must be on the alert to falling voter turnouts to take timely remedial actions. Low and falling voter participation suggests that a significant and growing proportion of the population thinks that their democracy is dysfunctional. In other words, they are disillusioned with and lost faith in the relevance and effectiveness of their democratic process.

The United States has been experiencing extremely low and falling voter participation. In the November 2014 midterm elections, voter participation fell to a record low of 36.4 percent, down from 40.9 percent in the 2010 midterm elections.[301] The democratic credentials of any country become doubtful if a majority of its voters no longer sees any utility in voting. In other words, about two thirds of US voters do not approve of the existing political arrangements; by boycotting elections, they are casting a negative vote on the entire democratic process as it stands. It also strongly suggests that the vast majority of Americans desire a centrist government, to the left of the current extreme right-wing agendas of the Republican and Democratic parties. To enhance voter participation, the political process must offer genuine political choice and adopt economic policies that serve the interests of the majority instead of the agendas of the ultra-rich.

Economic Policy Determination

Under capitalism, the two principal economic policy tools are fiscal and monetary policies. Moreover, under a capitalist democracy, these ought to be firmly under the control of the elected government and parliament (e.g., Congress). The US Federal Reserve, a private central bank, has declared itself "an independent central bank because its monetary policy decisions do not have to be approved by the President or anyone else in the executive or legislative branches of government."[302] This is a clear statement that monetary policy is outside any democratic process. Moreover, Chapter 10 illustrated that in dollar terms the majority of US fiscal resources now fall under the control of the Federal Reserve, not Congress. The Federal Reserve has allotted trillions of dollars to various banks and corporations, both domestically and internationally, without congressional approval, which demonstrates that democratic fiscal control is slipping too. These fundamental violations of democracy have left Congress with partial control over fiscal policy only, while the bulk of economic policy decisions have passed to the hands of unelected bankers.

Economic Inequality

Political democracy is meaningless without economic democracy. Moreover, a high degree of economic inequality is typically a consequence of undemocratic and regressive tax and public expenditure policies, which promote increasing income and wealth disparity. For our purposes, we shall use wealth concentration as a proxy for economic inequality.

Wars of Aggression

The great American leaders saw wars as theft and corruption.[303] The vast majority of Americans suffer multiple setbacks because of wars of aggression. First, such wars are crimes against humanity and result in needless deaths, permanent incapacities, and tragedies on both sides. Second, those wars divert resources away from much needed social services. Third, the bigger a war's cost is, the bigger the opportunity for theft from American taxpayers. Fourth, American taxpayers are required to pay for these wars with interest added. Hence, President Dwight Eisenhower famously warned against wars of aggression, which only serve the interest of the military-industrial complex and not the public's. Since World War II, America has waged too many wars, practically all without just cause. Accordingly, the frequency of wars of aggression indicates that self-interest is overwhelming *societal-interest* in public policy, symptomatic of a failing democracy.

Prison Population

Chapter 13 presented crime as a major negative economic and democratic externality.[304] Crime is also a barometer of social tension. A public policy that is insensitive to the needs of the majority is undemocratic, precipitating poverty and a high incidence of crime, whereas a compassionate policy improves the standard of living of the impoverished and curbs crime. History confirms this. Decades ago, when America was gentler, it was safer, and the social cost of crime was demonstrably less. Today, however, the United States has the largest prison population in the world, which suggests it has become less compassionate and less democratic.

Computing the Western Democratization Index

The democratic factors of the benchmark country are set to 100 percent, by definition; however, this does not imply a perfect score. For any one factor, the score of a country relative to the benchmark country can be less than or greater than 100 percent, depending on whether that country under study achieves lower or higher scores than the benchmark. The total score is arrived at by adding the score of individual factors, instead of multiplying them, to prevent a very low score in one factor from overwhelming the overall rating. For the same reason all six factors were given equal weight. The final democratic score is arrived at by totaling the score of the country under study and dividing it by 600 percent, the total score of the benchmark, to arrive at a standardized figure where the benchmark country has a total score of 100 percent.

The following illustrates the computation of the *Western Democratization Index*:

1. Political Choice: Germany currently has five significant political parties represented in the German Federal Parliament (the Bundestag), while the United States only has two parties represented in the Congress.[305]

   Accordingly, the score of the United States is: (2/5) = 40 percent.

2. Voter Participation: In Germany, 71.5 percent of the voters participated in the most recent election of the Bundestag, compared to 36.4 percent of American voters in the most recent congressional elections (in November 2014).

   Therefore, the score of the United States is: (36.4/71.5) = 50.9 percent.

3. Economic Policy Determination: In the United States, a private central bank, the Federal Reserve, is in charge of the monetary policy; it has also appropriated massive fiscal powers without congressional approval. In contrast, the German central bank is publicly owned and controlled and elected officials approve all fiscal expenditure. Accordingly, the United States gets nil for a democratically determined monetary policy and only ½ for its fiscal policy, compared to 2 for Germany.

   Hence, the US score is (0.5/2) = 25 percent.

4. Wealth Concentration: The richest 10 percent of the population in Germany and the United States owns 59.2 percent and 74.4 percent of all wealth, respectively.[306]

   Thus, the score of the United States is (59.2/74.4) = 79.6 percent.

5. Wars of Aggression as Proxies for Corruption: Since World War II, the United States has been engaged in more than ten conflicts, while

Germany has only participated in the War on Afghanistan at the insistence of the United States.[307]

Accordingly, the score of the United States is (1/10) = 10 percent.

6. Prison Population: Germany has 94 prisoners per 100,000 people, while the corresponding figure for the United States is 737 per 100,000.[308]

Therefore, the score of the United States is (94/737) = 12.8 percent.

Table 14.1 summarizes the scores of the United States relative to those of Germany, the benchmark country.

TABLE 14.1
Computation of Western Democratization Index

	Reference Country Germany	Target Country USA
Choice of Political Parties	100%	40.0%
Voter Participation	100%	50.9%
Economic Policy Determination	100%	25.0%
Wealth Concentration	100%	79.6%
Wars since WWII	100%	10.0%
Prison Population	100%	12.8%
Total	600%	218.2%
Democratization Index	100%	36%

The fact that the overall *Western Democratization Index* rating of the United States is 36 percent (relative to Germany) shocked the author and may shock others too. It is still more shocking because German democracy itself has been waning, with the growing power of its own *banking plutocracy*. Stated simply, the United States has a serious democracy deficit.

The low democratic rating of the United States indicates that there is a clear need for reforming and improving American democracy as a prerequisite for improving American public sector efficiency. Improving democracy at home should take center stage, without the distraction of attempting to improve democracy in the rest of the world. In any case, it is vain for a country to try to instill in other countries what it lacks itself.

It would be interesting to know the scores of other Western democracies (e.g., Greece, Spain, Great Britain, France, Sweden, Switzerland), and those of emerging ones (e.g., Argentina, Brazil, India, Russia).

———

Parts III and IV identified several critical negative externalities. However, identifying a problem is only half the solution. Hence, the focus of Part V is finance and tax measures that can resolve or minimize the negative effects of said externalities.

Part V

ALTERNATIVE FINANCING AND TAXATION

Fifteen

THE NEXT REVOLUTION IN EQUITY FINANCE

The decadent international but individualistic capitalism in the hands of which we found ourselves after the war is not a success. It is not intelligent. It is not beautiful. It is not just. It is not virtuous. And it doesn't deliver the goods. In short we dislike it, and we are beginning to despise it. But when we wonder what to put in its place, we are extremely perplexed.[309]

JOHN MAYNARD KEYNES

The unified theory of macroeconomic failure considers immoral usury—its products, institutions, and economics—a prime negative externality; Chapters 7 through 11 further explored the economic, cyclical, political, social, and human consequences of usury. Indirectly, those chapters also provided an explanation of what prompted Latin-speakers to associate *death* with *mortgage* (usury).[310]

The political environment has furnished debt with artificial but, nonetheless, decisive tax and legal advantages over equity, making debt pervasive. Assuming it is politically feasible to reverse or, at least, eliminate the tax and legal favoritism of usury over equity, the present chapter offers equity finance, the nemesis of usurious debt, as an economically superior alternative, using housing and the corporate sector for illustration. It also considers the implications of a broad shift to equity finance, away from debt, on the discount rate, banking, monetary policy, and government revenue.

Developing the field of equity finance fully will unleash a second equity revolution, no less. However, such a major development will require the imagination and ingenuity of numerous financial engineers to devise a broad range of equity products that will meet the full spectrum of financing needs. It will also require government support to eliminate the favoritism enjoyed by debt over equity.

Equity Participation Certificates

Aside from treasuries, mortgages constitute the largest long-term finance market, with maturities stretching to thirty years. Most homeowners are familiar with mortgages. Hence, it is a natural choice to use it to illustrate equity finance as a substitute for mortgages. Moreover, mortgage borrowers are hardly limited to homebuyers. Businesses use mortgages to acquire office buildings, warehouses, malls, hotels, factories, aircrafts, ships, earth-moving equipment, and a range of other long-lived assets. Therefore, the equity alternative to the home mortgage, with some modifications, has broad applicability.

The present tax system treats interest more favorably than dividends and profit, without rational justification. For example, the personal income tax code has an interest deduction provision that lowers the after-tax cost of mortgage interest but without a corresponding tax deduction for rent. This encourages indebtedness, a major negative externality. Such tax treatment is also unfair and regressive because the incomes of those who rent tend to be lower than those who have mortgages. Hence, removing this tax bias by giving comparable treatment to rent is not only economically more rational, but also fairer and less regressive.

Let us call this alternative financing *Equity participation certificates* (EPCs), such that the homebuyer and the finance provider share the risk of ownership. Depending on his (her) income and prevailing yields in the rental market, a homebuyer using EPC may need to provide 10 percent of the purchase price of a property to become a 10 percent owner and user of that property.[311] A bank would provide the balance of 90 percent of the purchase price to become a 90 percent joint-owner. Once the bank pools a sizable amount of such investments, it can then earn a fee by selling the pool as an *equity participation fund* (EPF), where the investors can be individuals, pension schemes, insurance companies, income funds, or other institutions. As part of the marketing or by law, the bank retains a small ownership stake, such as 2.5 percent, as a gesture of goodwill toward the investors. For a management fee, the bank also acts as manager of the EPF, collecting rents, passing them to the account of the EPF, and otherwise looking after the interests of the EPF.[312]

The EPC contract requires the owner-occupier (homebuyer) to enter into a five-year renewable lease with monthly rental payments. The rent is set at market less any cost savings resulting from the tenant being a longer-term owner-occupier, as will be explained shortly. Initially, the EPF and the homebuyer ownerships of say 90 percent and 10 percent, respectively, are entitled to similar shares in the rent, in line with their equity participations. However, the EPF retains 100 percent of the rent, applying the excess 10 percent toward partial repayment of its equity participation, thereby progressively reducing its ownership stake and increasing that of the homebuyer, and adjusting the future monthly shares in the rent accordingly. During periods of exceptionally low rental yields, the homebuyer would need to make a *supplementary principal repayment* of 1 percent to 2 percent per year to the EPF to ensure full principal repayment within thirty years or less.

Once every five years, independent appraisers reassess the rent and reappraise the price of the property based on the prevailing market conditions. Based on this reevaluation, a new rent applies for the following five years, the property price on the books is brought in line with its then current market price together with the dollar value of the ownership stakes of the two parties; the EPF capital repayment schedule is adjusted accordingly.

Should the owner-occupier fail, for any reason, to make the monthly rental payments (or the *supplementary principal repayments,* if any) then the EPF could evict the owner-occupier as a tenant and lease the property to a third party. To compensate the EPF for any shortfall in net rental income for the balance of that five-year tenancy term, the EPF would retain the home-owner's share of future rents until it fully recovers its loss. Subsequently, the rental sharing formula would resume.

In addition, in the event of payment interruption to the EPF and pro-vided the housing market is not depressed and the property has appreciated sufficiently since its purchase that the homebuyer does not suffer a loss, then the EPF could sell the property on an arm's-length basis and distribute the proceeds in accordance with the respective share of each party, after deduct-ing any lost income from the homebuyer's equity. Thus, aside from the rent recovery as per the tenancy agreement, unlike a mortgage agreement, the homebuyer's equity is not sacrificed to protect the interest of the provider of the funds because the reward and risk are shared.

Furthermore, the homebuyer has the right, at any time, to bid for the property and the EPF has the right of first refusal at the same price to thwart low bids. In addition, both parties can jointly sell the property, at any time, to take advantage of an overly inflated property market.

For comparison purposes, a ten-year tenancy is inappropriate because in the event of nonperformance by the homebuyer the payment obligation on the balance of a ten-year term would be onerous, making it similar to a mortgage, which defeats the object of the exercise. Moreover, a ten-year term offers a slightly lower internal rate of return (IRR) to the EPF, because the rent and price reviews are delayed by an extra five years.

EPC Rental Equivalence

The tables in this chapter use linked Excel spreadsheets. The figures pre-sented are hypothetical. It should be straightforward to replicate the results or to generate the results for alternative input values such as property price, rental yield, initial capital participations, expenses, etc. There are no restric-tions on the use of this model by purchasers of this book, provided due reference is given. Table 15.1 compares the net cash flow from a standard one-year lease with that of a five-year owner-occupier lease. In the interest of simplicity, the example assumes the property price is $100,000. It also assumes that a one-year lease yields 5.00 percent gross. Compared to a one-year renewable lease, a long-term owner-occupier lease saves the owners significant costs: periodic leasing fees, management fees, repainting, maintenance, and vacancy between tenancies. Accordingly, a $5,000 (5.00 percent) gross rental of a one-year lease is estimated to correspond to a $4,050 (4.05 percent) net income from a long-term owner-occupier lease. The cost saving of $950 ($5,000 minus$4,050) is passed as a rent reduction to the owner-occupier.[313] Table 15.1 shows how this equivalence is arrived at. Home insurance at about 0.3 percent to 0.5 percent per year of the property value, depending on such factors as the location and the insurance provider, has been excluded from the comparison of one- and five- year leases because in either case it is the responsibility of the owners.[314]

TABLE 15.1
Equivalent Lease Terms: Third Party vs. Owner-Occupier

	One-Year Lease %	One-Year Lease $	Five-Year Lease (PEC)
Property Price	100.000%	$ 100,000	$ 100,000
Gross Market Rental Yield	5.000%	$ 5,000	
Less Cost Savings:			
Maintenance @ 0.25% of Property Value		$ 250.0	-
Management Cost @ 4% of Rent		$ 200.0	-
Vacancy @ 5% of Rent		$ 250.0	-
Leasing Agency Fees @ 5% of Rent		$ 250.0	-
Total Long-Term Lease Cost Savings	0.950%	$ 950.0	-
Net Rental Income	4.050%	$ 4,050	$ 4,050

EPC Cash Flow Illustration

Table 15.2 uses the assumptions and results in Table 15.1 to summarize the initial cash flow assumptions used in Table 15.3. It assumes that the rent and the value of the property both appreciate at the rate of 1 percent per year, resulting in an increase of 5.10 percent in rent and the book value of the property at the start of successive five-year periods. The *supplementary principal repayment* in Table 15.3 is arrived at by using progressive approximations. In this example, full discharge of EPF ownership in thirty years requires a *supplementary principal repayment* of about 1.30 percent per annum. The internal rate of return (IRR) to the EPF of 4.35 percent is based on the net cash flow projections in Table 15.3.

TABLE 15.2

Equity Participation Certificate Assumptions

	Dollar Amount	Percent
Property Purchase Price	$ 100,000	100.00%
Initial Homebuyer Ownership Share	$ 10,000	10.00%
Initial EPF Ownership Share	$ 90,000	90.00%
Initial Net Annual Rent	$ 4,050	4.05%
Supplementary Principal Repayment Per Year	$ 1,302	1.30%
Annual Rent & Price Appreciation		1.00%
Rent & Price Increase Per Five-Year Review		5.10%
Internal Rate of Return		4.35%

Table 15.3 presents the book value of the property (adjusted to market price once every five years) and the corresponding year-end equity balances of the EPF and the homebuyer. It also shows the payments and cash flows for each year. It assumes that rental payments are annually in arrears instead of monthly in advance, as with standard rent.[315] Mortgage payments are also paid in arrears, although monthly. Monthly payments would have been more accurate; however, the table would have run for several pages, making it difficult for the reader to follow. The net effect of annual payments in arrears instead of monthly in advance is negligible, slightly delaying the receipt of payment by the EPF on the one hand, while slightly increasing the cash flow due to the EPF by delaying the recognition of its decreasing ownership stake on the other.

Table 15.3 presents two sources of principal repayment. First, the owner-occupier pays the rent, which the EPF retains in full, using the owner-occupier share of the rent as a partial principal repayment of the EPF capital contribution. Second, in this example the owner-occupier makes a *supplementary principal repayment* of $1,302 (1.3019 percent of the property purchase price) to ensure a full principal discharge within thirty years. An initial down payment greater than 10 percent would decrease the need for *supplementary principal repayment* or eliminate it if it is sufficiently large. Moreover, as the income of the owner-occupier increases over time, he or she could make additional principal repayments without penalty to bring the full repayment forward. Curiously, a higher rental yield would require a smaller *supplementary principal repayment* because the owner-occupier part of the rent retained by the EPF would be a larger dollar amount. The column titled "Total Principal Repayment" is the sum of the two sources of principal repayment: the homebuyer's share of the rent and the *supplementary principal repayment*.

The column titled "EPF Direct Expenses" refers to expenses born by EPF, namely its declining share of insurance at 0.3 percent of the property value and the bank management fee at 5 percent of the rental income attributable to the EPF. The final column titled "EPF Cash Flow" is the total of the columns "Net Rent," "Supplementary Repayment," and "EPF Direct Expenses." The internal rate of return to the EPF over the thirty-year period at 4.35 percent is calculated based on the cash flows appearing in the "EPF Cash Flow" column. This is slightly more attractive to investors than the current 3.8 percent interest on a thirty-year mortgage and without the risk of periodic mass defaults, which bankrupts many banks. It is also more attractive to homebuyers and more cost-effective because it is without the significant implicit cost of an event of default associated with borrowing. In the initial year, the owner-occupier total payment is $5,352 ($4,050 in rent + $1,302 in supplementary principal repayment), or 5.35 percent of the value of the property, which is comparable to the 5.00 percent gross yield of a one-year lease. In any case, it offers a lower cost option, net of principal repayments, for the homebuyer than a short-term lease.

TABLE 15.3
Equity Participation Certificates - Cash Flow

Year	Property Book Value	EPF's Equity	Home Buyer's Equity	Net Rent	Buyer's Share of Rent	Suppl. Repay. 1.3019%	Total Principal Repay.	EPF Direct Expens.	EPF Cash Flow
				A	B	C	B+C	D	A+C+D
0	$100,000	$90,000	$10,000						-$90,000
1	$100,000	$88,293	$11,707	$4,050	$405	$1,302	$1,707	-$452	$4,900
2	$100,000	$86,517	$13,483	$4,050	$474	$1,302	$1,776	-$444	$4,908
3	$100,000	$84,669	$15,331	$4,050	$546	$1,302	$1,848	-$435	$4,917
4	$100,000	$82,746	$17,254	$4,050	$621	$1,302	$1,923	-$425	$4,926
5	$100,000	$80,746	$19,254	$4,050	$699	$1,302	$2,001	-$416	$4,936
6	$105,101	$82,743	$22,358	$4,257	$820	$1,302	$2,121	-$414	$5,144
7	$105,101	$80,536	$24,565	$4,257	$905	$1,302	$2,207	-$416	$5,143
8	$105,101	$78,239	$26,862	$4,257	$995	$1,302	$2,297	-$405	$5,154
9	$105,101	$75,849	$29,252	$4,257	$1,088	$1,302	$2,390	-$393	$5,165
10	$105,101	$73,362	$31,739	$4,257	$1,185	$1,302	$2,487	-$381	$5,177
11	$110,462	$74,452	$36,011	$4,474	$1,351	$1,302	$2,653	-$376	$5,399
12	$110,462	$71,691	$38,771	$4,474	$1,458	$1,302	$2,760	-$374	$5,401
13	$110,462	$68,819	$41,643	$4,474	$1,570	$1,302	$2,872	-$360	$5,415
14	$110,462	$65,831	$44,631	$4,474	$1,687	$1,302	$2,988	-$346	$5,430
15	$110,462	$62,721	$47,741	$4,474	$1,808	$1,302	$3,109	-$331	$5,445
16	$116,097	$62,587	$53,510	$4,702	$2,032	$1,302	$3,334	-$322	$5,682
17	$116,097	$59,118	$56,979	$4,702	$2,167	$1,302	$3,469	-$314	$5,689
18	$116,097	$55,508	$60,589	$4,702	$2,308	$1,302	$3,610	-$297	$5,707
19	$116,097	$51,752	$64,345	$4,702	$2,454	$1,302	$3,756	-$279	$5,725
20	$116,097	$47,845	$68,252	$4,702	$2,606	$1,302	$3,908	-$260	$5,744
21	$122,019	$46,078	$75,941	$4,942	$2,905	$1,302	$4,207	-$245	$5,998
22	$122,019	$41,700	$80,319	$4,942	$3,076	$1,302	$4,378	-$232	$6,012
23	$122,019	$37,146	$84,873	$4,942	$3,253	$1,302	$4,555	-$210	$6,034
24	$122,019	$32,406	$89,613	$4,942	$3,437	$1,302	$4,739	-$187	$6,057
25	$122,019	$27,475	$94,544	$4,942	$3,629	$1,302	$4,931	-$163	$6,081
26	$128,243	$23,550	$104,693	$5,194	$4,024	$1,302	$5,326	-$141	$6,355
27	$128,243	$18,008	$110,235	$5,194	$4,240	$1,302	$5,542	-$118	$6,377
28	$128,243	$12,242	$116,001	$5,194	$4,465	$1,302	$5,766	-$90	$6,405
29	$128,243	$6,242	$122,001	$5,194	$4,698	$1,302	$6,000	-$62	$6,434
30	$128,243	-$1	$128,244	$5,194	$4,941	$1,302	$6,243	-$31	$6,464

This table is for illustrative purposes only. Market conditions fluctuate widely and could be materially different. The author assumes no responsibility as to the accuracy or completeness of the above assumptions or projections.

Standardization of the terms of the EPC agreement would facilitate their placement with large investors as pools of real estate investments, significantly expanding the funding available for this homeownership format. This would be one of the requirements of large potential investors such as Fannie Mae, Freddie Mac, insurance companies, and pension funds. Another likely requirement would be that the managing bank retains a small ownership stake in the EPF of some 2.5 percent to ensure its continued interest and to handle potential problems such as the owner-occupier vacating the property. An active secondary market in standardized pools of EPCs would provide liquidity to that market and, in time, a wide range of maturities to investors.

EPCs vs. Mortgage Finance

In an environment in which central banks aggressively manipulate interest rates, mortgage yields can fluctuate wildly over a full interest-rate cycle, with the greatest fluctuations occurring in variable-rate mortgages. As a result, mortgage yields can fall lower than property yields during periods of easy credit and rise higher during periods of tight credit. Thus, relative yields of mortgages versus rentals can change over a business cycle and over the longer credit cycle. To the extent interest rates in 2015 are at a low point after peaking in 1981, the odds are that the next long-term trend is for interest rates to rise, which could make EPCs relatively cheaper to homebuyers than mortgages.

Still, the cost of EPC is not directly comparable to the nominal cost of mortgage finance because in addition to its explicit interest cost a mortgage also carries a prohibitive implicit cost, which becomes explicit in the event of a default. Unlike mortgage finance, failure to meet the payments of EPCs does not culminate in the forced sale of a property in a weak market, wiping out the homebuyer's equity after years of savings. Indeed, the EPC option represents a far smaller financial risk than a mortgage to both the homebuyer and the finance partner, as will become clear.

The banks' foreclosure engine breaks down during recessions as unemployment soars, defaults peak, and property prices crash. At such times, selling a large inventory of foreclosed properties exacerbates the problems of the property market for all parties. In fact, foreclosed properties on bank balance sheets significantly diminish banks' capital adequacy ratios as defined by the central bank. This capital reduction drives banks to act like a mindless herd, against their own self-interest, by simultaneously disposing of hundreds of thousands, possibly millions, of foreclosed properties at the worst possible prices.

Foreclosures distort the housing supply curve, resulting in economic instability. A normal supply curve is positively sloping, where supply increases in response to higher prices. However, foreclosures artificially bend the supply curve to make it negatively sloping, where an increase in supply of foreclosed properties forces prices lower, leading to more foreclosures. Specifically, falling property prices act as a brake on new construction and economic activity, increasing unemployment and, with it, mortgage defaults and foreclosures, setting off a vicious cycle of falling prices and increasing foreclosures—hence, the intrinsic economic irrationality of mortgage financing. Indeed, a financially aware Consumer Protection Agency would have banned mortgage lending a long time ago for being a defective financing product. These periodic foreclosure tsunamis represent a significant incremental cost and risk not just to property owners but also to the mortgage providers and the economy at large.

Fair tax treatment of home rental payments that is comparable to that of mortgages is necessary for the successful transition away from mortgages to EPCs. Similarly, having Fanny Mae and Freddie Mac provide guarantees similar to those they provide for mortgages would expedite the secondary trading of pools of EPCs, increasing their liquidity.

Finally, with appropriate adjustments such as the cost recovery of maintenance and replacement parts, the EPC concept could be adapted to finance a variety of long-lived assets, including ships, aircraft, trucks, cranes, and earthmoving equipment.

Common Shares

Common shares are the foundation of company finance, representing corporate ownership and the full assumption of business risk.[316] Owning common shares is unconditional investing, without the promise of dividends, principal repayment, or a maturity date. Thus, they carry neither the risk of default to corporate issuers nor any incremental risk to the economy. The absence of a default risk permits corporations to assume greater business risk, which is conducive to faster economic growth and greater economic stability. Common shares can replace all other types of company financing, but no financing can replace them fully.

A single class of common shares is simplest to own and vote; it is also the most transparent form of ownership and the fairest because the complexity of multiple classes of common shares provides opportunities for abuse by unfair managements and powerful shareholders.

Convertible bonds give their holders the right to convert them into common shares, but until converted, they remain debt.

Preferred Shares

The closest financing instrument to common shares is preferred shares, but their market size is a fraction of that of common shares; hence, they typically trade over the counter. Unlike common shares, preferred shares characteristically can be for a limited period, requiring their corporate issuers to repay the principal at maturity. Sometimes preferred shares are convertible into common shares at a specified strike price. The preferred dividends are set as a percentage of the face value of the preferred shares, enjoy payment priority over common dividends, and offer a higher yield; preferred dividends are sometimes participating, meaning they become entitled to a higher dividend if the common dividend is increased.

Three attributes can make a preferred share resemble debt more than equity. First is a cumulative preferred dividend clause, requiring payment of all past-due and unpaid dividends before resuming dividend payments to common shareholders, even if the company did not realize any profit during the dividend-interruption period(s). Thus, a cumulative preferred dividend clause puts the dividend risk squarely on the common shareholders. Second, sometimes nonpayment of preferred dividends or principal permits revision of the original terms of the preferred, making nonpayment resemble an event of default under debt, especially if it gives the preferred shareholders more voting power and better financial terms. Third, a preference over common in capital distribution in the event of the liquidation of a company also makes the preferred resemble debt. Hence, a preferred share with a higher yield and preference over the common in the payment of dividends, but without a cumulative dividend clause, does not require renegotiating its terms in the event of nonpayment of dividends or principal; and without preference over the common in the event of corporate liquidation is a genuine equity rather than a hybrid.

The trade-off between preferred and common shares is that the former offers a lower risk of dividend interruption, a higher dividend yield, and a tentative principal repayment schedule in return for a more limited capital appreciation potential, except in the case of convertible preferred. These features satisfy the needs of certain types of investors, such as pensioners, income funds, and insurance companies, without the associated negative externalities of debt.

Eliminating the tax privileges of debt over equity will likely make preferred shares far more popular. Over time, investors will recognize enterprises with excellent preferred dividend and principal repayment records and will reward them with lower yields and longer maturities. Finally, preferred financing is less suited for highly cyclical corporations, but still a better option than debt because it avoids the credit risk to the issuer.

Charitable and Cooperative Lending
Both charitable and cooperative lending carry zero interest. Charitable lenders can be individuals or charities; they help those in need or extend interest-free loans with flexible repayment terms to fund micro businesses. The

clearest proof that such lending is in fact interest-free is that its total repayments do not exceed the original amount advanced. If a borrower's financial condition does not permit repayment, then a charitable loan should become a charitable gift, otherwise it would degenerate into an arduous loan.

Cooperatives can provide financing for a variety of needs, such as the purchase of durable goods or even housing. They operate as a club or society with each member paying a specific monthly amount for a predetermined period. To decide periodically who receives the required funds to make a purchase, a queuing system is preferable to a lottery because it is fairer.

The advantage of cooperative borrowing is that it carries zero interest. Moreover, a rapidly growing finance cooperative can significantly shorten the waiting period to obtain financing for a newcomer. Cooperatives are well adapted to financing the purchase of durable goods like cars, furniture, and white goods (i.e. appliances) because the waiting period between joining a financing program and obtaining financing is not excessive.

On the other hand, cooperative financing for the purchase of a property has three distinct disadvantages. First, a long waiting period must elapse before funding becomes available. Second, during the waiting period, the potential buyer must pay rent in addition to the monthly contributions to the cooperative. Third, property prices may rise in the interim, making the amount of the planned funding inadequate.

Short Rents

Asset rental is usually for short periods relative to the useful life of the asset because the need is temporary or for an uncertain duration. Thus, asset rental is flexible, does not require financing, and is easy to implement. Rented assets include residential units, offices, commercial spaces, ships, aircraft, cars, and heavy equipment.

However, rent can be a disguise for lending. A long rental period relative to the useful life of the asset, with a costly penalty for early termination and an option to buy for a relatively small sum at the end of the rental period, usually flags a financial lease (borrowing). The corporate income tax code permits full deductibility of rentals but only partial deductibility of financial leases because principal amortization is wrapped within the rental payments.

Tax-Exempt Municipal Bonds

Tax-exempt municipal bonds are a thinly veiled tax loophole for reducing the marginal income tax rate of the ultra-rich, hence, their strong political support for its preservation. If a lower marginal tax rate were appropriate for the rich, then it would be better to make it explicit and transparent.

Without this tax-loophole, the interest on municipal bonds would be higher, but the increase in federal and state personal income tax revenue would be larger still, which the federal government could use to help local authorities through direct transfers to offset the increase in interest cost.

To the extent that tax-exempt municipal bonds finance investments in income-generating projects, such as toll bridges and highways, and in the absence of tax preference for debt, preferred shares could serve the same purpose, without exposing local authorities to the risk of default.

The Discount Rate

The proponents of interest-bearing debt raise the concern that in the absence of interest it would be impossible to calculate the present value of future cash flows of investments and projects. This argument is flawed. Since neoclassical economics replaced Keynesianism in the late 1970s, government cyclical stabilization has shifted from fiscal to monetary policy, resulting in extreme interest rate gyrations driven by the Federal Reserve. Fed Chairman Paul Volker raised the federal funds rate to 20 percent in 1981; interest rates remained artificially high, though declining, up to the 1990s. Since then, a generally easy monetary policy has pushed interest rates to the other extreme, culminating in quantitative easing and near-zero interest rates. Hence, for decades, interest rates have been arbitrary instead of market driven, making them a misleading discount rate for evaluating investments.

The spillover effects of those monetary policies have also affected the market yields of equity and property investments. Still, those yields have been more stable than debt yields because the impact of monetary policy on them is secondary. Hence, in the absence of debt, the yield to maturity of EPCs, for example, is a more appropriate discount rate for evaluating property investments, while the yield to maturity of preferred stocks, without a conversion option, is more appropriate for discounting corporate cash flows of comparable risk and maturity.

Remodeling Banking

The difficulties confronting banking reform have echoes in a children's tale of two tailors that duped a king, his entourage, and the public into believing that the magnificent attire they had tailored for the king was invisible to idiots.[317] Hence, no one, least of all the king, dared say the outfit was invisible for fear of being taken for an idiot. Thus, the king went naked on a grand royal procession amid public adoration for his magnificent "attire."

Like those tailors, bankers have convinced the world that, without usury lubricating the world economic engine, capitalism cannot function. Economists, financial analysts, and political leaders have observed the repeated banking meltdowns in silence, not daring to declare banking defunct lest they are taken for idiots. Thus, the *theater of the absurd* continues to produce tragedies of Shakespearean proportions, with fate for director and bankers for lead actors, delivering dramatic performances on the dazzling stage of high finance to a world mystified by their impossible logic. Economics is not a mystery, but the experts we count on are lacking in assertiveness and self-confidence. Rescuing the banks from this fate of perpetual tragedy requires freeing them from the Ponzi trap that has ensnared them and the rest of the world for too long.

It is time to allow Joseph Schumpeter's creative destruction to run its course in the financial sector, as in the rest of the economy. Western governments have obstructed this process in the past as it relates to banking. This means they must now compensate for their past economic sins by gradually ending the support system that is keeping banking artificially alive, while simultaneously acting as midwife for the delivery of the new financial order. The existing parasitic banking model is an unstable Ponzi scheme that is obsolete and in desperate need of replacement, but banking interests have blocked the financial alternative for a long time, contrary to Western national economic interests. Reforming the financial system is essential for revitalizing Western economies. Indebtedness has reached such a degree in the West it is now impossible to forge a more efficient economic system without dispensing with usurious banking.

Ending the Ponzi scheme and resolving banks' chronic conflict of interest with their customers requires splitting banking into distinct lines of business à la Glass–Steagall, namely, investment banking, investment advisory services, and commercial banking. These distinct business models would permit specialist entities to emerge with a keen focus on their respective areas of specialty and a narrower scope for conflict of interest with their clients and, therefore, a better chance of delivering quality services.

Investment banks have had glaring conflicts of interest with the investing public. Moreover, the quality of their investment advice has been mediocre. Hence, it is best to restrict them to their primary business of raising capital and mergers and acquisitions, without operating as brokerage houses or providing investment advice other than in prospectuses and placement memoranda as part of their primary business. They also need to show the performance record of their past transactions relative to the market in the twelve months following its closing date, for the last five or ten years.

Investment advisory services would cater to the investing public, investment managers, investment banks, commercial banks, insurance companies, pension funds, and other institutional investors who in turn could share such advice with their customers where appropriate. They would also need to provide a verifiable record of their past advice over two stock market cycles, or since their inception if shorter.

Aside from investment banking and investment advisory services, which would have to be spun off as separate businesses, commercial banking would retain similarities to the present model, but with some distinct differences.

Its main business would gradually move away from lending to asset management and capital investing, without borrowing, derivatives, or short selling. However, they could issue preferred shares to finance a larger volume of business. Thus, banks would gradually stop new lending or paying interest on deposits, thereby progressively eliminating the exposure of their customers to their present financial risk.[318]

Banks would earn fees as managers of *equity participation funds* and other equity investment funds and earn a return on investing their capital. To the extent that banks would need to co-invest, to the tune of say 2.5 percent of the funds under their management, then total assets under their management could reach forty times their capital. With management fees of say 0.23 percent, total assets under management that would generate a return of 9.2 percent plus perhaps another 4 percent in return on their capital investments, giving the banks a total potential return of 13.2 percent before expenses and without leverage.[319] Matching the common equity with preferred shares yielding 6 percent would provide a net incremental return of 3.2 percent (9.2 percent minus 6 percent).[320] Hence, issuing preferred shares equal to five times the common equity would boost the total return on common equity to 29.2 percent before operating expenses, without risk of default.[321] Investment managers with steady performance records would likely be able to have higher levels of preferred shares at lower yields and those with a superior investment performance could potentially earn higher fees and vice versa.

The limited risk coupled with the attractive potential return is likely to attract more capital and competition over time to normalize the risk-adjusted return to that attainable in other parts of the economy. Nevertheless, it serves to illustrate the point. To protect investors from corrupt or incompetent operators, their audited investment performance record of all their current and discontinued funds needs to be available to potential investors.

In addition, banks would have a host of other sources of fee-based income including placement of asset pools, custody services, checking account, debit cards, transfers, and foreign currency exchange.

Fee-based instead of asset-based banking coupled with the absence of debt would dramatically cut banking risk, making banking crises largely passé. Federal Deposit Insurance Corporation (FDIC) fees would fall significantly, although it could provide better insurance cover for fraud and conflict of interest.

Finally, the anxious calls for reinstating Glass–Steagall are in vain because that never provided a real solution; it only attempted to manage the structural problem of banking; today, given the degree of overall indebtedness, it is hardly adequate even by the standards of the 1930s. In any case, the Ponzi-structured banks would never cease lobbying to repeal any reinstated Glass–Steagall, as the recent past has demonstrated.

Stability, Money Creation, and Monetary Policy

There are distinct advantages to the economy and the Treasury in remodeling banking as proposed in the previous section. First, the problem of banking crises and their associated costs—in the form of enormous bailouts, quantitative easing, and economic disruption—would cease, potentially saving the economy trillions of dollars. The business cycle would become smoother; hence, budget deficits during contractions would become smaller.

Intriguingly, banks would lose their present money-creating franchise under the fractional reserve system, which gives them license to create deposits (money) out of thin air to lend to their customers. This money-creation function would pass to the Treasury.[322] It would let the government capture the *monetary dividend* or the "free" revenue associated with increasing the money supply to accommodate economic growth and frictional inflation, a public windfall without taxation, borrowing, or inflation, thereby closing the loop of money creation.[323]

Given the major role of the dollar in the conduct of international trade and as an international reserve currency, the US *monetary dividend* would be greater still given the increase in the international demand for dollars to accommodate the growth in international trade and international reserves.

Without banking crises, central banks would lose their reason to exist, as lifesavers of big banks. Without lending, derivatives, or short selling, banking supervision would be simpler, and specialist sections within the Treasury could supervise financial institutions, including banks. Bringing any residual central bank functions within the Treasury would eliminate the schizophrenic conflicts between monetary and fiscal policies, a consequence of the so-called "independent" central banks conducting "independent" monetary policies.

For the United States, in particular, these measures would have the additional advantage of eliminating the daunting problem of a private central bank encroaching on government functions and undermining democracy, as discussed in Chapter 10. They would also result in significant savings to taxpayers by eliminating a bloated Federal Reserve bureaucracy.

In the absence of debt, a national economy would be better insulated against the vagaries of interest-rate fluctuations emanating from abroad. Federal, state, and local authorities wishing to finance income-generating projects, like airports or toll bridges, could use preferred stock, equity participation certificates, or build-operate arrangements for a defined term, with ultimate reversion of such projects to the authority concerned.

The role of monetary policy would be limited to accommodating growth and supporting fiscal policy. This is close to the vision of Milton Friedman of a steady growth in the money supply and no central bank with one major difference: fiscal policy would be responsible for cyclical stabilization in an environment substantially immunized against interest rate fluctuations.

In the final analysis, humanity surely deserves a more civilized, never mind a more efficient, financing model than the crude savagery of "a pound of flesh for a pound of gold," or any variation on it.

Sixteen

PUBLIC FINANCE AND INDIRECT TAXES

Note, besides, that it is no more immoral to directly
rob citizens than to slip indirect taxes into the
price of goods that they cannot do without.[324]

ALBERT CAMUS

Chapter 2 identified two instinctually rational drivers of economic behavior, *self-interest* and *societal-interest*, with the first driving markets and, ideally, the second driving public policy, but frequently otherwise. Self-interest is satisfied by maximizing profit and surviving the slings and arrows of the marketplace. *Societal-interest* is satisfied by the fair and efficient provision of public goods and their associated taxes. The choice of public goods and taxation requires a valid democratic process as the ultimate arbiter of the validity and fairness of public choice. Hence, anything that interferes with an efficient democracy degrades public choice and economic efficiency and vice versa.

The unified theory of macroeconomic failure identified several groups of chronic negative externalities that confront Western economies and, therefore, require public sector intervention. The discussion so far concerning the efficiency of public expenditure and taxation has been limited; a broader examination is now in order to permit a critical review. This chapter discusses public sector expenditure, taxation generally, and indirect taxes specifically. The three chapters to follow will examine corporate and personal taxation.

Before going any further, a word of caution is necessary about the unhappy state of affairs in the field of public finance, particularly to the students of public finance. If the previous discussions, especially concerning the role of academia, have illustrated that politics has corrupted macroeconomics, then we should emphasize that public finance has been a prime target of this perversion. For example, most public finance books and scholars are guilty of singing the praises of a "progressive" personal income tax instead of factually explaining that the present tax regime is regressive because it uses the wrong tax bases like taxing income from capital instead of capital proper. At the same time, the abundance of personal income tax loopholes, shelters, and exceptions has rendered any talk of progressivity misleading. Like macroeconomic theory, public finance has been a stagnant pond for too long and badly needs an overhaul. It is up to the students of public finance to bring their field into the 21st century.

The Need for Public Goods

Public goods are fundamentally different from private goods; hence, a market framework cannot provide them efficiently, if at all. The full benefits of pure public goods cannot be internalized through the market price because they are lumpy, it is not possible to exclude anyone, and their consumption does not diminish their availability to the rest of society. Examples of pure public goods include defense, police protection, the courts, the protection and enforcement of property rights, environmental protection, international relations, and democracy—a process for authorizing, funding, and administering a public-goods program. On the other hand, quasi-public goods like public health and education have characteristics of public goods, such as the spillover of benefits, as well as private goods, such as divisibility and lack of lumpiness, which permit the wealthy to treat them as private goods.

The following are some of the reasons that make the provision of public goods by the state necessary, as follows:

- Lumpiness, indivisibility, and huge cost make the public provision of pure public goods, like national defense, a necessity.
- Resolving conflicts and protecting property rights require an effective court system to ensure fairness and dispense justice, and a police force to enforce such decisions as well as to provide security.
- The production of negative externalities, such as pollution, requires public intervention through laws, taxes, and penalties to restrict their harmful effects on society.
- Improving income distribution helps alleviate poverty and *chronic underconsumption* to drive the economy closer to its production possibility frontier, thereby improving the performance and efficiency of the economy. Market forces cannot resolve such problems, requiring public intervention by replacing regressive taxes with progressive ones, providing more and better job opportunities to lessen unemployment, a higher minimum wage, training, education, transfer payments, public health, and other welfare programs.
- Maintaining competitive markets requires public intervention and regulation to prevent monopolies and curb oligopolies.
- The presence of natural monopolies, such as central banks and utilities, requires their public ownership or, at a minimum, satisfactory public regulation and oversight of their pricing, production, and operations.
- Improving the economic efficiency of decision-making requires the availability of reliable information about products, services, capital markets, and government statistics.
- Protecting the public against harmful products and practices in the marketplace requires product licensing and supervision by specialist agencies, such as the Food and Drug Administration (FDA).

- The production of positive externalities associated with quasi-public goods, such as public health and education, requires public intervention to encourage their consumption to capture their public benefits more fully.

Public Expenditure Efficiency

In recent decades, some economists have argued that improving economic efficiency and the rate of growth require reducing the size of the public sector. For example, Richard Rahn, originator of the Rahn curve, called for reducing the ratio of the public sector to GDP to the levels prevailing in the 1920s and in the 19th century.[325] This suggestion overlooks the history of US economic cycles summarized in Chapter 11, particularly the section titled "United States Cyclical Contractions (1785–2009)." A prime reason why economic contractions have become shallower and shorter since 1942 is the increase in the size of the government relative to GDP, following the growth of the welfare state. In addition, a satisfactory level of welfare is essential while a large segment of the population needs it, a requirement under a democratic system. Repudiation of essential welfare in the midst of poverty is tantamount to an abandonment of democracy. Moreover, improper privatization of certain government functions, such as the Federal Reserve and prisons, proved prohibitively costly to the government and taxpayers as well as detrimental to democracy itself.

The present anemic growth rate in the United States is the result of multiple causes, all invariably traceable to deteriorating democratic standards. The causes include a regressive tax system, tax discrimination against economic efficiency, tax subsidization of debt resulting in amplified cyclicality, falling competition, an overvalued dollar, and wasteful expenditures on wars of aggression and zombie banks. Thus, rationalizing public expenditure and improving the efficiency of taxation can dramatically reduce waste, increase public benefits, and raise efficiency, resulting in faster growth. In other words, the priority is increasing public sector efficiency by improving the public-expenditure tax mix rather than a blanket reduction in the size of government, as vividly demonstrated since 2009 by the disastrous austerity programs in Southern Europe.

Improving the efficiency of public sector expenditure requires resolving a variety of potential and actual issues, of which the list below is but a sample:

- High democratic standards are required to ensure the validity and legitimacy of public choice in formulating public expenditure and tax policies. For example, it is a contradiction of terms to speak of rich democracies having widespread poverty, homelessness, hunger, and depravation of their citizens; if such societies are rich, then they are not democratic.

- Which public goods and in what quantities does the public demand and need?

- Is the government provision of public goods cost-effective? For example, lack of serious competition in the United States has made the cost of US medical care much higher than in Japan, while the quality is materially inferior.[326] Reducing the inflated cost of public goods requires the breakup of monopolies and oligopolies and intensifying competition between public sector suppliers.[327]

- Is the government distributing the benefits and costs of public goods fairly and efficiently?

- Eliminating the structural conflict between fiscal and monetary policies is a necessary condition for an effective economic policy.

- Fiscal stabilization during contractions through the timely implementation of infrastructure projects maximizes the benefits per dollar expended, whereas tax cuts and quantitative easing are not cost-effective.

- Improving US competitiveness and growth requires the rejuvenation of the industrial sector, which in turn requires the end of chronic dollar overvaluation and trade deficits, because an overvalued currency is tantamount to a tax on exports and a subsidy for imports.

- Improving US international standing by pursing international peace, coexistence, and goodwill is infinitely cheaper than the prohibitively costly and futile wars of aggression.
- Public welfare would improve by reducing economic inequality and improving job opportunities, public education, health care, housing, and social services.
- Improving quality of life requires reducing crime and its associate costs through the elimination of poverty, better job training and job opportunities, and shorter and fairer sentencing.[328]

Tax Objectives, Efficiency, and Types

Taxes are the price of public goods and they are borne by people whether as consumers, workers, or capital owners. Taxes entail an excess burden when they misallocate resources, pervert a fair distribution of income, encourage the wrong activities, increase economic instability, entail waste, or promote economic inefficiency. Hence, it is the responsibility of economists to point out the flaws of the tax system, improve its efficiency, and lessen its burden.

As with public expenditure, there are several issues regarding the objectives, appropriateness, and efficiency of taxes, such as:

- Is a valid democratic process providing the constitutional and legal basis for taxation?
- Are taxes providing sufficient revenue to cover the cost of the required public goods?
- Are the benefits of the wealthy and high-income groups from the public expenditure commensurate with their level of taxation?
- Is taxation improving income distribution?
- Do tax loopholes and shelters make taxes unfair, undemocratic, and lacking in transparency?
- Is the tax code simple enough for taxpayers to understand and comply with it?

- Do taxes improve or detract from the efficient allocation of economic resources, with implications for economic growth?
- Do taxes amplify or dampen economic fluctuations?
- Are taxes reducing or increasing negative externalities?
- Is it possible to improve the efficiency of tax collection (diminish the cost of tax collection as a percentage of the revenue generated)?

There are two broad categories of taxes: direct and indirect. Direct personal taxes include personal income, capital gains, inheritance, transfer, and, in some jurisdictions, wealth taxes. The principal direct corporate tax is on corporate income.

On the other hand, indirect taxes, our focus in this chapter, are transactions based and levied on products and services. They are indirect because they are not specific to any individual or corporation and, in principle, avoidable by not consuming a good or service that is subject to tax.

The Case for a Pigovian Tax on Financial Pollution

Taxes can improve as well as detract from economic efficiency. The best example of the former is in curbing negative externalities. When the social cost of a good exceeds its private cost, the market is unable to internalize all the costs associated with its production or consumption, or both, indicating a market failure and a negative externality.[329] Correcting this market failure requires public intervention to curb the activity in question, typically by raising its private cost to match its social cost through taxation. Thus, taxes on petrol and diesel serve to curtail consumption of those goods to cut the incidental production of air pollution associated with their consumption. Such taxes are exceptional in that they simultaneously increase welfare and raise revenue; they are referred to as Pigovian taxes, after Arthur Pigou (1877–1959), the eminent English economist. Remarkably, Professor Pigou was also the first to consider welfare from the perspective of an externality.

Inexcusably, economists have invariably ignored the huge divergence between the public and private costs of interest-bearing debt, a divergence that requires classifying interest as a financial pollutant and, these days, the foremost negative externality. Bank lobbying for interest favoritism through the insertion of a multitude of clauses in the tax code, to permit interest deductibility from corporate and personal taxes, has made matters worse by encouraging indebtedness. This huge divergence between public and private costs explains the economic rationale for its ban by Jesus Christ, an affirmation of the consistency between morality and economic efficiency. Hence, banning usury was a mercy to the world from its belated economic, social, and political consequences, which too few fathomed at the time or since.

Why is the social cost of interest-bearing debt much higher than its nominal interest or private cost? Part III of this book provided a wealth of evidence of the huge consequential cost of interest-bearing debt, including prohibitively costly financial crises. For example, when a mortgage borrower defaults and the lending bank takes possession of his (her) house, the borrower loses the house equity he (she) accumulated over many years, an incremental cost that is over and above the nominal interest cost but it is not explicitly recognized as a large additional cost of debt. In addition, the personal traumas associated with debt are real costs that are not included in the interest on debt. Moreover, when mass defaults occur, triggering a financial meltdown as the sub-prime crisis demonstrated in 2008, the social cost of the interest negative externality becomes incalculable. Thus, whether the debt is for consumption or investment or whether the borrower is an individual, corporation, or government its nominal interest greatly understates its full social cost.

Worse still, the social cost of debt increases exponentially, as the pervasiveness of debt in an economy increases because it artificially amplifies cyclicality and its associated negative externality too. Thus, the sale of numerous repossessed houses crashes the housing market and halts housing construction, causing vast job losses, followed by further rounds of defaults. Comparable concerns apply to all types of borrowing. Recent experience in the United States and Western Europe has demonstrated yet again that these consequential public costs, including the amplified contractions, are in the trillions of dollars, a phenomenally high cost that is not included in the nominal interest.

Furthermore, the social cost of mass misery exacted by interest-bearing debt is impossible to estimate using current statistical tools. How deep is the pain of homelessness and broken families, following mortgage defaults? What are the economic as well as the emotional costs of losing a family business to a bank? The desperation of Indian farmers driven to suicide because they cannot withstand losing their lands and livelihoods for failing to meet a bank mortgage payment is unimaginable.[330] Suicides also increase with the rise of poverty, which *parasitic economics* spread. What is the dollar equivalent of making tens of millions of people desperate and miserable? Those public costs are enormous and real but unaccounted for because the presently available statistical and accounting methods are inadequate and primitive, preventing us from assessing the full cost of usury. It is testimony to the power of banks that most goods and services are subject to tax but not interest, despite its huge negative externality.

Pollution of the natural environment is physical while financial pollution is conceptual; nevertheless, the negative externality of financial pollution is far more extensive and economically more damaging than environmental pollution. Both require taxation to curb their respective negative externalities and improve economic efficiency and social welfare.

What is the appropriate rate for taxing financial pollutants? The social cost of interest-bearing debt runs into the trillions of dollars, making any tax on the nominal interest, however huge, too small. Hence, banning interest is economically logical. However, given the present pervasiveness of debt, weaning the economy from interest needs to be gradual to avoid jolting the economy. A very high tax on interest would eliminate all new lending instantly instead of gradually, whereas economies need time to adjust and adapt.

Hence, an initial financial-pollution excise tax of say 4 percent per annum applied to the face value of new debt is a small fraction of its social cost, but it is sufficient to discourage new borrowing without eliminating it outright. The rate ought to be raised in later years to discourage lending further. Moreover, for such a tax to achieve its objectives in the face of high interest rates, it would need to be the greater of 4 percent of the face value of the debt or 40 percent of its yield to maturity.

What should be the tax base of a financial-pollution excise tax? In addition to the face value of loans and bonds, the base should encompass all interest-bearing transactions such as deposits, inter-bank lending, and Federal Reserve transactions. Chapter 9 called for the prohibition of derivatives, warrants, and short selling, other than covered short selling for hedging production, exports, and the like. On the other hand, if naked short selling of securities and derivatives were to continue, it would be economically logical to impose a financial-pollution excise tax on these transactions. To discourage derivatives, the tax base would need to be the value of the potential assets that those contracts control at the time of their initiation, and not their negligible premiums.

Finally, preferred shares are a debt-equity hybrid instrument; if it resembles debt more than equity, then it ought to be subject to tax too because, like debt, it would entail an incremental risk to the economy.[331] The elimination of clauses concerning cumulative dividends, renegotiation of terms, and priority in net assets of a company could result in somewhat higher preferred dividend yields for some companies, but that is preferable because it makes the true cost of financing explicit instead of partially implicit.

The government could require lenders and brokers to collect the tax on its behalf in the same way that merchants collect sales tax and forward it to the government. Still, existing debt ought to enjoy a tax holiday for five to ten years to give the economy time to adjust. This tax holiday is necessary for a smooth transition to an equity-based economy that is free of debt.

Effect of Sales Taxes on Exports

Many countries, including all of Europe, have replaced their sales taxes with value added taxes (VAT). This is important for exports because under World Trade Organization rules, exporters are entitled to receive rebates of VAT, but not sales taxes. As a result, the exports of countries using sales taxes suffer a self-inflicted trade disadvantage corresponding to the rate of sales tax embedded in the goods they export.[332] In the case of the United States, this tax hurdle to exports compounds the competitive disadvantage of an overvalued dollar.

Repeal of Taxation of Essentials

High tax rates on luxuries such as Caspian Sea caviar, fine clothes, jewelry, expensive cars, private jets, and yachts is equitable because those who can afford opulent consumption can afford the higher taxes that it ought to attract. Similarly, the high rates of excise taxes on harmful, demerit, goods, such as alcohol and tobacco, have dual benefits; a fall in consumption lessens health and social problems, while an increase in tax revenue helps pay for the associated medical and social bills.

However, taxing the essential consumption of low-income groups—namely, taxing basic food, clothing, or heating—is unjustified because it is regressive and increases income inequality.[333] In recent decades, conservative political parties on both sides of the Atlantic have raised consumption taxes while reducing personal tax rates. For example, the VAT rate in many European countries is 20 percent or higher. This mode of taxation is regressive because it shifts more of the tax burden on consumers who cannot afford it.

Let us illustrate by using a hypothetical example of two consumers, Mr. Rich and Mr. Average, with annual net after-tax incomes of $1 million and $35,000 per year, respectively. To simplify the analysis, assume further that the annual consumption of Mr. Rich is $200,000 and that of Mr. Average is $35,000 (zero savings). Finally, assume that indirect taxes, including sales taxes and import duties, average 15 percent of all sales.[334] Accordingly, Mr. Rich pays $26,087 in indirect taxes (15 percent of $173,913) while Mr. Average pays $4,565 (15 percent of $30,435).[335] Thus, the consumption taxes are equivalent to a tax of 2.61 percent on the after-tax income of Mr. Rich ($26,087/$1,000,000) and 13 percent in the case of Mr. Average ($4,565/$35,000). In other words, relative to their incomes, the indirect tax rate of Mr. Average is five times that of Mr. Rich, flagging an absurdly regressive indirect taxation atop regressive direct taxes such as the social security tax, making the overall taxation of low-income groups most regressive, unfair, and economically illogical.

The lowering of personal tax rates on high-income groups in several Western countries while raising indirect taxes has stealthily implemented a *reverse Robin Hood* tax policy, symptomatic of democratic erosion and rising plutocratic power.

Conformity with the ability-to-pay principle requires banning all taxation of essentials; the tax shortfall can be recovered through higher taxation of luxuries, demerit goods, and various pollutants like coal, petrol, and interest, as well as by increasing the personal taxation of those who can afford it.

Taxing Fraudulent Gains

Four centuries ago, Gresham's Law implied that a morally lax environment promotes fraud.[336] The social cost of fraud, a negative externality, far exceeds the illegal gains of the fraudsters. The environment that has flourished under the *banking plutocracy* has been very harsh toward minor offenses but extraordinarily tolerant of serious fraud. Indeed, a hungry shoplifter stealing food to eat could face a jail term for a trivial sum while big institutions and their staffs who defraud their clients of billions of dollars only pay fines representing a fraction of their loot, without jail sentences and without admitting any wrongdoing. As with *usurious capitalism*, the *banking plutocracy* has hatched a dual sentencing standard: harsh punishment for minor offenses and no sentencing for serious fraud.

Mending this system requires reinstating public morality. It also requires removing the incentive for committing fraud by reducing its expected payoff to a negative value. Thus, if the regulators only detect 10 percent of fraud incidents, a fraud tax set at 1,000 percent of fraudulent gains would decrease the expected value from committing fraud to -10 percent.[337]

Furthermore, allocating part of the fraud tax to reward whistleblowers should improve fraud detection as well as increase public revenue, at least until the fraud subsides. Similarly, making corporate officers who partici-pate in fraud, their seniors, and their corporate entities jointly and severally liable for the fraud tax would deter participation. Prison sentences would help too. Moreover, the staffs of the supervising authorities who offer fraud-sters easy settlements without jail terms and fines representing a fraction of the looted sums, instead of enforcing the full powers of the law, deserve to be expelled and sued for gross negligence.

Seventeen

CORPORATE TAXATION

The genius of our ruling class is that it has kept a majority of the people from ever questioning the inequity of a system where most people drudge along, paying heavy taxes for which they get nothing in return.[332]

GORE VIDAL

The unified theory of macroeconomic failure identifies several taxes as causing negative externalities that interfere with economic efficiency, misallocate resources, promote inequality, increase instability, and hinder economic growth. Moreover, the large share of taxes in GDP amplifies their negative externalities. The efficiency of corporate taxation is particularly critical because it directly affects the largest productive sector in the economy.[339] No country can realize its full economic potential if its corporate taxes frustrate economic efficiency. Hence, the corporate sector deserves special attention. To the extent that similar negative externalities plague the corporate tax code of rest of the world, then reducing such externalities in any country holds the promise of improving its economic efficiency and growth prospects relative to the rest of the world for as long as other countries do not adopt similar reforms.

Tax Bias, Indebtedness, and Other Inefficiencies

The unified theory of macroeconomic failure identified debt and amplified cyclicality as two daunting negative externalities facing Western economies. Both externalities are attributable to a flawed tax system, which provides tax incentives for pervasive indebtedness and, consequently, amplified cyclicality. Resolving those negative externalities requires understanding their cause.

The principle of tax neutrality is important for maintaining economic efficiency. In general, taxes should not distort economic behavior by influencing, for example, the choice of financing, unless there is a compelling economic reason to do so. Unfortunately, several taxes violate this principle by providing incentives for using debt instead of equity financing and investing, such as:

1. Corporate income tax
2. Personal income tax
3. Tax-exempt municipal bonds
4. Dividend withholding tax

Economists have rarely voiced concern about the lack of tax neutrality with respect to interest. For example, the prominent economic scholar Friedrich von Hayek was an avid supporter of Pareto optimality and a keen student of economic cycles, yet he did not criticize the debt bias of the tax system or its role in economic instability.[340] His silence on the subject is puzzling given that he spent a lifetime advocating economic efficiency and studying economic cycles. If political ideology was not the reason behind his silence but rather that he simply did not detect the negative consequences of this tax bias, then this leaves us to speculate what his position might have been had he been aware of the problem.

The degree of interest bias in corporate income tax is directly proportional to the corporate income tax rate; the higher the tax rate, the greater the tax advantage of debt financing. Around the turn of the 20th century, the top corporate income tax rate in many industrialized countries was no more than 15 percent. However, the enormous costs of two world wars compelled many Western countries to increase their corporate income tax rate to more than 50 percent, making the after-tax cost of equity financing punitive, while the tax deductibility of interest provided a phenomenal tax advantage for debt financing. As a result, to recover their previously higher after-tax rates of return on equity, many corporations resorted to increasing their use of debt.

Indebted corporations must meet all the terms and conditions of their indenture at all times; these terms, besides demanding timely interest and principal payments, often entail the maintenance of liquidity and solvency ratios, cross-default clauses, negative pledges, and other conditions.[341] Violation of these terms can trigger an event of default and, hence, represent incremental risks to corporations, especially during recessions. Moreover, violations give lenders an opportunity to renegotiate debt terms to gain greater advantage, another tacit cost of debt.

The effect of interest tax deductibility is uneven across sectors, with its strongest negative impact falling on sectors with a natural tendency for wide cyclical fluctuations, particularly capital-intensive sectors with a high operating leverage. Several strategic sectors fall in this category, including the automotive, airline, and steel industries. Even without borrowing, the presence of debt in the economy magnifies cyclical fluctuations for these industries, increasing their business risk. Superimposed on this debt environment are inept monetary policies that exaggerate cyclicality and the chronic overvaluation of the dollar. Hence, many such companies go under during business downturns. For example, the steel industry practically became extinct in Cleveland, Ohio, after one such recession; foreign industrialists bought the idle plants for a song, dismantled them, and shipped them overseas, thereby providing fiercer competition to the unfortunate residual US steel producers.

Tax neutrality requires comparable treatment of interest and dividends. Thus, the German federal government permits dividends deduction from corporate income tax and refunds to shareholders the corporate income tax corresponding to the cash dividends they receive. Still, even complete tax neutrality between equity and debt is not economically efficient because debt is a negative externality.

Keynes argued that uncertainty increases economic instability and raises the normal rate of unemployment.[342] This rationale also implies that greater uncertainty curtails the capacity of corporations for business risk-taking, slows economic growth, and raises the rate of "normal" unemployment.

More generally, we would expect high indebtedness to be associated with the following:

1. Greater uncertainty
2. Higher interest rates
3. Currency overvaluation
4. Mounting trade and budget deficits
5. Industrial erosion
6. Falling industrial investment
7. Higher unemployment
8. Slower economic growth

In the case of the US economy, all of the above consequences have materialized over the past three-and-a-half decades, save one: high interest rates. Chapter 10 pointed to the role of the Federal Reserve in subverting a market-determined interest rate, which explains the present low interest rate environment despite heavy indebtedness. This makes the chronic dollar overvaluation, despite low interest rates and huge trade deficits, an economic anomaly that deserves further exposition.

The standard supply-and-demand framework cannot explain the inconsistency of a persistent overvalued dollar despite large trade deficits and low interest rates because this glitch is rooted in game theory. The problem of dollar overvaluation is, primarily, self-inflicted. Following the 1973 oil crisis, the United States insisted that the Organization of Oil Exporting Countries (OPEC) price its oil exports in dollars, artificially boosting the demand for the dollar and contributing to its overvaluation. The United States also persuaded several oil-exporting countries to invest their large trade surpluses in dollar-denominated assets, adding to the chronic dollar overvaluation. Furthermore, the United States has sought to maintain the dollar as the primary international trading and reserve currency, which, with the phenomenal growth of international trade, has steadily increased the demand for the dollar and sustained its overvaluation.

Finally, the principal exporters of industrial products to the United States, like China, Japan, and South Korea, have supported the dollar overvaluation by investing a substantial part of their trade surpluses in dollar-denominated debt despite the meager interest rates. From these countries' perspective, accepting a low interest rate is rational because an overvalued dollar preserves their trading advantage. This is not unlike the strategy employed by a company that cuts its prices and accepts a lower profit in the short term to drive some of its competitors out of business, thereby increasing its long-term market share and ultimate profit potential.

These factors have reduced the interest elasticity of the dollar exchange rate, which explains the inconsistency of dollar overvaluation with low interest rates and large trade deficits. The overvaluation, in turn, has contributed to perpetuating the huge US trade deficits, reducing US international competitiveness, and eroding the US industrial base. The dollar overvaluation also explains the lack of inflation in the United States despite an explosive growth in the monetary base.[343]

Since the dollar exchange rate is no longer sensitive to the rate of interest, correcting the chronic dollar overvaluation and the associated US trade deficit requires a gradual reversal of the aforementioned policies that caused the overvaluation in the first place, such as the insistence on pricing oil and investing the oil surpluses in dollars.

In addition, improving economic efficiency requires reversing the present corporate tax discrimination in favor of debt by making dividends tax deductible, instead of interest. This would lower the after-tax cost of equity while raising that of debt, thereby encouraging equity and discouraging debt financing. Consequently, corporate financial risk would fall, resulting in a fall in corporate bankruptcies and job losses, shallower recessions, greater capacity for business risk-taking, faster economic growth, and potentially saving the government tens of billions of dollars during recessions. Still, while these measures are steps in the right direction, they are not sufficient for reversing the US economic decline. What is required is a whole battery of additional measures to improve US economic efficiency, with a redesigned corporate tax as a cornerstone, thereby permitting the United States to steal a march on its international competitors.

Employers' Social Security Tax Contribution

An employer and an employee must each pay social security tax at 7.65 percent of an employee's income, bringing the total to 15.3 percent, while the self-employed must pay the full 15.3 percent, a stiff penalty for self-employment. The 7.65 percent tax rate is the total of two separate taxes, 6.2 percent required by the Federal Insurance Contribution Act (FICA) and a payroll tax at 1.45 percent. The latter has no salary ceiling. FICA, on the other hand, only applies to the social security wage base, which in 2014 was set at $117,000, exempting salaries in excess. The social security tax also has a mélange of exemptions regarding minor sources of income.[344]

The benefits that the social security tax provides are essential but inadequate. However, it is a very regressive tax because it exempts incomes exceeding a ceiling under FICA instead of exempting meager incomes. Moreover, some analysts warn that the social security system is underfunded because as the longevity increases, the number of beneficiaries will increase and the outgoings will exceed the revenue.

The most serious criticism of the social security tax is that by taxing labor it discriminates against labor and employment, falling most heavily on labor-intensive industries and lightly on capital-intensive ones. It also results in major misallocation of resources because it favors the substitution of labor with capital. This was probably a minor concern when the original legislation was passed in the 1930s. In recent decades, however, robotics and artificial intelligence have been displacing labor in car manufacturing, bank ATMs, and barcode-readers at retail checkouts, to name a few, and the testing of driverless trucks is underway. This systematic displacement of labor by capital is likely to increase dramatically over time.

Given rising chronic unemployment and falling real wages, the social security tax discrimination against labor is an acute negative externality: imposing a social security tax on labor while depreciation of capital investment shelters capital from taxation, only accelerates and accentuates these problems. The process of increasing automation is unstoppable, but a slower transition would give the economy and labor more time to adjust through improved education and learning new skills to compete better in the face of this onslaught of new technology. From the perspective of business too, robots do not represent customers, hence, an orderly transition is in everybody's interest. Indeed, there is a case for taxing automation to increase employment during this transition phase because unemployment is a negative externality.

It is economically more efficient in terms of resource allocation to stop discriminating against labor by incorporating employers' share of the social security tax within a general tax on the corporate sector that does not specifically target labor. The section "Computation of a Corporate Capital Tax Rate" to follow explores such tax integration. A capital tax would also decrease the cost of compliance because employers would only need to inform the Treasury about their employees and their salaries once a year.

Erosion of the Corporate Income Tax Base

The corporate income tax base is suffering rapid erosion as more corporations discover that engaging in global trade provides a legal means of tax avoidance, at a time when there are record budget deficits on both sides of the Atlantic. Lower effective corporate income tax rates have been achievable by simply shifting corporate profits from a high to a low tax jurisdiction, and there is no shortage of tax havens worldwide.

Let us illustrate how this works using two examples. Assume an American company manufactures electronic products in Southeast Asia for export to North America and Europe. It acts as a manufacturer, intermediary, and seller in different tax jurisdictions. To minimize its global corporate income tax liability, it needs to lower its reported profit where the tax is high and increase it where the tax is lowest. This requires minimizing its profit in the manufacturing domicile by minimizing its inter-company export price to a tax haven. It then jacks up its re-export price from the tax haven to the final destinations, thereby minimizing its reported profits in the high-tax jurisdictions. Thus, US corporations have been reportedly accumulating hundreds of billions of profits in tax havens, which will remain untaxed until repatriated to the United States, if ever.

The second example is that of a US company that exports coffee beans from a tax haven to its large chain of cafes in the UK. The UK tax authorities complained to the company that its corporate income tax liability was too low. The coffee exporter responded promptly by reducing its export price to the British market, thereby increasing its profits and taxable income there. This illustrates how some corporations are in effect setting their own tax rates.

The same rationale applies to foreign corporations that have US manufacturing plants because they can inflate the prices of their imported parts and components, thereby reducing their US corporate income tax liability.

Domestic corporations with overseas subsidiaries and foreign corporations with US manufacturing plants are enjoying a significant tax advantage over US companies without overseas subsidiaries. Hence, US corporations are paying corporate income tax at widely varying rates. This has contributed to the deindustrialization of the United States because domestic industrial producers pay a higher effective corporate income tax rate than those that move their plants abroad. Furthermore, it is less economical or uneconomical for smaller companies, the most important source of job creation in the US, to engage effective but costly tax experts to cut their tax liabilities.

In theory, governments can use transfer pricing for goods that cross borders to assess corporate income tax; in practice, this can be highly arbitrary. Moreover, with the mushrooming of corporations that are involved in international trade and the extensive bag of tricks available to multinational corporations, including relocating their domiciles, transfer pricing is not a satisfactory tax remedy.

Pricing Public Goods for the Corporate Sector[345]

Corporations enjoy the benefits of public goods, including defense of their property against foreign invaders, a legal system that protects their property rights and a police force that enforces such rights, an education system that provides them with skilled labor, a health system for their workers and customers, and a transportation system for their customers, workers, and products. These and many more public goods are essential for the proper functioning of a modern corporate sector and taxes are the price of such public goods. A rational and fair corporate tax prices public goods in proportion to the benefits that corporations derive from them.

Naturally, larger corporations derive bigger benefits from public goods than smaller ones by virtue of their size. Hence, corporate size is a logical tax base for pricing public goods` to the corporate sector. This raises the question of what is the most appropriate measure of corporate size between six identifiable measures: *sales volume, number of staff, income, total assets, shareholders' equity (net worth),* and *capital (shareholders' equity + debt).*

Sales volume is an unsatisfactory measure of size because it overstates the size of some small corporations with huge sales volumes but little value added, as in the wholesale trade, while vertically integrated corporations have high value added per dollar of sales and, thus, sales tend to understate their true size.

Number of staff is also inappropriate because some very large corporations use high capital intensity and automation, and scant labor. Besides, a tax based on the size of the labor force discriminates against employment and encourages the substitution of labor with capital, a self-defeating measure under conditions of chronically high unemployment and low wages. Such a tax would also place an excess burden on labor-intensive industries such as fast food, retailing, and agriculture, while corporate giants in capital-intensive industries like oil refining, chemicals, and automated steel production would substantially escape the tax.

Income is another poor indicator of corporate size because certain small companies are highly profitable while some large ones are only marginally so. Moreover, corporate profits fluctuate widely over the business cycle, while corporate size remains relatively stable. In addition, corporate income tax suffers from several defects, like the erosion of its tax base, as discussed in the previous section.

This leaves three measures: *total assets, shareholders' equity (net worth),* and *capital (shareholders' equity + debt).* The three have similarities. However, *total assets* would overstate the real size of some industries like retail and wholesale trades because these carry relatively large inventories and accounts receivable, which would overburden them with excessive taxation along with their customers, given the potential for tax shifting.

Shareholders' equity is also not an ideal proxy because some industries, such as utilities, have historically employed a lot of debt. Hence, shareholders' equity on its own seriously understates their true size.

Finally, *capital (shareholders' equity + debt)* is a compelling indicator of size because it is based on the size of long-term corporate resources, regardless of its composition in terms of equity or debt. A *capital tax* is also preferable to a *tax on shareholders' equity* because the latter would encourage the replacement of equity with borrowing to lower the tax bill, thereby inheriting a key defect of the present corporate income tax. Accordingly, *capital* would seem to be the most robust indicator of corporate size and a logical tax base for pricing public goods to the corporate sector.

The Relative Economic Efficiency of a Corporate Capital Tax

Before declaring a corporate capital tax a suitable replacement for corporate income tax, one needs to assess its relative economic efficiency and its effect on the corporate sector. Table 17.1 presents the tax consequences of a corporate income tax versus a corporate capital tax on two purposely very similar corporations: A and B.

Table 17.1 begins by listing the assumptions regarding companies A and B. They have identical shareholders' equity, number of shares, and price-earnings multiples (PE), and, for simplicity, both are debt free. They only differ in their profitability: Company A has a 16 percent pretax rate of return on equity compared to 8 percent for Company B.

Also, for ease of comparability, the rates for the two taxes—corporate income and corporate capital taxes—are revenue-neutral such that both taxes generate the same total tax revenue; however, the incidence of the two taxes on each company varies considerably, as illustrated in Cases I & II in Table 17.1.

Case I illustrates the imposition of a 40 percent corporate income tax; it taxes Company A twice as heavily as it taxes Company B because Company A is twice as profitable.[346]

Case II illustrates the imposition of a 4.8 percent corporate capital tax that generates the same total tax revenue as the corporate income tax. In this case, both companies pay the same amount of tax because they have equal shareholders' equity given that both have no debt.[347]

Table 17.1 demonstrates the economic irrationality of the corporate income tax, because by using profitability as its tax base, it taxes corporate efficiency. Indeed, under the corporate income tax the more efficient a company is, the greater is its tax penalty, while an inefficient company earning no profit or incurring losses completely escapes the tax, permitting corporate free riders to enjoy the benefits of public goods without paying for them.

TABLE 17.1

Revenue Neutral

Corporate Income Tax vs. Corporate Capital Tax

(U.S. Dollars)

Assumptions	Company A	Company B	Total (A+B)
Shareholders' Equity	$100,000,000	$100,000,000	
Number of Shares	10,000,000	10,000,000	
Pre-Tax Profit	$16,000,000	$8,000,000	$24,000,000
Pre-Tax Rate of Return on Equity	16.0%	8.0%	
PE Multiple	10	10	
Case I: Corporate Income Tax			
Corporate Income Tax Rate	40%	40%	
Tax Liability	$6,400,000	$3,200,000	$9,600,000
After Tax Profit	$9,600,000	$4,800,000	$14,400,000
Earnings Per Share (EPS)	$0.96	$0.48	
Share Price at PE Multiple of 10	$9.60	$4.80	
After Tax Rate of Return on Equity	9.6%	4.8%	
Equivalent Capital Tax Rate	6.4%	3.2%	
Case II: Corporate Capital Tax			
Corporate Capital Tax Rate	4.8%	4.8%	
Tax Liability	$4,800,000	$4,800,000	$9,600,000
After Tax Profit	$11,200,000	$3,200,000	$14,400,000
Earnings Per Share (EPS)	$1.12	$0.32	
Share Price at PE Multiple of 10	$11.20	$3.20	
After Tax Return on Equity	11.2%	3.2%	
Equivalent Income Tax Rate	30.0%	60.0%	

The following compares the economic effects of using a corporate income tax with those of a corporate capital tax:

1. A corporate income tax is economically irrational on two counts. It is a poor proxy for the public goods consumed by corporations and it penalizes efficiency, falling most heavily on the highest rates of return in the economy, hence, it is economically irrational. By

contrast, a corporate capital tax is economically rational because it taxes permanent corporate resources, a proxy for the public goods consumed by a corporation, without penalizing efficiency.[348] Indeed, a corporate capital tax favors efficiency and penalizes inefficiency by acting like a corporate income tax that varies inversely with profitability, falling as a percentage of income as profitability increases and rising as profitability falls.

2. The losers under a corporate income tax are the shareholders of the most profitable companies, their employees, suppliers, customers, and the national economy because it is a penalty on collective efficiency.

3. Since a corporate income tax favors inefficient companies, it misallocates resources and, therefore, entails a larger excess burden than a corporate capital tax.

4. Switching from a corporate income tax to a corporate capital tax raises the after-tax rate of return (*marginal efficiency of capital* in Keynesian terminology) of above-average profitability (i.e. efficient) companies and lowers it for below-average profitability (i.e. inefficient) companies.

5. The tax switch also increases the number of viable investment opportunities, thereby inducing a higher level of investment.

6. It also increases the after-tax resources available to efficient companies and decreases them for inefficient ones.

7. A corporate income tax blurs the distinction in the profitability of companies, rendering capital markets less efficient, whereas corporate capital tax accentuates this distinction, rendering capital markets more efficient. Even with the PE ratios of the two companies remaining constant, as assumed in Table 17.1, the tax switch raises the stock prices of efficient companies and lowers it for inefficient ones. Thus, the signals to the capital market become sharper, improving capital market efficiency and capital allocation. More likely, the PEs of efficient companies will expand while those of inefficient ones will shrink because the growth of the former will accelerate

relative to the latter, making capital markets even more efficient by further increasing the capital availability to efficient companies and reducing it to inefficient ones.

8. The simultaneous rise in the after-tax profitability of investment opportunities available to efficient enterprises, coupled with the rise in their after-tax resources and their increased availability of funds through the capital markets, tends to increase the level of investment in the economy, accelerating economic growth.

9. Unlike corporate income tax, eliminating the tax deductibility of interest would tend to shrink corporate indebtedness and the financial risk in the economy, thereby dampening economic cycles, increasing the capacity of the corporate sector for business risk-taking and achieving faster economic growth.

10. To the extent that a corporate capital tax results in faster economic growth and lower unemployment, it would increase tax revenue and diminish certain budget expenditures such as unemployment benefits. Where a budget surplus results and in the absence of any urgent spending programs, including national debt repayment, it is possible to cut the corporate capital tax rate with further positive ramifications for the economy.

11. The burden of a corporate capital tax falls most heavily on poorly utilized corporate resources, inducing enterprises to ration their idle and excessive assets by paying off their debts, reducing their capital, increasing their dividends, and generally shrinking their bloated balance sheets to minimize their corporate capital tax bill. A corporate capital tax would also encourage enterprises to improve their capital efficiency by becoming more specialized, focusing on their most profitable core operations, and spinning off nonessential businesses as independent entities or selling them to third parties. The net effect on the economy would be greater resource dynamism and improved resource allocation, releasing low-productivity resources to other parties that can better utilize them. Thus, a corporate capital tax is an effective antidote to corporate

resource hoarding by fostering a more efficient use of society's scarce resources and limiting the negative impact of the liquidity trap during recessions.

12. To the extent that a country adopts a corporate capital tax while other countries retain corporate income taxes, there would be a tendency, over time, for highly profitable investments to migrate to the corporate capital tax domicile and for low-profitability investments to migrate to the corporate income tax domicile, both motivated by the desire to minimize their tax bills. Thus, a corporate capital tax would attract the most profitable and efficient use of capital, while a corporate income tax would attract the least efficient. A country that adopts a corporate capital tax instead of a corporate income tax would likely enjoy significant favorable long-term effects on its growth, employment, and tax revenue.

In 1997, Don Fullerton and Gilbert E. Metcalf estimated the excess burden of the corporate income tax at 35 percent due to its inefficiency.[349] In other words, a corporate income tax creates large economic distortions and dislocations. The total economic distortion is likely higher still because Fullerton and Metcalf did not explicitly address all the potential inefficiencies of corporate income tax.

In conclusion, a corporate capital tax would likely accelerate economic growth with benefits accruing to corporate shareholders, labor, customers, and the public purse. It is especially suited for stimulating the mature economies of the West, where economic growth is languishing and deficits and chronic unemployment are high.

The Incidence of a Corporate Capital Tax

Tax incidence is concerned with who ultimately bears the tax burden: consumers, workers, or shareholders, or a combination of these in varying degrees. In theory, a company would likely attempt to shift its tax burden, at least partially, away from its shareholders. It shifts the tax forward to its customers by raising the price of its products and services or backward to its suppliers and labor by reducing the prices it pays for their inputs.

Tax incidence is a function of the elasticities of demand and supply. The more elastic the demand for a company's products and services, the less it can shift the tax forward. Similarly, the more elastic the supply of its inputs, the less it is able to shift the tax backward, including to its own labor force. On the other hand, the more inelastic the demand for a company's products and the supply of its inputs, including labor (by limiting pay raises), the easier it is for a company to shift the tax forward and backward, respectively. However, one should also keep in mind that elasticity increases over time as competitive substitutes become available to consumers and suppliers (including labor) find alternative buyers. Hence, because it tends to change over time, the analysis of tax incidence is most relevant for the short-term.

In the case of a corporate capital tax replacing a corporate income tax, we can draw certain tentative conclusions *a priori*. To the extent that the tax bill increases for low-profitability companies, presumably with less pricing power, they would be less able to shift the tax forward. However, they might be able to shift it backward, in part or in full. Hence, there is a reasonable expectation that the shareholders of low-profitability companies, and possibly their suppliers (including labor), would bear a larger share of the tax burden rather than their customers.

By contrast, the adoption of a corporate capital tax would lower the tax liability of high-profitability companies relative to corporate income tax. However, to the extent that such companies have significant pricing power, it is possible they would be less inclined to pass the tax reduction to their consumers by lowering their prices. Hence, the profitability of such companies would likely improve further, at least in the short term, with further favorable repercussions on economic growth.

Effect on Corporate Indebtedness

The tax base of the corporate capital tax is shareholders' equity plus debt. Hence, it carries no corporate tax incentive to replace equity with debt.

Furthermore, it favors neither interest nor dividends, because neither enters into the calculation of the tax liability. Thus, a corporate capital tax is tax-neutral with respect to debt versus equity.

Cyclical Stabilization

Some public finance textbooks and articles mistakenly praise the so-called "automatic stabilization" of corporate income tax. The term refers to the variability in corporate income tax revenue over the economic cycle, falling during recessions when corporate profits fall and peaking at the height of expansions when profits peak. This analysis arrives at the wrong conclusion because it takes a secondary effect, tax revenue, as the only effect while over-looking the larger, primary, but opposite effect. Indeed, corporate income tax, through the tax deductibility of interest, encourages corporate indebtedness and therefore induces greater cyclicality, dwarfing any marginal advantage of a cyclical rise and fall in tax revenue.

In the case of corporate capital tax, to the extent that the value of the assets of a company rises and falls over a cycle and with it the market valuation of its capital (shareholders' equity plus debt), this provides some automatic stabilization through a corresponding rise and fall in the tax bill. This occurs without encouraging indebtedness, and therefore, without inducing amplified cyclicality.

In any case, it is easy enough to give a corporate capital tax additional automatic stabilization features, if required. For example, giving corporations the option to make prepayments against their future corporate capital tax liability (up to two or three years in advance) would provide such a counter cyclicality feature. This is especially helpful to the highly cyclical sectors such as the extractive, petrochemical, transportation, and high-capital-intensity industries generally. Indeed, a case can be made for making such tax prepayment a requirement for such industries to partially shield them from the impact of a downturn.

To encourage corporations to use this option, the tax prepayment could be treated, fully or partially, as an expense instead of a prepaid expense, thereby slightly reducing the corporate capital tax base and with it the tax bill. Implementing this option would tend to increase tax collections during boom times and lower it during contractions, providing an additional source of automatic stabilization without the negative consequences associated with increased indebtedness under a corporate income tax. A wide exercise of this option by corporations would entail a reduction in tax revenue, which would require a corresponding adjustment to the tax rate to ensure that this option is revenue neutral over a business cycle.

Effect of Inflation

Today, inflation seems like a distant memory, but the huge rate of expansion in the money supply, along with other factors, could bring it back, swiftly. Inflation distorts various taxes in different ways. In the absence of replacement cost accounting, inflation increases the replacement cost of assets such as inventories, equipment, plants, and buildings above their historical cost, the cost basis for computing depreciation and income, thereby automatically raising the effective marginal corporate income tax rate as inflation rises.

This problem is most acute in the case of long-lived assets such as buildings, plants, and equipment because, over several years, the cumulative effect of inflation results in a large discrepancy between historical and replacement costs. The overstatement of taxable income raises the effective corporate income tax rate without any constitutional authorization. Hence, under inflationary conditions, the effective corporate income tax becomes arbitrary. Sometimes governments secretly welcome this effect because it raises additional tax revenue by stealth.

Economically, this stealthy income tax hike under inflationary conditions lowers the corporate real after-tax rate of return, discourages investment, curtails increases in supply, and inhibits growth. It also discriminates against investing in long-lived high-capital-intensity assets because these are riskier. Generally, inflation adds to the general risk in the economy and lowers the real after-tax rate of return on investments.

In the case of a corporate capital tax, inflation has the opposite effect because the book value of corporate assets tends to understate their replacement cost, thereby reducing the effective corporate capital tax and increasing real return. This effect tends to curb a government's incentive to perpetuate inflation. On the other hand, periodic asset revaluations could update the current value of long-lived corporate assets, particularly buildings and lands, albeit, with a time lag.

Corporate Capital Tax Avoidance

Regardless of the form of corporate taxation, a growing tendency among companies is to relocate their domicile to minimize their tax burden. Some economists have argued that the solution to this is reducing corporate tax rates generally. This opinion has some validity in exceptionally high tax-rate environments. Nevertheless, the existing competition among tax jurisdictions for lowering their tax rates to attract more companies is a loser's game. The ultimate outcome is a tax rate that is too low to pay for the cost of a satisfactory level of public goods in major economies, although it might be more than adequate for tax havens and quasi tax havens that provide small quantities of public goods. The immediate solution to this problem is to ban the relocation of corporate domiciles. The long-term solution is global tax harmonization as proposed by Professor Piketty.

The other concern is about the pricing of international inputs. Under a corporate income tax, an international manufacturer with a domestic manufacturing facility is motivated to overstate the cost of international inputs to siphon more of the profits tax free to a lower tax jurisdiction. Under a corporate capital tax, there is no such enticement. Instead, the tax-minimization strategy becomes to streamline the capital invested, reducing the domestic plant as far as possible to an assembly operation that requires smaller capital. In the absence of international tax synchronization and tariffs, maintaining vertical industrial integration would have to fall on a fair exchange rate that stops the subsidization of imported inputs and curtails excessive international sourcing.

Computation of a Corporate Capital Tax Rate

What should the rate be for a corporate capital tax? If the initial target is to maintain the current corporate tax revenue, then the calculation of the rate of a flat corporate capital tax is straightforward, as follows:

Corporate Capital Tax Rate= (ΣCurrent Corporate Tax Revenue)[350] / (ΣCorporate Shareholders' Equity + ΣCorporate Debt)

The term "ΣCurrent Corporate Tax Revenue" ought to include all current direct corporate taxes. For example, a previous section titled "Employers' Social Security Tax Contribution" proposed integrating employers' share of social security tax contributions with the primary corporate tax. This implies the following:

ΣCurrent Corporate Tax Revenue= ΣCorporate Income Tax Revenue + ΣEmployers' Social Security Tax Contributions + ΣOther Corporate Tax Revenue

The term "ΣOther Corporate Tax Revenue" represents: all other corporate taxes, including those that only apply in some jurisdictions, such as a possible corporate wealth tax or a corporate capital gains tax, as the case may be. However, it should not be interpreted literally to include government charges, fees, or taxes limited to specific activities, companies, or sectors, such as licensing fees, a pollution tax, and the like.

Adapting a corporate capital tax to permit tax credits for foreign corporate income tax while maintaining the same overall tax revenue, is also relatively simple, as follows:

Corporate Capital Tax Rate = (ΣCurrent Corporate Tax Revenue + ΣInternational Tax Credits) / (ΣCorporate Shareholders' Equity + ΣCorporate Debt)

The above calculation provides a means for giving international tax credits to corporations up to a ceiling represented by their corporate capital tax on their international corporate capital tax base (International Shareholders' Equity + International Corporate Debt).

Finally, to encourage the formation of small businesses, it would be wise to exempt the first $1 million or more of corporate capital from the tax. Hence, the tax rate computation would be as follows:

Corporate Capital Tax Rate = (ΣCurrent Corporate Tax Revenue + ΣInternational Tax Credits) / (ΣCorporate Shareholders' Equity + ΣCorporate Debt - ΣCorporate Exemptions of $1 Million per Company)

Naturally, to avoid double or multiple counting of a corporate capital tax, it needs to be synchronized for companies with large ownership stakes in affiliates and subsidiaries by crediting them with the tax levied on their ownership stakes in such affiliates and subsidiaries. This approach should not affect the tax revenue generated by a corporate capital tax because it merely eliminates the multiple counting of the same capital. The corporate income tax has adopted an approximately similar methodology.

One transitory problem deserves consideration. In recent years, many enterprises have resorted to buying back their own stock at prices that far exceed their book value per share. This practice has artificially decreased corporate net worth, sometimes to zero or even a negative amount, which results in substantially escaping a corporate capital tax.[351] One way to overcome this problem is to treat the average premiums per share paid over book value for stock buy-backs during the past twenty-five years as an *intangible asset per share* that needs to be added to the current book value per share of existing shares, thereby augmenting shareholders' equity for purposes of calculating the taxable amount. Alternatively, such corporations could elect at the time of the adoption of a corporate capital tax to use the excess of the market value of their shares over their book value as the proxy for such *intangible assets*. The *intangible assets* would be amortized over, say, twenty-five years to give corporations sufficient time to increase their shareholders' equity, the major component of the tax base, to a reasonable level. Incidentally, this measure would encourage future pro-rata share redemptions at book value, which would be fair because all shareholders, both large and small, would enjoy similar treatment. It would also encourage increasing dividend payouts.

Corporate Capital Tax Collection and Compliance

One measure of the efficiency of a tax is its cost of collection as a percentage of the total tax revenue it generates. The cost of tax collection incurred by the Treasury as well as the cost of compliance incurred by corporations is an economic waste that is best minimized. The simpler the tax code, the lower the cost of tax collection, permitting the Treasury to retain more of the revenue it collects while reducing the cost of compliance for corporations too and vice versa. The corporate income tax code is extremely complex, and its complexity continues to surge as special interests lobby to amend it to cut their tax bills. It is especially burdensome to small and midsize corporations, the source of most of the economic growth and job creation. Finally, a complex tax code, by providing multiple opportunities for inserting tax loopholes and exemptions, makes taxation less transparent, unfair, and undemocratic.

Income, a flow concept, makes estimating corporate pretax income costlier and much more intricate than assessing a corporate capital tax, a stock concept. Corporate income is defined as total corporate revenue (sales plus other sources of revenue such as fees, royalties, interest, etc.) less total corporate expenses (salaries, wages, raw materials, power, light, fuel, maintenance, depreciation, amortization, depletion, advertising, fees, bad debts, travel, communications, interest expense, miscellaneous expenses, etc.). Within a single tax year, billions of revenue and expense items go into the determination of a large corporation's taxable income, an overwhelming task. By comparison, the determination of its net corporate asset values and liabilities is a vastly simpler task, only requiring the identification of corporate assets and liabilities and their book values or prices, as the case may be. Thus, the cost of collecting and complying with a corporate capital tax should be a small fraction of the corresponding cost of a corporate income tax, resulting in significant cost savings to both the government and the corporate sector. The assessment of a corporate capital tax could be once a year, semiannually or quarterly. The first option is the simplest and the least costly.

Charities, Charitable Foundations, and Charitable Assets

The definition of charitable assets ought to be restricted to assets that are dedicated to charitable activities. Thus, free or low-cost shelters for the deprived that cover its reasonable operating costs and earn no profit represent charitable assets. Similarly, a hospital, school, or university that charges no more than its reasonable operating cost, without realizing a surplus, holds charitable assets and is properly exempt from a corporate capital tax. On the other hand, charities and foundations that realize surplus revenue over reasonable costs can either increase their subsidy to needy recipients or pay a pro rata corporate capital tax on a portion of their assets that is earning a surplus. The tax would discourage abuse of the charitable label by taxing assets that are not fully dedicated to charitable service and ensuring efficient use of societal resources by charging partial charities a fair share of the cost of public goods. Prime examples of abuse are universities that charge exorbitant fees to their students and earn significant surpluses while claiming to be charitable, whereas they ought to have their capital resources taxed like any other profit-seeking enterprise.

Dividend Withholding Tax

The United States currently imposes a 30 percent tax on dividends while exempting interest. It is one of the many irrational biases against equity in the present tax system. In this case, tax neutrality is achievable by either imposing an equivalent withholding tax on interest or eliminating the tax for both.

———

In conclusion, the economic advantages of replacing a corporate income tax with a corporate capital tax are numerous and significant, yet a corporate capital tax is unjustifiably unpopular, even if it is revenue neutral compared to a corporate income tax. The underlying reasons are definitely not economic but a result of enthusiastic corporate lobbying by the less efficient corporations and a lack of sufficient lobbying by the efficient ones.

Eighteen

REGRESSIVE PERSONAL TAXATION

*You know, gentlemen, that I do not
owe any personal income tax.
But nevertheless, I send a small check, now and then, to the
Internal Revenue Service out of the kindness of my heart.* [352]

DAVID ROCKEFELLER[353]

Egotistic immorality, a negative externality, is the primary driver behind regressive taxation. The overall tax system or a single tax is regressive when it falls lightly or not at all on those best able to pay and heavily on those less able to do so. Taxes can be regressive because of the choice of tax base, like taxing labor while exempting capital. Moreover, frequently taxes only seem progressive with higher tax rates for higher incomes, whereas in reality tax loopholes, shelters, exemptions, and alternative rates create gaps between the stated and effective rates. Hence, the effective personal income tax rate of the wealthy is lower than that of the middle class. Worsening economic inequality and regressive taxation are symptoms of deteriorating morality and sinking democratic standards.

Principles of Personal Taxation

A tax is personal if it is borne by an individual or a family rather than a corporation, institution, or foundation. Direct personal taxation includes personal income, capital gains, social security, wealth (in some jurisdictions), inheritance (estate), and gifts (asset transfers).[354]

In theory, one can escape an indirect sales tax by not consuming, but not a direct tax; in reality, one can escape a direct personal tax by using tax loopholes and tax shelters or not realizing a profit on an asset. Hence, the details of the tax code can subvert its declared purpose.

There are four widely accepted tax principles for upholding the efficiency and fairness of personal taxation:

1. *Simplicity*: This is the easiest principle to apply but the most frequently violated because complexity is necessary to obscure the low effective tax rates borne by the extremely wealthy. To ensure fair taxation, elected assemblies should avoid passing complex and incomprehensible tax legislation that is only understood by a microscopic minority of tax experts. Thus, in Switzerland, perhaps the world's most democratic state, laws need to pass a comprehension test by a suitable sample of Swiss citizens.
2. *The ability to pay*: This principle requires those with a greater ability to pay to bear a larger share of the tax burden than those who are less able to do so; it is the impetus behind a progressive income tax, whereby higher tax rates apply to higher incomes.
3. *Equity*: This principle requires persons in similar economic circumstances to have similar tax burdens.
4. *Neutrality*: This principle seeks to maintain economic efficiency by avoiding or minimizing tax interference with economic choice and distortion of resource allocation.

Arguably, there ought to be two additional tax principles, as follows:

1. *The Laffer principle*: The Laffer curve, popularized by Arthur Laffer (b. 1940), illustrates a marginal tax rate that maximizes tax revenue

such that a higher or a lower rate would reduce tax revenue.[355] In 1963, President Kennedy proposed reducing personal and corporate income tax rates.[356] The legislation passed in 1964, after his assassination, reducing the top personal income tax rate from 90 percent to 70 percent and the lowest rate from 20 percent to 14 percent. It also lowered the corporate income tax rate from 52 percent to 48 percent.[357] The tax cuts sustained a fast economic growth rate at 5.5 percent until 1969, while inflation remained restrained at 1 percent. Most remarkably, the tax cuts increased tax revenue materially, suggesting that excessively high tax rates had resulted in *chronic underconsumption,* holding back the economy below its production possibility frontier. The increase in tax revenue also suggests that the tax cut moved the fiscal policy from a restrictive posture to a more neutral one and diminished the tax-disincentive for work.[358]

2. *Justifiable tax burden:* The benefits derived from public goods must correspond to their cost, the overall tax burden. In a failing democratic system, these benefits typically fail this test because public goods are not supplied in a sufficiently competitive manner and they represent a wrong mix of public goods by including, for example, wars of aggression.

A Regressive Personal Income Tax

Taxation of wealth, land, and produce is steeped in history, while personal income tax is a relatively recent innovation, only becoming moderately significant in the second half of the 19th century. In the United States, such taxation began with the Civil War at 3 percent. A major reason for not adopting it earlier was its considerable complexity; that aspect continues to this day as one of its many drawbacks, although it presently generates more revenue than any other personal tax.

There is a prevailing impression that the US personal income tax is fair, with progressive tax rates, and those with higher incomes pay higher tax rates; in reality, it is highly regressive. This unfair distribution of the income tax burden has prompted Warren Buffet, one of the very richest in the world, to complain that his secretary's personal income tax rate was double his own, although, clearly, he should be subject to a higher tax rate than she. The words of David Rockefeller—one of the wealthiest people in America—at the start of this chapter are further evidence that the personal tax regime is terribly regressive.

The marketing of the personal income tax has brainwashed the public mind into believing it is progressive, whereas it is regressive, inequitable, undemocratic, and violates all the fundamental principles of taxation.

In part, the unfairness of the personal income tax is rooted in its base, personal income. In addition, over the years, numerous tax loopholes, shelters, and fiddling have rendered it still more biased against earned incomes while sheltering income from capital sources. It is a testament to the unfairness and absurdity of personal income tax that a person on a modest salary must pay his share of income tax while a billionaire earning tens of millions in interest from municipal bonds is exempt.

To the extent that the tax code treats capital gains more favorably than yield on investments, it encourages risky investments over safer ones, resulting in speculative bubbles followed by huge losses, as demonstrated by the bursting of the dot-com and other bubbles. Similarly, continuation of the oil-depletion tax allowances accelerates oil depletion at a time of ample international oil supplies, thereby squandering a strategic reserve instead of preserving it for future emergencies. It also makes the development of clean energy sources, such as solar energy, less attractive than otherwise, thereby contributing to environmental pollution and global warming. The personal income tax also interferes with free choice and efficient resource allocation by favoring debt-financed property ownership over rental through allowing a tax deduction of mortgage interest without comparable treatment for rent. Its favorable treatment of the interest expense of business partnerships and proprietorships encourages debt financing, with major negative economic consequences.

In a Senate debate, Ted Kennedy famously complained about the Republican refusal to raise the minimum wage while giving considerable tax breaks to billionaires by saying, "Where does the greed stop?"[359] To the extent that personal taxes of all forms, including social security taxes, diminish the incomes of wage earners who have a high propensity to consume, it dampens economic activity. In contrast, taxes that distribute the tax burden more fairly would be economically beneficial to all segments of society: lower income groups would have more after-tax dollars to spend and the rich would benefit because their corporations would have more sales and profits and the value of their stock holdings would appreciate.[360]

Moreover, the personal income tax falls mainly on the savings of salaried people. Consider someone who consumes 80 percent of his (her) pretax income and is subject to total direct personal taxes at 20 percent (social security tax at 7.65 percent plus income tax at 12.35 percent). The tax is tantamount to a 100 percent tax on his (her) savings. As such, it is a precipitous barrier to building a nest egg through savings, falling heavily on marginal changes in wealth instead of on wealth itself. Thus, the personal income tax is a formidable impediment to vertical social mobility, frustrating the American dream for the majority of citizens. Perhaps, students of sociology may have more to say about the role of taxation in stifling American vertical social mobility.

Personal income tax also has subtle negative effects on demographics. To the extent that it cuts the resources available to low- and middle-income families, it discriminates against child bearing, given the high cost of bringing up children and seeing them through college. This is a critical problem in several European countries and Japan, where reproduction rates have fallen below the levels necessary for maintaining their populations. Thus, personal income tax has increased the risk of the progressive extinction of some nations and races.

The following identifies how the present personal income tax code violates the six tax principles cited earlier:

1. Instead of a simple code, it is highly complex; its opaqueness facilitates its regressive nature. It is accessible to only a few prohibitively expensive tax advisers who have dedicated their lives to deciphering its mysteries.

2. The tax base, taxable income, is only a partial indicator of ability to pay. It also violates the taxable income yardstick because the loopholes permit those with very high incomes to have lower effective tax rates than those with middle incomes.
3. It violates the equity principle because it treats income from capital sources more favorably than income from labor. For example, someone earning $500,000 in salary would pay a higher tax rate than someone making a similar amount in capital gains, and worse still the latter could simply pay nothing by not realizing any capital gain.
4. It violates the tax-neutrality principle because it discriminates against labor by its non-uniform treatment of different sources of income. It also has a strong bias in favor of debt financing.
5. It violates the Laffer principle because closing the tax loopholes would yield substantially higher tax revenue, making it feasible to lower tax rates.
6. It violates the principle of fair pricing of public goods by charging rich taxpayers significantly less than the benefits they derive from public goods.

In conclusion, the personal income tax code is complex and unfair, it violates tax neutrality, it causes economic dislocations, and it's detrimental to economic efficiency.

Capital Gains Tax

Capital gains tax is the other significant personal tax as measured by the revenue it generates. It is payable pursuant to the realization of net capital gains in a given financial year. In practice, this is an elective tax for the wealthy, because it is avoidable by not realizing capital gains, just as a sales tax is avoidable by not making a purchase. Indeed, the investment strategy of many successful investors is to continue holding assets with huge unrealized capital gains for years or even decades. In a debate on Bloomberg on

November 6, 2010, the distinguished economics professor Nouriel Roubini aptly summarized the capital gains tax in an illuminating comment, ".... for Warren Buffet, and others, unrealized capital gains are taxed at zero percent."

In the absence of a personal capital tax, unrealized capital gains should be taxable annually instead of leaving it to the discretion of the individual to postpone it indefinitely by not selling appreciated assets. Unrealized capital gains are a central tax loophole for the rich.

Capital gains tax is also regressive because its rate is lower than the top rates on earned income for no justifiable economic reason. It is more regressive still because the tax rate on long-term capital gains is lower than that on short-term gains, and since the wealthy can hold their investments longest, its higher rate targets those with limited resources.

The excuse for taxing those with limited means at a higher rate than the rich is that short-term gains are speculative and should be discouraged, overlooking that those with limited means cannot hold on to their investments for as long as the wealthy. This argument is without merit because institutions conduct the bulk of the speculation and they are subject to corporate taxes, not personal capital gains tax.

Finally, a capital gains tax seriously violates Pareto optimality because it prompts a lock-in effect on appreciating assets; hence, it diminishes capital market liquidity and capital mobility, distorts securities prices, and interferes with the efficient allocation of capital.

Employees' Social Security Tax Contribution

US social security tax targets the poor in particular; it is 7.65 percent as a percentage of the income of working people.[361] In 2014, the largest component of the social security tax, the 6.2 percent FICA tax, only applied to the first $117,000 of the gross compensation, whereas a smaller flat rate without an income ceiling would have been less regressive.[362] Most unfairly, the social security tax is without regard to the official poverty threshold.[363]

In Chapter 17, the section titled "Employers' Social Security Tax Contribution" discussed the social security tax as it applies to corporations and proposed merging it with the general tax on corporations to eliminate its discrimination against labor. Similarly, employees' share of the social security tax is regressive, which requires incorporating it within a single tax on labor income to permit exempting low incomes, as discussed in the next chapter. [364]

Expenditure Tax

An expenditure tax, sometimes referred to as a consumption tax, is a tax on the total annual consumption of an individual. At present, it is not applied anywhere and has rarely been used in the past. Nevertheless, from time to time, some recognized economists have proposed it; hence, it is useful to put it in perspective. Like all taxes on consumption, except perhaps those on super-luxuries, it is regressive because those with low income consume a much higher percentage of their incomes than those with high incomes. Thus, in principle, it would fall most heavily on lower- and middle-income groups and lightest on high-income groups. Hence, along with the poll tax, it is one of the most regressive taxes ever devised, although generous exemptions for low consumption levels would make it less so. Still, it would always be light on the rich because they consume least as a percent of their income.

It is also economically inefficient and irrational. To the extent that the rich consume a small percentage of their income and to the extent that an expenditure tax would discourage their consumption further, it would accentuate the problems of economies suffering from *chronic underconsumption*, causing them to operate well below their production possibility frontier, precipitating higher unemployment, lower profits, and slower economic growth.

Nineteen

PROGRESSIVE PERSONAL TAXATION

*...I think that people at the high end—people
like myself—should be paying a lot more in taxes.
We have it better than we've ever had it.*[365]

WARREN BUFFETT

There are many ways to make the tax regime more regressive, by increasing the revenue from regressive taxes such as sales taxes, targeting wage earners using the social security tax, exempting capital from taxation, the best indicator of ability to pay, increasing the tax loopholes and tax shelters, etc. For example, personal income tax has higher rates on large incomes that do not apply in practice due to a multitude of tax exemptions, loopholes, and shelters. Another example is the optional capital gains tax, which wealthy taxpayers can avoid indefinitely by not realizing capital gains and then to pay the lower tax rate on long term gains while small investors typically pay the higher rate on short-term gains.

These technical problems are easy to fix by revising the tax bases, closing tax loopholes, and using alternative taxes. The real problem is the waning of democratic standards.

Basil Al-Nakeeb

The Politics of Income Distribution

Harvard professor Thomas Piketty's scholarly and best-selling book *Capital in the Twenty-First Century* offers conclusive evidence of the serious income inequality in the West over the past 250 years, with special reference to France.[366] Almost two centuries earlier, Vilfredo Pareto (1848–1923) arrived at similar findings, concluding that an income pyramid is not an accurate portrayal of income distribution, which more closely resembles a dart atop a flat surface.[367] Previous chapters discussed the causes of poverty and the circumstances that forced change in income distribution; however, some elaboration seems appropriate now.[368]

Historically—even before the pharaohs and the pyramids—plutocracies implemented *parasitic economics* to exploit the masses, resulting in painful income maldistribution. On rare occasions, income distribution did improve, but that typically followed cataclysms such as epidemics, famines, wars, or revolutions, not plutocratic benevolence.

In the late 18th century, certain influential social philosophers like Voltaire began alerting the world to the unhappy state of the vast majority of people, enlightening European mass consciousness, and calling for change. Plutocracies readily ignored their pleas, and without plutocracies' cooperation, there was no peaceful means of effecting change. Following its involvement in the Seven Years War and the American War of Independence, France became heavily indebted; King Louis XVI sought to increase taxes, which coincided with several poor agricultural harvests and increasingly hungry French peasants. The tax hike in 1789 was the last straw; it ignited the French Revolution and broke the back of the French monarchy and plutocracy. To ensure lasting change, the revolutionaries struck at the power base of their feudal oppressors by confiscating their lands and property.

The French Revolution has inspired many uprisings since, invariably to improve income distribution. In 1848, revolutions swept across Europe. The counterstrategy of European plutocracies was to calm the revolutionary fervor by offering concessions, but to rescind them gradually once the storm had passed. The fruits of these revolutions mostly dissipated. However, they did serve as rehearsals for the mother of revolutions, the 1917 Communist

326

Revolution in Russia, which confiscated all wealth—and not just that of the feudal lords as the French Revolution had done. It was a mortal threat to Western plutocracies and their scandalous wealth, and they recognized it as such. Hence, between 1917 and 1922—despite the human, psychological and economic exhaustion from World War I—Western plutocracies financed and armed a terrible civil war in Russia and mobilized a quarter-million-strong invading force to reinstate a Russian plutocracy, but without success.[369] Communism took root.

In the 1930s, during the Great Depression, widespread unemployment and worsening poverty swelled the ranks of the dreaded communists in the West. In the United States, President Franklin Roosevelt initiated the New Deal to improve the condition of the working class and to promote economic democracy, which, among other things, legalized unions. Unfortunately, the impact of those reforms, in the midst of the Great Depression, the continued adoption of neoclassical economics, and very high rates of unemployment, was marginal.

Western plutocracies' desperate drive to improve the condition of the impoverished masses came later. At the end of World War II, a communist tsunami swept across Eastern Europe and reached distant corners of the globe as far as China. Eyeing the prospect of losing everything, as had happened in many countries, anxious Western plutocrats orchestrated sweeping reforms that included Keynesian economics, political and economic democratization, raising the standard of living of the working class, welfare programs, and progressive taxation. The rise in the purchasing power of the masses cured the chronic problem of underconsumption that had plagued economies for millennia, thereby propelling a powerful consumption-driven economic boom. It lasted almost three decades—until a costly Vietnam War and the first oil crisis in 1973 stopped in its tracks.

Western economic and political democracy plateaued in the 1970s and with it the standard of living of the majority. The tide turned in the 1980s, following the appearance of cracks in the economies of the communist bloc, signaling a receding communist threat. Western plutocracies concluded that the preservation of their regimes was no longer in doubt and, therefore, the reforms implemented after World War II were no longer necessary. Margaret Thatcher, the Prime Minister of Great Britain, and Ronald Reagan, the President of the United States, initiated a *counter-revolution* to reestablish the *Ancien Régime*.[370] They used neoclassical macroeconomics as a complement to their reactionary political ideology. The ultraconservatives initiated tax reductions for the wealthy, raised indirect taxes, cutback welfare for the underprivileged, undermined trade unions, and adopted measures that steadily increased the income and wealth of the super-rich and decreased the standard of living of the majority. They also supported the rise of a powerful *banking plutocracy*, which sought to permeate economies with debt. The rest of Western democracies followed this Anglo-American lead in varying degrees.

Democracy Tax[371]

Professor Piketty notes the worsening inequality in the West during the past three decades, which he considers a characteristic of capitalism that is not reversible without state intervention. He attributes the growing inequality since the early 1980s to a rate of return on capital (r) that has exceeded the rate of economic growth (g) such that r>g has resulted in a growing concentration of income and wealth.[372] Doubtless, his math correctly depicts conditions during the past three decades. However, there is another possible explanation: The rising rate of return on capital and the falling growth rate were not the cause of worsening inequality but rather a consequence of rising plutocratic power.

Capitalism run by a frightened plutocracy had improved economic democracy, equality, and growth that launched an economic boom from the mid-1940s to the late 1960s. Ironically, it was the ideal environment for the wealthy too because their ownership rights became more secure and the US economy achieved high growth rates, which in turn increased their profits and wealth. On the other hand, a confident plutocracy in the early 1980s began dismantling those reforms, curtailing economic and political democracy, increasing inequality and indebtedness, and stifling economic growth.

Two Centuries of Parasitic Economics

The increasing monopoly elements in the goods market and monopsony in the labor market raised the rate of return on capital (r) and, simultaneously, lowered real wages for the majority of people. Falling labor purchasing power resulted in the reemergence of *chronic underconsumption* and rising unemployment, which together with an overvalued currency, deindustrialization, and rising indebtedness, caused economic growth (g) to fall. In other words, the changes in the relative values of r and g, first from the mid-1940s to the mid-1970s and then after 1980, were in essence a reflection of the ebb and flow of the power of plutocracy and its exercise of such power in the economic sphere.

Do plutocracies know what is in their best interest? Regrettably, plutocracies tend to focus on either the demand or the supply side of the economic equation not both at the same time—acting as profit maximizers or cost minimizers, losing sight of the economy as a whole. Hence, they perceive the economy as a zero-sum game, failing to see that monopsonists stifle the growth of the economy and profits. Something similar is at work in the goods markets in the case of monopolies. Stated differently, plutocrats are economically myopic, unable to gaze beyond the static short-term to perceive the economy as a dynamic win-win game. Hence, they cannot see that improving the lot of the workers is in their best interest because it yields two windfalls, the multiplier effect and economies of scale, which improve the profitability of their capital and speed its growth.

Plutocracies are unreliable because they renege on the concessions they promise once a crisis passes. Karl Marx sought a permanent solution by socializing all wealth. His draconian prescription was a "cure" that kills the patient, economic efficiency. It achieved neither an efficient economy nor a democracy and it was not permanent. The capitalist system is economically efficient in principle, but left to its own devices without regulation, it degenerates into inefficient monopolies that want to take over everything, and not just markets. To prevent it from spawning *parasitic capitalism*, capitalism requires balancing self-interest against *societal-interest* through regulation and taxation. The balancing mechanism is a populist democracy that must navigate between the dual threats of a proletarian dictatorship on the extreme left and a plutocratic dictatorship on the extreme right.

A 2014 study by Professors Martin Gilens of Princeton University and Benjamin Page of Northwestern University concluded that the United States has already passed from a democracy to a plutocracy. Their study observes that "…rich, well-connected individuals on the political scene now steer the direction of the country, regardless of or even against the will of the majority of voters."[373] The BBC considered this study important enough to report it.[374] If political power has indeed passed irretrievably to the plutocracy, then the present book is thirty years too late. On the other hand, was it possible thirty years ago to foresee where the *counter-revolution* was heading?

Professor Thomas Piketty has proposed a one-time tax on wealth to pay off the national debt, a brave suggestion and a reasonable interim solution for the problem of indebtedness.[375] Nevertheless, the more pressing problem is that of excessive plutocratic wealth and power and their effect on democracy and the economy, a concern that Professor Piketty shares.

Bertrand Russell saw wealth as latent political power.[376] Therefore limiting excessive political power requires limiting wealth, the root cause of many excesses of the capitalist system. Plutocracy is, of course, a negative externality and taxes are ideally suited for handling externalities, whether in the goods market or the political marketplace. It would also require better public awareness and a superior political leadership to match. Hence, a democracy tax, by limiting wealth, simultaneously protects democracy and ensures that public choice is valid, a prerequisite for an efficient capitalist system. The task is delicate: eliminating excessive plutocratic wealth to check plutocratic power while preserving the self-interest motive. Populist political leaders who care about the national interest can best determine the limit on excessive plutocratic power and, therefore, wealth.

Sustaining self-interest is not difficult to achieve because a democracy tax would only apply to less than 1 percent of 1 percent of the population who have excessive wealth. However, it would give a clear signal to everyone that democracy is not for sale to the highest bidder. Moreover, provided a democracy tax applied once yields the desired political effect—without the need to lower the limit on wealth and apply the tax again—then it should have no more than a transitory negative effect on incentives, if any. At the same time, to the extent that it improves public sector choice, tax efficiency, fairness, and breaks up monopolies and increases competition, it improves the opportunities and reinforces the self-interest motive for the vast majority of people. Thus, a democracy tax is the first building block of an efficient capitalist system and a genuine democracy.

There remains the question of preserving democracy thereafter, by preventing future plutocratic encroachment on the political process. This is best achieved through a redesigned inheritance (estate) tax.

Inheritance Tax

The objective of an estate tax is to prevent intergenerational cascading of wealth, as well as to provide reasonable tax revenue; regrettably, plutocratic meddling has foiled both objectives. Today, foundations, trusts, and generation skipping allow the extremely wealthy to escape the estate tax, making it redundant. The Tax Foundation has noted that effective estate planning can avoid the estate tax, falling only on those who do not plan for it or use incompetent tax advisers.[377] Taking advantage of tax loopholes requires costly tax advice, making it uneconomical except in the case of large fortunes.

Aside from invading the privacy of bereaved families, estate tax is unfair, falling onerously on the moderately wealthy, who have enough wealth to be subject to the tax but not enough to avoid it by implementing and maintaining costly tax-avoidance schemes in perpetuity. If the wealthiest, armed with superior advice on estate planning, escape the estate tax, then its only imaginable purpose is to give the public the illusion of a progressive tax regime.[378]

On the other hand, a reformed estate tax can play a useful role as a complement to the democracy tax discussed in the previous section, permitting the latter to be a one-time event instead of a periodic tax. Any tax revenue generated would be incidental to the primary objective of inhibiting potential plutocratic encroachment on the political process and maintaining democracy. Thus, the exemption per individual beneficiary should be generous to restrict the tax to the largest fortunes, sparing the vast majority of families the need to plan for the tax.

Shifting the tax base from the size of the estate to the size of the individual inheritance would make it more appropriate to relabel the tax as an inheritance tax (not an estate tax). An inheritance tax ought to have the following features:

- All tax shelters, loopholes, and generation skipping need to end. In addition, family and personal foundations and trusts need to dissolved and their net assets distributed to their rightful beneficiaries to hold in their names directly with full visibility.
- The level of tax exemption needs to be generous, preferably several hundred million dollars per beneficiary, because the objective is to limit excessive political power and not tax revenue.
- To limit the intergenerational cascading of wealth, the estate tax exemption needs to consider a beneficiary's total wealth: present wealth plus the amount inherited.
- The progressive tax rate on excessive wealth ought to be such as to prevent the reemergence of plutocracy in the future.

Identifying Personal Tax Bases

The fundamental flaw in the concept of personal income tax is that it attempts to tax the two factors of production, labor and capital (including land), using a single tax base. Resolving this problem requires disentangling the two factors of production by using a distinct tax base for each.[379] This does not imply increasing the overall tax burden but rather giving it a measure of rationality. Accordingly, the natural tax base for taxing labor is labor income. On the other hand, the intuitive tax base for capital is either the income it generates or capital proper. The sections to follow will discuss these matters in more detail.

Labor Income Tax

The natural tax base for taxing labor is all sources of labor income. Unlike a personal income tax, dividends, interest, rent, capital gains, and the like would be exempt from this tax because their source is not labor income. Hence, the tax code for a labor income tax is simple, freeing the majority of people from the yoke of complying with a complex code.

A labor income tax, like the present personal income and social security taxes, can be regressive unless handled carefully. Nevertheless, provided labor enjoys a reasonable standard of living, a tax on labor income is justified as labor's contribution toward the cost of public goods.

A tax on labor income ought to have the following characteristics:

- The tax base is all sources of income accruing from labor, including self-employment, family businesses, salaries, wages, bonuses, stock options, the value of benefits in kind that accrues from employment, royalties, the net proceeds from the sale of creative work, and any other monetary benefits.
- In the interest of efficiency, transparency, and simplicity, a single tax would replace the multitude of taxes on labor income, including personal income tax, social security tax, and health insurance contributions. The tax code should contain no tax shelters, loopholes, or interest deductibility, and should make no distinction between taxpayers based on their marital status.
- Since a labor income tax is regressive for low-income groups, it is important to provide for a reasonable exemption to make it progressive at the low end of the income scale.
- Similarly, regressive taxation of essential foods, clothing, housing, utilities, schooling, and medication constitutes a high rate of indirect taxation of labor income and should cease.[380] On the other hand, excise taxes and taxation of luxuries and excessive consumption of utilities ought to continue.
- The tax threshold should be significantly above the definition of poverty line to avoid repeating the contrived disincentives to work

in the present tax regime. For example, under the present system, those who accept low-income jobs face cutbacks in social assistance on the one hand and taxation of their meager income on the other (e.g., social security tax), subjecting them to a strong disincentive to work.

- In 2015, a $50,000 tax-exemption is probably sufficient to cover the cost of modest living such as housing, utilities, food, transportation, schools, medical bills, an emergency fund, and a little saving. It is also consistent with what President Franklin Roosevelt called "a living wage."
- The following attempts to make the taxation of labor income fair, using a simple tax schedule with few tax brackets, no loopholes, and a reasonable peak tax rate:
- $0 < 0% >= $50,000
- $50,000 < 10% >= $250,000
- $250,000 < 15% >= $500,000
- $500,000 < 20% >= $1,000,000
- $1,000,000 <25%

The above tax schedule tries to achieve the following objectives:

1. Permit those with meager incomes (below $50,000) to have the opportunity to pursue a worthwhile life that is free of the burden of unfair taxation.
2. The tax code is simple (e.g., without regard to marital status) and transparent because it eliminates the multiple taxation of labor (personal income tax, social security tax, indirect sales taxes on essentials).
3. To give labor a strong incentive to work and a chance to participate in the American dream, the tax rate on labor income needs to rise gently and to peak at a level that is not punitive and significantly lower than the stated theoretical rates of the present personal income tax, which the wealthy escape in any case.

4. A reasonable labor income tax ought to make an important contribution toward the cost of public goods enjoyed by labor. Such a contribution will increase automatically as the living standards of labor improve.[381]

Personal Capital Tax

The tax base for capital could be either the income it generates or the capital itself. Income from capital includes rent, business profit, stock dividends, and capital gains. However, taxing the income from capital, as with corporate income tax, discriminates against the efficient use of capital by falling markedly on its highly profitable (efficient) use and lightly on its marginally efficient use, with unprofitable and unproductive uses completely escaping the tax. Thus, taxing income from capital is tantamount to making capital efficiency a tax base, which discriminates against efficiency and is seriously detrimental to the economy and growth. More fundamentally, since taxes are essentially the price of providing public goods, the tax base needs to reflect the amount of benefits derived from public goods, which in the case of capital is proportional to the amount of capital held by its owners.[382] Moreover, a tax on capital does not imply an increase in the overall tax burden if, together with a tax on labor income, they generate the same revenue as the current personal taxes.

In October 2014, Credit Suisse Research Institute estimated the total wealth in the United States at $83.7 trillion[383] with 10 percent of the people holding 74.4 percent of the wealth.[384] Thomas Piketty advises that in Europe 10 percent of the people hold 60 percent of the wealth.[385] Piketty's proposal for a global wealth tax to contain the growing wealth inequality is economically rational, but the ultra-rich and their lobbyists have criticized it unfairly.

Let us begin by examining the logic of taxing the income of two individuals. Assume that in a particular financial year an executive (Mr. Executive) earns $150,000 while a wealthy individual (Mr. Rich) suffers a slight loss on his investment portfolio and earns no current income. Under the present personal income tax regime, Mr. Executive is required to pay income tax, but not Mr. Rich. Without information about their relative abilities to pay, this seems fair. Let us further assume that the net worth of Mr. Executive is $500,000, split between $200,000 in home equity and $300,000 in a shares portfolio. Mr. Rich, on the other hand, has a net worth of $5 billion. Clearly, imposing a tax on Mr. Executive and exempting Mr. Rich is outrageously unfair.

Those with more assets benefit proportionately more from public goods than those with fewer or no assets.[386] Hence, personal capital is the best indicator of the amount of public goods consumed by capital owners, whereas earning a profit or suffering a loss on capital has no bearing on the amount of public goods consumed by capital owners.

A personal capital tax is more advantageous than a tax on capital income to those who earn a higher return on their capital because it leaves them a higher after-tax return and vice versa. [387] Those earning a mediocre return on their capital could respond by selling or redeploying their idle and unproductive assets, distributing excess assets to their offspring and charities, or improving the rate of return on their capital (e.g., by choosing better investment managers).

Furthermore, with reference to the tax principles cited earlier, let us consider the effects of replacing a personal income tax with a personal capital tax, as follows:

1. In terms of the simplicity and transparency principle, a personal capital tax is simplicity itself because it only entails the valuation of assets less liabilities, requiring a few simple accounting computations, and wealth is more readily identifiable than income.
2. Based on the ability-to-pay principle, wealth is a far better indicator of the ability to pay than income; it is only intuitive that the greater the wealth, the greater the ability to pay. Clearly, a billionaire has

a far greater ability to pay taxes than most salaried persons do even when he (she) incurs a net loss in a particular year. Hence, a personal capital tax conforms better to the ability-to-pay principle than a personal income tax while overlooking wealth violates this critical tax principle.

3. The equity tax principle requires those in similar economic circumstances to have similar tax burdens. A billionaire and an average salaried person clearly do not have similar economic circumstances but the personal income tax is blind to the glaring economic discrepancy between the two by not considering the difference in their wealth. In addition, a personal capital tax should not distinguish between different forms of wealth, so that those who have comparable fortunes should be subject to the same amount of tax, regardless of the composition of their assets.

4. The fourth tax principle requires the maintenance of tax-neutrality to retain economic efficiency. Personal income tax, by taxing different types of income at different rates, interferes with and distorts economic decisions, while a personal capital tax is neutral.[388] Personal income tax also distorts economic decisions by treating interest more favorably than dividends although both are rewards for providing capital financing.

Excluding wealth from the tax base is the ultimate tax loophole. Indeed, some of the super-rich are satisfied with living on a modest budget and a modest salary. Without a personal capital tax, more of the tax burden inevitably shifts from the wealthiest to those with fewer resources and less ability to pay.

Moreover, a flat personal capital tax is progressive, while the seemingly progressive personal income tax, by disregarding wealth and employing numerous tax loopholes and exemptions, is in fact very regressive.

The arguments against capital gains tax were discussed in the previous chapter and do not warrant repeating; it is sufficient to remember that it is an elective tax at the discretion of the wealth holders.

Computing the Rate of a Flat Personal Capital Tax

Calculating the tax rate of a revenue-neutral proportional personal capital tax, in conjunction with a labor income tax, is straightforward; however, let us first make explicit the assumptions used in the calculation, as follows:

- The proposed flat, personal capital tax and labor income tax would replace all existing personal taxes, with the exception of an inheritance tax, as discussed previously.

- The revenue generated from a flat personal capital tax and a labor income tax is equal to the combined revenue generated from all direct personal taxes (with the exception of an inheritance tax). Hence, the overall tax burden is unchanged because the new taxes are revenue-neutral; however, the relative tax burden would shift to make personal taxation progressive, one of the declared objectives of the tax system.

- Exempting the first $250,000 of personal capital for each taxpayer from a personal capital tax adjusted for future inflation seems sufficient to cover essential personal assets such as a modest dwelling, a car, personal belongings, and an emergency fund, or a family business. This exemption would make the personal capital tax more progressive as well as greatly simplifying compliance by the majority of taxpayers and reducing its cost of collection. Such an exemption would also encourage the formation of small businesses, an important source of job creation and growth.

- The tax base would include all tangible and intangible assets registered to individuals, including overseas holdings (to prevent a tax bias favoring foreign assets) minus the aforementioned personal capital exemption and minus personal debt and debts that finance personal assets.

- To prevent recreating the tax loopholes and shelters found in the personal income tax, all wealth must be taxable and at the same rate. Accordingly, all personal and family trusts, and foundations (except dedicated institutional charities) need to be dissolved and their assets distributed to the beneficiaries to permit taxation of the assets they hold.

Accordingly, calculation of the personal capital tax rate is as follows:

The Personal Capital Tax Rate =
($\sum$Revenue from (Personal Income Tax + Personal Capital Gains Tax + Labor's Share of Social Security Tax & Health Insurance Contributions + All Other Personal Taxes Excluding Estate and Transfer Taxes) - $\sum$Revenue from Labor Income Tax)/ ($\sum$The Net Value of Personal Tangible and Intangible Assets- $\sum$Personal Capital Exemptions)

The key variable in the above equation is *"$\sum$Revenue from Labor Income Tax."* Reducing the revenue from the *labor income tax* results in a higher *personal capital tax rate* and vice versa. Deriving excessive revenue from *labor income tax* makes it regressive, increases income disparity over time, and results in too little consumption demand in the economy, which is detrimental to growth and profits. On the other hand, too little revenue from *labor income tax* could make the tax on the personal capital excessive and detrimental to capital formation and growth. The proposed top rate of labor income tax seems fair and economically reasonable, but precise fine-tuning, as the Kennedy Tax cut revealed, is only possible subsequently.

The Economic Efficiency of a Personal Capital Tax

The following analysis assumes that revenue-neutral personal capital and labor income taxes would replace the present personal income, social security, and capital gains taxes, as detailed in the previous sections. The implementation of a personal capital tax is economically superior to the present arrangements for the following reasons:

1. Tax Base: Taxes are the price of public goods and the means for recovering the same. Wealth holders ought to pay for the benefits they receive from public goods; such benefits are in proportion to the net value of their personal assets (personal capital), whereas return on capital is not a valid indicator of such benefits but rather a function of the efficiency or otherwise of their capital utilization.

2. Free-Rider Problem: The free-rider problem occurs when some parties enjoy the benefits of public goods without paying for them. The free-rider problem is incurable when the design of a tax fosters it. For example, a capital gains tax permits the owners of capital not to pay any tax simply by not realizing any capital gains, however large. A personal capital tax has no such built-in free-rider problem.

3. Tax avoidance and Evasion: These serious problems are undermining the revenue base of the existing tax regime and making it more regressive. A personal capital tax is more difficult to avoid than a capital gains tax or a personal income tax, bypassing their intricate and opaque tax determination, estimation, exemptions, loopholes, and tax shelters. It is also more difficult to evade than a tax on income from capital sources because it is more difficult to hide assets than income.

4. Revenue Efficiency: As a percentage of the total revenue generated from a tax, the cost of assessing and collecting a personal capital tax is far less than that for personal income, capital gains, and other personal taxes.

5. Income Distribution: A personal capital tax falls only on those with substantial wealth. Thus, it is consistent with improving income distribution.

6. Vertical Social Mobility: The personal income tax is a formidable hurdle to saving and wealth accumulation, falling on savings and marginal changes in wealth rather than wealth proper; hence, it is a major impediment to vertical social mobility.[389] Stated differently, the present regressive personal income tax perpetuates the restricted membership of the club of the wealthy by imposing hefty dues on aspiring members who cannot make use of its various tax-avoidance features. On the other hand, the combination of a personal capital tax and a labor income tax improves vertical social mobility by making it easier for savers to accumulate wealth. In addition, it makes it more difficult to stay wealthy for those who do not employ their

capital productively. Thus, it potentially increases vertical social mobility in both directions.

7. Hoarding: A personal capital tax provides a powerful disincentive for hoarding because it progressively eradicates idle capital over time.

8. Economic Efficiency: To the extent that wealth is both a private property and part of society's scarce resources, society benefits from its productive employment, not its idleness. A personal capital tax penalizes owners of idle, underutilized, or badly utilized social resources, providing a strong incentive to improve the marginal efficiency of capital in the economy. In the absence of tax loopholes and tax shelters, highly productive uses of capital would be taxed more lightly than under the present "theoretical" personal tax rates, increasing the after-tax resources available for efficient, high-return investments and improving the prospects for faster economic growth. Efficient use of capital is consistent with Pareto optimality.

9. Adoption of New Technology: The lockup effect of a capital gains tax is detrimental to Pareto optimality and the efficient allocation of resources. By contrast, a personal capital tax eliminates this lockup effect, thereby improving capital mobility and investment in new technologies. This effect is conducive to a more dynamic economy with faster germination, dissemination, and adoption of new ideas, products, and industries. [390]

10. Chronic Underconsumption: To the extent that a personal capital tax lessens the tax burden of labor, it improves income distribution and acts as an antidote to *chronic underconsumption*, reduces unemployment, and provides an impetus for the growth of the economy and profits. [391]

11. Asset Prices: The adoption of a personal capital tax would depress the prices of less productive assets and raise the prices of productive assets, thereby further rewarding efficiency. In addition, the price rise of high-return assets would direct more investments toward similar assets, thereby improving resource allocation and economic growth.

12. Property Bubbles: Property bubbles preceded the Great Depression, the Great Recession of 2008, and numerous other financial contractions. A personal capital tax is ideally suited to curtail bubbles because the tax burden increases with the inflation of asset prices. The gifted and well-liked American economist Henry George (1839–1897), in his bestselling economics book, *Progress and Poverty*, used broadly similar reasoning to justify a land tax.[392] Additionally, in 1977, Professor Joseph Stiglitz (b. 1943), an American economist and recipient of a Nobel Prize, supported the idea under certain conditions.

13. International Effects: All taxes provide a motive for capital flight, unless they are plagued by loopholes that make them more cosmetic than real. Moreover, the present tax regime with its present tax rates, loopholes, and shelters is unsustainable in the long run, because it is not generating sufficient revenue to pay for public expenditure. Thus, any increase in tax revenue would encourage tax migration, regardless of the form of tax. However, for the same amount of increase in tax revenue, economically efficient and fair taxes are economically preferable to inefficient and unfair taxes.

14. Long-Term Effects: To the extent that a personal capital tax would result in faster economic growth and lower unemployment, it would decrease a budget deficit or increase a budget surplus. In the latter case, absent compelling spending programs, it could lessen national indebtedness and, eventually, make possible a reduction in the tax rate.

15. Unless the wealthy plutocracy bears a fair share of the tax burden, instead of largely escaping it as at present, they will continue to have little incentive to improve the efficiency of public expenditure by curtailing wars of aggression, halting the periodic bailing outs of zombie banks, and pork barrel programs, and increasing competition in the provision of public goods.

Administration of a Personal Capital Tax

A personal capital tax requires identification of all the assets belonging to individuals, their values less related liabilities. Quoted securities are valued annually at market. Unlisted securities are valued with reference to their closest comparable listed securities. Properties would need periodic valuations such as once every five years with annual adjustments based on local property indices, but they need more frequent valuations when markets fluctuate wildly or following a major shift in the inflation rate in either direction.

Tax Migration

The growing problem that tax authorities have to contend with is the tax migration of capital. With the dismantling of restrictions on international capital transfers, a progressive trend has emerged worldwide of large fortunes changing their domiciles to tax havens, sometimes together with their owners. Professor Thomas Piketty proposed a global capital tax as a solution. This requires international enforcement, most effectively undertaken by the U.N. Security Council. That, however, must await the emergence of less confrontational and more cooperative international relations, which is likely to be a long wait.

The political power of the plutocracy is a logical explanation of the problem of regressive taxation, but not the only one. Labor is less mobile than capital because its tax domicile is its country of employment. Moreover, the less skilled the labor, the less choice it has regarding its domicile. In other words, labor cannot readily change its domicile to minimize its tax burden. Capital, on the other hand, can more readily relocate for tax purposes, legally as well as illegally. For example, it came to light that thousands of wealthy US citizens hold secret Swiss bank accounts. This is also true of wealth holders from other nationalities.

In other words, the response of capital to fair taxation is migration. On the other hand, a sustainable reduction in tax rates requires improving the efficiency of economic decisions generally, as will be explained in the next section.

Reducing the Tax Burden

Reducing the overall burden of taxes and tax rates is an important economic objective. It is achievable by improving public expenditure decisions, which in turn requires improving democratic standards , as follows:

1. Improving the efficiency of the political, economic, and social decision-making process requires reducing the influence of the plutocracy and improving democratic standards, which in turn requires a democracy tax.
2. The adoption of efficient, rational, and fair taxation is conducive to eliminating *chronic underconsumption,* promoting economic efficiency, and accelerating economic growth, thereby increasing tax revenue without resorting to increasing tax rates.
3. Improving the efficiency of public decisions requires factual and accurate national statistics that do not show the cost of negative externalities as additions to GDP.
4. Competitive pricing of exports, imports, and import substitutes requires a competitively priced dollar exchange rate, a key factor in reviving US industry. This will increase tax revenue, one prerequisite for reducing tax rates.
5. Taxes are the price of public goods. A prerequisite for reducing tax rates is reducing the cost of public goods, which in turn requires more competitive pricing of their supply, and, therefore, the breakup of oligopolies.
6. Similarly, reducing public expenditure requires ending costly wars of aggression.
7. In the same vein, reducing public expenditure requires stopping absurdly costly financial crises through the imposition of a financial-pollution excise tax to decrease indebtedness.
8. It also requires reducing and, eventually, eliminating national debt.
9. Reining in the escalating cost of crime and realizing important cost savings will require nationalizing prisons, adopting shorter sentencing (especially for nonviolent poverty-driven crimes), and improving rehabilitation programs and job prospects.
10. Reducing public expenditure also requires the elimination of wasteful pork barrel programs.
11. The nationalizing of the Federal Reserve is also essential to eliminate its prohibitive explicit and implicit costs, to ensure the

synchronization of fiscal and monetary policies, and to improve the democratic process, thereby improving overall economic performance.

12. The progressive replacement of fractional reserve banking will provide the government with an annual windfall of extra revenue through the painless process of the increase in money supply.

These measures would achieve ample savings in the cost of public sector expenditure, improve economic efficiency, accelerate growth, and increase tax revenue without the need for increasing tax rates. The long-run effect of these measures on tax revenue and public expenditure would be to lessen the need for taxation over time, thereby facilitating sustainable taxation at significantly lower tax rates, which is the most effective long-term solution to the problem of tax migration.

Part VI

Outlook

Twenty

The Gathering Storms

Economics is a very dangerous science.

John Maynard Keynes

For some vague reason, postal stamps appear not individually but as sets, as do many other things. Casual observation suggests that good and bad events seem to cluster, although I am unaware of any empirical testing that supports or refutes this idea. Still, let us indulge our minds by speculating on the possibility that it might exist, for if it does then it can help explain the gathering of storms over the shores of the North Atlantic.

One ticking storm is the sheer passage of time. The US economy last peaked in 2007. By the end of 2015, more than eight years had passed, a ripe old age for a business cycle. Two powerful factors have extended its life beyond that of an average cycle: zero interest rate and a sharply lower oil price. The ultralow interest rates have permitted the economy to coast along for a while longer by pumping a bigger bond bubble than anything the world has ever seen. We can only imagine what will happen when this bubble bursts, as inevitably it will. Thus, the bond bubble is a second ticking storm. Probably more stimulative have been the effects of a sharply lower oil price, with the opposite of the effects of the 1974 oil crisis. While the oil price may dip below $30 per barrel, such a low price is not sustainable and its eventual reversal will have important contractionary effects. Aside from economic factors, faced with the prospect of bleeding to death, the Russian Federation, the world's largest hydrocarbon exporter, is likely to take matters in its own hands. Thus, the direction of the oil price is a third ticking storm. Hence, with every passing day, the odds increase that the cycle peak was yesterday. A global contraction is drawing closer, but it is too chancy to predict when. It is also chancy to predict its severity, but we can attempt this lesser challenge, provided the reader takes it with a grain of salt.

The West today is staring at its old unresolved problems. Massive and rapidly escalating indebtedness, budget deficits, industrial erosion, high unemployment, poverty in the midst of plenty, anemic growth, and social tensions—each one a gathering storm—have been left to fester and compound for more than eight years. Why have Western governments not reformed their economies in the wake of the Great Recession of 2008? Perhaps Western plutocracies are reactionary and not inclined to reform voluntarily.

Sophocles, the ancient Greek tragedian, once said, "Foolishness is indeed the sister of wickedness."[393] Myopic and uncaring governments with unsustainable debt, in Greece, Portugal, Spain, Italy, and other nations, have made matters worse by listening to neoclassical economists, their bankers, and international institutions. Instead of stimulating their economies and unloading the debt burden onto their creditors, they imposed austerity and increased their debt, thereby navigating their sinking ships into deeper waters. The mass exodus of the unemployed youth has been increasing the debt per person of working age who remained behind. In Greece and elsewhere in Southern Europe, this is another ticking storm.

The economic problems of Iceland surfaced in 2008 and those of Greece shortly after in 2009, but their leaders pursued diametrically opposite solutions. A shrewd and brave government of tiny Iceland shrugged off bankers' warnings and threats, especially from the Bank of England, and decided to break away from the herd; it took the plunge, letting its irresponsible zombie banks fold, wiping out their capital and mountain of debt with one stroke of the pen. The Icelandic government established new banks to replace the ones it buried, with fresh capital, new shareholders, new managements, and new policies. Shortly thereafter, as a deepening gloom and malaise engulfed Europe, the Icelandic economic miracle surfaced. Since Iceland took control of its destiny, it has been basking in its achievements. Today, it is the fastest growing economy in Europe. Meanwhile Greece lingers in debt negotiations, unrelenting austerity, and depression, a prisoner of its creditors without a prospect of release, the tragic consequence of governments that serve plutocrats instead of the people.

The Eurozone

Yesterday, the euro seemed like an ingenious idea. Today, millions complain that it is a nightmare. What economic sins transformed the euro from a blessing to a curse? Germany, the economic captain, had set sail with Europe on a grand economic voyage without a map.

Euro bank notes began circulating in January 2002, at the height of the neoclassical seduction. The euro conception included a large dose of neoclassical dogma. Neoclassical economists' record since before the Great Depression illustrates a distinct inability to learn from the economic fiascos they seed. Without valid economics, the euro was ill-fated long before its launch.

A subtle consequence of following neoclassical economics is that German leaders did not heed the advice of John Maynard Keynes in searching for an economic advisor: "…good, or even competent, economists are the rarest of birds. An easy subject, at which very few excel…He [the master-economist] must reach a high standard in several different directions and must combine talents not often found together. He must be mathematician, historian, statesman, philosopher—in some degree…He must study the present in the light of the past for the purposes of the future."[394] Instead, German leaders entrusted the fate of the euro to advisors who did not comprehend an easy subject, at which very few excel! That was the original German sin. Thus, the tally of Europe's terrible economic set began.

Germany's second economic sin was to let a ghost from its past haunt its present economic policies. Memories of *hyper-stagflation* from the 1920s, an economically lethal combination of hyperinflation and massive unemployment, have tormented the German economic psyche ever since. *Hyper-stagflation* had played a role in inciting political disorder followed by dictatorship, culminating in war and Germany's devastation. Unable to put those specters to rest, Germany's understandable but misplaced inflation phobia and bias for an appreciating currency were another major negative influence in the management of the euro.

This background explains the obsession, for a long time, of the European Central Bank (ECB), the monetary authority governing the eurozone, with controlling inflation. It transformed the euro into a quasi-gold standard, accepting the inflexibilities of that ill-fated standard and overlooking why the world abandoned it in the first place. The ECB neoclassical ideology made for irreconcilable policies, at once conservative in running the euro and liberal in its tolerance of indebtedness. These policy inconsistencies were irrational, untenable, and foolish.

Given the constraint of self-imposed monetary inflexibility, the eurozone desperately needed greater fiscal flexibility to compensate. This of course was not a neoclassical option. Germany should have insisted on eurozone candidates to overhaul their fiscal systems to improve their chances of surviving future economic shocks. However, fiscal measures were anathema to Germany's neoclassical advisors, admitting that Keynes was right and they were wrong is something they could never confess. With the option of fiscal measures removed, neoclassical economists had tied Germany's hands: inflexible monetary and fiscal policies. Is it any surprise the euro is in trouble? Policy paralysis was Germany's third economic sin. One storm was spawning another.

Many of the tax reforms mentioned in the previous chapters were as pertinent then as now, particularly three tax measures. Foremost is scrapping the corporate income tax because it penalizes efficiency; replacing it with a corporate capital tax offers a more rational pricing of public goods to the corporate sector and favors economic efficiency. This change would have been conducive to faster economic growth, thereby augmenting the future stream of tax revenue instead of increasing indirect taxation of the middle and lower income classes and precipitating *chronic underconsumption* and anemic and negative growths.

The second fiscal measure is the institution of a financial pollution excise tax to discourage borrowing and encourage equity financing. This tax would have decreased indebtedness and encouraged equity financing in the private sector, making the economies of the eurozone financially robust, and immunized against financial crises.

Third is scrapping the existing personal taxes (e.g., personal income tax, capital gains tax) and replacing it with a labor income tax and a personal capital tax. These superior tax handles, with appropriate amendments to include the global capital of taxpayers, would have greatly diminished the possibility of, and the incentive for, the endemic tax evasion in Southern Europe and elsewhere. These three tax measures alone would have gone a long way toward curing the chronic budget deficits of the eurozone countries and reversed the worsening trend of economic inequality

Still, overlooking structural fiscal reforms was hardly the last of the German economic sins. Why did the European Union not link its regional fiscal aid more tightly to the fiscal responsibility of the recipient countries? Why did Germany not reward fiscally responsible countries by using tax incentives to encourage German companies to invest there?

The rapid shift in the world trade balance further exposed the neoclassical central bankers' lack of economic comprehension. The ECB, the Fed, and the Bank of England, among others, misread the long-term economic repercussions of the low-priced Chinese exports. Thus, the ECB imagined that the reduction in the cost of imports and the associated balance of payment improvements were a permanent windfall to the eurozone, permitting its members to enjoy a combination of an appreciating currency, falling rates of inflation, and rising standards of living. For a decade or so, this policy was politically popular, but, ultimately, it was a recipe for loss of economic competitiveness.

The ECB management should have realized that those cheap imports and their associated eurozone trade surpluses and rising living standards were without a corresponding growth in the exports in much of the eurozone, indicating an overvalued currency and loss of competitiveness. The ECB should have gradually devalued the euro to allow the eurozone as a whole to regain trade competitiveness and to use the cheap imports to cushion any imported inflation resulting from the devaluation.

There is also the problem of the eurozone's excessive indebtedness that needs a structural solution, not just a superficial fix. James M. Buchanan (1919–2013), an American economist and recipient of a Nobel Memorial Prize in 1986, argued that even in democratic societies, future generations might not repay the debts of earlier generations if those debts supported past consumption instead of providing lasting benefits.[395] That line of reasoning has universal applicability.

Sovereign debt turns cancerous when its growth rate outstrips the rate of economic growth; it is then only a matter of time before it overwhelms taxpayers. This raises a puzzling question as to why banks, the presumed experts in finance, accommodate excessive borrowing to the detriment of nations and themselves. Or is there more to it?

Bankers' avarice overwhelms their judgment. Instead of assisting borrowers, they compensate for the deterioration in credit by raising the interest rates they charge, driving further credit deterioration. The kind explanation is they are ignorant. The other is that higher interest increases the pressure on sovereign borrowers to surrender their valuable natural monopolies to the lenders, such as utilities, railways, airports, ports, public hospitals, and lands, in exchange for some debt relief. However, the surrender of such strategic assets usually compounds the problems of indebtedness because sovereign borrowers will have to contend with the gouging of their citizens by foreign investors and the transfer abroad of excessive dividends, thereby replacing the burden of debt with a more intimidating predicament. Hence, across Europe today, many influential voices are complaining about financial totalitarianism.

The overvalued euro slightly dented German exports, but it rendered many eurozone members uncompetitive, constraining their growth and, with excessive indebtedness, sealing their economic fate. The misguided ECB made matters worse by attempting to save the lending banks instead of the eurozone.

The cumulative impact of these neoclassical economic policy errors is now tearing the European Union apart. It is driving the rich regions across Europe to secede from their motherlands, and not just from the eurozone. Thus, Scotland in the United Kingdom; Catalonia in Spain; Alsace and Corsica in France; Sardinia, South Tyrol, and Venice in Italy; and Bavaria in Germany want to break away to escape austerity and improve their economic lots. If they do, the economic situation of the residual regions will become unsustainable; sacrificing the interest of the banks for the greater good is the only solution, but conservative governments have blocked this remedy.

In the stricken regions too, harsh economic conditions are driving voters to rebel against their conservative political masters that promise nothing but unrelenting austerity. John Kenneth Galbraith, in his sweeping review of modern Western history, aptly observed that when reform from above became impossible, revolution from below became inevitable.[396] The extremists on the left previously and the extremists on the right currently have both demonstrated their redundant economics and undemocratic practices. A landslide is brewing in the West to replace the agenda of extremist right-wing conservative governments with centrist economic policies.

Present conditions are indefensible. The ECB's pathetic solution of quantitative easing is no more effective than giving an aspirin to a patient with a brain tumor. With the prospect of never-ending austerity, certain countries will be compelled to exit the eurozone, revert to their national currencies, and reflate their economies. In doing so, they will likely repudiate some or all their debt and, if necessary, use inflation to shrink the real value of any debt that remains. Once eurozone members resort to such measures, not only will the eurozone disintegrate, but probably the European Union as well. Thus, the stark choice facing the German leadership today is the prospect of debt repudiation and the breakup of the eurozone and the likely disintegration of the European Union against Germany's wishes or else debt repudiation with Germany's blessings and preserving the eurozone and the European Union.

Even at this late hour, Germany can still salvage the European Union and the eurozone, albeit in a modified form. This will require taking the following steps:

- For one time only, the ECB pays off the euro-denominated sovereign debt of eurozone members, without recourse to these countries. In return, eurozone members agree not to borrow in euros in the future and preferably not to borrow at all.
- All eurozone members reintroduce their national currencies for use in domestic transactions.
- To preserve the euro, eurozone members continue to use it for their international transactions.

Indeed, Germany had successfully operated a dual currency system in the 1930s, one for domestic and the other for international transactions. These measures will have several positive effects. Naturally, the euro will fall perceptibly relative to national currencies; by letting the euro take the fall, the prices in eurozone countries denominated in their national currencies will be more stable, insulating them against an inflation epidemic. The value of national currencies will adjust relative to one another to help the weaker economies become more competitive. Once free from the chains of debt, eurozone members will regain control over their economic destiny, end austerity, and reflate their economies. These measures will save the eurozone and the European Union.

The banks will shoulder a large share of the shrinkage in the real value of the euro-denominated debt. In reality, without constant government support, many banks are bankrupt in any case and must fold. New banks with fresh capital must take their place, à la Iceland. Furthermore, many poor countries outside the eurozone are also excessively indebted and need debt reduction

Two Centuries of Parasitic Economics

or repudiation. The Vatican has urged the cancelation of the debt of all poor countries.[397] There have been similar demands in the United States and elsewhere.[398] Sadly, it has mostly fallen on the deaf ears of conservative Western governments. Debt relief is negative for the banks but positive for Europe and the world because it would help revive world growth, and with it European exports. Indeed, the cancelation of the national debt of African countries and assistance for Africans to pursue positive economic development (instead of subjecting them to financial imperialism) can preempt the human waves from Africa that will otherwise overwhelm Europe later this century.

A wise Chinese once said, "Problem is opportunity." Judging by the size and variety of problems confronting Europe, there is no shortage of opportunities, if only Europe can figure out how to use them.

Conflict and the Price of Oil

The 2015 terrorist attacks against France paralyzed tourism and disrupted normal life there. The French home front faces blowback from the actions of French governments, which destabilized governments and facilitated and supported terrorism under and over the table in Libya, Syria, African Sahara, and elsewhere, yet another demonstration of the unintended consequences of immoral policies. The French leadership presumed it was possible to sow terrorism and to harvest something pleasant. This rising risk of terrorism inside Europe comes at a time when Europe is already economically vulnerable. Putting the terrorism genie back in the bottle may be a protracted process unless the West and NATO are ready to abandon, indeed to reverse, its past policies that led to its present muddle.

Chapter 11 pointed out that since the mid-1970s, unexpected surges in oil prices have caused or at least contributed to recessions. By contrast, the sharp fall in oil prices in 2015 has provided relief to Western economies and postponed the inevitable contraction.

Since the US invasion of Iraq in 2003, followed by the war on Libya, conflict has been raging in Arab countries. From West to East, Al-Qaeda and

357

its affiliates are now waging wars on Algeria, Tunisia, Libya, Sudan, Egypt, Yemen, Lebanon, Syria, and Iraq. Taken together these represent about 85 percent of the Arab population. These conflicts are prone to spread to the remaining 15 percent, which includes major oil producers; disruption of oil supplies could send oil prices to $200 per barrel, seeding a great depression in the West comparable to that of the 1930s.

The United States

European structural economic problems were less evident in 2008. Europe was coasting along when the financial meltdown in the United States dragged it into the vortex of the Great Recession; now it seems the tables are turned, and Europe will likely drag the United States into the next economic cyclone. Both regions have no shortage of economic problems such as excessive debt, overvalued currencies, and gross economic mismanagement. Members of the eurozone have surrendered control over their monetary policy to the ECB. The United States, on the other hand, has surrendered its monetary policy to the bankers. Thus, both are in serious trouble.

The Great Recession of 2008 was an alarm bell, calling for an orderly retreat away from the economic cliffs, but the mainstream economists and their political masters have been in denial mode. Lacking the will and expertise to solve these problems, they resorted to understating and dismissing them, leaving them to fester and grow more intractable.

Thus, Western governments find themselves today waiting passively for the next crisis to hit. Its trigger could be anything, a reversal in the oil price or an overly indebted European country deciding to exit the eurozone, followed by others. Given deeply interlocking indebtedness in the form of loans, deposits, credit default swaps, and other derivatives across both sides of the North Atlantic, the financial tsunami would be difficult to contain within European shores. It would likely be worse than 2008, with potentially colossal bank failures and correspondingly larger rescue packages, seeding an even bigger financial collapse of the West a few years hence.

An Alternate Reality

The gathering storms are an accumulation of colossal errors. Covering the errors with plausible explanations is a process of denial. When it is widespread it becomes an alternate reality. To illustrate the point, the following is a slightly-exaggerated version of the reality that Western plutocracies and their media project to their audience and themselves:

Western plutocracies know best and are best fit to rule because they are socially responsible. Their business interests do not conflict with *societal-interest*. They lobby to close tax loopholes, promote fair taxation, and increase the budgets for public education, public health, and social welfare. Hence, Western governments are making excellent public choices. The participation of eligible voters is increasing, steadily. Thus, Western democracy is getting stronger.

Markets became nearly perfectly competitive following deregulation; oligopolies have no negative effects. The capital markets are discounting all available information, eliminating market surprises and inducing fair and efficient pricing of securities; hence, cutting the budgets for the supervision of securities markets is rational. Banking is a viable business; in future, it will not need colossal sums to rescue it. Central banks serve the public interest, not the big banks; their shrewd monetary policies have smoothed economic cycles and preempted financial crises.

High moral standards are rising; hence, greed and fraud in banking, credit agencies, accounting firms, investment management, business lobbying, and bids for government contracts are fading. The mainstream media is a bastion of democracy; it echoes all political views, delivers impartial and objective information and does not censor or bend the truth. The tax system is progressive, efficient and fair; hence, income distribution is improving. Unemployment, poverty, homelessness, and hunger are personal choices of lazy individuals who stubbornly refuse to take job opportunities with good pay, training, and incentives. In the social sciences, the universities are citadels of excellence in learning. Society is looking after the weak; hence, crime is falling and prisons are emptying.

Guided by neocons and their ideology, Western democracies are peace loving nations. The wars they engage in are for noble causes like promoting world peace, democracy, freedom, liberty, prosperity, compassion, humanity, goodwill, and love of the weak. The peoples of Vietnam, Cambodia, Laos, Iraq, Syria, Somalia, Libya, and many others all unequivocally attest to this.

This is the manifest reality; those who disagree are, doubtless, conspiracy theorists.

The Struggle for Valid Economics

The principal error of classical economic theory, on the extreme right, was that it disregarded morality, the key to understanding a host of negative economic externalities that continue to plague economies to this day. This led to its second error of assuming that self-interest was the sole economic driver, and overlooking the other driver: *societal-interest*. The third error flowed from the second by assuming self-interest on its own would give rise to "efficient markets" that need no regulation, a forlorn hope because monopolies in the goods markets and monopsonies in the labor market plagued their economies, producing desperate poverty and *chronic underconsumption* that stifled economic growth and fueled revolutions. Classical economics influence has continued through its updated version of neoclassical economics and its associated *parasitic economics*, thereby contributed to perpetuating *parasitic capitalism*.

Marxist economics on the extreme left was a reaction to and a rejection of classical theory. It made the opposite error. It assumed that the people in the perfect society it envisioned would be driven by morality to the exclusion of all else. Its second error flowed from the first by implicitly assuming that *societal-interest* was as a sufficient economic driver and that self-interest was a negative influence on society, requiring its purge from mass consciousness. The third error was a consequence of the second: developing an economy without conventional markets.

Neither side was willing to look at the economic picture from the opposite perspective, preventing their reconciliation and the emergence of a more comprehensive economic theory. Morality, whether by disregarding it or exclusively relying on it, became the Achilles heel of both camps. Dismissing *societal-interest* or self-interest relegated both theories to dogmas in support of political ideologies, if with generous sprinklings of economics. Hence, both sides carried the seeds of their inevitable economic miscarriage.

Marxist economics has demonstrably failed. In 1989, the Soviet Union initiated the process of discarding the Marxist dogma. Today, even the once ardent supporters of Marxist economics have given up on fixing it.

Classical (and, subsequently, neoclassical) theory was a lesser failure, but a failure nonetheless, that has precipitated monopolies, monopsonies, poverty, unemployment, mass unrest, wars, Marxism, revolutions, grave depressions, and, most recently, the Great Recession of 2008. The neoclassical dogma has made a comeback since the 1980s, not because its theory improved since its grand failure during the Great Depression but because it served the political agendas of the Reagan- and Thatcher-led *counter-revolution*. It has been stifling economic rationality and precipitating progressively harsher economic conditions, while the *counter-revolution*aries progressively constrain political choice. The pending demise of the neoclassical dogma is a prerequisite for the reemergence of centrist economics (that recognizes both self-interest and *societal-interest*) and the resumption of economic and political democratization that gained momentum following World War II, which the *counter-revolution* interrupted.

The Struggle for Democracy

Democracy requires strong moral leaders to stand by the weak, a perilous posture. The timeless struggle for democracy is a battle to displace plutocracy with its uncanny skills for retaining power. The Roman senators who assassinated Julius Caesar (100 BC–44 BC) claimed they did it to preserve democracy; it is the widely accepted version, but not the only one. No doubt,

Julius Caesar was a dictator, but he was also a prolific and populist reformer. The Roman Senate was a club of wealthy landowning plutocrats and Caesar was their nightmare. His love for Rome drove him to make Rome stronger. He was planning to expand the Senate to include ordinary Roman citizens. He was also contemplating the ultimate sin: distributing the lands of the feudal senators to ordinary Romans, thereby eliminating the power base of the plutocracy and replacing it with a genuine political and economic democracy. He saw democracy as a pillar for perpetuating Roman power, which required shrinking the political power of the plutocracy. Passing such fundamental reforms required him to have dictatorial powers, which he demanded and the Roman Senate granted him. Caesar's assassination aborted his reforms, preserved the plutocracy, and postponed Western democracy for two millennia. Such is the calculus of plutocracies.

Had that assassination plot failed, world history would have taken a decidedly more contented course. Furthermore, Caesar's assassination is relevant for our times because it appears to parallel Kennedy's mysterious assassination. Did JFK's plans frighten the plutocracy as Caesar's did? Following Caesar's assassination, Roman politics veered to the right, increased plutocratic power and aborted Caesar's plans for a democratic Rome for good. Following the two Kennedy assassinations, US politics also veered to the right and increased plutocratic power, but would it succeed in permanently aborting America's democracy?

Democratic trappings aside, Roman democracy was a government of the plutocracy, by the plutocracy, and for the plutocracy. So was the romanticized democracy of ancient Athens. So was the exalted British democracy of the 19th century. To a lesser degree, so have been Western democracies during most of the 20th century, with one notable exception: the mid-1940s to the mid-1970s when a budding democracy was replacing plutocracy. Since then a few genuine democratic oases have so far survived in Northern Europe, Iceland, and Switzerland.

Plutocratic avarice drives *parasitic capitalism*. Plutocracy is not just anti-democratic; it is also anti-capitalist because it breeds monopoly just as communism was a monopoly, the ultimate monopoly, and hence its failure.

The pain of the approaching economic crisis would not be in vain if it were to be the birth pangs of an authentic Western democracy and a *moral capitalism*. Irony aside, this time is different.[399] Technology and a discredited mainstream news media have loosened plutocracies' grip on the dissemination of information and the formation of public opinion. Today, the Internet, social media, mobile phones, and some of the international media have launched a communications revolution that is elevating mass awareness. The viewership and influence of the plutocratic media is plummeting because the public has discovered more reliable information sources. At the same time, the present inefficient parasitic model is ill equipped to meet the fierce international competition and the banks are squeezing Western masses to desperation.

The West is standing at the crossroads of egotism and morality, the same crossroads where Caesar once stood. The Achilles heel of Western plutocracies is the *parasitic capitalism* they practice, which has left a void for China, India, Russia, Iran, and others to fill at the expense of the economies of Japan, Europe, and the United States. Arresting the decline will require eliminating the democracy deficit to instill moral, rational, and centrist economic decisions in the public sector and competition in the private sector. In turn, this will require a Western Spring to power political reforms to restrict the power of the extremely wealthy to the economic sphere by limiting their wealth.

The alternative is more of the same; the West will continue to slide into economic irrelevance amid crises and, with it, a progressive erosion of Western plutocratic power. The cancerous growth of the usurious sector alone will spread the economic rot. Parasitic usury is incapable of limiting its own growth; hence, there is no limit to its potential for economic devastation. The biological analogy is that of a parasite growing and spreading until it overwhelms its host. Usury has sapped the vitality of a once vigorous West, rendering it the sick man of the world. We only need to contemplate the degree of indebtedness in the West following the next crisis and the one to follow to realize that the usurious system will collapse under its own weight.

The next crisis carries the potential for greater hardship should the plu-tocracy persist in their present policies. On the other hand, it also holds the promise of becoming the great cleanser, if plutocracy's grip on power slips. Remarkably, both paths, of more plutocracy or less plutocracy, point to the decline of Western plutocracy. Call it the march of time. After lasting millennia, the Western plutocratic license to pillage, exploit, and oppress is about to expire.

Alas, the world cannot fully appreciate many things without experi-encing their opposite. Thus, it takes darkness to appreciate light, evil to value kindness, and debt saturation to understand the blessings of a debt-free economy. Similarly, only deepening plutocratic crises will convince the world of the necessity for the transition to post-plutocracy. For three-and-a-half decades, the West has endured the ravages of the rising tide of pluto-cratic immorality. Sadly, it must endure still more before its final deliverance from plutocracy: costlier misadventures, bigger budget and trade deficits, outrageous indebtedness, continued erosion of industry, loss of interna-tional competiveness, worsening unemployment and income inequality, stagflation, deepening economic crises, vanishing growth, increasing bank-ing power, and failing democracies. The insidious policies of the *counter-revolution* are undermining the state itself; hence, Europe is on the verge of breakups and secessions. In the recent past, the communist economic failure precipitated the breakup of the Soviet Union. The neoclassical macroeco-nomic failure represents a comparable threat to the West.

The *counter-revolution* adopted and inspired several "Neo" labels: neo-classical macroeconomics, neocons, neo-imperialism, and neo-feudalism. These "Neo" labels proved to be seals of unmitigated disasters. The grand fiascos they have spun in every direction have made the next Hegelian swing in the pendulum of history toward morality almost inevitable. The West is itching for a tidal wave of morality to wash away past barbarism, regain its soul and usher in an era of civilized social and international relations, effi-ciency, vitality, dignity, democracy, centrism, and *moral capitalism*. Parasitic psychopaths representing a small percentage of humanity have subjugated the rest for as far as the eye could see. It is time their reign comes to an end and their yoke is lifted.

In parting, let us contemplate a few perceptive words someone once said:

There are those who make things happen.
There are those who watch things happen.
And there are those who wonder what happened.[400]

In the midst of the next economic crisis, Western plutocrats will be wondering, "What happened?"

Appendix: Identifying Usurious Lending

If the environment should turn unfavorable to usury through taxation or otherwise, some moneylenders might resort to dusting off the old Renaissance deceptions or devise new ones. Hence, spotting usury disguised as "profit" becomes important to interested parties. The following is a guide for detecting concealed usurious debt that uses misleading terminology, re-labeling interest as profit and loans as investments or trade.

Generally, lenders insist on receiving interest and principal repayment regardless of whether their counterparties profit or suffer losses, whereas genuine equity investments entail the sharing of business risk. Usurious debt masquerading as equity must retain some, if not all, the characteristics of usury, as follows:

1. Nonpayment of profit (interest) is an event of default, regardless of the nonrealization or unavailability of profits for distribution.
2. Non-repayment of principal is an event of default, regardless of the availability of funds.
3. Nonpayment of profit (interest) during any period makes the liability *cumulative* (e.g., cumulative preferred dividends).
4. The profit (interest) rate is set with reference to the yield on debt, such as the three-month London Inter-Bank Offered Rate (LIBOR) or bond yields.

5. In the event of corporate dissolution, usurious debt attempts to take precedence over equity investments in the payment of past profits (interest) and principal.
6. In debt financing concealed as trades, the delayed payment price for a good or service is noticeably higher than the cash price.[401]

The contrived complexity of some trade contracts often flags the likelihood of a usurious nature and the need for careful analysis.

The more an instrument takes on hybrid characteristics of equity and debt the more it is difficult to judge where it belongs. Genuine equity investments in the form of common stock, most preferred stock,[402] venture capital, partnerships, equity participations, and other equity instruments have characteristics that distinguish them from debt, as follows:

1. Nonpayment of dividends does not constitute an event of default.[403]
2. Non-repayment of principal does not constitute an event of default.
3. Preferred dividend distributions are contingent on and limited to the availability of profits during any financial period.
4. Non-repayment of a preferred principal amount should only become a contract violation if the issuer is able, but unwilling, to honor the contract.
5. Equity investors of all classes are residual owners with equal rights to the net assets of a company in the event of its dissolution or liquidation.

Selected Bibliography

Adams, Ian and Dyson, R.W., *Fifty Major Political Thinkers* (Routledge, 2007)

Ahamed, Liaquat, *Lords of Finance: The Bankers Who Broke the World* (Penguin Books, 2009)

Badiou, Alain, *The Rebirth of History: Times of Riots and Uprisings* (Verso, 2012)

Barofsky, Neil, *Bailout: An Inside Account of How Washington Abandoned Main Street While Rescuing Wall Street* (Free Press, 2012)

Beckett, Ian F. W., *The Making of the First World War* (Yale University Press, 2014)

Bernstein, Peter L., *Capital Ideas: The Improbable Origins of Modern Wall Street* (John Wiley & Sons, 2005)

Bloom, Howard, *The Genius of the Beast: A Radical Re-Vision of Capitalism* (Prometheus Books, 2010)

Bonner, William and Lila Rajiva, *Mobs, Messiahs and Markets: Surviving the Public Spectacle in Finance and Politics* (John Wiley & Sons, Inc., 2007)

Bremmer, Ian, *The End of the Free Market: Who Wins the War Between States and Corporations* (Portfolios, 2010)

Brown, Ellen Hodgson *The Web of Debt: The Shocking Truth About Our Money System and How We Can Break Free* (Third Millennium Press, 2007)

Brown, Stephen R., *Merchant Kings: When Companies Ruled the World 1600-1900* (Thomas Dunne Books, 2010)

Brussee, Warren, *The Great Depression of Debt: Survival Techniques for Every Investor* (Wiley & Sons, 2009)

Buchanan, Patrick J, *Suicide of a Superpower: Will America Survive to 2025?* (Thomas Dunne Books, 2011)

Buffet, Mary & Clark, David, *Warren Buffet and the Interpretation of Financial Statements* (Simon & Schuster, 2008)

Cassidy, John, *How Markets Fail: The Logic of Economic Calamities* (Penguin Books, 2009)

Chang, Matthias, *The Shadow Money Lenders and the Global Financial Tsunami* (21st Century Strategic Studies, 2008)

Cholle, Francis P., *The Intuitive Compass: Why the Best Decision Balance Reason and Instinct* (Jossey-Bass, 2012)

Chomsky, Noam, *Making The Future: Occupations, Interventions, Empire and Resistance* (Penguin Books, 2012)

————, *Hopes and Prospects* (Penguin Group, 2010)

————, *Power Systems: Conversations on Global Democratic Uprisings and the New Challenges to U.S. Empire* (Metropolitan Books, 2013)

Claman, Liz, *The Best Investment Advice I Ever Received* (Business Plus, 2006)

Cooker, Mark, *Rivers of Blood, Rivers of Gold: Europe's Conquest of Indigenous Peoples* (Grove Press, 1998)

Cooper, George, *The Origin of Financial Crises: Central Banks, Credit Bubbles and the Efficient Market Fallacy* (Vintage Books, 2008)

Cunningham, Lawrence, *The Essays of Warren Buffet: Lessons for Investors and Mangers* (John Wiley & Sons, 2002)

De Mesquita, Bruce Bueno, *Prediction: How to See and Shape the Future with Game Theory* (Vintage, 2010)

Derman, Emanuel, *Models Behaving Badly* (Free Press, 2012)

Drobny, Steven, *Inside The House of Money* (John Wiley & Sons, 2009)

Feierstein, Mitch, *Planet Ponzi* (Transworld Publishers, 2012)

Ferguson, Charles H., *Predator Nation: Corporate Criminals, Political Corruption, and the Hijacking of America* (Crown Business, 2012)

Ferguson, Niall, *The Great Degeneration: How Institutions Decay and Economies Dies* (Allen Lane, 2012)

Frank, Robert F., *The Economic Naturalist: Why Economics Explains Almost Everything* (Virgin Books Ltd., 2008)

Friedman, George, *The Next Decade: Empire and Republic in a Changing World* (Anchor Books, 2012)

Gladwell, Malcolm, *The Tipping Point: How Little Things Can Make a Big Difference* (Little, Brown and Company, 2000)

Gombrich, E.H., *A Little History of the World* (Yale University Press, 2008)

Graham, Benjamin, *The Intelligent Investor* (Harper, 2006)

Heuvel, Katrina Vanden, and The Nation editors, *Meltdown: How Greed and Corruption Shattered Our Financial System and How We Can Recover* (Nation Books, 2009)

Kessler, Andy, *Wall Street Meet My Narrow Escape from the Stock Market Grinder* (HarperBusiness, 2004)

King, Stephen D., *Losing Control: The Emerging Threats to Western Prosperity* (Yale University Press, 2010)

Krugman, Paul, *End This Depression Now* (W. W. Norton & Company, 2012)

Lessig, Lawrence, *Republic Lost: How Money Corrupts Congress-and a Plan to Stop It* (Twelve, 2011)

Levitt, Steven D., and Stephen J. Dubner, Stephen J., *Freakonomics: A Rogue Economist Explores the Hidden Side of Everything* (William Morrow, 2005)

Lewis, Michael, Ed. *Panic: The Story of Modern Financial Insanity* (Penguin Books, 2008)

————, *Boomerang* (Allen Lane, 2011)

————, *The Money Culture* (Norton, 2011)

————, *Liar's Poker* (Holder & Stoughton, 1989)

Lovell, Julia, *The Opium War: Drugs, Dreams and the Making of China* (Picador, 2011)

Lowe, Janet, *Warren Buffet Speaks: Wit and Wisdom from the World's Greatest Investor* (John Wiley & Sons, 2007)

Lowenstein, Roger, *The End of Wall Street* (The Penguin Press, 2010)

Mahar, Maggie, *Bull: A History of the Boom and Bust, 1982-2004* (Harperbusiness, 2004)

McDonald, Lawrence G., and Robinson, Patrick, *Colossal Failure of Common Sense: The Inside Story of the Collapse of Lehman Brothers* (Three Rivers Press, 2009)

Michaelson, Adam, *The Foreclosure of America* (Berkley books, 2009)

Minsky, Hyman P., *Stabilizing an Unstable Economy* (McGraw Hill, 2008)

Moore, Michael, *Here Comes Trouble: The Making of an American Agitator* (Penguin Books, 2012)

Moyo, Dambisa, *How the West Was Lost: Fifty Years of Economic Folly and the Stark Choices Ahead* (Penguin Books, 2012)

Napoleoni, Loretta, *Maonomics: Why Chinese Communists Make Better Capitalists Than We Do* (Seven Stories Press, 2011)

Oliver, Jamie, & Goodwin, Tony, *How They Blew It: The CEOs and Entrepreneurs behind some of the World's most Catastrophic Business Failures* (Kogan Page, 2010)

Olusoga, David and Erichsen, Casper W., *The Kaiser's Holocaust: Germany's Forgotten Germany* (Faber and Faber, 2011)

Perkins, John, *Confessions of an Economic Hit Man* (Crown Business, 2009)

Phillips, Kevin, *Bad Money: Reckless Finance, Failed Politics, and the Global Crisis of American Capitalism* (Penguin Books, 2008)

Piketty, Thomas, *Capital in the Twenty-First Century* (The Belknap Press, 2014)

Reinhart, Carmen M. and Rogoff, Kenneth S., *This Time Is Different: Eight Centuries of Financial Folly* (Princeton University Press, 2009)

Riverbend, *Baghdad Burning: Girl Blog from Iraq* (The Feminist Press at the City University of New York,2005)

Krepinevich, Andrew F.,*7 Deadly Scenarios: A Military Futurist Explores War in the Twenty-First Century* (Bantam books, 2010)

Rogers, Jim, *Street Smarts: Adventures on the Road and in the Markets* (Crown Business, 2013)

Rousseau, Jean-Jacques, *The Social Contract* (Oxford University Press, 2008)

Sarkar, Saral, *The Crisis of Capitalism: A Different Study of the Political Economy* (Counterpoint, 2012)

Schui, Florian, *Austerity: The Great Failure* (Yale University Press, 2014)

Skidelsky, Robert, *Keynes the Return of the Master* (Penguin Books, 2010)

Soros, George, *The Crash of 2008 and What It Means: The New Paradigm for Financial Markets* (Public Affairs, 2008)

Stiglitz, Joseph, *Freefall: Free Markets and the Sinking of the Global Economy* (Penguin Books, 2010)

———, *The Price of Inequality* (Allen Lane, 2012)

Wedel, Janine R., *Shadow Elite: How the World's New Power Brokers Undermine Democracy and the Free Market* (Basic Books, 2009)

Zuckerman, Gregory, *The Greatest Trade Ever: How One Man Bet Against the Markets and Made $20 Billion* (Penguin Books, 2010)

Notes

1. Introduction

1. http://www.brainyquote.com/search_results.html?q=intelligence&pg=2

2. https://www.youtube.com/watch?v=A7wKHIYysjY

3. Professor Joseph Schumpeter (1883–1950) was a famed innovations cycle theorist.

4. *Groundhog Day* is a bizarre, but charming, movie in which the days and their events repeat endlessly with only slight variations, imparting reflections on the rhythm of life and even a little wisdom.

5. https://en.wikipedia.org/wiki/Decolonization

6. The International Monetary Fund report is based on purchasing power parity.

7. Many of these comments concerning Western economies also apply to Japan.

8. Throughout, the terms *business cycle* and *economic cycle* are used interchangeably.

9. Although 1979 marked the start of the parting with Keynesian economics and the progressive adoption of neoclassical economics, for convenience the text refers to the 1980s as the start of this process.

10. BRICS is short for Brazil, Russia, India, China, and South Africa. The G-7 was established in 1973 as five countries; it evolved into the Group of Seven, or G-7, by 1975. These seven countries represented the largest

and wealthiest nations at the time—namely, the United States, Japan, Germany, France, Britain, Italy, and Canada.

11. *The West* here and henceforth refers primarily to the advanced economies of Western Europe, North America, Australia and New Zealand. Occasionally, it implies Japan and South Korea as well.

12. The economic contraction began in 2007, but very few felt any pain before 2008; hence, we will adhere to the public's perception.

13. http://en.wikipedia.org/wiki/Financial_crisis_of_2007%E2% 80%9308#Role_of_economic_forecasting Wikipedia, Financial crisis of 2007–08, Bezemer, Dirk J (June 2009). "No One Saw This Coming: Understanding Financial Crisis Through Accounting Models." Munich Personal RePEc Archive. Retrieved October 23, 2009.

14. Plutocracy is the rule of the wealthy, as defined by Merriam Webster's Internet dictionary.

15. http://www.brainyquote.com/quotes/authors/l/leonardo_da_vinci. html#WcrI0DF4mEoyVFTz.99

16. Chapter by Noble laureate Joseph E. Stiglitz, p. 376-377, *Lives of the Laureates*, sixth edition, edited by Roger W. Spencer and David A. Macpherson, The MIT Press, 2014.

17. http://www.brainyquote.com/search_results.html?q=Voltaire

18. Refer to Chapter 4, the section titled "Viscount Takahashi's Macroeconomic Revolution."

19. This is discussed further in Chapter 5 in the section titled "MPT versus Dynamic Portfolio Theory."

20. Refer to Chapter 6.

21. http://www.sanders.senate.gov/newsroom/press-releases/the-fed-audit

22. All references to $, dollar, or dollars implies the US dollar, throughout.

23. http://en.wikipedia.org/wiki/2008%E2%80%9311_Icelandic_financial_crisis

24. Refer to Chapter 9, the section titled "Usurious Capitalism."

25. "Charlie Rose Show" (Bloomberg TV, July 27, 2012).

26. https://en.wikiquote.org/wiki/John_Maynard_Keynes#Quotes

27. http://www.brainyquote.com/search_results.html?q=truth

28. Unless indicated otherwise, the term *monopolies* here and subsequently refers to all forms of restriction of trade, including monopoly, duopoly, oligopoly, cartels, and trusts on the demand side, and monopsony on the supply side.

29. The publication of *The Wealth of Nations*, in 1776, marks the start of classical economics; 1873 was the year that John Stuart Mill, the last of the classical economists, passed away.

2. Classical Economic Theory

30. www.brainyquote.com/

31. In his book, *Economic Thought of Islam: Ibn Khaldun* (1964), Joseph J. Spengler suggested that the Father of Economics is Ibn Khaldun (1332–1406).

32. https://en.wikipedia.org/wiki/David_Ricardo#Parliamentary_record

33. https://en.wikipedia.org/wiki/Jean-Baptiste_Say

34. This is discussed in Chapter 4.

35. https://en.wikipedia.org/wiki/John_Stuart_Mill

36. https://en.wikipedia.org/wiki/Thomas_Robert_Malthus

37. Refer to Chapter 4, the section titled "Jean Charles Léonard de Sismondi."

38. Other similar concepts that border on instinct include intuition, inspiration, creativity, hunches, super-consciousness, and insight. See the super-conscious mind at http://www.youtube.com/watch?v=vYz0eREf9f0

39. For brevity, man is referenced here, though women are implied as well.

40. http://www.brainyquote.com/search_results.html?q=intelligence&pg=2

41. Given his undoubted intelligence, reflected by his excellent investment performance, and moral positions on critical economic issues, we shall use Warren Buffet repeatedly as one benchmark for intelligent and moral economic behavior.

42. Its slope is positive because progressively larger amounts of wealth accumulation are necessary to provide the same utility. For example, an additional hundred thousand dollars in wealth hardly provides the same satisfaction when the wealth accumulator has $100 million as when he or she had just one million.

43. Robert Skidelsy, "Keynes and the Ethics of Capitalism," https://en.wikiquote.org/wiki/John_Maynard_Keynes#Quotes.

44. Bertrand Russell, "Power," http://www.amazon.com/Power-Bertrand-Russell/dp/0415094569/ref=sr_1_2?s=books&ie=UTF8&qid=1411370548&sr=1-2&keywords=bertrand+russell+power.

45. Czarist Russia only abolished serfdom, the selling of peasants along with the lands they cultivated, in 1861. The French Revolution formally abolished the remnants of feudalism on August 4, 1789. By 1793, there had been a major transfer of wealth and income from large landowners and the church to the peasants. See http://en.wikipedia.org/wiki/Feudalism.

46. Prime examples are the Opium Wars.

47. Denis Nowell Pritt, *The Labour Government, 1945-1951* (pub. 1963).

48. *The Holy Bible* (Mark 8:36, KJV).

49. The English Poor Laws were codified in 1587–98 for the relief of the poor.

50. See http://en.wikipedia.org/wiki/Corn_Laws.

51. John Kenneth Galbraith: "Age of Uncertainty, Episode I" (BBC video series).

52. Reverend Desmond Tutu explained the imperialist hold over the church well in stating, "When the missionaries came to Africa they had the Bible and we had the land. They said, Let us pray and we closed our eyes. When we opened our eyes, we had the Bible and they had the land."

53. https://en.wikipedia.org/wiki/Collective_unconscious.

54. See http://www.brainyquote.com/quotes/quotes/a/abrahamlin110340.html.

55. Refer to Chapter 6.

56. Nassim Talib, *The Black Swan: The Impact of the Highly Improbable* (Random House, 2007).

57. See http://www.brainyquote.com/quotes/topics/topic_war. html#Cdw bGwZMwOHH8WxD.99.

3. *The Rise and Fall of Marxist Economics*

58. The *Communist Manifesto* was published in 1848. In 1988, Mikhail Sergeyevich Gorbachyov launched glasnost, the start of the dissolution of the Soviet Union; this led to the Soviet Union's formal termination in 1991.

59. http://www.brainyquote.com/search_results.html?q=Religion+is+what +keeps+the+poor+from+murdering+the+rich.

60. http://en.wikipedia.org/wiki/Black_Death.

61. "Masters of Money - Karl Marx" (BBC documentary).

62. An import tax.

63. The aristocracy owned most of the land.

64. https://en.wikipedia.org/wiki/Winston_Churchill

65. *Trattato di Sociologia Generale*, 1916, and published in English as *The Mind and Society* by Harcourt, Brace and edited by Arthur Livingston, 1935.

66. Ian Adams and R. W. Dayson, chapter on Karl Marx in *Fifty Major Political Thinkers* (Routledge, 2007).

67. The causes of an increase in demand for a normal good include a change in tastes, an increase in incomes, a rise in the price of a substitute, and a decline in the price of a complementary good.

68. E. Carroll pointed out in *An Introduction to Economics with Emphasis on Innovation* (2006) that "Joseph Schumpeter argued that technological innovation created transient monopolies with abnormal profits, a necessary incentive for innovation, until imitators drove down profit."

69. Similarly, a century earlier, famine in the British Isles and fear of revolution had prompted the British parliament to repeal the Corn Laws, thereby scrapping the tariff on the import of grains.

70. More precisely, the condition of labor already began improving following the Russian Revolution in 1917. The New Deal in the 1930s partly reflected this, however it was minor compared to the major social reforms after World War II.

71. Andrew Mack, Why Big Nations Lose Small Wars: The Politics of Asymmetric Conflict, page 181. http://web.stanford.edu/class/polisci211z/2.2/Mack%20WP%201975%20Asymm%20Conf.pdf

72. https://en.wikipedia.org/wiki/Wind_of_Change_(speech)# Background.

73. https://en.wikipedia.org/wiki/Wind_of_Change_(speech)#Cold_War_politics_and_.the_ fear_of_communism.

74. Georg Wilhelm Friedrich Hegel (1770–1831) was a German philosopher. Hegel used "dialectic" speculative logic and "absolute idealism" to influence both his admirers and his critics. One French philosopher, Paul-Michel Foucault (1926–1984), asserted that philosophers were "doomed to find Hegel waiting patiently at the end of whatever road we travel."

75. The rich enjoyed personal income tax cuts, while the poor suffered higher indirect taxes, such as value-added tax (VAT).

4. Keynesian Cyclical Stabilization

76. The year 1819 marked the publication of de Sismondi's *Nouveaux principes d'économie politique*. In 1979, 160 years later, Great Britain, under Thatcher, reverted to neoclassical macroeconomics and discarded Keynesianism.

77. See http://www.brainyquote.com/search_results.html?q=truth.

78. This topic is explored further in Chapter 11, section titled "Stages of a Business Cycle."

79. For more details, refer to Chapter 10.

80. Ambrose Evans-Pritchard, "Japan's economic revolution rocks the world," *Sydney Morning Herald*, Jan. 22, 2013, http://www.smh.com.au/business/world-business/japans-economic-revolution-rocks-the-world-20130122-2d3w2.html.

81. The cobweb supply-demand model was proposed by Nicholas Kaldor.

82. For example, Keynes was a successful investor who did not think markets were rational. Moreover, some investors have outperformed markets over long periods, which is inconsistent with the market's

efficiency and rationality. A more crucial issue is that there is no assurance that those charged with economic management are good investors and, therefore, good predicators of the market's future direction. This seems to have been one of the problems facing Federal Reserve Chairman Ben Bernanke in the years leading up to the 2008 crisis.

83. The multiplier effect refers to a ripple effect in the economy, where an increase (or decrease) in spending triggers a cycle of increases (decreases) in spending. The multiplier tends to be greater in relatively closed economies where international trade is smaller relative to GDP and, therefore, represents a smaller leakage. For the US economy, the total economic stimulus (or dampening), after a time lag, exceeds the original amount spent (or withheld) by a factor of about 0.75 times. In other words, the US multiplier is about 1.75.

84. John Maynard Keynes, *The General Theory of Employment, Interest and Money*, February 1936.
    This chapter also makes use of some of the concepts contained in *The Return of the Master* by Robert Skidelsky, Penguin Books, 2010.

85. Pursuant to the 1973 oil crisis, the author's 1975 MSc. Dissertation, "A Proposed Scheme for Recycling Surplus Oil Funds," suggested a means of increasing capital absorption in the Middle East region to speed up the process of recycling surplus funds.

86. See http://en.wikipedia.org/wiki/List_of_recessions_in_the_United_States.

87. In his 1975 MSc. dissertation in financial economics at the University of Wales (Bangor), this author proposed solving the stagnation side of the problem by accelerating the global recycling of surplus Arab petrodollars by reducing the risk of nationalization in capital-deficient Arab countries and increasing investments there. The dissertation was titled "A Proposed Scheme for Recycling Surplus Oil Funds."

88. Myung Soo Cha, "Did Takahashi Korekiyo Rescue Japan from the Great Depression?" *Journal of Economic History*, Vol. 63/No. 1 (Mar. 2003): 127–44. Also see http://en.wikipedia.org/wiki/Great_Depression#cite_note-74

89. Part V discusses these issues at length.

90. In this chapter and elsewhere, criticisms of neoclassical economics imply neoclassical macroeconomics.

5. The Fall and Rise of Neoclassical Macroeconomics

91. William Stanley Jevons's *Theory of Political Economy* and Carl Menger's Principles of Economics were both published in 1871. By 1931, the severity of the Great Depression made it plain that neoclassical macroeconomics was inadequate. However, it was revived starting in 1979 and continues, at present, despite growing uncertainty about its relevance.

92. See http://www.goodreads.com/quotes/tag/monopoly.

93. Throughout, reference to Western countries or simply the West implies the twenty-eight member countries of the European Union, the United States, Canada, and European countries generally considered part of the West although not members of the European Union, most notably Norway, Switzerland, and Iceland. Moreover, many of the economic arguments herein apply to the present state of the Japanese economy as well.

94. "On Friedrich Hayek's Prices and Production," in *Collected Writings, Vol. XII*, p. 252, https://en.wikiquote.org/wiki/John_Maynard_Keynes#Quotes.

95. J. Bradford De Long, *"Liquidation" Cycles: Old Fashioned Real Business Cycle Theory and the Great Depression*, National Bureau of Economic

Research, Working Paper No. 3546, p. 1, https://en.wikipedia.org/wiki/Great_Depression#cite_ref-nber.org_28-0.

96. Lawrence White, "Did Hayek and Robbins Deepen the Great Depression?" *Journal of Money, Credit and Banking*, Vol. 40/No. 4 (June 2008): 751–768, http://en.wikipedia.org/wiki/Great_Depression#cite_ref-nber.org_28-0.

97. The Sherman Act 1890, the Clayton Act 1914, and the Federal Trade Commission Act 1914, http://en.wikipedia.org/wiki/United_States_antitrust_law.

98. Milton Friedman's prize in 1976 resulted in international protests accusing him and the University of Chicago of supporting the military dictatorship in Chile. Moreover, four Nobel Prize laureates—George Wald, Linus Pauling, David Baltimore, and Salvador Luria—made similar protests to the New York Times in October 1976.

99. See http://en.wikipedia.org/wiki/List_of_recessions_in_the_United_States.

100. Chapter 10 discusses these problems further.

101. The efficient market hypothesis (EMH), where markets are efficient with securities prices reflecting all available information, is consistent with the *rational expectations hypothesis* (REH).

102. https://en.wikipedia.org/wiki/Modern_portfolio_theory#Criticisms.

103. http://www.thetao.info/quote/tao5395.htm

104. The efficient market hypothesis is part of the modern portfolio theory.

105. In the 1920s, Charles Ponzi (1882–1949) became famous as a con artist in the US. His "Ponzi scheme" promised a high return and used

pyramiding—that is to say, taking money from new investors to pay earlier ones. The scheme worked for a few years, but was exposed when new money dried up.

106. For further elaboration on this point, refer to Chapter 12's section titled "Corporate Reporting."

107. Chapter 12 discusses this progressive deterioration in market efficiency.

108. See Ross Ashcroft's interview of Prof. Steve Keen on the occasion of Keen's newly published book *Debunking Economics: The Emperor Dethroned?* (Zed Books, 2011). Ashcroft is with the "Renegade Economist Show." See http://www.youtube.com/watch?v=7F2FKxxN_IE.

109. Refer to Chapter 9's section titled "The Banking Model."

110. Refer to Chapter 6.

111. http://www.brainyquote.com/quotes/quotes/v/voltaire118641

112. Refer to Chapter 11, which deals with economic cycles.

113. Refer to Chapter 2.

114. See http://www.brainyquote.com/quotes/authors/a/albert_einstein.html.

6. The Unified Theory of Macroeconomic Failure

115. http://www.brainyquote.com/quotes/quotes/j/johnmaynar385471

116. Gresham's Law applies mostly to gold and silver coinage and, to a lesser extent, to copper coins. When some part of society scraps coins, in effect, stealing a little from the legal tender, the currency in circulation

is debased. Once some debased coins are accepted as legal tender then, soon, all coins become debased; hence, bad money drives out good money. Forty years earlier in Poland, Nicolaus Copernicus made similar assertions. Earlier still, Al-Maqrizi (1364–1442), a Muslim jurist and historian, developed a similar concept in his work *Study of the Monetary System*. See http://en.wikipedia.org/wiki/Gresham%27s_law.

117. Luke 6:3.

118. See http://en.wikipedia.org/wiki/Golden_Rule#Christianity.

119. Regrettably, the author is not sufficiently familiar with other religions to include them in the discussion.

120. The New Testament.

121. Theodore Roosevelt, *Theodore Roosevelt: an autobiography* (New York: Macmillan, 1913).

122. Al-Hussein ibn ʿAlī ibn Abī Ṭālib, http://en.wikipedia.org/wiki/Husayn_ibn_Ali.

123. See http://en.wikipedia.org/wiki/Psychopathy.

124. Don Fitz, "Inside the Psyche of the 1%," Truth-Out, November 3, 2013,

123. http://truth-out.org/opinion/item/19776-inside-the-psyche-of-the-1.

125. See http://en.wikipedia.org/wiki/Technological_dualism.

126. On Feb. 18, 2015, Al-Mayadeen TV reported that the Iraqi ambassador to the United Nations informed the Security Council that ISIS was financing its activities in part by selling human organs.

127. The economics literature recognizes the Protestant work ethic as a significant factor in promoting economic development. The focus here is broader.

128. See http://en.wikipedia.org/wiki/Sophism.

129. https://en.wikipedia.org/wiki/Bertrand_Russell#First_World_War.

130. https://en.wikipedia.org/wiki/Galileo_Galilei.

131. In 1918, the British authorities imprisoned Bertrand Russell for his opinions. Refer to Bertrand Russell's Power (Routledge, 1995), introduction by Kirk Willis, http://www.amazon.com/Power-Bertrand-Russell/dp/0415094569/ref=sr_1_2?s=books&ie=UTF8&qid=1411370548&sr=1-2&keywords=bertrand+russell+power

132. http://www.brainyquote.com/quotes/topics/topic_power.html#lfitBch5KHm3AYCC.99.

133. https://en.wikipedia.org/wiki/Classical_conditioning.

134. Chapter 1's section titled "In Search of Reliable Signposts."

135. For those unfamiliar with the concepts involved, consult any standard public finance textbook for a detailed explanation.

136. In what follows, where appropriate, consumption will mean production also and goods include services.

137. Public cost equals private cost plus the externality, if any.

138. In some instances, the estimated total benefit compared to the cost of reducing pollution from coal-burning utilities was ten to one or higher.

139. A somewhat similar concept that refers to the confusion of battle is the fog of war.

140. See http://www.brainyquote.com/quotes/authors/w/winston_churchill.html.

141. Chapter 4, section titled "The Golden Age of Keynesianism."

142. Henri Bergson, *The Meaning of War* (London: T. Fisher Unwin Ltd., 1915), p. 45. Also see
https://books.google.ae/books?id=0LcKAwAAQBAJ&pg=PA45&lpg=PA45&dq=Bismarck+might+is+right&source=bl&ots=Lq5_l7SXJC&sig=WedvPLNjibKDn6MbkG_imsoqd3Y&hl=en&sa=X&ved=0ahUKEwi3-5KakKLKAhUEKw8KHZYaAgQQ6AEIQDAH#v=onepage&q=Bismarck%20might%20is%20right&f=false.

143. David Olusoga and Casper W. Erichsen, *The Kaiser's Holocaust* (Faber and Faber Ltd., 2011), p. 55.

144. Adam Hochschildthat, *King Leopold's Ghost* (Mariner Books, 1998). This bestseller exposes the atrocities committed under the rule of Belgium's King Leopold II in the Congo. Even a century or longer after those crimes, the truth is not widely known, or is twisted or suppressed. Nine of the first ten publishers who saw the manuscript refused to publish it. See also http://en.wikipedia.org/wiki/King_Leopold%27s_Ghost.

145. Chapter 3, section titled "Nineteenth-Century Poverty and Plutocracy in Europe."

7. Usury: Conquest by Stealth

146. http://www.brainyquote.com/search_results.html?q=Man+is+born+free%2C+and+everywhere+he+is+in+chains

147. Usury is lending for interest, the mainstay of the banking business.

148. Supplementary Convention on the Abolition of Slavery, the Slave Trade, and Institutions and Practices Similar to Slavery, 226 U.N.T.S. 3, entered into force April 30, 1957, Human Rights Library, University of Minnesota. See http://www1.umn.edu/humanrts/instree/f3scas.htm.

149. Under Islam, a charitable loan is a loan to Allah. See Surat Al-Muzzammil, 73:20, Holy Qur'an.

150. Regrettably, the author is not sufficiently familiar with other religions, although some might also hold usury in contempt.

151. Refer to Chapter 6.

152. The Renaissance was from the 14th to the 17th century, a period in which major cultural and religious transformations took place in Europe.

153. Chapter 15 presents examples of equity alternatives to usurious lending.

8. *The Ascent of Banking*

154. http://www.brainyquote.com/search_results.html?q=We+cannot+solve +our+problems+with+the+same+thinking+we+used+when+we+created +them

155. Monopsony is a market situation in which there is a single buyer for a product or service and many sellers. Unlike a monopoly, which exploits the buyers, a monopsony exploits the sellers, typically, labor.

156. This brings the total immoralities of banking to four: (1) usury itself, (2) the dishonesty of lending nonexistent funds, (3) the betrayal of the

public trust by putting depositors' funds at risk, and (4) unloading sub-par credit onto their clients. In reality, the moral violations associated with usury, its products and institutions are innumerable, as will become clear in due course.

157. Short selling and margin lending are covered in Chapters 10 and 11, respectively.

158. See Chapter 11.

159. Hyman P. Minsky, "The Financial Instability Hypothesis" (Working Paper No. 74), the Jerome Levy Economics Institute of Bard College, May 1992.

160. The term "counterrevolution" was used earlier by Naomi Klein with reference to Milton Friedman's free market experiments in Chile and elsewhere in her penetrating book "The Shock Doctrine: The Rise of Disaster Capitalism," Henry Holt and Company, 2008.

161. Robert Luongo (b. 1949) astutely draws similarities between Shakespeare's portrayal of plutocracy in ancient times and recent trends. See *The Power Template: Shakespeare's Political Plays*, http://www.amazon.com/Power-Template-Shakespeares-Political-Plays/dp/1463659520/ref=sr_1_1_title_0_main?s=books&ie=UTF8&qid=1313339020&sr=1-1.

162. In 1913, the Federal Reserve Act was passed. In 1932, the first "Glass–Steagall Act" was passed. In 1979, Margaret Thatcher became the British prime minister. In 1981, Ronald Reagan was elected US president. The British Conservative Party and the American Republican Party share a similar ideology.

9. Bank Instability, Products, and Economics

163. See www.brainyquote.com/.

164. For an interesting history of financial crises, see "Financial crisis" in Wikipedia, http://en.wikipedia.org/wiki/Financial_crisis.

165. This section draws heavily on the extensive documentation of economic and financial crises in Carmen M. Reinhart and Kenneth S. Rogoff's seminal work, *This Time Is Different: Eight Centuries of Financial Folly* (Princeton University Press, 2011).

166. Table 13.1, This Time Is Different.

167. *This Time Is Different: Eight Centuries of Financial Folly.*

168. See Chapter 11's section titled "Stages of a Business Cycle."

169. Ibid.

170. Rising interest rates tend to lower the prices of fixed-interest loans and bonds and vice versa.

171. Roger Lowenstein, *When Genius Failed: The Rise and Fall of Long-Term Capital Management* (New York: Random House Trade Paperback, 2000).

172. The first round was following the first oil crisis in 1973.

173. For more on the problems of Citigroup, see the chapter titled "Steel's Turn" in Roger Lowenstein's *The End of Wall Street* (Penguin Press, 2010).

174. F. William Engdahl, "Oil Wars: Pop! Goes the Weasel," Jan. 27, 2015, *New Eastern Outlook*, http://journal-neo.org/2015/01/27/pop-goes-the-weasel.

175. The London interbank offered rate (LIBOR) is the reference rate used by borrowers and lenders (worldwide) to set the interest rate on international currencies that they should pay or receive. Barclays's LIBOR fiddling and fixing illustrates that the concept of a free money market is a myth, encouraged by its beneficiaries because, under a free market, participants cannot fix LIBOR to suit their interests.

176. Japan has one of the highest ratios of debt to GDP, and its serious consequences will surface more visibly in future.

177. *Fortune Magazine*, Europe Edition, June 7, 2012, p. 44.

178. *Foreign Affairs*, March/April 2010 issue.

179. See www.TheFinancialCoach.com.

180. Alexander Nahum Sack (or Aleksandr Naumovich Zak) (1890–1955) formalized the odious debt doctrine (unjust national debt) through his work *Effects of the Transformations of the States in Their Public Debts and Other Financial Obligations* (*Les effets des transformations des Etats sur leurs dettes publiques et autres obligations financières: traité juridique et financier*), Recueil Sirey, Paris, 1927.

181. Patricia Adams, "Odious Debts: Loose Lending, Corruption, and the Third World's Environmental Legacy."

182. Seema Jayachandran and Michael Kremer, "Odious Debt," *American Economic Review*, March 2006.

183. John Perkins, *Confessions of an Economic Hit Man* (Penguin Group, 2004), http://www.amazon.com/Confessions-Economic-Hit-John-Perkins/dp/0452287081.
Also see http://en.wikipedia.org/wiki/Confessions_of_an_Economic_Hit_Man

184. See http://en.wikipedia.org/wiki/Conspiracy_theory.

185. See http://en.wikipedia.org/wiki/Plausible_deniability.

186. See *Watching the Hawks*, RT, April 7, 2016, for recent accusations of USAID participating in funding turmoil and regime change in several countries, including former Yugoslavia, Georgia and Ukraine.

187. Seehttp://www.brettonwoodsproject.org/2014/10/impact-brics-contingent-reserve-arrangement-cra-new-development-bank-ndb.

188. This is sometimes referred to as frictional inflation.

189. Refer to Chapter 10's section titled "Democracy and the Federal Reserve."

190. For an interesting exposé of how derivatives bankrupted the Long-Term Capital Management hedge fund, see Roger Lowenstein's *When Genius Failed* (New York: Random House Trade Paperbacks, 2000).

191. Nassim Nicholas Taleb discusses the problem posed by outliers at length in his book *The Black Swan: The Impact of the Highly Improbable*.

192. For an inside story of the rise and fall of Countrywide Home Loans and the mortgage crisis, see Adam Michaelson's *The Foreclosure of America* (Penguin Group, 2009).

193. The term Machiavellian derives from Niccolò di Bernardo dei Machiavelli (1469–1527), a Florentine political philosopher best known for his book *The Prince*, which many consider the final authority in real politique.

194. Vilfredo Pareto (1848–1923), an Italian economist, first introduced the concept. One of the arguments for banking deregulation was that free and competitive markets would improve economic efficiency, edging closer to a Pareto optimal resource allocation.

10. The Federal Reserve as an Extension of Banking Power

195. http://www.brainyquote.com/search_results.html?q=We+the+people+are+the+rightful+masters+of+both+Congress+and+the+courts

196. Refer to Chapter 9's section titled "Usurious Capitalism."

197. "Who owns the Federal Reserve?" (November 2, 2014), see http://www.federalreserve.gov/faqs/about_14986.htm

198. "Income and Expenses of the Federal Reserve Banks, 1914–2013," Table 11, pp. 300–302, http://www.federalreserve.gov/publications/annual-report/files/2013-annual-report.pdf

199. Chapter 5's section titled "The Monetarist School."

200. Criticism of the Federal Reserve, Wikipedia, http://en.wikipedia.org/wiki/Criticism_of_the_Federal_Reserve#Private_ownership_or_control.

201. Wikipedia, History of Banking: http://en.wikipedia.org/wiki/History_of_ banking# Great_ Depression.

202. For a more detailed discussion, refer to the section titled "Misdiagnosis of Stagflation (1979–1982)" in Chapter 5.

203. See http://en.wikipedia.org/wiki/Paul_Volcker.

204. See http://en.wikipedia.org/wiki/Regulation_Q.

205. Table A.4.1 "Banking Crises: Historical Summaries, 1800–2008," *This Time Is Different.*

206. Abraham Lincoln's Gettysburg Address, http://en.wikipedia.org/wiki/ Gettysburg_Address.

207. "Who owns the Federal Reserve?" http://www.federalreserve.gov/faqs/ about_14986.htm.

208. *Business Insider,* http://www.businessinsider.com/fed-is-unconstitutional-2010-11.

209. *Business Insider,* http://www.businessinsider.com/fed-is-unconstitutional-2010-11.

210. The Dodd–Frank Wall Street Reform and Consumer Protection Act, signed into federal law by President Barack Obama on July 21, 2010.

211. See http://www.sanders.senate.gov/newsroom/press-releases/the-fed-audit.

212. See http://www.sanders.senate.gov/imo/media/doc/GAO%20Fed%20 Investigation.pdf.

213. Russia Today, February 25, 2015.

11. Amplified Business Cycles

214. BrainyQuote://www.brainyquote.com/quotes/topics/topic_war. html#CdwbGwZMw OHH 8WxD.99

215. Allowing for the complex effects of shorter and longer cycles, this is not far from the estimate of a cycle's duration of seven to eleven years

by French economist Clement Juglar. Refer to Chapter 4, the Section titled "Durations and Stages of Economic Cycles."

216. See http://en.wikipedia.org/wiki/Year_Without_a_Summer.

217. I first heard of a link between sunspots and the weather in 1986 from the ingenious American climatologist, the late Dr. Iben Browning (1918–1991). Presenting a paper at a conference organized by the National Committee for Monetary Reform and Wealth Magazine in Montreal, Canada, he explained how severe droughts preceded many momentous conflicts and population movements in history, including the Mongol expansion.

218. Refer to Chapter 6's section titled "Chronic Negative Externalities."

219. Robert Lenzner, "The Recessions of 1973, 1980, 1991, 2001, 2008 Were Caused by High Oil Prices," *Forbes*, Sept. 1, 2013.

220. Irving Fisher, "The Debt-Deflation Theory of Great Depressions," *Econometrica*, 1(4), pp. 337–357.

221. Steve Keen, "Finance and Economic Breakdown: Modelling Minsky's Financial Instability Hypothesis," *Journal of Post Keynesian Economics*, Vol. 17, No. 4, 607–635,1995.

222. For a country that imports 6 million barrels of crude oil per day, a $30/barrel fall in the price of crude oil stimulates the economy to the tune of $65.7 billion/year, excluding the secondary effects via the multiplier. However, a sharp fall in the price of oil also carries a negative impact on the domestic oil industry, if any.

12. Private Sector Inefficiency: Competition and Information Quality

223. See   http://www.brainyquote.com/quotes/keywords/monopoly.html# mp5ZlIQ3XfD0ul1I.99.

224. Ernest Ezra Mandel (1923–1995), in his book *Late Capitalism*, takes a similar view.

225. See http://en.wikipedia.org/wiki/Rent_seeking.

226. President Barack Obama, 2016 State of the Union Address.

227. See   http://en.wikipedia.org/wiki/Health_system#International_ comparisons.

228. See http://www.forbes.com/sites/dandiamond/2015/09/22/greedy-pharma-executive-cancels-5000-price-hike-but-he-didnt-fix-the-real-problem.

229. For a broader discussion of tax issues and their effect on employment, refer to Chapters 19, 20, and 21.

230. https://en.wikipedia.org/wiki/History_of_union_busting_in_the_ United_States#cite_ note-Smith_88-89-17.

231. "Breaking the Set," Russia Today, October 16, 2014.

232. See http://en.wikipedia.org/wiki/Underconsumption.

233. Refer to Chapter 1's section titled "In Search of Reliable Signposts."

234. See   http://www.brainyquote.com/search_results.html?q=market+ information.

235. Interview on "Russia Today," April 11, 2012.

236. See Chapter 10.

237. https://en.wikipedia.org/wiki/Credit_rating_agency#Explanations_of_ flaws.

238. https://en.wikipedia.org/wiki/Enron.

239. Since then, WorldCom in 2002, and Lehman Brothers in 2008, have broken Enron's record bankruptcy.

240. The archaic governing rules permit companies to submit different accounts to the IRS, the SEC, and the shareholders.

241. Maggie Mahar, *Bull: A History of the Boom and Bust, 1982–2004* (Harper Business, 2004), Chapter 16, "Fully Deluded Earnings."

242. Mitch Feierstein, *Planet Ponzi* (Bantam Press, 2012), p. 17.

13.   Public Sector Inefficiency: Plutocracy vs Democracy

243. http://www.brainyquote.com/search_results.html?q=America+will+ne ver+be+destroyed+from+the+outside.+If+we+falter+and+lose+our+free doms%2C+it+will+be+because+we+destroyed

244. http://www.brainyquote.com/quotes/authors/l/leonardo_da_vinci. html#EIEQkE8ifuC0Q 7cK.99

245. https://en.wikipedia.org/wiki/Fairness_Doctrine

246. Six corporations are said to control the bulk of US news media: Rupert Murdoch's News Corp., Time Warner, Viacom, Walt Disney, CBS Corporation, and NBC Universal.

247. "Breaking the Set," Russia Today television program on July 8, 2014.

248. For example, the media blocked news of the Occupy Movement for a long time.

249. The Big Picture with Thom Hartman, RT, March 30, 2016

250. https://en.wikipedia.org/wiki/File:FDR%27s_1941_State_of_the_Union_(Four_Freedoms_speech)_Edit_1.ogg

251. https://en.wikipedia.org/wiki/Oxfam

252. https://en.wikipedia.org/wiki/Poverty#Wealth_concentration

253. The US Bureau of Justice Statistics and http://en.wikipedia.org/wiki/Incarceration_in_the_United_States.

254. http://www.brainyquote.com/search_results.html?q=crime.

255. https://en.wikipedia.org/wiki/Economic_inequality#cite_ref-119. Jerome L. Neapolitana, "A comparative analysis of nations with low and high levels of violent crime," *Journal of Criminal Justice*, Vol. 27, Issue 3, May–June 1999, p. 260. Also "Political structure, economic inequality, and homicide: a cross-national analysis," *Deviant Behavior*, Vol. 20, Issue 1, 1999, p. 50.

256. "Rough Justice," *The Economist*, July 24, 2010 and "Too Many Laws, Too Many Prisoners," July 30, 2010.

257. See http://www.leaderu.com/orgs/probe/docs/crime.html#.

258. Fareed Zakaria, on CNN, March 30, 2012 (quotation appearing in Wikipedia, "Incarceration in the United States").

259. Andrew D. Leipold, "Why Grand Juries Do Not (and Cannot) Protect the Accused," Cornell Law Review, Vol. 80, Issue 2, January 1995, Article 10, p. 274.

260. For firsthand commentary on US prisons, see the interview with ex-CIA officer and Associate Fellow at the Institute of Policy Studies, John Kiriakou: http://rt.com/shows/watching-the-hawks/259861-shooting-cia-whistleblower-prison.

261. http://www.brainyquote.com/quotes/topics/topic_war.html# CdwbGwZMwOHH8WxD. 99.

262. Maj. Gen. Smedley Butler, *War Is a Racket* (Round Table Press, 1935), https://archive.org/details/WarIsARacket.

263. American Airlines Flight 11, crashed in the of the North Tower of the World Trade Center at 8:46:40 Eastern Time (https://en.wikipedia.org/wiki/American_Airlines_Flight_11). Fifty-one minutes later, American Airlines Flight 77 crashed in the Pentagon at 9:37 a.m. Eastern Time (https://en.wikipedia.org/wiki/American_Airlines_Flight_77).

264. http://en.wikipedia.org/wiki/Colin_Powell#Secretary_of_State.

265. Joseph Stiglitz and Linda Bilmes, *The Three Trillion Dollar War* (W.W. Norton, 2008).

266. Riverbend, Baghdad Burning: Girl Blog from Iraq (The Feminist Press at the City University of New York,2005)

267. For example, although a convicted bank thief was sentenced in Jordan to a 22-year jail term for ingeniously plundering his own bank there, the Anglo-American occupation entrusted him with running Iraq's financial affairs.

Basil Al-Nakeeb

268. Certainly, they also hold Iraqi citizenships to permit them to rule Iraq, whereas no self-respecting country, to protect itself against conflict of interest, permits dual nationals to hold the leading positions of the state such as that of president, prime minster, key ministries, etc.

269. For a glimpse of the ongoing American confusion that has resulted from the unintended consequences of the War on Iraq, refer to: https://www.youtube.com/watch?v=DFph7-L-Jug.

270. http://www.brainyquote.com/quotes/quotes/n/napoleonbo103585

271. https://en.wikipedia.org/wiki/Suez_Crisis

272. Curiously, two events that proved disastrous in Iraq's history, the coup in 1958 and the Mongol ravaging of Baghdad in 1258, are precisely seven centuries apart.

273. The original quotation by Abraham Lincoln was: better to remain silent and be thought a fool than to speak and to remove all doubt.

274. The American volunteer army is one of the unintended consequences of the Vietnam War.

275. https://en.wikipedia.org/wiki/Vietnam_War#Impact_on_the_U.S._military.

276. *The Baker-Hamilton Report* (Vintage Books, 2006).

277. On May 14, 2013, CNN reported a video showing a well-known rebel leader eating the heart of a dead Syrian soldier. Human Rights Watch commented, "…the atrocious act in the video is inexcusable." See http://edition.cnn.com2013/05/14/world/meast/syria-eaten-heart/

278. https://en.wikipedia.org/wiki/Abu_Ghraib_torture_and_prisoner_ abuse.

279. Rebecca Gordon in her recent book, *American Nuremberg: The U.S. Officials Who Should Stand Trial for Post-9/11 War Crimes*, Skyhorse Publishing, 2016, makes a persuasive case for putting key figures in the Bush administration on trial.

280. Robert Fisk, "Why is David Cameron so silent on the recapture of Palmyra from the clutches of Isis?" The Independent, March 27, 2016.

281. See ISIS is Us: The Shocking Truth Behind the Army of Terror, ProgressivePress.com, San Diego, California, 2016

282. Financial Times, April 15, 2016

283. Francis Fukuyama, *The End of History & Last Man*, First Avon Books, 1993.

284. https://en.wikipedia.org/wiki/Muslim_world.

285. http://www.brainyquote.com/quotes/keywords/stupidity. html#9A2gAv1CstQOll3X.99.

286. For a thorough discussion, refer to Chapter 6's section titled "The Unified Theory of Macroeconomic Failure."

287. NATO, the North Atlantic Treaty Organization, is a military alliance established in the wake of World War II to check the communist military power in Europe, but since the collapse of communism it has evolved into an instrument for imposing Western hegemony on the rest of the world.

288. http://www.brainyquote.com/quotes/quotes/n/napoleonbo124809

289. Although the wars on Vietnam, Laos, and Cambodia preceded the formal emergence of the neocons, nevertheless Henry Kissinger, who had a senior role in the conduct of those wars, was a neocon in everything but name.

290. On June 28, 1914, the assassination of Austria's Archduke Franz Ferdinand in Sarajevo had a butterfly effect, setting off a chain of events that culminated in World War I. https://en.wikipedia.org/wiki/Assassination_of_Archduke_Franz_Ferdinand_of_Austria.

291. Turkey's shooting down of a Russian bomber in late 2015 was hardly the first salvo fired by Turkey.

292. "The Big Picture with Tom Hartman," Russia Today, October 10, 2014.

293. Refer to Chapter 6's section titled "Psychopathic Plutocracies."

14. *Measuring Democracy*

294. http://www.brainyquote.com/search_results.html?q=The+people+who+cast+the+votes+decide+nothing.+The+people+who+count+the+votes

295. See http://en.wikipedia.org/wiki/List_of_United_States_political_party_platforms.

296. For an alternative definition of democracy, see Wikipedia: http://en.wikipedia.org/wiki/Democracy.

297. See http://en.wikipedia.org/wiki/List_of_freedom_indexes.

298. Bundestag: http://en.wikipedia.org/wiki/Bundestag
Also, German Politics: http://en.wikipedia.org/wiki/German_politics

299. See http://en.wikipedia.org/wiki/List_of_political_parties_in_the_United_States#Parties_with_ federal_representation

300. http://www.brainyquote.com/quotes/quotes/n/napoleonbo110029

301. See http://en.wikipedia.org/wiki/United_States_elections,_2014#Turnout.

302. See "Who Owns the Federal Reserve?," http://www.federalreserve.gov/faqs/about_ 14986.htm.

303. Refer to Chapter 13's section titled "Wars of Aggression."

304. Refer to Chapter 13's section titled "The Crime Externality."

305. This is the number of political parties represented in the latest federal election in 2013. German voter participation is based on the same reference. See http://en.wikipedia.org/wiki/German_federal_election,_2013.

306. Credit Suisse Research Institute, *Global Wealth Data Book 2014*, p. 16. See http://publications.credit-suisse.com/tasks/render/file/index.cfm?fileid=5521F296-D460-2B88-081889DB12817E02

307. Professor William Blum estimated that the United States has engaged in more than seventy wars since 1945.

308. See http://news.bbc.co.uk/2/shared/spl/hi/uk/06/prisons/html/nn2 page1.stm.

15. *The Next Revolution in Equity Finance*

309. Keynes was referring to the British economy after World War I. https://en.wikiquote.org/wiki/John_Maynard_Keynes#Quotes.

310. Refer to Chapter 7's section titled "Religion and Usury."

311. For full ownership of the property in thirty years, a lesser initial percentage ownership is financially feasible if rental yields are sufficiently high or if additional principal periodic repayments are possible.

312. Refer this chapter's section titled "Remodeling Banking."

313. Conceivably, the cost saving could pass fully or partially to the owner-occupier, depending on market conditions.

314. See http://www.thesimpledollar.com/best-home-insurance/#choosing-the-best-homeowners-insurance-company.

315. Rental payment in arrears makes the timing of cash flows easier to compare with mortgage payments.

316. Common shares are also referred to as common stock and common equity.

317. https://en.wikipedia.org/wiki/The_Emperor%27s_New_Clothes.

318. For further details, refer to Chapter 16's section titled "The Case for a Pigovian Tax on Financial Pollution."

319. A bank management fee of 5 percent of revenue is equivalent to 0.20 percent of the assets under management at the inception of an EPF

portfolio, using their original cost, rising to 0.232 percent after ten years and 0.51 percent after twenty years. Accordingly, 0.23 percent is a reasonable approximation of the bank management fee as a percent of EPF assets under management.

320. See http://www.dividendyieldhunter.com/preferred-stocks-sorted-yield.

321. This is calculated as follows: 13.2 percent return on common equity + 21.6 percent net return on preferred shares (7.2 percent X 3) = 34.8 percent.

322. Chapter 7's section titled "The Evolution of a Ponzi Scheme."

323. In an interview on April 4, 2014, on "Boom Bust," Russia Today, Dr. Ann Pettifor stated that all noted economists, including Keynes, have recognized that private banks created money.

16. *Public Finance and Indirect Taxes*

324. See http://www.brainyquote.com/search_results?q=taxes.

325. See http://freedomandprosperity.org/2010/videos/the-rahn-curve-and-the-growth-maximizing-level-of-government.

326. "Infant Mortality Rate," *CIA: The World Factbook*, archived from the original on December 18, 2012. "OECD Health Data 2009: Frequently Requested Data," Oecd.org. https://en.wikipedia.org/wiki/Health_system#cite_note-datasource-38

327. For a comprehensive look at the progressive privatization of government services and the dismantling of competitive bidding and related topics, an informative reference is Janine R. Wedel's *Shadow Elite: How The World's New Power Brokers Undermine Democracy, Government, and the Free Market* (Basic Books, 2009).

328. Refer to Chapter 13 for a detailed discussion.

329. A good here implies a good or service.

330. https://en.wikipedia.org/wiki/Poverty#Financial_services

331. Refer to Chapter 15's section titled "Preferred Shares."

332. See http://www.theamericanconservative.com/articles/how-to-lose-an-empire.

333. Depending on the elasticity of supply and demand for a good or service, a tax, including a corporate income tax, could be partly or fully shifted to lower income groups as consumers of that good or service or workers engaged in its supply.

334. Indirect taxes include sales taxes, local surtaxes, plus import duties, excise taxes, user fees, etc. In several European countries, VAT is 20 percent or higher.

335. The purchases of Mr. Rich before the 15 percent tax are $200,000/1.15 = $173,913. Accordingly, a 15 percent tax amounts to $26,087. Thus, the cost of his purchases, including the tax, amount to $173,913 + $26,087=$200,000. On the other hand, the purchases of Mr. Average before the 15% tax are $35,000/1.15 = $30,435. Accordingly, a 15 percent tax amounts to $4,465. Thus, the cost of his purchases, including the tax, amount to $30,435+ $4,465=$35,000.

336. Refer to Chapter 6's section titled "The Unified Theory of Macroeconomic Failure."

337. A fraud tax at 1,000 percent of fraudulent gains and a detection rate of 10 percent would reduce the total expected fraud payoff significantly.

For detected fraud: -1000 percent (fraud tax) X 10 percent (probability of discovery) = -100 percent (of the value of fraud). For undetected fraud: 100 percent (in fraudulent gains) X 90 percent (probability of non-discovery) = 90 percent (of the value of fraud). Thus, the total expected fraud payoff becomes negative: -100 percent + 90 percent = -10 percent

338. See http://www.brainyquote.com/search_results?q=taxes.

17. Corporate Taxation

339. This chapter draws heavily on an article by this author: "Growth, Unemployment, Inflation and Some Aspects of Islamic Economics," *Oil and Arab Cooperation*, Vol. 7/No. 4, 1981, Organization of Arab Petroleum Exporting Countries.

340. For a discussion of the effect of debt on the business cycle, refer to Chapter 11.

341. A cross-default clause makes the default of a borrower on any loan an event of default on the present loan as well, thereby greatly magnifying the financial risk to the borrower. A negative pledge clause requires a borrower not to pledge any of its assets to a third party, thereby greatly restricting a borrower's room for maneuvering in a financial emergency.

342. Robert Skidelsky, *Keynes: The Return of the Master*, (Penguin, 2010), page xix.

343. In 2005, Ben Bernanke attributed the low US interest rates to what he described as a savings glut. See http://en.wikipedia.org/wiki/Ben_Bernanke.

344. https://en.wikipedia.org/wiki/Social_Security_(United_States).

345. This section draws on a 1979 article in Arabic published by the author in the *Economic Journal of OAPEC* (Organization for Arab Petroleum Exporting Countries) titled "Growth, Inflation, Unemployment and Some Aspects of Islamic Economics."

346. In 2010, the marginal US federal corporate income tax was 34 percent at $75,000 rising to 35 percent at $100,000. In addition, states, on average, levied another 6.5 percent on corporate income, bringing the top tax bracket to 41.5 percent of pretax income.

347. The equivalent corporate capital tax rate shown here is calculated as follows:
Corporate Capital Tax Rate = Total Corporate Income Tax Revenue/ (Total Capital of A + B)
= $9.6 million/$200 million = 4.8 percent

348. Since the greater the profitability, the greater the tax burden, the tax base, in effect, is economic efficiency.

349. Don Fullerton and Gilbert E. Metcalf, "Environmental Taxes and the Double-Dividend Hypothesis: Did You Really Expect Something for Nothing?" *NBER Working Papers* (w6199): 42, Sept. 1997.

350. More precisely, the numerator should include all direct corporate taxes, including those at the federal, state, and local levels to permit their apportionment accordingly.

351. Moody's Corporation annual reports for the years 2000–2003 and 2007–2009.

18. *Regressive Personal Taxation*

352. See http://www.brainyquote.com/quotes/quotes/d/davidrocke164629. html?src=t_income_ tax.

353. The Forbes 2015 wealth survey estimated the wealth of David Rockefeller, Sr., at $3 billion. See http://www.forbes.com/forbes-400/list/#version:static_tab:oldest_sortreverse:true.

354. Some economists have proposed, without success, replacing the personal income tax with an expenditure tax; this is potentially the most regressive tax because the rich would substantially escape it given that they save a higher percentage of their income than the rest of society.

355. Arthur Laffer, "The Laffer Curve: Past, Present and Future," The Heritage Foundation, June 1, 2004. Arthur Laffer was a member of President Ronald Reagan's Economic Policy Advisory Board (1981–1989). Laffer points out that the concept first appeared in The Muqaddimah by Ibn Khaldun (1332–1406), a Tunisian philosopher and one of the founding fathers of modern sociology, historiography, and economics. Arthur Laffer did not refer to his Laffer curve as the Laffer principle; however, the author finds this terminology appropriate for the present purpose.

356. See http://en.wikipedia.org/wiki/John_F._Kennedy#Economy

357. See Chapter 18's section titled "Principles of Personal Taxation."

358. Refer to Chapter 12's section titled "Monopsony and Chronic Underconsumption."

359. "The Big Picture with Tom Hartman," Russia Today, October 10, 2014.

360. Robert Reich, *Aftershock* (Penguin Random House, 2010).

361. https://en.wikipedia.org/wiki/Social_Security_(United_States)

362. https://en.wikipedia.org/wiki/Federal_Insurance_Contributions_Act_tax#Social_Security_ regressivity_debate

363. In the United States, the poverty level for 2014 was set at $23,850 (total yearly income) for a family of four. See http://en.wikipedia.org/wiki/Poverty_in_the_United_States.

364. Refer to Chapter 16's section titled "Repeal of Taxation of Essentials."

19. Progressive Personal Taxation

365. See http://www.brainyquote.com/search_results?q=taxes.

366. Thomas Piketty, *Capital in Twenty-First Century*, translated by Arthur Goldhammer (Belknap Press of Harvard University Press, 2014).

367. Refer to Chapter 3's section titled "19th-Century Poverty and Plutocracy in Europe."

368. Refer to Chapter 8.

369. This pattern has repeated many times since, most recently in Syria, even though it is not a threat to Western plutocratic wealth.

370. This French term is often used to refer to reestablishing the old status quo once the monarchy was reintroduced in France following the battle of Waterloo and the defeat of Napoleon Bonaparte, the last vestige of the French Revolution.

371. For a broader discussion of the subject, refer to Chapter 13's section titled "The Negative Externality of Excessive Plutocratic Wealth."

372. See http://en.wikipedia.org/wiki/Capital_in_the_Twenty-First_Century.

373. See http://talkingpointsmemo.com/livewire/princeton-experts-say-us-no-longer-democracy.

374. See http://www.bbc.com/news/blogs-echochambers-27074746.

375. Capital in the Twenty-First Century, Chapter XVI, The Question of Public Debt.

376. Refer to Chapter 2's section titled "Wealth, Power, and Insecurity."

377. See http://en.wikipedia.org/wiki/Estate_tax_in_the_United_States#cite_note-Tax_ Foundation-52.

378. During the presidency of George W. Bush, the estate tax was set to 0 percent, while during Obama's administration the exemption was set at $5 million.

379. For tax purposes, it is convenient to treat land as a form of capital since one is easily convertible into the other.

380. Refer to Chapter 16's section titled "Repeal of the Taxation on Essentials."

381. A full contribution would make the tax regressive, because labor has fewer resources than the wealthy and does not earn a profit from government contracts.

382. Refer to the discussion on the corporate capital tax in Chapter 17, particularly the section titled "The Relative Economic Efficiency of a Corporate Capital Tax."

383. Credit Suisse Research Institute, *Global Wealth Data Book* 2014, p.145. See http://publications.credit-suisse.com/tasks/render/file/index.cfm?fileid=5521F296-D460-2B88-081889DB12817E02.

384. Ibid, p.16.

385. Capital in the Twenty-First Century.

386. Refer to Chapter 16.

387. The total rate of return includes the total of capital appreciation, dividends, rent, and interest per annum divided by the amount of capital employed.

388. Islam requires the payment of Zakat at the rate of 2.5 percent of total personal wealth per lunar year, with exemptions covering a reasonable dwelling, transport, a wife's jewelry, and personal effects.

389. The author first learned about this concept from the late sociology professor, Khaldun Al-Nakeeb, whose PhD dissertation researched vertical social mobility in the United States.

390. Refer to Chapter 4's section titled "Durations and Stages of Economic Cycles."

391. John Maynard Keynes.

392. Henry George, *Progress and Poverty: An Inquiry into the Cause of Industrial Depressions and of Increase of Want with Increase of Wealth… the Remedy* (1879). This book sold over three million copies.

20. The Gathering Storms

393. See http://www.brainyquote.com/search_results.html?q=foolishness.

394. https://en.wikiquote.org/wiki/John_Maynard_Keynes#Quotes.

395. Seema Jayachandran and Michael Kremer, "Odious Debt," *The American Economic Review*, March 2006.

396. John Kenneth Galbraith, *The Age of Uncertainty* (Episode I, BBC video series).

397. See http://www.indcatholicnews.com/news.php?viewStory=7626.

398. See http://www.catholicnews.com/services/englishnews/2014/jubilee-campaign-for-debt-relief-gains-momentum-allies-in-the-vatican.cfm.

399. The irony here refers to Carmen M. Reinhart and Kenneth S. Rogoff's *This Time Is Different: Eight Centuries of Financial Folly* (Princeton University Press, 2011).

400. Mindtools.com claims that the author of this popular investment proverb is Mary Kay Ash, an American businesswoman.

401. For some noncash transactions like trade sales and rentals, nonpayment can still trigger repossession and damage claims.

402. Preferred stock is equity, but the adoption of certain features can make it more akin to debt.

403. An event of default could precipitate the seizure of assets and the dissolution of an enterprise.

Index

HSBC, 149
J. P. Morgan, 166
JP Morgan Chase, 182
Lehman Brothers, 145
Morgan Stanley, 182
Union Bank of Switzerland, 149
Wells Fargo, 182
Bank of England, 167-168, 350, 353
Banking model, 144-145, 154, 276
Bankruptcy, 4-5, 31, 177, 214, 239
Barbarism, 1, 37, 43, 50-51, 92, 96, 114, 223, 240, 364
Basel Committee on Banking Supervision, 154
Behavior:
compulsive, 27
conformist, 99, 100, 102, 235
herd, 24-25, 39, 103, 147, 192, 270, 350
psychopathic, 28, 30, 34, 38, 40, 95. See also Economic drivers - emotional behavior, Irrationality
Behavioral economics, 39
Benevolence, 6, 116, 137, 142, 238, 326
Bezemer, Dirk, 6
Big banks, 5, 11, 111, 135, 139, 141-142, 145, 163, 166, 174, 176-177, 179-180, 183, 203, 220, 243, 250-251, 279, 359. See also Government type - banking plutocracy

Bilmes, Professor Linda, 229
Bismarck, Chancellor Otto von, 113-115, 230, 240
Black Death, 41
Black, Fischer, 78
Black-Scholes model, 78, 146
Bonaparte, Napoleon, 41, 230, 249, 252
Bondage, 27, 30, 121-122, 139. See also Slavery
Borrower(s), 10-11, 28, 121, 128, 135, 139-140, 148, 153, 156, 182, 212-213, 249, 262, 273, 287, 354
Bretton Woods system, 61, 167-168
BRICS countries, 4, 154
Britain, 4, 14, 21, 54, 56, 61, 69, 99, 113, 117, 146, 167, 193, 197, 230-231, 234, 237, 245, 248-249, 251-252, 257, 328. See also British Empire, England
British Corn Laws, 20-21, 33, 42, 116
British Empire, 50-51, 231. See also Britain, England
British Foreign Office, 64, 231-234
British Parliament, 20, 33, 42, 61, 1673
British PM:
Cameron, David, 237
Margaret Thatcher, 137, 328
Tony Blair, 236, 249
Buchanan, James M., 354

Communist party, 46, 94, 117, 176, 219, 247

Confessions of an Economic Hit Man (Perkins), 152

Conflict of interest, 134, 161-162, 170, 176, 212-213, 276, 278

Conservative agendas, 32, 50, 70, 99, 137-138, 220, 237, 248-249, 290, 328, 352, 355, 357

Conspiracy theory, 153, 229, 237, 360

Construction, 10, 56, 147-148, 191, 245, 270, 287

Consumer protection agency, 93, 99, 221, 270

Cooperatives, 21, 272-273

Cornell Law Review, 225

Corporate democracy, 109, 222-223, 246

Corporate profits, 4, 112, 197, 207, 210, 299, 302, 309

Corporate reporting, 110, 213, 215

Credit rating, 4, 81-82, 110, 212

Crime, 7, 28, 31, 34, 38, 70, 85, 95, 103, 110, 161, 181, 207, 212, 224-228, 235-236, 254, 285, 344, 359. See also Poverty

Crisis, 4-6, 8-9, 12, 21, 48, 54-55, 62, 74, 77, 83, 102, 122, 128, 134, 141, 145, 148, 168, 179, 181, 190-191, 194-196, 200, 213, 231, 287, 297, 327, 329, 350, 358, 363-365. See

also Financial bubble, Great Depression, Great Recession

Cycle type:
Juglar cycle, 55
Kitchin cycle, 55
Kondratiev cycle, 55
Kuznets cycle, 55
Schumpeter's creative destruction cycle, 12, 55, 108, 275

Cycles:
business cycle, 15, 21, 54-55, 80, 110, 194-195, 199, 269, 278, 302, 310, 349
contraction, 21,54, 57-58, 62, 68, 72, 74, 84-87, 106, 151, 174-176, 188-189, 191-193, 197, 199-200, 208-209, 278, 283-284, 287, 310, 342, 350, 357
credit cycle, 190, 192-193, 269
depression, 4-5, 7, 12-13, 30, 53, 56, 58-59, 62, 64, 66, 69, 74, 84-85, 117, 133, 136, 141, 143, 167, 175-177, 179, 181, 188, 190-191, 197, 199, 205, 209, 327, 342, 351, 358, 361
expansion, 53-54, 56, 58-59, 65, 72, 85-86, 106, 151, 155, 174-176, 188-189, 191, 193-195, 209, 213, 231, 309-310
stock market cycle, 79, 276

Social cost, 92, 104, 121, 136, 164, 189, 204, 225, 254, 286-288, 291. See also Externalities, Public goods, Taxes

Social mobility, 321, 340-341

Socrates, 95

Solvency, 135, 146, 209, 295

Somalia, 236, 360

Sophists, 98-99

Soviet economy, 51, 210

Soviet Union, 3, 47, 51, 102, 210, 237, 240, 247, 252, 361, 364

Spain, 4, 154, 193, 210, 257, 350, 355

Speculative, 10, 38, 135, 142, 148, 158, 163, 174, 177, 191-193, 196, 197, 320, 323

Spillover effects, 97, 103, 105, 112, 117, 238, 275

Standard of living, 33, 49, 209, 212, 254, 327-328, 333

Statistics, 4, 93, 153, 200, 210-212, 224, 282, 344

Suicide, 30, 224, 235, 239, 288

Sunspots, 187

Syria, 101, 153, 221, 228, 230-237, 239-240, 250, 357-358, 360

T

Tax avoidance, 299, 311, 340

Tax base, 153, 281, 289, 299, 301-303, 308, 310, 313-314,

317, 322, 325, 332-333, 335, 337-339

Tax burden, 51, 150, 200, 307-308, 311, 318-321, 332, 335, 337-338, 341-343

Tax cut, 60, 86, 209, 220, 249, 251, 284, 319, 339

Tax haven, 299-300, 311, 343

Tax incidence, 307-308

Tax loopholes, 274, 281, 285, 314, 317-318, 320, 322-323, 325, 331, 337-338, 341, 359

Tax migration, 342-343, 345

Tax neutrality, 294, 296, 316, 322

Tax principles, 318, 321, 336

Tax rate, 60, 274, 290-291, 295, 298-300, 303, 305-306, 310-313, 317-320, 322-323, 325, 332, 334, 338-339, 341-345

Tax shelters, 318, 325, 332-333, 340-341

Tax shifting, 302

Taxation:
progressive, 281-282, 317-321, 327, 331-333, 337-338, 341, 343, 345, 359, 361, 363
regressive, 96, 219, 221, 253, 262, 281-283, 290-291, 298, 317, 319-321, 323-325, 333, 337, 339-340, 343

Basil Al-Nakeeb

Made in the USA
Charleston, SC
03 July 2016